PC Music Composing with Cubasis VST & Notation

Vera Trusova

Evgeny Medvedev

PC Music Composing
with Cubasis VST
& Notation

A-LIST, LLC

295 East Swedesford Rd.

PMB #285

Wayne, PA 19087

702-977-5377 (FAX)

mail@alistpublishing.com

http://www.alistpublishing.com

This book is printed on acid-free paper.

PC Music Composing with Cubasis VST & Notation
By Vera Trusova, Evgeny Medvedev

   ISBN: 1-931769-10-9

Printed in the United States of America

03 04 7 6 5 4 3 2 1

A-LIST, LLC titles are distributed by Independent Publishers Group and are available for site license or bulk purchase by institutions, user groups, corporations, etc.

Book Editor: Jessica Mroz

Contents

To our loving parents

INTRODUCTION

When anything is possible,
you must know exactly what you want.

The Computer — a New Musical Instrument

The wider the capabilities of an instrument, the more difficult it is to master. In order to use the computer for creating music to the *fullest extent possible*, one must not only understand the principle of the software's operation, but also be *musically literate*. This book is meant to act as a "bridge" connecting these two areas of knowledge. Therefore, it is meant for readers of various ages and educational backgrounds:

❏ For beginners as well as advanced users who want to get closer to music, understand the laws of musical language, and use the computer in their creative activities

❏ For musicians that want to master certain computer technologies and learn to create and write music on the computer

The material of the book may also be useful for those working with *other* musical software, since many principles here concern the *basic approaches* of using a contemporary musical instrument — the computer.

Cubasis Software — the First Step in Cubase Software Mastering

It is not possible to study higher levels of mathematics if you don't know the multiplication tables. Likewise, it is just painful to see beginners trying to master Cubase VST when they possess neither a sufficient musical nor computer background.

As a rule, the results are sad: "worn out" by Cubase VST, they either reject it in favor of less complicated and *limited* software, or use only *a few* of the capabilities of the multifunctional and powerful Cubase system from the Steinberg Company.

We propose that readers start mastering the musical computer environment in the traditional manner: from simple to difficult. The best choice is the Cubasis VST and Cubasis Notation software — "simplified" versions of the professional Cubase VST and Cubase Score software from Steinberg.

The software products described in this book have the following advantages for beginner musicians:

☐ They are very easy to master.
☐ They allow you to obtain high-quality results.
☐ They have the same basic advantages as their professional versions (Cubase VST and Cubase Score).
☐ Having mastered the basic principles, you will be able to move on to the next level of the Cubase family software.

If You Read This Book, You'll Be Able to Play Music

Learning notes is no more difficult than learning to read, and you will begin to understand this when reading certain sections of *Chapters 2, 3*, and *4*.

Those who are already familiar with notation will find it much more convenient to create music with the help of the computer. *Even a basic knowledge of musical notation* makes it possible to use Cubasis Notation as:

☐ A "musical translator" that can write down a part you played, or play the selected notes
☐ A "personal music teacher", helping you to play without mistakes

Contemporary computer technologies help people who have never learned music to overcome the gap between the theory and practice, and, having repaired the problem, score their musical ideas using musical software.

The mere mastering of notation is only half the work. The main idea is to clearly understand the laws of how combinations of sounds become music. And neglecting these laws, even out of ignorance, is the same type of imprudence as erecting a building neglecting important rules of construction.

Along with the explanations of the main principles of the software's operation, a large portion of *Chapters 2, 3*, and *4* is allotted to the basics of musical language.

Knowledge is Power

How interesting it is to submerge yourself into the virtual world, where — like a great maestro — you have your own orchestra with virtual musicians eager to implement all your musical plans!

Professional musicians often treat the computer as a toy not to be used for creating "real" music. Such an opinion was formed mainly because, among examples of computer music, there used to be very many low-grade products full of monotony, endless loops, unjustified noise effects, etc.

But it is not possible to appreciate the quality of the instrument if a (normal) first-grader is playing a Stradivarius violin, is it?

To tell you the truth, *the computer can do anything*. To be more precise, it can do anything a human being tells it to do via commands. And who but the professional musician, with a subtle sense of music, will know *how* to use all the capabilities of this perfect instrument?

Unfortunately, musicians often have no idea of the technologies that have been developed *esspecially for them*. This gap is easy to fill, though: choose *worthy* software, learn to work with it, and enjoy the latest achievements in this area.

The computer can not only be a performer. If used skillfully, it becomes the *co-author* — it generates new rhythm patterns and offers unusual melodic and harmonic moves. In the software that we describe, these capabilities become possible due to the application of both *rhythmical quantization* (*Chapter 2*), and *scale quantization* (*Chapter 4*).

One of the main features of the Cubasis Notation software is the fact that the score here can be *adapted* — represented as the musician wants to see it: either extremely concisely, or in maximum detail (with respect to all the rhythmical nuances of the performance).

Structure of the Book

The most important aspects are presented in the book according to the leading learning methods, which enable you to study the material in full with the least amount of intellectual expense. The essence of this method is that, before a difficult aspect is approached, the basis for its understanding has already been laid out. We recommed that beginners read the book from the very beginning. The material is laid out from simplest to most complicated. For convenience' sake, the brief overview of the operations in the Key Edit and Score Edit editors is given in the illustrated tables in *Sections 2.23* and *3.9*.

Chapter 1 (Cubasis VST):

❑ You can use the computer as a "multichannel tape recorder", with additional capabilities.

❑ The technique of working with audio in the arrangement window is presented: recording, editing.

❑ Special attention is paid to additional methods of editing in the VST Pool window.

❑ The use of ReCycle files for creating diversity in loops is presented.

❑ The virtual mixer and virtual effect connection and capabilities (Insert and Send) are considered.

❑ The methods of mixing the composition (Export Audio) into one file to be processed in professional editors and put on the Audio CD are considered.

Chapter 2 (Cubasis VST):

❑ MIDI technology capabilities: selecting a timbre, methods of recording, methods of editing recordings.

❑ A detailed description of the Key Edit editor used for "explaining" to the computer the subtleties of a performance.

❑ The basics of rhythm: lengths, differences in meters (simple and complex).

❑ MIDI sound enlivening algorithms, step-by-step and real-time recording from the MIDI keyboard.

❑ Special attention is paid to ways of creating a complex rhythm, as well as correction of rhythmical errors during the performance (the features of the rhythmical quantize application).

❑ The List Edit editor, which enables you to make amendments on the command level if necessary.

❑ And as a summary, a table of the main editing operations in the Key Edit editor.

Chapter 3 (Cubasis Notation):

❑ The basics of notation, features of note and octave designation in MIDI numeration

❑ Work with notes in the Score Edit editor: recording using the mouse and MIDI keyboard, and all methods of editing

❑ Score adaptation

❑ Score layout

❑ Score printing

❑ Enlivening MIDI sound in the Score Edit editor

Chapter 4 (Cubasis Notation):

❒ Intervals
❒ Chord building
❒ Alphanumeric symbols for chords
❒ Figurings in the Score Edit editor
❒ Scale
❒ The 21 scales of the Cubasis Notation program (from major and minor to Japanese, Chinese, Hungarian, etc.)
❒ Scale quantization

Chapter 5 (Cubasis VST):

❒ VST Instruments
❒ VST technology. MIDI conversion into Audio

Chapter 6 (The Sound Forge 6.0 and WaveLab 4.0 audio editors):

❒ Joint use of Cubasis VST and the audio editor
❒ The main methods of audio processing in the Sound Forge 6.0 and WaveLab 4.0 audio editors
❒ The technology of mastering and burning CDs

CHAPTER 1

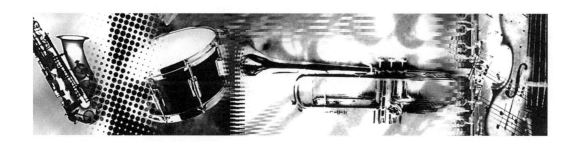

Working with Audio in Cubasis VST

1.1. Connecting the Microphone and Synthesizer to the Sound Card

The sound card is the voice of the computer. Without this device, the computer will not be able to digitize and reproduce sound, or receive and transmit MIDI events.

The assortment of sound cards is being constantly expanded. The modern market features examples of quality that go far beyond the multimedia class in their characteristics. There are no fireworks, and no festive chimes, but this evidences the beginning of the great era of *professional sound on PC.*

Today, almost every musician can buy a sound card featuring professional technical characteristics for quite a reasonable price.

One of these is M-Audio Audiophile 2496 (www.midiman.net). Although it is rather inexpensive, this sound card supports the ASIO, GSIF, and EASI interfaces, has high-quality converters integrated into it, and provides the short latency that is integral to "live" recording and the use of virtual synthesizers.

The SB Audigy sound card (the new implementation of the classic "sound blaster" from Creative Labs) is now also supported by special ASIO drivers (which we will describe later in *Section 1.2*).

Let's take a look at the ways in which it can be used in the home studio for beginners.

There are ADC and DAC converters on the sound card, which are necessary for the computer to work as a digital recorder. Thanks to the algorithms of these converters, we can record and play back sound on the computer as we would on a regular tape recorder, with the only difference being that no tape is used: the recording is done in an audio file on the hard disk.

Multimedia sound cards have several inputs and outputs. You can therefore connect the microphone to a separate microphone input, but this option is suitable only in the first stage of acquaintance with the powerful PC capabilities for virtual sound processing.

The quality of the sound will be much better if you use an analog mixing console connected to the linear input of the sound card. This allows you to use microphones of higher quality, and is convenient for acoustic control (monitoring) and preliminary mixing of several sources of sound.

Some sound cards (such as SB Audigy) have an integrated MIDI synthesizer or sampler. You can operate this device from the MIDI interface of the sequencer software. Cubasis VST and Cubasis Notation, which are described in this book, are examples of such software.

The graphic interface of sequencer software enables you to enter musical messages using the mouse (e.g., set the notes in the Score Edit editor or draw key imprints in the Key Edit editor). In most cases, however, it is more convenient to use "keys": the MIDI keyboard or a synthesizer with a MIDI output. For this purpose, there is a special connector provided — the external MIDI port.

It should be mentioned that some sound cards do not have full MIDI interfaces, and therefore require an *additional cable adapter.*

The SB Audigy sound blaster, for example, belongs to this type of sound card. Owing to its "gamer" specifics, there is a standard game port provided for joystick and MIDI cable adapter connection. In order to connect the external MIDI synthesizer to the sound card, its MIDI OUT should be connected to the MIDI IN of the sound card, and the MIDI OUT of the sound card to the MIDI IN of the synthesizer.

When the synthesizer is connected, its audio (linear) output must be connected to the analog mixer or to the linear input of the sound card.

These connections allow you to record MIDI events from the synthesizer directly to the sequencer software (to the MIDI tracks of Cubasis VST and Cubasis Notation) and edit them. The signal from the synthesizer will go through the integrated mixer of the sound card and will be heard in the control active acoustic systems that should be connected to the output of the sound card. For this, an audio system or headphones will do.

Later, the edited MIDI material is re-recorded to the Audio tracks. This is done via the same external synthesizer or special MIDI synthesizer module (a separate device having no keyboard). This operation is mandatory, since you can only get the final product (an Audio CD) on the computer after *mixing down* to the final audio file. Then you can process this file with special software such as WaveLab. Each of these stages will be considered separately.

1.2. Software Setup

The Cubasis VST software is a simplified version of the professional Cubase VST software, and thus the main technical features of its "big brother" — Cubase — are retained here. The Cubasis VST software is also an ASIO application. This means that it interacts with the sound card via the ASIO driver.

 Note

ASIO is the abbreviation for Audio Stream Input/Output.

We will mention only the most important details here, in order not to scare beginning musicians.

❐ Owing to the various imperfections of the Windows operating system, sound processing in real time was practically impossible, due to large delays in the sound signal. In order to eliminate this problem, the ASIO professional program interface was developed. As a result, the modern virtual studio technology (VST technology) implemented in the Cubase system software (Cubase VST, Cubasis VST, and Nuendo) is based on the ASIO interface.

❏ Cubasis VST, like an ASIO application, can interact with professional sound cards via special ASIO drivers (which come with the sound card).

▶ *Note*

Of course, the audio flow routing abilities in Cubasis VST are considerably limited when compared to the Cubase VST and Nuendo software.

❏ In order for the software to interact with multimedia sound cards that are not supported by special ASIO drivers, the Cubasis VST package comes with ASIO adapter drivers — ASIO Multimedia Driver and ASIO DirectX Driver.

By default, Cubasis VST uses ASIO Multimedia Driver. It automatically sets the driver up, and in most cases, these settings need not be changed.

❏ If you have an SB Audigy sound card, it is best to use its specialized ASIO driver (Creative EMU 10K ASIO). This will reduce the latency (or in other words, the delay between the command and its sound). As a result, you will be able to use the advantages of the VST technology in full — i.e., work with the virtual synthesizer *in real time* from the MIDI keyboard, or play the VST instruments.

Nowadays, virtual instruments are gaining wide recognition: their sound is no worse than that of real electronic instruments, they are inexpensive, and don't occupy much space at all. If you decide to put your money on them, you will always be in the front line of sound technologies (see more details in *Chapter 5*).

Now let's move on to some practice. There is a special Audio System Setup window for setting the audio parameters of Cubasis VST (Fig. 1.1). It is opened in the Audio menu with the System option.

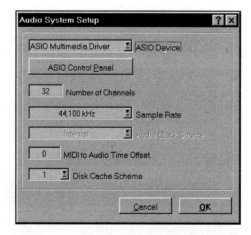

Fig. 1.1. The **Audio System Setup** window

Select the ASIO driver from the ASIO Device drop-down list (Fig. 1.2). The example shows the selection of the specialized ASIO driver of the M-Audio Audiophile 2496 sound card, which provides the minimal delay for this card.

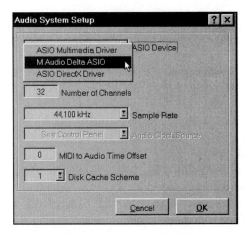

Fig. 1.2. Selecting the ASIO driver

The selection of the ASIO driver affects not only the latency. A specialized ASIO driver allows you to use the capabilities of the sound card in full, which is shown in Fig. 1.3.

Two variants of the VST Inputs window are shown (it is opened in the Audio menu with the Inputs option). The upper example (A) is with the specialized M Audio Delta ASIO driver, and the lower example (B) is using the typical ASIO Multimedia Driver.

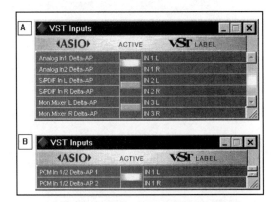

Fig. 1.3. Compare the configuration of VST inputs
with different types of ASIO drivers

You can see from the example that the specialized ASIO driver provides more possibilities, since you can do the recording from more inputs.

The settings in the VST Inputs window are very simple. The left <ASIO> column contains the list of the available ASIO ports, and the right column (VST Label) contains the tags of the VST inputs of the virtual mixer. If you click on the Active button, the VST input becomes active and available in the virtual mixer window (and in the Inspector panel of the Audio track).

► **Tip**

We recommend that you name the icons of the VST inputs (Fig. 1.4) to avoid difficulties when selecting the VST input for each channel.

Click on the **Input Selector** button with the <Ctrl> key pressed to determine the VST input, and select from the drop-down list that opens (Fig. 1.4).

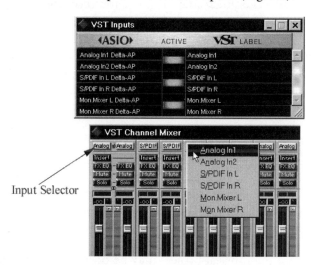

Fig. 1.4. Selecting a VST input with convenient names for the VST tags

Return to the **Audio System Setup** window (Fig. 1.2). The number of *virtual channels* is specified in the **Number of Channels** field.

► **Note**

Like MIDI channels, virtual channels are used for Audio tracks in Cubasis VST. See details below.

The maximum number of audio channels in Cubasis VST is 32. The Sample Rate drop-down list is used to set the sampling rate. If you plan to release the composition on CD, the sampling rate should be set to 44,100 kHz.

Note

Selecting this rate will avoid a quality loss when re-sampling (recalculating the audio file into another sampling rate), since 44,100 Hz is the standard sampling rate for Audio CD. This topic is considered in detail in our book "Live Music on Your PC", A-LIST Publishing, 2002.

The Audio Clock Source field is intended for professional equipment that supports external synchronization. The MIDI to Audio Time Offset field is used to compensate for the constant lag between MIDI and Audio that may occur with some MIDI equipment.

The Disk Cache Scheme drop-down list contains three points, marked as 1, 2, and 3. This is the necessary setup for optimizing the work of the disk subsystem: the tracks are played from the hard disk and require a high operating speed.

❑ The *Virtual Tape Recorder* chart is used for recording long audio parts. Here, Cubasis VST is used as multitrack digital recorder.

❑ The *Audio Sequencer* chart uses Cubasis VST as an audio sequencer — a device for playing phrase loops. Loops are audio files that contain a musical phrase (a groove), which can be looped, i.e., multiplied on an audio track.

❑ The *Virtual Tape Recorder + Audio Sequencer* chart is the "happy medium" intended for use when the project contains both long audio parts and loops.

1.3. The *Arrange* Window

We'll begin with a creative comparison. The structure of the musical data presentation in Cubasis VST recalls a book for notation that possesses "magic virtual capabilities".

The *song* is the book itself, and the *arrangement* is the pages of this book. The *multitrack* is the staves where the *parts* are positioned. It is the multitrack that presents the musical information the user works with.

The sections of the musical project may be positioned either in one arrangement (the Arrange window), or in several arrangements of the song.

You can save different sections of the project — separate parts, arrangements, or the whole song. The file extensions correspond to the information being saved: ALL (song), ARR (arrangement), PRT (parts). See more details in *Section 1.14*.

There are two main classes of tracks used in Cubasis VST — the *Audio track* and the *MIDI track*. The data recorded on Audio and MIDI tracks is different. So, the name of the track class means that the track contains *only* Audio information, or *only* MIDI data.

Since all "music machines" — including the PC — understand only commands, all sounds are encoded: they are presented as instructions sent from one instrument to another as MIDI events. Therefore, you could say that the MIDI interface (Musical

Instrument Digital Interface) is the language that electronic musical instruments use to communicate among themselves and interact with the computer.

The MIDI tracks of the Cubasis VST software contain parts with MIDI events recorded from the MIDI keyboard or MIDI synthesizer.

There are Audio parts on the Audio tracks that result from the recording and digitizing of an *analog* signal, e.g., a voice recorded from a microphone, or an acoustic instrument.

MIDI events can be recorded from a MIDI instrument or "written in with the pencil" in one of the editors — as notation in the Score Edit editor, or as keyprints in the Key Edit editor.

It should be mentioned that the method of recording music as MIDI events (described in *Chapters 2* and *3*) has many advantages. For example, you can correct the MIDI recording by adding or removing notes and changing their pitch and length. A MIDI part created in this way can be easily converted to an Audio part, and *all* features of virtual audio processing (effects, etc.) will be applicable to this part. After the sound is corrected, you will be able to transfer the resulting Audio file to a CD, or record it on a cassette. This chapter, however, deals with Audio. MIDI is described in *Chapter 3*.

Now let's turn to Cubasis VST.

When Cubasis VST is launched, the start def.all file of the song is loaded from the folder in which the software is located. The song contains one starting arrangement window, named def.arr by default. The maximum number of arrangements in the song is 16.

The **Arrange** window consists of three main parts (Fig. 1.5).

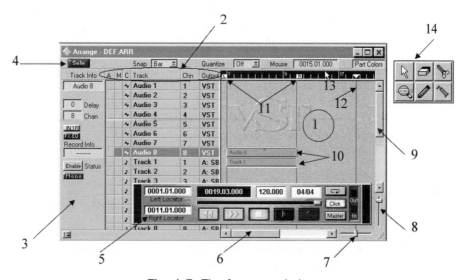

Fig. 1.5. The **Arrange** window

The bigger part of the window is the Part Display section. It is marked with the number 1 in the illustration. The musical material is presented as parts in the part section on MIDI and Audio tracks.

In the middle, there is the Track Columns section consisting of 6 columns where the track parameters are specified. It is indicated in the illustration with the number 2. The area consisting of the track and part sections will be referred to as the *multitrack* from now on.

You can navigate the multitrack using sliders 6 and 9. The scale is changed using regulators 7 and 8, or the <H> and <G> keys (horizontally) and the <Shift>+<H> and <Shift>+<G> keys (vertically).

On the left, there is the Inspector panel (indicated by the number 3) (see more information on the Inspector panel in *Section 1.8*). Here the information of the selected object (the part or the whole track) is displayed. The appearance of this panel is changed, depending on which selected object data are displayed: Audio track, Audio part, MIDI track, or MIDI part. (A part is always of a *higher priority* than a selected track. So if both these objects are selected, the information on the part will be displayed on the Inspector panel).

You can hide the Inspector panel by clicking on the ▦ button (in the bottom right corner), or in its immediate vicinity on the vertical bar. Clicking on this button again calls the panel back.

► ### *Tip*

You need to hide the **Inspector** panel in order to free up screen space for the multitrack. For this very purpose, you might want to hide some of the columns in the **Track Columns** section. Place the cursor on the border of the multitrack and the **Track Columns** section (the "hand" will appear); then drag the border to the left.

In the upper part of the window, you see the Status Bar (indicated by the number 4). Here also is the Solo button for listening to the selected track with the others muted. There are also 4 fields here:

❑ Mouse — shows the mouse cursor position.

► ### *Note*

Snap sets the "step" by which the multitrack cursor can be moved (**Bar** — bar line, **1/2** — half beat, **1/4** — quarter beat, etc.) in beats. This function is used for accurate part editing. See the details on bars and beats in *Chapter 2, Section 2.8.4*.

❑ Quantize — in the drop-down list of this field, you can select the lengths for rhythmic quantization (moving a length to certain rhythmic positions of the bar). This function works *only* with MIDI and is described in detail in *Section 2.20*.

❏ Part Color — allows you to color the parts various colors. The principle of its work is simple: the selected color is applied to the selected object.

❏ If a part is selected, then only its color is changed; if a track is selected, then *all the parts* on this track will change color. If you need to color a group of parts positioned at *different* places of the multitrack, first select them, and then select the color in the drop-down list of the **Part Color** field. There is also another method of selecting parts: press and hold <Shift>, and then click on each part. When the parts are moved, the selected color is retained.

Fig. 1.5 shows the **Transport** bar (№ 5) with the buttons and fields intended for working with the material (recording, playback, tempo change, etc.). Many functions are duplicated by hotkeys. For example, here you find the Click button, used for switching the metronome on and off. The **Transport** bar can be moved around the screen, hidden, and opened using several methods, such as pressing the <F12> key.

The *toolbar* of the **Arrange** window is marked with the number 14 in the illustration (it is outside of the window's borders). You can open the panel by clicking and holding the right mouse button in the part section. It consists of 6 tools: **Arrow, Eraser, Scissors, Magnifying Glass, Pencil,** and **Glue Tube.** In order to switch from one tool to another, move to the required icon holding the right mouse button pressed.

Unlike the other tools, the **Arrow** tool is called by simply clicking with the right mouse button in the part section.

1.4. Multitrack

The multitrack is the virtual space that holds the parts on its tracks. The "width" of the multitrack is the number of tracks created by the user, and its "length" can be very large, and is limited only by the hard disk space.

Parts. Fig. 1.5 shows two *different* parts corresponding to MIDI and Audio tracks (indicated by the number 10). You can perform various operations with parts: move, copy, delete, multiply, cut, etc. These operations will be described later. There are several methods of creating a part: by clicking with the **Pencil** tool in the part section on one of the created tracks, by dragging it from right to left, or by double-clicking with the left mouse button (arrow) between the L and R locators when L is *to the left* of R.

The software automatically names the parts. These names repeat the name of the track. If you want to rename the part, hold the <Alt> key, double-click on the part, and enter the new name in the window that opens. The renaming is completed by pressing the <Enter> key or by clicking outside of its borders.

Ruler. Above the part section, you will find the Ruler (marked with the number 13 in Fig. 1.5). It is divided into bars, each fifth one marked with a number. Thanks to the

Ruler, all editing operations with the parts — cutting, copying, moving, etc. — can be done in accordance with the meter size.

L and R locators. The two vertical lines crossing the part section are the **Left Locator** and **Right Locator** (markers). They are always marked on the **Ruler** with the letters L and R (marked with the number 11 in the illustration). They can be moved by clicking on the **Ruler** with the left and right mouse buttons, respectively. The locators define the working area of the project and are necessary for various operations, such as when parts of a specified duration are created, or when loop borders are defined. If you want to set the locators with utter precision, enter the required parameters in the **Left Locator** and **Right Locator** fields on the **Transport** bar. The order of the numbers means the following: bar number, meter beat, tick (see details in *Sections 2.8.4 and 2.9.2*).

Mouse cursor and multitrack cursor. The "mouse cursor" — a white arrow — is very widely used in the software. It is positioned on the **Ruler** in the illustration (see number 13). The "classical" mouse cursor is used only outside of the multitrack.

Note

The same kind of white arrow within the multitrack is the **Arrow** tool.

The mouse cursor is used for many things. After double-clicking in a number field (e.g., **Left Locator** or **Right Locator** on the **Transport** bar), the new values are entered from the keyboard. Using the mouse cursor, the tracks are dragged in the **Track Columns** section, etc.

The vertical line marked with the number 12 is the *multitrack cursor*. It shows the current position of the song during recording and playback, and serves for other operations as well, such as the place to insert the copied material.

There are several methods of moving the multitrack cursor: the <Page Up> and <Page Down> keys, and entry of new values in the **Position Indicator** field highlighted in black on the **Transport** bar. See details in *Section 1.7*.

The **Track Columns** section is used for operations with tracks: creation, moving, and parameter setting. There are 6 columns in it (Fig. 1.6).

A	M	C	Track	Chn	Output
		♦	Audio 1	1	VST
		♦	Audio 2	2	VST
		♦	Audio 3	3	VST
		♪	Track 1	1	A: SB Liv..
		♪	Track 2	2	A: SB Liv..

Fig. 1.6. The **Track Columns** section

1.4.1. The *Track* Column

By default, Cubasis VST creates the arrangement window with 8 Audio tracks and 16 MIDI tracks.

A new track is created either with a double-click on the left mouse button in the **Track** column field in the blank area (*under the existing tracks*), or with the **Create Track** command of the **Parts** menu. If necessary, you can change the class of the created track, i.e., convert a MIDI track into an Audio one and vice versa (this is described in *Section 1.4.2*). This operation is applicable only to blank tracks that contain neither Audio nor MIDI information.

The **Track** column contains the names automatically assigned to the tracks. They consist of the words *Audio* and *Track*, which determine the class of the track, and its number among the tracks of *this* class.

You can change the name of a track. Double-click on it with the left mouse button in the **Track** column and enter the new name in the window that opens. Complete the entry by pressing the <Enter> key or by clicking with the mouse outside of this field.

▶ *Tip*

It is better if you rename the track *before* you create parts on it. They will then automatically be assigned the name of the track.

You can move the tracks (the parts move along with them). This operation is simple: grab the name of the track in the **Track** column and drag it up or down, holding the left mouse button pressed. Thanks to this operation, you can quickly and efficiently place tracks on the multitrack.

If you don't need the track any more, you can delete it. Select it by clicking the left mouse button in the **Track Columns** field and press the <Delete> or <Backspace> key. If the track contains parts, the software will ask for a confirmation ("Delete track?"), and you must press Yes.

1.4.2. The *Class* Column

There are two types of tracks marked with icons in the C (Class) column: the note symbol corresponds to a MIDI track, and the sound wave fragment means that the track belongs to the Audio class. You can easily change the class of the track in this column. Click on the icon and make your selection in the drop-down list (Fig. 1.7, Example B).

▼ *Warning*

You can change the class of the track *only when there are no parts on it* (or they are blank). Methods for transferring MIDI to Audio will be described in *Chapter 5*.

Pay attention to the fact that, after the class of the track is changed, its name and the name of the part on it remain the same (compare Examples A and C in Fig. 1.7).

► *Tip*

In order to avoid a mess when the track's class is changed, we recommend that you don't postpone renaming it in accordance with its new status.

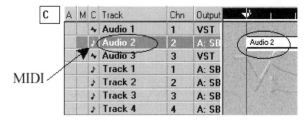

A	A	M	C	Track	Chn	Output		**B**	A	M	C	Track	Chn	Output
			♪	Audio 1	1	VST						Audio 1	1	VST
			♪	Audio 2	2	VST						MIDI Track	2	VST
			♪	Audio 3	3	VST						Audio Track	3	VST
			♪	Track 1	1	A: SB					♪	Track 1	1	A: SB
			♪	Track 2	2	A: SB					♪	Track 2	2	A: SB
			♪	Track 3	3	A: SB					♪	Track 3	3	A: SB
			♪	Track 4	4	A: SB					♪	Track 4	4	A: SB

C	A	M	C	Track	Chn	Output	
			♪	Audio 1	1	VST	
			♪	Audio 2	2	A: SB	Audio 2
			♪	Audio 3	3	VST	
MIDI			♪	Track 1	1	A: SB	
			♪	Track 2	2	A: SB	
			♪	Track 3	3	A: SB	
			♪	Track 4	4	A: SB	

Fig. 1.7. Changing the track class in the **Class** column

The special Audio Mix class track, created automatically and used for automation data recording, is considered in *Section 2.5.3*.

1.4.3. The *Active* and *Mute* Columns and the Solo Mode

The column marked with the letter A (Active) displays the track's activity. If a signal comes from the track, there is a horizontal indicator fluctuating in it.

A	M	C	Track	Chn	Output			
			♪	Audio 1	1	VST	Audio 1	Mono
			♪	Audio 2	3*	VST	Audio	Stereo

Fig. 1.8. The activity indicator for **Mono** and **Stereo** tracks

The column with the letter M (Mute) is used to mute one or more tracks. In order to mute a track, just click in the M column field on the level of the track (a muted track is marked with a black circle). Another click cancels the muting.

The Solo button on the Status Bar leaves the sound of only the *selected* track, *simultaneously* muting all the rest of the tracks. If the Solo mode is active (the Solo button is highlighted), then any selected track will automatically be switched to this mode.

Fig. 1.9 shows variants of track muting:

❐ All tracks sound, since none are muted in the M column (Example A). Their activity is displayed in the A column.

❐ Only two tracks (Voice and Guitar) are heard at playback, since they are not muted in the Mute column (Example B).

❐ Only one track (Drum) is heard at playback, since the Solo mode is active (Example C).

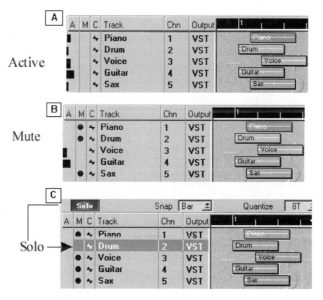

Fig. 1.9. The Active, Mute, and Solo modes

1.4.4. The *Chn* and *Output* Columns

The Chn (Channel) column is used to assign an Audio channel to an audio track. By default, the number of the track corresponds to the number of the channel. This condition is not mandatory, however: the numbers of the track and channels need not coincide.

Tracks and Channels: Distinctions

You should make sure that you know the difference between a track and a channel. The concept of a virtual audio channel is implemented in the Cubasis VST software. You can create however many tracks you want, and their number can exceed the number of channels. But it is the *channels* where the work with sound happens — work such as mixing in the virtual mixer — and each channel can "play" several tracks.

There are two methods of assigning another channel to a track (Fig. 1.10):

❏ For *any* track: click in the Chn column of the Track Columns section and select the number of the channel from the drop-down list

❏ Only for a *selected* track: click in the Chan field on the Inspector panel and make your selection from the drop-down list

After the channel has been changed using any of the methods, the values in the Chn column and Chan field will also be changed simultaneously.

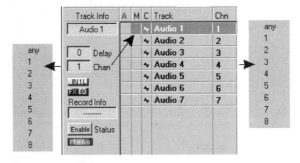

Fig. 1.10. Assigning a channel to an Audio track

By default, the software creates only mono channels. In order to convert a mono channel into stereo *before recording* and import a stereo audio file, do the following:

1. Select the track (by clicking in the Track column).
2. Call the list of channels by one of the methods described above (e.g., by clicking in the Chn column).
3. Select an *odd-numbered* channel from this list (1, 3, 5, or 7).
4. Switch the mono mode to stereo by clicking on the Stereo/Mono button in the bottom of the Inspector panel (pointed to by an arrow in the illustration).
5. Switch the stereo mode back to mono by clicking on this button again.

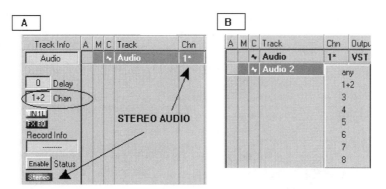

Fig. 1.11. Switching an audio channel from Mono to Stereo

Fig. 1.11 shows that after this operation is done, the stereo channel is marked with an asterisk in the Chn column (pointed to by the arrow). The message in the **Chan** field of the **Inspector** panel is changed to 1+2. Thus, in Cubasis VST, there is always a pair of channels reserved for stereo audio: an odd number + even number.

Channels linked into a stereo pair can not be used separately by the rest of the tracks. Fig. 1.11 (Example B) shows that the channels 1 and 2 make up a stereo pair and *cannot* be used separately as mono channels.

Now it is time to say a few words about the subtleties of channel selection.

Suppose several blank tracks were assigned to *the same* mono channel (for example, 1). Then let's say that this channel was converted into stereo, and that these changes will be valid for *all* tracks assigned to this channel.

Warning

If at least one track has a *mono audio clip*, it will be impossible to convert the corresponding virtual channel into stereo.

When a mono channel is converted into stereo, it "takes as a partner" the next (even) channel.

If, however, the next channel *is already reserved* for a track with the mono audio clip, its conversion into stereo will be impossible. So you will not be able to convert a mono channel with the number 5 into stereo if a mono audio clip is assigned to the next channel (6).

Therefore, when you select a channel for stereo, you should remember that:

❏ It should have an *odd* number.
❏ It should not have a mono audio clip track assigned to it.
❏ The following channel (with an even number) should also be clear.

Now let's consider the features of the **any** channel. It is mainly used for work with the multichannel sound card. Its advantages, however, may be used in a configuration with a common multimedia sound card, since it enables you to place several audio clips assigned to *different* channels to one track. This function is very useful. Fig. 1.12 shows that two stereo clips and one mono clip were copied from the three upper tracks to the lower one, containing the **any** channel. As a result, when the clips are played back, the channels are *automatically switched.*

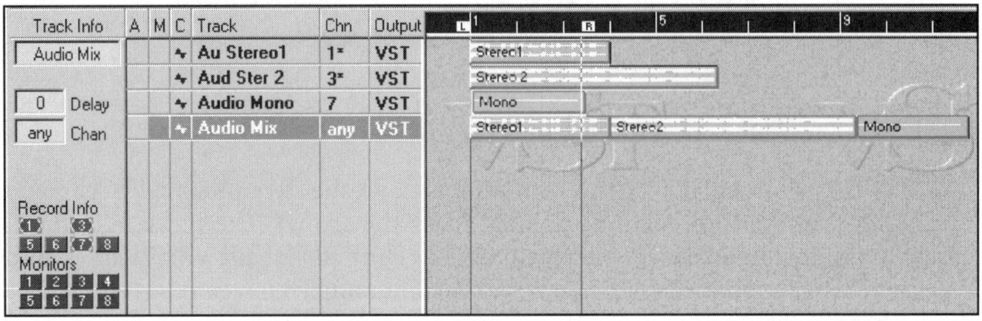

Track Info	A	M	C	Track	Chn	Output	L	R	5	9
Audio Mix				Au Stereo1	1*	VST	Stereo1			
				Aud Ster 2	3*	VST	Stereo 2			
0 Delay				Audio Mono	7	VST	Mono			
any Chan				Audio Mix	any	VST	Stereo1	Stereo2		Mono

Record Info

Monitors

Fig. 1.12. Using an **Any** channel

Since the **any** channel enables you to place clips assigned to *different* channels to *one* track, it is best to use it to introduce diversity into the sound (see *Section 1.15.4*).

The **any** channel is assigned in the usual way (in the Chn column or Chan field). However, it may automatically appear at a *blank* track for which the mono channel has been "withdrawn" for organizing stereo on another track. Fig. 1.13 shows that the Audio 1 track had the first mono channel, and the Audio 2 track had the second mono channel. After the first track was converted into stereo, the second had an **any** channel automatically assigned.

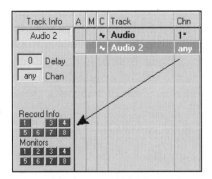

Fig. 1.13. Automatic assignment of the **any** channel

Finally, pay attention to the fact that the *same channel can be simultaneously* assigned several tracks, but remember that if two or more tracks are assigned to the one channel, the clips (parts) *compete* for it. In such cases, it is best to avoid assigning tracks to one channel. The dotted line in Fig. 1.14 shows the border of the clip's intersection, and the parts that are not to be played are crossed out.

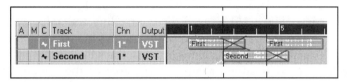

Fig. 1.14. Audio clips competing for a channel

Sound control of the channels is done in the virtual mixer of the software (VST Channel Mixer) abbreviated in the Output column as VST.

The virtual mixer is opened in the Audio menu with the VST Channel Mixer command, or using the <Ctrl>+<*> (on the additional keyboard)> key combination.

Fig. 1.15 shows two different virtual channels as channel cells in the VST Channel Mixer window (unlike in the illustration, they are positioned close to each other in the VST Channel Mixer window).

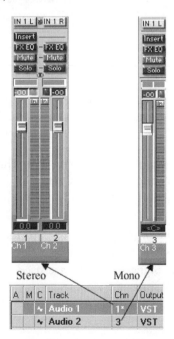

Fig. 1.15. Mono and stereo channels on the track and the mixer

The stereo channel cell is a doubled mono cell, since it is presented as *two* mono channels (1 and 2) controlled by two doubled sliders. Mono channel number 3 has only one control slider. Working with the mixer is described in detail in *Section 1.15.1.*

1.5. The *Transport* Bar

The Transport bar (Fig. 1.16) is used for controlling the software as a "virtual tape recorder". You can open and close it in the **Windows** menu using the **Show Transport Bar** and **Hide Transport Bar** commands, or with the <F12> key.

The Transport bar occupies a rather large area of the screen, and therefore you often have to move it. Grab it at any free place (not by the buttons or fields), and when the cursor changes to the "hand", drag the bar to the new place.

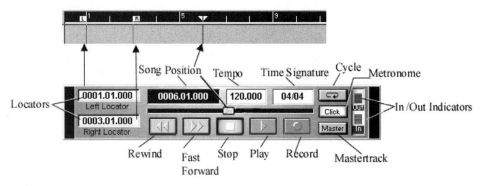

Fig. 1.16. The **Transport** bar

There are 8 buttons, 2 indicators, and 5 active fields for data display on the Transport bar (Fig. 1.16).

□   The **Left Locator** and **Right Locator** fields show the positions of the left and right locators and serve for changing these values.

□   The **Song Position** field shows the position of the multitrack cursor and is used for entering new values.

□   The slider in the middle of the panel is used to move quickly along the multitrack (together with the cursor of the multitrack).

□   The **Tempo** and **Time Signature** fields are used to display and change the meter and tempo of the *whole* song at once.

 Note

All the main musical notions are described in *Chapters 2* and *3*.

❑ The Cycle button switches the looped playback mode on and off. When this button is pressed, the fragment between the left and right locators (L and R) is played without pauses until the playback is stopped with the Stop button. The use of the cycle modes will be considered later.

❑ The Click button switches the metronome (**Metronome**) on and off, measuring the beats with even clicks.

❑ Setting up the metronome is done in the **Metronome** window, which is opened either in the Options/Metronome menu or with a double-click on the Click button. There are two varieties of clicks, depending on what option is checked: **Audio Click** or **MIDI Click** (if both fields are checked, two metronomes click). In order to make the audio metronome sound louder or quieter, change the value in the **Audio Click Level** field (by clicking with the left or right mouse button). The number of bars counted by the metronome *before* the recording is specified in the Bars field. See details on setting up the metronome in *Section 2.5.1.*

❑ The Transport Bar's In/Out indicators show the MIDI signal input and output activity.

❑ The Master button is used for switching on the tempo control mode from the special **Mastertrack**. Double-clicking on this button opens the **List Mastertrack** window, in which you can change the meter and tempo.

▶ *Note*

See details on changing the meter and tempo in the **List Mastertrack** window in *Section 2.15.3.*

❑ The Record, Play, and Stop buttons are used for switching on the record, playback, and stop modes, respectively.

❑ The Rewind and Fast Forward buttons are used to quickly move the multitrack cursor.

1.5.1. *Transport* Bar Buttons
Duplicated by Hotkeys

❑ In spite of the fact that you cannot do without the functions of the Transport bar, sometimes it irritates the user by taking up too much space on the screen. You can remove it from the screen using the <F12> key, and then just use the hotkeys (Fig. 1.17).

▼ *Warning*

The keys of the *additional* keyboard are marked with *braces* in the illustration.

❏ It can be seen that the "main buttons" — Stop, Play, and Record — can be switched on and off with two keys: one on the main keyboard, and another on the additional one. In order to accelerate the "rewinding", press the <Shift> key together with the <Page Up> and <Page Down> keys.

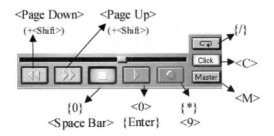

Fig. 1.17. Duplicating the **Transport** bar buttons

1.6. Five Methods of Changing Values in Number Fields

Below are the methods of changing the values in the fields of the Transport bar. It is worth mentioning that practically all of them can be used to change values in any of Cubasis VST's fields.

❏ Click with one of the mouse buttons on the figure to be changed. The left mouse button reduces the value, while the right button increases it.

❏ Click and hold one of the mouse buttons. The value will be smoothly changed. If you hold the <Shift> button pressed as well, the changes will be quicker.

❏ Press and *hold* one of the mouse buttons while clicking with another. Using *two mouse buttons* at the same time, you can change the values quicker in larger steps.

❏ Press and hold the <Ctrl> key, click on the figure to be changed, and drag it horizontally up or down outside of the field holding the mouse button pressed. The values in the field will be changed as if you were using a vertical slider.

❏ Enter the new value from the keyboard. Double-click on the field with the left mouse button and enter the new value in the field. Press <Enter> to complete the entry. This method will be described in more detail.

The values in three fields — Left Locator, Right Locator, and Song Position — are shown as three numbers separated by periods. The first one is the number of the bar, the second is the number of the beat in the bar, and the third is the tick.

▶ *Note*

A *tick* is a part of the musical beat in the "computer" measurement of the Cubasis VST program. A whole note corresponds to 1536 ticks (a quarter note to 384 ticks, an eighth note to 192 ticks, etc.).

You can open the fields for them using the following keys: <L> for Left Locator, <R> for Right Locator, and <P> for Song Position.

These three fields with "big numbers" have their own peculiarities when it comes to entering values.

If you enter *one digit* from the keyboard in the opened field (such as 5), this will mean the start of the fifth bar (the number of beat and tick is set automatically by the software): 0005.01.000.

If you want to enter a value consisting of several figures (e.g., 17th bar, 3rd beat, 20th tick), then the numbers can be entered in short form — without zeros. To do this, type them on the main or additional keyboard using "+" or "−" (e.g., 17+3+20), and complete the entry with the <Enter> key. The following will then appear in the field: 0017.03.020.

1.7. Moving the Multitrack Cursor and *L* and *R* Locators

The multitrack cursor is used very often. We already mentioned that it can be moved with the slider in the middle of the Transport bar and by changing the value in the Song Position field.

There are additional service features that you can use to move it that are provided in the software.

❑ The <Home> key moves the multitrack cursor to the leftmost point of the window.

❑ The <Page Up> and <Page Down> keys move the cursor to the right and left, respectively.

Instantaneously moving the multitrack cursor is done with the keys of the additional keyboard:

❑ The <1> and <2> keys set the cursor in the position of the left and right locators, respectively (Fig. 1.19).

❑ The <9> key moves the cursor to the point of its last stop.

❑ The <3>, <4>, <5>, <6>, <7>, and <8> keys can become "bookmarks" (markers) for moving to certain cursor positions. In order for these keys to work, they must be assigned to certain points of the multitrack: set the cursor to the required position and press one of these keys on the *additional* keyboard holding the <Shift> key pressed.

❏   You can use the ▭ (Stop) button of the Transport bar to move the cursor.

❏   *Repeatedly clicking* on the Stop button *after* the playback is stopped moves the cursor to the left locator.

▶ **Note**

If the multitrack *was already positioned to the left* of the **L** locator, it will turn out to be at the beginning of the song when you perform this operation.

❏   If you *double-click* on this button *after* the playback is stopped, the multitrack cursor will end up at the beginning of the song.

Now we should probably say a few words about moving some no less important elements of the multitrack — locators. They can also be moved using several methods.

The locators are controlled with the left and right mouse buttons (for the left and right locators, respectively) on the **Ruler**. You just need to click with the mouse button to put one of the locators at that location. If you hold one of the mouse buttons pressed, you can drag the locator along the **Ruler**.

In most cases, it is more convenient when the locators are moved *precisely* by metric beats. To do this, you must make the necessary settings in the **Snap** field.

If the **Off** value is set, the locators can be positioned in any place. If another value is selected, there are fewer permitted positions:

❏   **Bar** — bar line (beginning of the bar)

❏   1/2 — half beat

❏   1/4 — quarter beat

❏   1/8 — eighth beat

❏   1/16 — sixteenth beat

Fig. 1.18 shows that if the "largest" step is set in the **Snap** field — equal to a bar — the locators and the multitrack cursor can be positioned only at the beginning of the bar (and not more often).

▶ **Note**

These settings are also valid for positioning the mouse cursor, which is displayed in the **Mouse** field.

Do not confuse the parts of the bar and metric beats. For example, if the meter is *six quarters* (6/4), a locator can be set to *six* positions of the bar, each of them determining the beginning of the quarter beat. If the meter is *four eighths* (4/8), then the locator will be set only on two positions, corresponding to the beginning of the quarter beats, since *four eighths* is the same as *two quarters*.

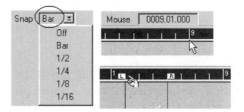

Fig. 1.18. The limits in the **Snap** field
within which a locator can be moved

▶ *Tip*

Using the <Shift>, <1>, and <2> hotkeys on the additional keyboard, you will be able to quickly move the cursor to the position of any of the locators, and vice versa (Fig. 1.19).

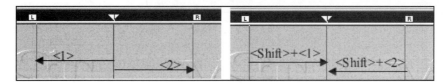

Fig. 1.19. Moving the locators and the multitrack cursor

This very convenient function is applied with the <Alt>+<Ctrl>+<P> key combination. It sets the locators precisely at the borders of one selected part or on the opposite borders of the two *outermost* parts of the selected group (Fig. 1.20).

This enables you to quickly limit the area for further editing.

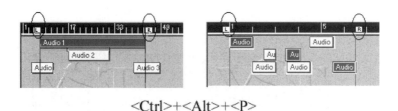

<Ctrl>+<Alt>+<P>

Fig. 1.20. Setting a locator on the borders
of the selected part (parts)

Note

To select several parts, click on them with the left mouse button, holding the <Shift> key pressed.

1.8. Toolbar

The toolbar is opened by clicking and holding down the right mouse button in any place of the parts section. As soon as the right mouse button is released, the panel is hidden. This solution allows you to always have the tools at hand without occupying the working area of the screen.

To select a tool, move to the required icon holding the right mouse button pressed (Fig. 1.21).

Fig. 1.21. Toolbar buttons

Let's now take a look at the features of the **Arrange** window tools.

1.8.1. *Arrow*

Arrow is the most functional tool, so, besides the traditional method, it can be called by clicking the right mouse button on the multitrack.

Note that the Arrow tool and the regular mouse cursor both take on the appearance of a white arrow (Fig. 1.22). The difference is that the **Arrow** tool works within the parts section, while the mouse cursor works outside the borders of this section.

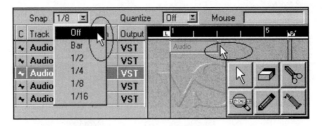

Fig. 1.22. The **Arrow** tool and the mouse cursor

Any tool, when outside of the parts section, is *automatically* changed to the standard mouse cursor. When this tool is within the parts section, it takes on its former appearance. From now on, we will just call the standard mouse **Arrow** when it is within the multitrack, since in practice their difference is insignificant.

Within the multitrack, the Arrow tool is used to manipulate parts and tracks. Using this tool, you can:

❏ *Create a track and a part.* Track creation is done by double-clicking in the **Track** column. To create a blank part, double-click on the multitrack opposite the created track and between the locators (the L locator should be positioned to the left of the R one).

❏ *Select the track and one or several parts, and cancel the selection.* One click selects one part. If you want to select several parts, click on each of them holding the <Shift> key pressed, or drag the Arrow tool diagonally, framing the parts. To cancel the selection, click *outside* of the area of the selected objects.

❏ *Move the track and/or part.* Grab the object (the arrow will turn into a "hand") and drag it to the new place. The track is moved vertically, but the part can be moved in any direction, even onto the free space in the parts section. A track of the corresponding class with the same channel will be created automatically.

❏ *Open the field for renaming the part or track.* To rename the track, double-click on its name in the **Track** column of the track section. To rename the part, you need to double-click on it while the <Alt> key is pressed.

❏ *Copy a part or group of parts* by dragging the selected objects, keeping the <Alt> or <Ctrl> keys pressed. (When the <Ctrl> key is pressed, "imaginary copies" are created, which we will describe later.)

Using the arrow — the mouse cursor — you can perform the standard operations outside of the borders of the multitrack: select values from the Inspector panel, Status Bar, and menu options, change values in all the fields, control the buttons on the Transport bar, move the locators on the Ruler, control the scale sliders, etc.

1.8.2. *Eraser*

The Eraser tool is used to delete parts. Working with it is very simple: click with the Eraser on the part, or drag it across several parts, to erase (delete) it (them). There are peculiarities, however, related to using it with the <Alt> key:

If you hold the <Alt> key pressed while erasing, not only the clicked part will be deleted, but *all the parts* to the right on this track as well (Fig. 1.23, Example B).

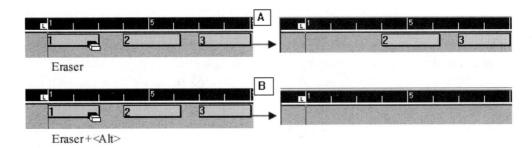

Eraser

Eraser+<Alt>

Fig. 1.23. Various ways of using the **Eraser** tool

1.8.3. *Scissors*

The Scissors tool is used for cutting parts. This is done with one click of the mouse button on the part. The increment by which the Scissors tool moves depends on the value in the Snap field.

If you click with the Scissors tool with the <Alt> key pressed, the part will be cut *along its full length into equal parts* (Fig. 1.24, Example B).

The length of the parts depends on the value specified in the Snap field, and on the distance of the cut line from the starting edge of the part. If Bar is set, as in Fig. 1.24, you will be able to cut the part precisely by bars (along the bar lines); if 1/2 is specified you can do it by half beats, etc.

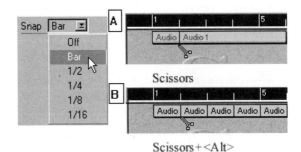

Scissors

Scissors+<Alt>

Fig. 1.24. Various ways of using the **Scissors** tool

▶ *Tip*

This function is extremely useful for quick and accurate montage of the musical material. For example, the original instrument parts are cut precisely into parts of the specified length in the **Snap** field, and the new part is mounted from the resulting parts.

1.8.4. *Magnifying Glass*

The Magnifying Glass tool is used to audition the part's contents. The methods of audition vary:

❒ In order to listen to an *audio part*, click on it with the Magnifying Glass and *hold the left mouse button pressed*. The playback will start from the point that the mouse cursor was at, and continue until you release the mouse button.

❒ In order to listen to a *MIDI part*, drag the Magnifying Glass across the part from left to the right, or vice versa — from the end to the beginning. The tempo of the playback depends on the speed at which the Magnifying Glass is moved across the part.

1.8.5. *Pencil*

The Pencil tool is used to create a part, as well as to copy it and change its size.

To create a part, click with the Pencil tool on a free area of the track.

You can also create parts if you drag the Pencil tool on the track to the left or to the right (Fig. 1.25, Example A). With this method, the points at which the part starts and ends will depend on the values set in the Snap field.

If you drag the Pencil tool with the <Alt> key pressed, this musical part will be equal to one bar (Fig. 1.25, Example B).

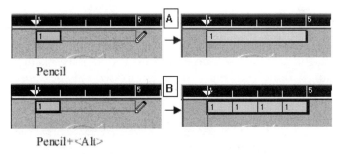

Fig. 1.25. Ways of creating parts using the **Pencil** tool

Using the Pencil tool, you can also either lengthen or shorten a part.

❒ In order to shorten a part, click on it with the Pencil tool, or move it closer to the center by dragging its final border (the new position depends on the value in the Snap field).

❒ In order to lengthen the part, grab one of its borders and move it *away from the center.*

❒ Copying is a method of multiplying parts using the Pencil tool. To perform this operation, drag the border with the <Alt> key pressed. Fig. 1.26 shows that with this method, the border cannot be in just any place: it must be at a spot that is divisible by the part being copied (which corresponds to each *third* bar in the example). If you perform this operation with the <Ctrl> key pressed, ghost copies will be created.

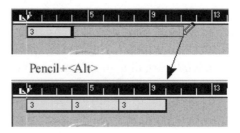

Fig. 1.26. Copying with the **Pencil** tool

Tip

To multiply a part repeatedly, you can drag the **Pencil** tool (with the <Alt> key pressed) to the right edge of the **Arrange** window, or outside of its borders. The window will automatically start scrolling. After the mouse button is released, the window will automatically return to the original position.

1.8.6. *Glue Tube*

This tool links the cut parts of the clips (musical parts, Fig. 1.27). If you click with this tool on a part, the next part will be "glued" to it (compare Examples A and B). If the same operation is done with the <Alt> key pressed, all the *subsequent* parts on this track will be linked to the current one (compare Examples A and C).

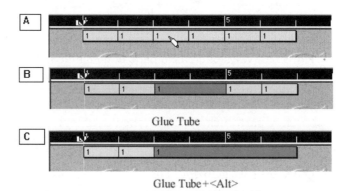

Fig. 1.27. Part linking with the **Glue Tube** tool

1.9. The *Inspector* Panel

In the left part of the Arrange window, you will find the Inspector panel. It is used to *virtually* edit one or more parts. Changes on the Inspector panel can be introduced *at any stage of work* on the project, since they are *non-destructive* (they do not harm the original).

This panel displays the parameters (properties) of the selected object: track (MIDI, audio) or part (MIDI, audio). Working with MIDI objects is described in *Chapter 3*.

If one part is selected, its properties are displayed on the panel, and all changes will concern this part only. If several parts are selected, all the changes will be applied to the group. When the track is selected (and there are no selected parts in the Part Display section), the changes on the Inspector panel will affect *all the parts on this track*.

The part has priority: as soon as at least one of them is selected, the Inspector panel *automatically* "switches" to it.

Let's look at the Inspector panel. Its external differences — for track or for a part — is expressed only in its name (Fig. 1.28).

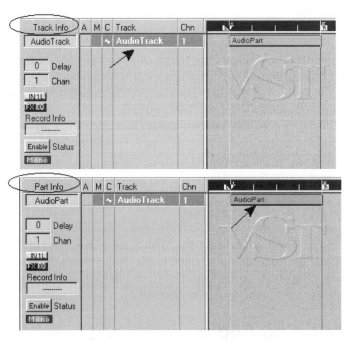

Fig. 1.28. The **Inspector** panel for audio tracks and parts

The upper **Track/Part Name** field shows the name of the selected object. You can enter a new name here after a double-click. Changing the "name" will affect the object itself (the track or part).

You can set the delay value of the track or part relative to the others in the **Delay** field. The values here vary from –256 to 256. A negative value means an advance, and a positive one indicates a delay.

The number of the channel is shown in the **Chan** (channel) field. A mono channel is marked with one digit, whereas a stereo channel is marked with the sum of some digits, the first of which is always odd. The stereo/mono mode is switched with the lower **Mono/Stereo** button. In order to reassign the channel, click in the **Chan** field and select the new channel from the drop-down list.

The **Input** button is used for switching the monitoring mode of the assigned audio channel on and off.

If you click on this button with the <Ctrl> key pressed, you can select the VST input from the opened list. (The number of the VST inputs depends on the type of the sound card, settings in the VST-**Inputs** window, and the type of ASIO driver used.) This button is duplicated by the **Input Selector** for each audio channel in the VST **Channel Mixer** window.

The **FX/EQ** buttons (the FX Send to the effects and equalizer) are used for opening the VST **Channel settings** window, which is an expanded view of the channel cell of the VST mixer.

The **Record Info** field shows the name of the audio file being recorded. Double-clicking in this field opens the **Audio Files Folder**, which contains a list of the audio file recorded in the song. Use this window to select or create a new folder for the audio files, completing the dialog with the **Select** button.

The **Enable** button of the **Status** field is used for switching on recording on the track. The **Enable** button of the selected track is switched on automatically together with the **Rec** button on the **Transport** bar.

Now let's get a little practice.

1.10. Audio Recording

To be able to work with audio clips, first you must place them on the multitrack. You can do this in a number of ways: import the audio file to the software, record the audio clip from the input of the sound card, or convert a MIDI clip into an audio clip using a VST instrument (see details in *Chapter 5*).

1.10.1. Importing Audio

To import an audio file, do the following:

1. Select the track in which the imported file is to be placed. The channel of the track must correspond to the file (mono or stereo).

Warning

If you want to place a stereo file on a blank multitrack, select a track with an odd channel number, and it will automatically be converted into stereo. You can not place a stereo file on a track with an even channel number.

2. Set the left locator to the point at which the imported file is to start.
3. Select the Import Audio File option from the File menu.
4. Select the required file in the Import Audio File window that opens, and press the Open button. (Files may have either the WAV or AIF extensions.)

Apart from common Audio files, you can import special ReCycle files with the REX extension into Cubasis VST. These files are phrase loops created in the separate Steinberg ReCycle application.

You can import a REX file the same way you would an Audio file — by using the File/Import ReCycle File command. A remarkable feature of ReCycle files is that their playback tempo changes along with the project tempo, just like MIDI clips (see more details on ReCycle files in *Section 1.15.4*).

1.10.2. Recording from a Microphone

Recording from a microphone in Cubasis VST is done in almost the same was as on a regular tape recorder, with some additional features.

1. Make the necessary connections and settings (connect the microphone to the input of the sound card, and select the microphone recording input on the sound card's mixer).

Note

See details on the mixer settings in *Section 1.10.3*.

2. Create (and leave selected) the audio tracks on which the recording will be done.

Tip

It is best to rename the track at once, in accordance with its future contents. Remember that the parts are automatically named according to the name of the tracks.

3. Open the Inspector panel (if it has been removed from the screen). This is done by clicking on the ▓▓ button in the bottom left part of the screen.
4. According to the planned type of recording — mono or stereo — press the Mono/Stereo button on the Inspector panel (an odd channel should be assigned

for stereo recording). When recording from the microphone connected to the sound card input, Mono mode is selected. However, if the microphone is connected to external editing devices with stereo outputs, Stereo mode may be required).

5. Set the L locator at the point of the multitrack from which the recording should start, and the R locator a bit further towards the presumed end of the recording. *Attention: If the multitrack cursor crosses the right locator (R), the recording is automatically interrupted.*

6. Set the recording level using the mixer of the sound card. The recording level is controlled in the VST Channel Mixer or VST Channel Settings windows. The VST mixer is called with the VST Channel Mixer option of the Audio menu, or with the <Ctrl>+<*> key combination on the additional keyboard. You can use the FX/EQ button on the Inspector panel to open the VST Channel Settings window for this track. For the indicator to display the level of the input signal, the In button should be pressed. The recording level must not exceed 0 dB, and at the same time should not be too low, since the quality will worsen.

7. If necessary, switch on the metronome on the Transport bar by clicking on the Click button (or the <C> key).

Note

By default, the metronome "clicks" two introductory bars. See details on the metronome settings in *Section 2.5.1*.

8. Specify the tempo and meter on the Transport bar using the mouse buttons (see details on the changing the values in the fields in *Section 1.6*).

9. Press the Rec button on the Transport bar (or the <9> key).

Warning

The **Cycle** button should be switched off, since the previous audio part will be deleted with repeated recording.

10. Play the part.

11. Press the Stop button on the Transport bar. The recorded part will appear on the multitrack.

12. Listen to the part. You can do this by holding the Magnifying Glass over it, or by clicking on the Play button on the Transport bar (<Enter> on the additional keyboard). You can switch off the metronome during the audition (the <C> key).

If the recorded take didn't turn out the way you wanted, you can delete the part with the Eraser tool, or use the Undo option of the Edit menu. If you do, the part will be deleted *from the arrangement window only*. In order to delete the audio file that the part refers to from the hard disk, select this part and use the <Ctrl>+<Backspace> key combination. The software will ask you to confirm your decision in a window. If you click on the Yes button, the file will be deleted from the hard disk.

If you press the Cycle button on the **Transport** bar before the recording, recording will be done in the Loop mode. See details in *Section 1.13.*

1.10.3. Re-Recording MIDI to Audio

In order to be able to apply virtual audio processing to MIDI parts, you need to either re-record them onto Audio tracks or use VST instruments (described in *Chapter 5*). The MIDI part, in turn, can be recorded either in the **Arrange** window (from the MIDI keyboard), or in any of the editors: Key Edit, Score Edit, or List Edit.

 Note

Users familiar with notation can write the score with the mouse in the Score Edit editor of the Cubasis Notation software. (The Note editor of this software has more features than Score Edit of the Cubasis VST software). A score thus created can then be opened in Cubasis VST. Working with both MIDI and the notes will be described later.

Before we begin describing the recording algorithm, we'd like to say a few words about the sound card mixer. Its settings affect the signal input.

Basically, the mixer structure of various sound cards is very similar. There are differences in the appearance, however. Below is an example of the mixer of a common and rather inexpensive sound card — Sound Blaster Live (Fig. 1.29).

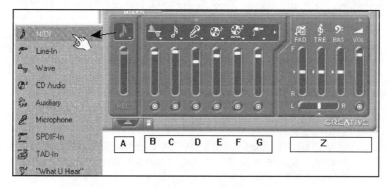

Fig. 1.29. A sound card mixer

It is opened with the **Start/Settings/Audio HQ/Mixer** command.

Select the source *from* which the recording will be made in the REC section (marked with the letter A in the illustration). If we plan to re-record the MIDI part, the MIDI icon — a note — should be here. Click on the icon and make your selection from the drop-down list. (The element that is already selected is *missing* from the list, but in the illustration we duplicated MIDI in the list for clarity.)

The round buttons under the sliders (marked with the letters B, C, D, E, F, and G) are used for switching the corresponding signals on and off. Since we are working with MIDI and Audio, the B and C buttons should be lit.

 Note

If an Audio recording was made from a microphone, the **D** button, as well as the **B** button, should be lit, and the **Microphone** command should be selected in the list. The mixer of the SB Live sound card makes it possible to *independently* control the recording and playback levels.

General parameters, such as volume (VOL.) and panorama (L and R), are controlled from the Z section.

In order to regulate controls in the mixer window during recording or playback, check the Play in Background option in the Options menu of Cubasis VST.

Suppose there is a MIDI part on the multitrack. Below is the algorithm for re-recording it into an Audio clip.

1. Select the audio track where the recording will be made.

Note

If there is no free Audio track, create it by double-clicking the left mouse button in the **Track** column. If you get a MIDI track as a result, change its class to Audio by setting the sound wave icon in the **C** column.

2. If necessary, assign the channel for the Audio track (mono or stereo is switched using the Mono/Stereo button on the Inspector panel).
3. Set the locators at the edges of the future part.

Warning

The recording will start *precisely* from the left locator and will end at the right locator. Therefore, to be on the safe side, it is better to set the **R** locator a little bit to the right, and cut it once the part is recorded.

4. Switch off the looped recording mode if it was on (release the Cycle button on the Transport bar.
5. Press the Rec button of the **Transport** bar (or the <*> key on the additional keyboard).

6. After the multitrack cursor crosses the right locator, the recording will be stopped, and the part will be created on the multitrack. Playback will continue.

7. Stop playback with the **Stop** button (or with the <Space> or <0> keys of the additional keyboard).

8. Set the cursor at the beginning of the recorded part (the <1> key on the additional keyboard).

9. Listen to the recording by switching on the **Solo** mode with the button of the **Status Bar** of the recorded track (the track should be selected).

As a result of using any of the possible methods of recording, the files turn out to be not only on the multitrack, but also segments on the "cutting table" of the software — in the VST Pool window. This provides additional features that can be used for creative work with the audio material. If the recording is done in looped mode (if the Cycle button is pressed), this window will retain all the takes in the form of separate segments (see *Section 1.13*).

In order to maximally simplify your work in the Arrange window, you should know well all the basic operations that will be described in general below (in *Sections 1.11* and *1.12*). We hope that after you have an idea of the tools and elements of the Arrange window, all of them will seem simple, familiar, and clear.

1.11. Creating Tracks and Parts

There are several methods of creating tracks and parts.

1.11.1. Creating Tracks

Variant 1. In order to create a track in the blank Arrange window, perform one of the following operations:

- ❏ Select the **Create Track** option from the **Parts** menu
- ❏ Press the <Ctrl>+<T> key combination
- ❏ Double-click with the left mouse button in the Track column

▌ Attention:

❗ A track created in the blank **Arrange** window will always have the MIDI class (Fig. 1.30, Example A).

In order to convert the created MIDI track into an Audio track, change its class in the C column (Fig. 1.30, Example B).

► ***Tip***

In order to avoid confusion, it is best to rename tracks. To rename the track, double-click with the left mouse button on its name in the **Track** column, and type in the new name in the field that becomes available (Fig. 1.30, Example A).

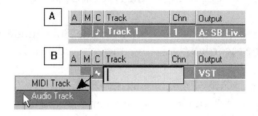

Fig. 1.30. Creating an audio track (Variant 1)

Variant 2. If there is one or more tracks in the **Arrange** window, then in order to create a new track, double-click with the left mouse button in the Track column (under an existing track). The class of a track thus created will *be the same as the previously selected track.*

Fig. 1.31 shows that a track of the *Audio class* is created under a previously selected *Audio track.*

Fig. 1.31. Creating an Audio track (Variant 2)

Variant 3. If the part is placed on a free area of the multitrack (where there is no track) either by dragging or copying (i.e., dragged with a pressed <Ctrl> or <Alt> key), then the track will be automatically created by the software (Fig. 1.32).

Fig. 1.32. Creating an Audio track (Variant 3)

1.11.2. Creating Parts

As we already mentioned, Audio parts are created automatically when an Audio file is imported, or during recording onto an Audio track. Let's consider other ways of creating parts.

Variant 1. If you select the **Create Part** option from the **Parts** menu (or press the <Ctrl>+<P> key combination), a MIDI class part and track will appear in the blank **Arrange** window. The beginning and end of the part will coincide with the positions of the left and right locators, respectively.

In order to use the created track for work with Audio, change the track's class in the C column.

Variant 2. If you double-click on the **Arrow** tool in the **Part Display** section between two locators on the track level, you will create a part whose edges coincide with the position of the locators.

Note

Attention: the **L** locator must always be to the left of the **R** one. You can set the locators by clicking the left or right mouse button on the **Ruler**. If utter precision is necessary, enter the required parameters on the **Transport** bar in the **Left Locator** and **Right Locator** fields (Fig. 1.33).

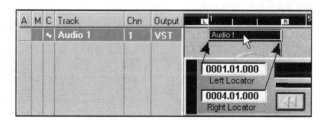

Fig. 1.33. Creating an Audio part with the **Arrow** tool

❑ *Variant 3.* You can create blank parts of various duration using the Pencil tool.

Note

A part will be created if you click with the tool in the part section.

If you drag the Pencil tool across the multitrack (to the right or to the left), you can create a longer part, but its start and end will depend on the authorized values in the Snap field (Fig. 1.25, Example A). If you drag the Pencil tool to the right with the <Alt> key pressed, a sequence of parts will be created.

The methods used for creating blank parts are the same for both Audio and MIDI, but creating a blank clip makes much more sense for work with MIDI — for example, to be able to record notes in the Score Edit editor, etc.

An Audio part appears on the multitrack as a result of recording or importing.

1.12. Editing Parts

Editing in the **Arrange** window means moving, cutting, gluing, and deleting. These operations are available only with parts that have been *selected*. The editing operations are demonstrated in this chapter using Audio parts.

1.12.1. Selecting

You can select one part by clicking the **Arrow** tool.

To select several neighboring parts, drag the **Arrow** tool across the multitrack holding the left mouse button pressed; in doing this, you frame the parts. This method also enables you to select partially framed parts (Fig. 1.34, Example A). The selected parts differ in color: they are always darker.

If you want to select several parts that are positioned far from each other, click on each of them with the **Arrow** tool while holding the <Shift> key pressed (Fig. 1.34, Example B).

To cancel a selection, click on any free area of the multitrack.

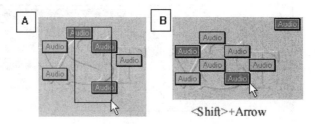

Fig. 1.34. Selecting several parts

1.12.2. Moving and Copying

Moving a part can be done in several ways. The simplest one is to grab the part and move it to any place on the Audio track.

▼ *Warning*

You can move the part only to a track of the same class. If you try to move an Audio part to a MIDI track, the software will give you a warning.

The moving interval depends on the value in the Snap field (Fig. 1.35):

☐   If Off is selected, the part can start at any point (at the start of any tick)
☐   Bar — only at bar lines
☐   1/2, 1/4, 1/8, 1/16 — at the beginning of beats (half, quarter, eighth, sixteenth)

▶ *Tip*

We do not advise you to select **Off** if there is no good reason for doing so, since you can lose synchronicity among parts on different tracks as a result of "free" moving.

You can move a *group of selected parts*. Grab one of them with the Arrow tool and drag them to the new place.

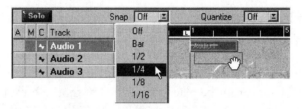

Fig. 1.35. Moving a part with the **Arrow** tool

You can also move parts using the Edit menu options:

1. Select a part by clicking on it.
2. Select the Cut option (or press the <Ctrl>+<X> key combination).
3. Set the multitrack cursor to the point from which the part should begin after you have moved it.
4. Paste the part with the Paste option (or the <Ctrl>+<V> key combination).

This same method can be used for moving a group of parts.

Unlike the moving feature, the original part remains in its position when copied, and one (or several) copies of it appear on the multitrack.

There are two types of copies: "*regular*" (Copy) and "*imaginary*" (Ghost Copy). They look different: the name of a ghost copy is written in italics. Fig. 1.36 shows the part (A), its copy (B), and its ghost copy (C).

The regular copy (from here on referred to as simply a "copy") is a copy of the original part. The *ghost copy* is a reference to the original part containing the information concering at what time position the original part should be reproduced.

In this software, ghost copies are useful when working with MIDI (see details in *Section 2.3.1*).

Fig. 1.36. A part, its copy, and its ghost copy

Let's take a look at some of the features of the *Audio part* that ghost copies use. This copy is *automatically* transformed into a regular part if it is processed with tools (e.g., if its size is changed with the Pencil tool, if it is cut with the Scissors and glued with the Glue Tube). If the name of the original part is changed, this would entail a change in the names of all of its ghost copies.

There are two methods of creating copies of both types.

❏ Grab the selected part with the **Arrow** tool and drag it to a new place, holding one of the function keys pressed:

- If the <Alt> key is pressed, a regular copy will be created.
- If the <Ctrl> key is pressed, a ghost copy will be created.

The copy will appear in the place where the left mouse button was released. When this method of copying is used, the beginning of the copy depends on the value in the **Snap** field.

❏ The second method consists of several operations:

1. Select the part.
2. Press the **Repeat** option in the **Parts** menu (or the <Ctrl>+<K> key combination).
3. Specify the required number of copies in the **Number of Copies** field of the **Repeat selected parts** window (to create ghost copies, check the **Ghost Copies** field).

As a result, the copies will be attached to the original part (Fig. 1.37).

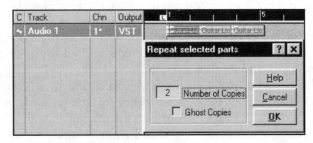

Fig. 1.37. Copying via the **Repeat/Parts** option

In our previous book, we debated why some compositions live for centuries and why others die before they are born. Along with a discussion of non-verbal intelligence, we spoke about the reasons for the groundless use of repeated fragments in contemporary electronic musical compositions. We are not going to go back to this theme in this chapter. (Those interested can find it in *Chapters 1*, *2*, *3*, and *6* of our book *Live Music on Your PC*, A-LIST Publishing, 2002).

We will, however, warn beginner musicians against the danger that lurks in computer technologies. It is very easy to repeat a musical phrase on the computer. But you should remember that unjustified repetition makes music meaningless, mechanical, and insipid. (The methods of introducing motivated diversity into the musical material are considered in the sections dealing with sound processing and working with takes in the VST Pool window during cycle recording, and also in *Chapters 2* and *3*).

1.12.3. Cutting, Gluing, and Deleting

To cut a part (or its copy), click on it with the Scissors tool. We already mentioned that the accuracy of the cutting line's positioning depends on the value in the Snap field. If this operation is done with the <Alt> key pressed, the part will be cut into equal parts along the entire length. The length of the cut parts depends on the distance between the cutting line and the beginning of the part.

After the part is cut, each of its parts becomes "independent": as a separate part, it can be moved, deleted, glued, copied, etc.

Remember, though, that if you click on a part with the Glue Tube tool, the current part will be glued to the next one. If this operation is done with the <Alt> key pressed, all the subsequent parts of this track will be linked to the current one (see Fig. 1.27 in *Section 1.8.6*).

To delete one or more parts, select them and press the <Delete> or <Backspace> key, or apply the Delete Parts command from the Edit menu.

If you want to delete a whole track along with all the parts on it, use the Delete Track command from the Edit menu, and confirm your decision in the window that appears by pressing Yes.

1.13. The *VST Pool* Window. Additional Editing Features

Now it is time to reveal a "secret": the parts on the multitrack don't contain Audio files, but rather references to them. In Cubasis VST, these references are called *segments* (Fig. 1.38).

Fig. 1.38. A part and its segment

 Note

> The editing method that is implemented on the principle of working with references to files rather than the original Audio files themselves is called *non-destructive editing*. In some professional brands of audio software, such as Nuendo or SAWStudio, these references are called *regions*.

You know that Audio files are quite large in size. Therefore, working directly with them will lead to an unpractical waste of space on the hard disk and the considerable slowdown of such operations as copying and deleting a selected area of an Audio file. This kind of editing is called *destructive*. With this kind of editing, you need physical copies of Audio files for storing the undo levels, and — what is most important — there is the danger of irreversible damage to the original material.

This is the reason why the *non-destructive* method appeared, which became available only with the appearance of the appropriate computer technologies. When this method is used, none of the original files are affected, since all the operations are done not with the files, but with their "virtual images": their references that contain the information as to where in the multitrack a particular part (segment) of the Audio file is to be reproduced. As a result, the musical project's file contains a sequence of commands that occupy considerably less disk space.

Working with segments provides additional possibilities of editing in the VST Pool window. Suppose you imported an Audio file into Cubasis VST. The software automatically creates an equal segment and places it inside the Audio Part "container" and positions it on the multitrack.

At the same time, the segment appears and is displayed in the structure of the VST Pool window (Fig. 39). This registration of the file in the software as a segment is *necessary for all audio files* of the project.

Cases where the segment and part length coincide are marked in Figs. 1.39 and 1.40 with an equals sign.

Due to further operations, this equality may be violated. For example, when parts are edited on the multitrack — e. g., cut with the Scissors tool with the deletion of one of the parts — the size of the segment in the VST Pool window is also changed (compare Examples A and B in Fig. 1.40).

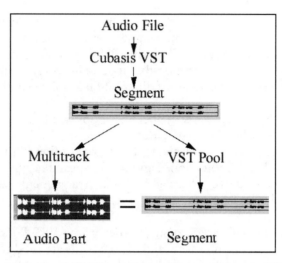

Fig. 1.39. Displaying an Audio file on the multitrack and in the **VST Pool** window

The fact that when the segment size is changed virtually in the VST Pool window a corresponding change in the Audio contents *within the part* takes place is also important (compare Examples A and C in Fig. 1.40). Note that the segment of the part has been reduced, but the part itself (the "container") remains the same size.

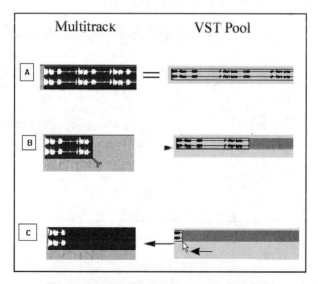

Fig. 1.40. The interconnection of objects in the **VST Pool** and **Arrange** windows

You should also keep in mind that the segment *cannot be changed irreversibly*: you can always return it to its full size by moving its borders in the VST Pool window, and the previous sound will also be returned, which will definitely affect the contents of the part.

To conclude, we should mention that if you glue several parts with the **Glue Tube** tool, there will be several segments of different files in the resulting part, as it should be in a "container".

Working with the segments in the VST Pool window considerably expands the editing options described in the previous sections.

The VST Pool window is opened with the Pool option in the Audio menu, or with the <Ctrl>+<F> key combination. Figuratively speaking, this is sort of the accounts department of the software, where all files and arrangement segments of the song are strictly registered. You can move *any* segment into *any arrangement* of the song from this window.

All the project details are in a strict order in the VST Pool window. The original Audio file here serves as a directory, and the segments are subdirectories. A triangle icon comes before the name of the file, and a speaker comes before the segments (Fig. 1.41).

The segments are the main "building material" of the arrangement. You can listen to them, change their size, copy them, and delete them in the VST Pool window. If you use cycle recording, every new take will appear in this window as a segment (see the details at the end of the chapter). Segments that you obtain in this manner can be freely moved to the multitrack in the form of parts. These operations can be compared to preparing the ingredients for the final audio product.

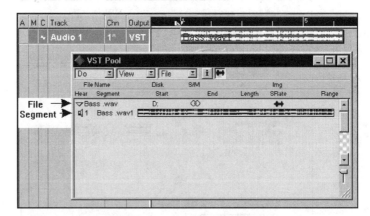

Fig. 1.41. A file and a segment in the **VST Pool** window

All work with the part in the **Arrange** window will be accompanied with synchronous changes in the VST Pool window. So, if a part is cut, each of its parts will contain an independent segment. You can independently change its size (Range), and then use it in the arrangement in various ways (Fig. 1.42).

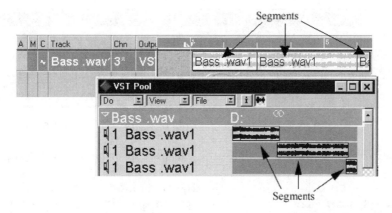

Fig. 1.42. Displaying an Audio file and segment in the **VST Pool** window

The information on the file and segments differs in content. This can be seen in the names of the columns: the upper line gives a title to the file's information, and the lower one deals with the segments (for clarity, "unnecessary" lines are colored white in Figs. 1.43 and 1.44).

File Name	Disk	S/M	Resolution	Img	Length	Date	Time
▷ Bass .wav	D:	◯◯	16 Bit	◄►	1,837K	16.09.98	12:20 AM

Fig. 1.43. File information in the **VST Pool** window

The VST Pool window holds the following information on the file (Fig. 1.43):

❑ File name
❑ Disk
❑ Stereo/Mono (S/M)
❑ Resolution
❑ Status of the Audio file's soundwave image
❑ Size in KB (Length)
❑ Date and Time

There is a triangle pointer before the file name. When it is pointed at the file name, the file's directory is closed, and the segments are not visible in the window. If you click on it, the triangle will change its position, and the list of the segments of this file will open below (compare Figs. 1.43 and 1.44).

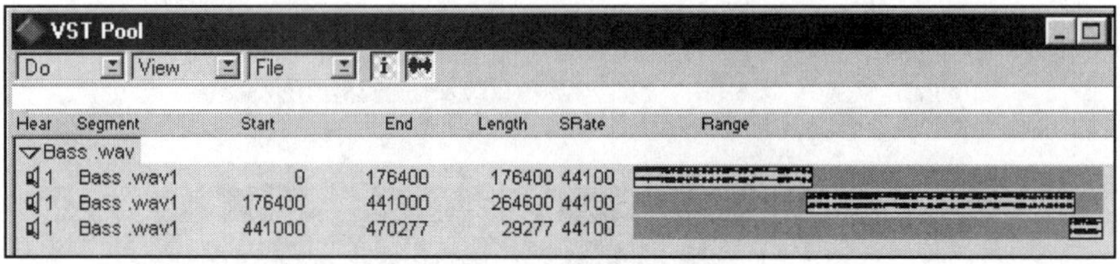

Hear	Segment	Start	End	Length	SRate	Range
▽ Bass .wav						
◁)1	Bass .wav1	0	176400	176400	44100	
◁)1	Bass .wav1	176400	441000	264600	44100	
◁)1	Bass .wav1	441000	470277	29277	44100	

Fig. 1.44. Segment information in the **VST Pool** window

The VST Pool window contains the following information on the segments:

- ❑ Hear — this column contains the triangle pointing at the "head" file from which the segments were formed, as well as the speaker icon used for listening to the segment. To do this, press and hold the mouse cursor on the icon.
- ❑ Segment — the name of the segment. The segment name is assigned automatically, but you can change it if necessary (double-click on it and type another name on the keyboard.
- ❑ Start — the starting point of the segment. As in the three next columns, this value can be displayed differently, depending on what is selected in the drop-down list.
- ❑ ViewEnd — the end point of the segment.
- ❑ Length — the length of the segment.
- ❑ SRate — the sampling rate of the file.
- ❑ Range — the range of the segment represented visually.

The segment may be shown in two views in the VST Pool window. If the button in the upper part of the window is pressed, the waveform will be visible in the illustration. If it is switched off, the segment is shown as a lightly colored rectangle (Fig. 1.45).

▶ *Note*

You can listen to the segment if the mouse cursor is held on the segment image (**Range**). The playback will start from the point at which the cursor is set.

You can minimize the information in this window by releasing the i (information) button. Clicking again shows detailed information (compare Figs. 1.42 and 1.45).

We already mentioned that the segment size in the VST Pool window can be changed. This is very convenient for later Audio montage, since you can select the required area of the Audio file to be played back by moving the edges of the segment.

In order to move one of the edges, grab it with the mouse cursor and move it to a new place (compare Example A in Fig. 1.46 with Examples B and C).

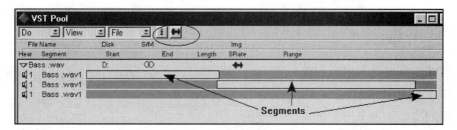

Fig. 1.45. The window's appearance with released **i** and waveform buttons

If you grab the segment with the <Ctrl> key pressed, you can move the whole segment to a new place (Example D).

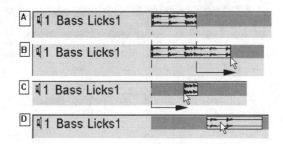

Fig. 1.46. Changing the segment borders

There is yet another important detail. No matter how the segment edges are changed, on the multitrack, it will always start from the *starting edge of the part*. If you shift the left edge of the segment, the rest of the contents will be moved to the starting edge of the part (compare Examples A and B in Fig. 1.47).

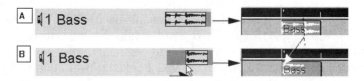

Fig. 1.47. Cutting the beginning of the segment

▼ Warning

The segment size change will *simultaneously affect all parts* in which it is used. If this is not what you want, you can copy the segment with the **Duplicate Segment** option in the **Do** menu, and change its size without worrying about affecting the material of the multitrack. Then drag the resulting segment to the multitrack.

The main operation when doing Audio montage from segments is the copying of the segments from the VST Pool window. This is very simple. Grab the *name* of the segment and drag it to one of the Audio tracks of the multitrack (Fig. 1.48). Thus, each segment can be placed in *any* Arrange window.

There is a number before the segment name in the VST Pool window. It indicates the number of times the segment is used in the Arrange windows (in Fig. 1.48, the Violin segment is used twice in 2 arrangements).

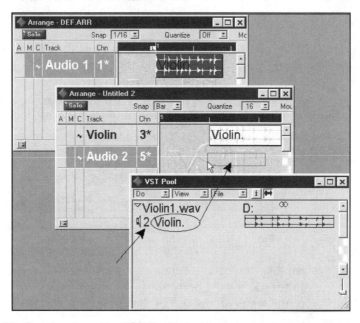

Fig. 1.48. Copying from the **VST Pool** window to various arrangement windows

The rest of the operations with the segments are done via the Do, View, and File menus in the upper part of the VST Pool window. Their drop-down lists contain commands that enable work with files and segments, and you can also make the settings for the object info display in the VST Pool window in them (Fig. 1.49).

The Do menu is used for work with segments.

❑ The Duplicate Segment option duplicates the segment in the VST Pool window, which gives you more ways in which the segments can be used. After this operation, you can fearlessly change the size, since this editing will not affect the existing parts.

❑ This operation is very simple: select a segment (by clicking on its name in the Segment column), and then select the Duplicate Segment option. Then you can grab the segment name and drag it to the multitrack, thus creating a new part.

❏ The Purge Segment option automatically deletes all the segments not used in *any* of the Arrange windows of this song.

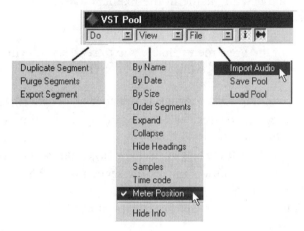

Fig. 1.49. The **Do**, **View**, and **File** menus of the **VST Pool** window

Note

Be reminded that the figure beside the speaker icon indicates the number of times this segment is used. If there is no figure, the segment is not used in any of the arrangements (Fig. 1.50). Consequently, just like the other segments, it will be deleted by the **Purge Segment** command.

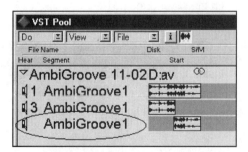

Fig. 1.50. A segment not used in an arrangement is deleted by the **Purge Segments** command

❏ The Export Segment option allows you to save the segment as a *separate Audio file*. To do this:

1. Select the segment.
2. Select Export Segment.

3. Confirm your decision in the window that opens by clicking the **Yes** button after the program asks if you would like to "Save as a discrete file?"
4. Type in the new file name in the **Exporting Segments** window that will open, and press the **Save** button.

The options of the **View** menu enable you to represent the information on the files and segments in the VST Pool window in a different manner.

❏ The **By Name** option sorts the files in alphabetical order.
❏ The **By Date** option orders the files according to the time of their creation (the most recent one is at the top of the list).
❏ The **By Size** option sorts the files by size. The largest one is at the beginning of the list.
❏ The **Order Segments** option moves the segments in the list, positioning them in the sequence that they are in in the file.
❏ The **Expand** option opens the directories of all the files, opening the lists of the segments as well.
❏ The **Collapse** option minimizes the list structure, leaving just the names of the files
❏ The **Hide Headings** (**Show Headings**) option hides (shows) the headings of the VST Pool window.

▶ *Tip*

This function is very convenient, since it enables you to leave *only the necessary information* in the window. Remember that you can hide information using the **i** button, or increase the scale with the slider (Fig. 1.51).

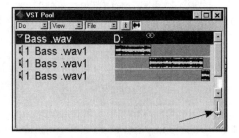

Fig. 1.51. Optimizing the information in the **VST Pool** window
with the **Hide Headings** option

❏ The **Samples**, **Time Code**, and **Meter Position** options switch the segment information display mode in the **Start**, **End**, and **Length** columns:
 • Samples — in samples

- Time Code — in time units (minutes:seconds:frames:subframes)
- Meter Position — in musical meter units (bars/beats/ticks).

❏ The Hide Info/Show Info option duplicates the i button (hides or shows some of the information in the VST Pool window).

The File menu is intended for three operations.

❏ The Import Audio option allows you to import a file without leaving the VST Pool window (i.e., it partially duplicates the Import Audio File option of the File menu).

❏ The Save Pool option allows you to save the configuration of the VST Pool window. We should mention that the contents of this window are fully saved with the song in a file with the ALL extension (or partially, in ARR and PRT files). But you can only save some of the segments using this function.

To perform this operation, select in the VST Pool window only the ones that are to be saved (click on their names with the <Shift> key pressed). Then select the Save Pool option and confirm it by pressing the Selected button in the window that opens (if the All button is pressed, all segments will be saved). Next, name the created POL file in the Saving Pool window that opens.

▌ *Warning*

This method saves not the Audio files themselves, but just the references to them. Therefore, if the files were deleted or moved, loading the segment will become impossible.

❏ The Load Pool option enables you to load the saved segments.

Using segments in cycle recording. The VST Pool window allows you to make editing more comfortable. This also applies to cycle recording. Let's consider an example.
To switch on cycle recording, you need to:

1. Select the audio track on which the recording will be done.
2. Limit the recording area with the L and R locators (the L locator should on the left).
3. Set the tempo and meter on the Transport bar and switch on the metronome if necessary (the Click button).
4. Switch on the Looped mode with the Cycle button (circled in Fig. 1.52).
5. Start recording (with the Rec button on the Transport bar, or the <*> on the additional keyboard). After two (default) bars of introduction, the Play button will be lit, the cursor will cross the border of the left locator, and the recording will start. (You can change the number of intro bars. See details in *Sections 1.5 and 2.5.1.*)

After the cursor crosses the right locator, it will return to the beginning of the fragment. This will continue until the musician stops recording (with the **Stop** button on the **Transport** bar or with the <0> key on the additional keyboard).

Each time the multitrack cursor passes between the locators, the software creates another take. These takes are saved in the **VST Pool** window as regular segments. An extra convenience here is that they are sorted: the upper segment is the recording of the whole part without dividing it into takes (which are shown with the arrow). Below are the segments of each take (circled). They are numbered and positioned in order of "freshness": the upper one was recorded last. By default, it is it positioned in the part on the multitrack.

Thanks to the **VST Pool** window, you can use the take collection as you like, using the same methods used to work with segments.

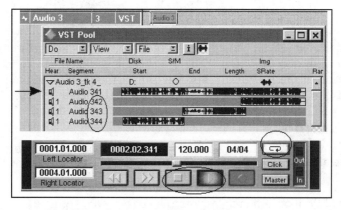

Fig. 1.52. Creating a region in cycle recording

1.14. Saving the Song's Structure

Saving the material is an operation that can hardly be overestimated. In Cubasis VST, you can not only save a whole song, but also its parts. Files with different extensions are used for this purpose. They are easily memorized, since the letter combination has a significance: ALL (for saving the entire song), ARR (for the arrangement), and PRT (for parts).

▼ Attention:

The methods described in this section do not pertain to saving the Audio file itself, but only to its segments (references). If the original WAV file is deleted from the hard disk (or renamed), you will not be able to play the material back.

Below is a sequence of saving operations that beginners can use (Fig. 1.53):

1. Select the Save As option from the Edit menu.
2. Select the folder in which the file will be saved in the Save File As window that opens. Fig. 1.53 shows the buttons you can use to navigate the directory's structure, which are circled. The folder is selected by clicking in the list (which is pointed to with the arrow). The file will be saved in the folder whose name is in the Folder field.
3. Type in the name of the file being saved in the File Name field.
4. Select the corresponding extension in the File Type field. There is a special extension for each type of file, and the number of saved parameters depends on this extension.
5. Press the Save button.

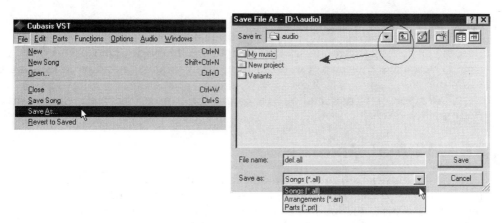

Fig. 1.53. Saving the song and its parts

If you decide to save the file with the ALL extension, the project (song) will be saved with the *maximum amount of data*: all the arrangement windows, the Setup settings, and the references in the VST Pool window.

If the ARR extension is selected, only *active* (open) Arrange windows that contain the parts and their corresponding segments will be saved.

Files saved with the PRT extension will contain information on one or more parts of the arrangement.

In order to load files thus saved, click on the Open option in the File menu (the <Ctrl>+<O> key combination), select the required extension from the drop-down list of the Files of type: field, and click on the name of the required file.

If a file with parts (PRT) is loaded, they will be inserted in the arrangement window at the position of the *left locator*. (The relative distance between the parts will be retained.)

If you want to create a new **Arrange** window or song to load the previously saved material, use the New option (the <Ctrl>+<N> key combination) or the **New Song** option (the <Shift>+<Ctrl>+<N> key combination) in the **File** menu.

Very often, the labor spent on creating a musical project costs much more than the medium on which this information is stored. In order not to lose the product due to technical problems, we urgently recommend that you make a copy of the information: save it on floppy disks, a CD-ROM, etc.

There are special applications — archivers — that allow you to increase the reliability of saving the information on floppy disks and also reduce the space it takes up. To compress the most bulky parts of the project (WAV files) with the purpose of saving space, for example, on a CD, the best archiver among the ones that we know of is the WinAce application (version 2.03 and later) (www.winace.com), which efficiently compresses 32-bit Audio files.

1.15. Audio Processing

It would be no exaggeration to say that computer technologies can work wonders with sound. Nowadays, musicians can create almost any kinds of audio patterns using the computer.

Contemporary virtual audio technologies fully meet the requirements of the computer musician.

1.15.1. Virtual Mixer

Imagine the musicians of a big orchestra randomly wandering on stage playing their parts without paying attention either to the other parts or to the conductor's instructions. This is the kind of cacophony that will ensue if the step of mixing and Audio processing is skipped after the project is recorded.

Mixing is the process of converting the original multichannel phonogram into one meeting the technical requirements of the commercial audio carrier format (Audio CD, audiocassette, etc.). In other words, the multichannel phonogram should be converted (mixed) into a common stereo phonogram.

The mixing console is the main technical device that allows you to do such conversion. This sophisticated and expensive device is substituted in Cubasis VST by its virtual analog — the VST mixer.

Using the VST mixer, the computer musician can correct the volume of each part, change the timbre characteristics if necessary, apply special effects to each part, and, as a result, create a finished musical composition.

There are two types of the virtual mixers in Cubasis VST: those that work with MIDI, and those that work with Audio. This chapter deals with the VST mixer that works with audio that is invoked with the **VST Channel Mixer** option of the **Audio** menu, or with the <Ctrl>+<* on the additional keyboard> key combination.

The mixer consists of vertical *channel strips* that correspond to mono or stereo channels. Each of them can be separately regulated (Fig. 1.54). The rightmost section is the Master section, where all the virtual channels are mixed (it will be described later). Note that the parameter changes may be automated.

 Note

> Between the last channel strip and the **Master** section, you will find channel strips of the connected virtual VST instruments (described in *Chapter 5*).

You can change the size of the VST Channel Mixer window in the usual way: grab at one of its borders and expand or reduce. There is a slider in the bottom of the window used for scrolling the channel strips. The window may be moved around the screen by dragging the upper panel that contains the name.

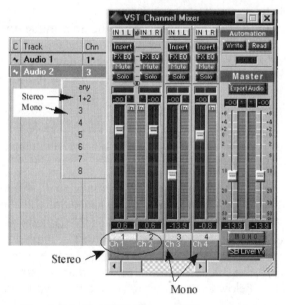

Fig. 1.54. The **VST Channel Mixer** window

Let's take a look at the structure of a channel strip, with its elements indicated by numbers in Fig. 1.55.

❏ The name of the channel strip (1). It can be changed after you double-click on it.
❏ The number of the virtual channel (2).
❏ The Fader level indicator field (3), where the positions of the volume regulators (Fader) (4) and panorama (Pan) (7) are displayed in their *numerical equivalents*.

You can change the values in this field using the mouse buttons the same way you do for all numerical fields of the software.

❏ Fader is the channel volume regulator (4). It is simply dragged with the mouse. For precise regulation, hold the <Shift> key pressed. To set the fader to the 0 dB position, click on it with the <Ctrl> key pressed. Separate regulation of stereo channel strip faders is done with the <Alt> key pressed.

❏ The channel signal level meter (5). The meter contains the In button, which switches it to VST input for the recording level control.

❏ The overload indicator — Clip indicator (6). The maximum level of the signal is 0 dB. If it goes any higher, the overload indicator will begin working. To avoid distortions, ensure that the signal level never exceeds the maximum level of 0 dB.

❏ The panorama regulator (Pan) (7) is used for panning the mono signal in a stereo environment. As with the fader, *all the key combinations* with <Ctrl> and <Shift> are applicable to the panorama regulator.

❏ The Solo button (8) is used for switching the Solo mode on and off. Switching on the Solo mode automatically mutes the rest of the channels. You can switch on the Solo mode for several channels simultaneously. Clicking on any active Solo button with the <Ctrl> key pressed clears the Solo mode for the rest of the channels.

► *Tip*

If you press the **Solo** button with the <Ctrl> key pressed, you will not need to clear the Solo mode from the channels in which it was set before. With this method, the Solo mode will be transferred to the selected channel.

❏ The Mute button (9) is used for muting the channel volume. The Mute button works with the <Ctrl> key in the same way as the Solo button.

❏ The double FX/EQ button (10) opens the VST Channel Settings window, which shows the expanded channel strip. The VST Channel Settings window also contains the Send routing section and the EQ parametric equalizer (which we will describe later). The FX/EQ button of the channel strip is duplicated on the Inspector panel. Below are the methods that allow you to reduce the number of some operations:

• Clicking the FX button with the <Ctrl> key pressed turns the Sends section on and off (duplicates the Enable button)

• Clicking the EQ button with the <Ctrl> key pressed turns a previously pressed Enable button of the equalizer on or off (or both at once)

❏ The Insert button (11) is used for connecting an Insert effect in a break in the channel. In other words, the channel seems as if it were broken at a point, and the additional processing module — a plug-in — is inserted at this point of breakage.

❑ The **Input Selector** button (12) enables you to determine the VST input from which the recording will be done. Just click on it with the left mouse button with the <Ctrl> key pressed and make the selection in the list.

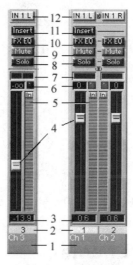

Fig. 1.55. Channel strip controls (mono and stereo)

The signal from all channel strips goes to the **Master** section of the VST mixer, and parameter changes affect the general sound. Its structure partially resembles that of the channel strips, but there are also considerable differences (Fig. 1.56).

❑ The **Write** and **Read** buttons (1) are used for switching on and off the recording mode and that of reading data from the special automation Audio Mix track, where the changes of the VST mixer parameters and those of the connected plug-ins are recorded.

❑ The **Export Audio** button (2) is used for mixing (song recalculation) into the audio file (mix). This is the final operation, which completes the process of mixing the project.

❑ The **Mono** button (3) is used for controlling the stereo and mono compatibility during the mixing. Such control is necessary, since the phonogram can be used (replicated or broadcasted) in mono mode, too. And mono playback should not be distorted: all the elements of the composition should be heard.

❑ The **Output menu** field (4) is used for selecting the sound card output. If there are several outputs on the sound card, their list will be opened after you click in this field.

So, the virtual mixer is a device necessary for many important operations during mixing. You cannot do without it when working with effects, for example.

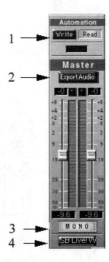

Fig. 1.56. The **Master** section

1.15.2. Connecting Effects

In virtual audio technologies, audio processing is done by means of so called "plug-ins", which are installed on the computer in the same way as software.

In Cubasis VST, you can process the signal from each virtual channel with effects, and this processing may relate either to the *whole signal* (this will be described in the first method), or can affect *a part of the audio stream* (this will be described in the second method).

A signal not processed by effects is called "dry". Therefore, the processed signal is "wet".

First method — connecting Insert Effects. This method is also known as connecting effects *at the breakpoint*, since it seems as if the channel breaks, and that the effect is inserted at this breakpoint. In this case, the *entire* signal of the virtual channel that comes from the channel strip of the mixer to the Master section is processed. Inserting an effect is done in the VST Inserts window opened with the Insert button of the channel strip.

The scheme (Fig. 1.57) illustrates the difference in audio streams from the strip to the Master section of the mixer:

❏ In the first case, the signal is dry. You can control it only with the volume and panorama sliders.

❏ In the second case, the whole audio signal is processed with the Insert effect (it is connected in the VST Inserts window).

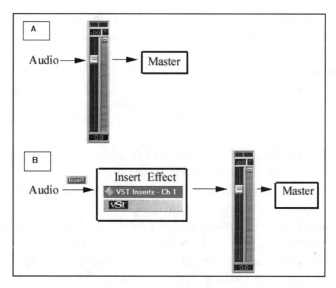

Fig. 1.57. Stages of audio signal control with an Insert effect

Below is a sequence of operations for connecting an Insert effect (Fig. 1.58).

1. Click on the Insert button on the channel strip of the VST mixer. The **VST Inserts Ch** *N* window will be opened (where *N* is the number of the channel).
2. Click on the No Effects field (Example A) and select the effect in the list that opens (Example C). This list contains only the effects installed on the computer.

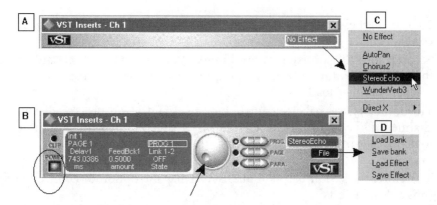

Fig. 1.58. Connecting an effect with the **Insert** button

3. Switch on the effect by clicking on the POWER button (which is circled in the illustration). The name of the effect is shown in the upper left field. In the example, this is Stereo Echo.

4. The effect is regulated with the mouse cursor (on the manipulator shown with the arrow) or by *switching programs* using the PROG button nearby. The interface of the connected effects may differ, but the general principles remain the same. See *Section 1.15.3* for details on working with the programs and automating the effect's controls.

5. The created settings may be saved (and loaded later). To do this, click on the File button and select the required option from the drop-down list:
    *   Save Effect and Load Effect — save and load separate *programs* into files with the FXP extension (Effect Program)
    *   Save Bank and Load Bank enable you to save and load *banks* containing *several programs* into files with the FXB extension (Effect Bank)

6. You can change the effect without leaving this window. To do this, open the list again by clicking on the field with the name of the effect, and select another name. To switch the effect off, select the No Effect option.

Second method — connecting Send effects. This method differs from the previous one.

Imagine a situation where an effect or group of effects with the same settings is intended for simultaneous use in different channels. The reverber effect can serve as an example. If we solved this task by inserting the effect, we would have to connect the same plug-in as an Insert effect *many times*. Of course, such a solution is *not rational*, and the reasons for this are not to be taken lightly:

❑ First of all, these effects will occupy *the only* slot each channel has for Insert effect connection.

❑ Second, the CPU's resources are limited, and you must be careful about using them efficiently. Multiplying the plug-in when it doesn't make sense to do so will create *additional* load.

❑ Third, the dry/wet balance control between the dry and processed signals of each channel will be performed inside the Insert effect. This is much more convenient to do on the virtual mixer.

Therefore, the VST mixer of Cubasis VST has the option of connecting the same plug-ins as Send effects.

This connection method makes each Send effect *common* for all channels.

For connecting with Send effects, there is another, additional mixer, consisting of channel strips and a Master section, within the main virtual mixer.

This additional mixer is represented by a special Sends section in the VST Channel Settings window (Fig. 1.59) and the VST Send Effects virtual rack (Fig. 1.62).

The channels of this additional mixer are called "routes" or "sends", since it is as if the channel signal were sent to a general effect, called a Send effect. The process of forming the route is called Send routing.

There are separate controls of the Sends section in the VST Channel Settings window for controlling the signal sent to the Send effects (Fig. 1.59).

Fig. 1.59. The **Sends** section
in the **VST Channel Settings** window

To the left in the window, there is a channel strip in the form displayed in the VST Channel Mixer window, in the middle is the section for sending the signal to the effects (Sends), and on the right are two sections for setting the parametric equalizer (EQ).

Three ⟨Enable⟩ buttons are used for switching the sections on and off.

Sends consists of two of the same sections, each of them used for forming a separate Send route. Each of them has 4 controls:

❑ The On button switches on the sending of the signal to the effect.

❑ The Pre (Pre Fader) button changes the pattern of the Send route. If the Pre button is pressed, the signal sent to the Send effect does not depend on the fader position or the state of the Mute button. In other words, the sent signal branches off *before* the fader and the Mute button.

❑ The Effect Send Amount regulator determines the level of the signal sent to the Send effect. In other words, this regulator specifies the dry/wet balance for each channel. If you raise the send level, the level of the wet signal processed by the Send effect will also be raised for this channel. Thus, one Send effect simultaneously serves several channels, but you can set an *individual* dry/wet balance for each of them.

❏   If a plug-in with an *integrated* dry/wet regulator is used as a Send effect, this regulator should be set in the 100% wet position.

❏   The drop-down list of the **Effect type** field is used for selecting the route to the connected Send effect (Fig. 1.60).

Fig. 1.60. Connecting effects via the **Sends** section

Send effects are connected via the **Effects** option of the **Audio** menu.

So, to make sure that a Send effect works, it should be *connected* and *activated* with the following operations.

1.   Call the **Effects** option in the **Audio** menu.
2.   In the opened **VST Send Effects** window, click on the **No Effect** field and select the effect from the drop-down list. Using this method, you can simultaneously connect two effects.
3.   Press the **Power** button to activate the effect.

Cubasis VST supports plug-ins of two standards: VST and DirectX. Some manufacturers release their plug-ins in two standards at once, such as Ultrafunk fx (www.ultrafunk.com) (Fig. 1.61).

Fig. 1.62 shows the **VST Send Effects** window with two plug-ins connected (**Chorus 2** and **Stereo Echo**). The upper plug-in is active, since its **Power** button is pressed.

4.   After the effect is connected and activated, determine the route the signal should be sent by.

   •   If only the On button is pressed in the Sends section, the sent signal *will be affected* by the signal regulated by the fader of the channel, as well as the state of the Mute button (Fig. 1.63, Example A).

- When both the On and the Pre buttons are lit, the signal sent to the Send Effect is not affected by the change of the fader position and the Mute button (Fig. 1.63, Example B).

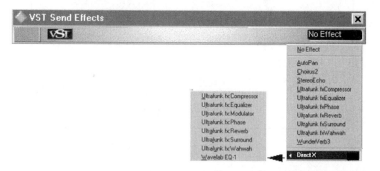

Fig. 1.61. Selecting Send effects in the **VST Send Effects** window

Fig. 1.62. Two connected Send effects (the lower is not active)

▶ *Note*

Remember that the **Effect Send Amount** control determines the dry/wet balance between the dry and the processed signal. The lower the sent level, the weaker the processing.

When the VST Channel Settings window was described, we promised to return to the equalizer sections. They are on the right in Fig. 1.64.

The *equalizer* is the device that enables you to change the timbre of the signal and form its gain-frequency response. Consider the organization of the EQ equalizer.

❑ The Enable buttons switch on the EQ sections.

❑ The Gain (level) control is used for the intensification/suppression of the frequency band.

❑ The Frequency control changes the central part of the frequency range.

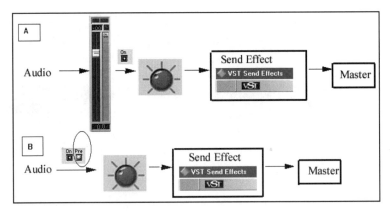

Fig. 1.63. Signal routing scheme

□ The Q (quality) control determines the width of the frequency range. The higher the Q parameter, the narrower the band.

□ The Hi, Mid, Hi Mid, and Lo Mid buttons specify the frequency range in which the regulation is done.

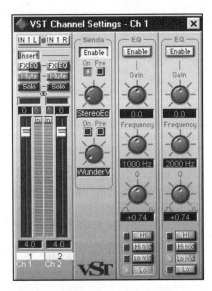

Fig. 1.64. The **VST Channel Settings** window.
Setting up the equalizer

This does not at all cover the features of Cubasis VST. The parameters of the Insert and Send effects, as well as those of the virtual mixer, may be automated.

1.15.3. Automating Sound Processing (the Automation Track)

Automation is used for recording the audio processing parameters' change over time, which will be repeated by the software when played back later.

Let's examine two methods of performing this operation. In the first case, we will set the multitrack cursor to a specified position and set the required processing parameters to this point. In the second method, the regulation is done "on the move": the mixer and effect regulators are moved during the playback, and the change of their positions is recorded.

In both cases, the software records our operations on the special Audio Mix track of the Audio Mix class placed on the multitrack under the lowest track. (If necessary, Audio Mix can be moved in the usual way — by grabbing the name (Fig. 1.65).)

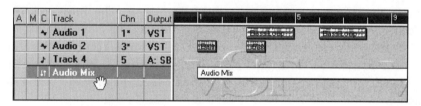

Fig. 1.65. Moving the Audio Mix track

Controlling recording and playback from the **Audio Mix** track is done with the Write and Read buttons positioned in the upper part of the **Master** section of the virtual mixing console (Fig. 1.66). This track is created automatically when the automation data recording mode is switched on with the **Write** button. In order to "read" the automation track, press the **Read** button. If both buttons are pressed, recording is done simultaneously with the reading of the previously recorded automation data.

Fig. 1.66. The **Write** and **Read** buttons

To end the topic of automation, let's take a look at the features of using *virtual effects programs* (Effect programs). We'd like to mention that the internal structure of plug-ins varies, but their control interface in Cubasis VST has common elements and principles of control.

Fig. 1.67 shows two plug-ins. From the point of view of their interfaces, it doesn't matter what kind they are: Insert or Send effects. For the sake of illustration, effects with different configurations are shown: the lower module has its own control panel, opened with a click on the Edit button; the upper module contains a separate display showing the setting parameters.

To change the parameter, select it from the display and move the cursor vertically, holding the left mouse button pressed. You can also use the Value Dial regulator. It is not possible to have all the parameters on the display at once, so they are distributed on pages. To navigate through the pages, there is a double **Page** button. To navigate through the effect parameters, use the **Para** button. The **Prog** control is used for switching presets.

The programs, in turn, are consolidated into banks. You can save both banks and programs in separate FXB and FXP files, respectively. Program switching is also automated. This allows you to form a preset bank beforehand and automate their switching.

A musician can form a bank on his or her own. The current settings of the effect are automatically saved in the selected program. If you want to save them, select another program in the bank and start the setting process anew. When there are no more free programs, just save the bank in an FXB file.

We recommend that you name the programs. To do this, click in the upper left corner of the display (on the word "Init") and type in the name from the keyboard.

The VST plug-in parameters can be automated. This means that you can "turn" the effect's "knobs", and the software will save their positions (Write mode) and play them (Read mode).

Automating program switching is very convenient for plug-ins of the DirectX type. The algorithm is the same. First form the bank, and then switch the programs in the automation recording Write mode. Then the same DirectX plug-in can be applied in different places of the project with different settings.

▼ *Warning*

The automation recording Write mode is switched off when the **VST Channel Mixer** window is closed. So, if you want to save this mode, we recommend that you only *minimize* the window.

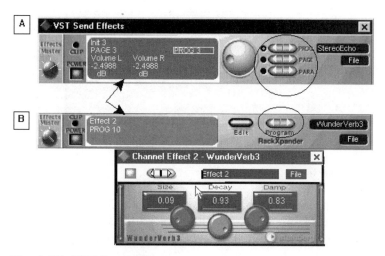

Fig. 1.67. VST Send Effects automation using program switching

1.15.4. Features of Sound Processing ReCycle Files

ReCycle files are special Audio files with the REX extension (the REX 1 format) created in the Steinberg ReCycle software. Their main advantage lies in the peculiarities of their internal structure: their musical phrases are split into slices. Thanks to this, you can perform additional operations with such files, such as changing the tempo, or, as described in this section, *applying separate sound processing to each slice.*

ReCycle files are used for constructing music from loops. Since the phrase cutting lines fall at moments of the *signal attack,* they are most often used for creating phrase loops for percussion instruments: drumloops and bassloops. And this is understandable, since — for the drumloops, for example — each slice will begin with a *percussion* sound.

We already mentioned that the unjustified repetition of a musical phrase is harmful to music. The use of ReCycle files *combined with the capacities of Cubasis VST* enables you to overcome this problem: you can introduce considerable diversity into repetition using the complex sound processing and automation of the VST mixer.

The technology of the ReCycle file sound processing is very simple.

1. Create an Audio track and set the **Any** value for it in the **Chan** column.
2. Using the **File/Import ReCycle File** menu, import the ReCycle file to this track. The software will open the **Make Recycle File Polyphonic** window (Fig. 1.68).

Fig. 1.68. The **Make ReCycle File Polyphonic** window

There are two fields in this window:

❑ Specify the number of virtual channels the ReCycle file will be split into when played in the **Divide the Recycle File into Channels** field

❑ Specify the first virtual channel from which the splitting will start in the **Starting with Channel** field

By default, Cubasis VST offers the optimal number of channels in the **Divide the Recycle File into Channels** field for a particular ReCycle file. In reality, you can specify *any number* no more than 31 (since this is the maximum number of channels in Cubasis VST). Besides which, when this parameter is selected, you should take into account the *free* channels available in the project.

After the selection is done, complete it by pressing the OK button. The ReCycle file will be on the Audio track as a part (its starting position coincides with the position of the L locator).

As a result of this operation, *each slice* will be played via a *separate virtual channel of the VST mixer*. An *order* will be observed, beginning from the channel with the number specified in the **Starting with Channel** field. Remember that such a service is possible only on the special any track.

This process is cyclical: the channels and slices change in strict sequence. For example, if there are four channels specified in the **Divide the Recycle File into Channels** field, then the program will cyclically switch them from the first to the fourth.

The new technology provides new options for the audio processing of phrase loops, since any slice of a ReCycle file is provided with a *separate* virtual channel with its own processing parameters: volume and panorama, the level and route of the send, and an Insert effect.

If you record the change in the effect's parameters on the automation track after the multiple copying of the ReCycle part, the monotony of the loop fragment may be hidden behind complicated sound processing.

Fig 1.69 shows an example of processing a ReCycle file by four channels of the VST mixer.

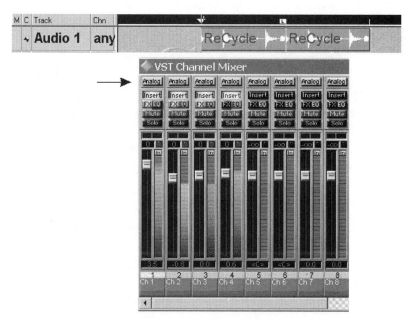

Fig. 1.69. The VST mixer when a ReCycle file is processed

The sound gotten as a result of multichannel processing should be mixed down into one Audio file using the Export Audio function to free the virtual channels.

1.16. Mixing down to a File.
Export Audio

The reason for the Export Audio operation — which consists of mixing down to the final Audio file — is so that the Audio parts positioned on different tracks can be mixed to a separate audio file with all the virtual processing and automation. In other words, what we hear during playback should be accurately repeated when the final Audio file is played.

Let's make it a little clearer as to why we need to do this. The programs intended for Audio CD mastering, such as, WaveLab 4.0 (described in *Chapter 6*), do not work with songs of the Cubasis VST program, in which the project is stored in many different kinds of files, but only with Audio files.

The Audio files used in a PC working in Windows have the standard WAV extension. Thus, in order to make an Audio CD, *the project must be converted into a WAV Audio file.* The Export Audio function of Cubasis VST is used for this purpose.

Apply this function after all of the material is mixed, and the sound of the project attains the required quality.

This operation is done with the Export Audio button in the Master section of the virtual mixer. The sequence of operations is the following.

1. Prepare the material for Audio export:
    - Set the L and R locators so that they embrace the whole project.
    - If necessary, switch off the Audio tracks that do not take part in the operation (Mute them in the M column).
2. Call the virtual mixer (<Ctrl>+<* of the additional keyboard>) or select the Export Audio File command from the File menu.
3. Click on Export Audio in the Master section.
4. In the opened Export Audio File window (Fig. 1.70):
    - Select the folder in which the file will be saved.
    - If necessary, rename it in the File Name field.
    - Check the Mono or Stereo option (according to the file being created).
    - Check the Add created file to current Song option (if you want the file to be exported back to the song, as well as to the selected folder).
    - Press the Create File button.

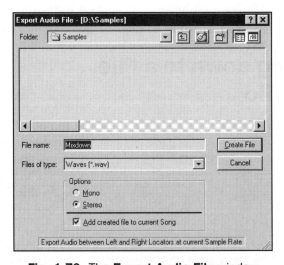

Fig. 1.70. The **Export Audio File** window

As a result of the operations, the new MixDown track with the imported part will appear on the multitrack. Except for its origins, it is no different from regular parts. This means that there is a slice in the VST Pool window that corresponds to it, which you can use for further operations (Fig. 1.71), such as grabbing the multitrack by its name and dragging it, etc.

 Note

A mixed Audio file needs to be imported back to the song only if you are performing what is called *intermediate mixing*. This method is used for mixing the parts of the project to a file in order to free up computer resources or to convert MIDI tracks into Audio tracks (using the VST technology described in *Chapter 5*). In Cubasis VST, we recommend that you only use intermediate mixing for VST instruments and split ReCycle files. If high-quality audio processing is necessary, connect the Sound Forge 6.0 or WaveLab 4.0 editor to the software.

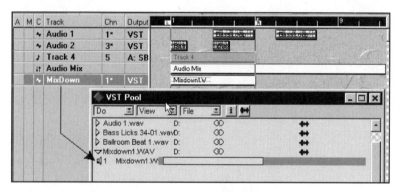

Fig. 1.71. Creating a MixDown track
as a result of the Export Audio procedure

Before the **Export Audio** function is applied, check the output level on the meter of the **Master** section. The signal level should not exceed 0 dB; the Clip indicators should not be lit. If necessary, the output level should be reduced using the faders of the **Master** section. You can find more details on ways of processing a file received as a result of export to the Audio editors in *Chapter 6*.

Now, let's turn to working with MIDI.

CHAPTER 2

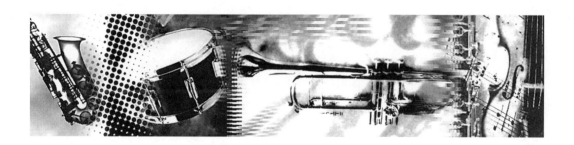

Working with MIDI
in Cubasis VST
and Cubasis Notation

2.1. The MIDI Interface

Communication is only possible if the participants speak the same language. A language is a system of signs that allow you to transfer information. Strangely enough, a language of communication is necessary not only for the living beings of our planet, but for electronic devices as well.

The Musical Instruments Digital Interface — or MIDI — is the digital interface necessary for musical instruments to "understand" each other. Thanks to MIDI, the transfer of the following commands, for example, is possible: what key to press and when, what force to employ for pressing, and when the key is to be released.

In other words, MIDI — from the user's point of view — is musical notation for computer software. It has many advantages over Audio, but also many drawbacks.

The essence of MIDI is that music is "split" into certain commands, such as how long the note will sound, what patch will be used, etc.

Its incontestable advantages are:

- High recording accuracy
- Reproducing the sound of various instruments, changing the tempo without a loss in the sound quality
- Detailed editing of the recorded part: for example, "drawing" a note or parameters of the sound, changing the duration (length) of one note, moving it to a new pitch or rhythmic position, etc.

Thanks to MIDI, synthesizers can be networked, which enables you to conduct a whole orchestra of MIDI instruments from the keyboard of just one of them.

The ancestors of the modern MIDI synthesizer were the simplest musical machines: musical boxes, street organs, and mechanical pianos. The "musical commands" in them were also coded, and the code was transferred to the instrument via mechanical devices (cylinders, punched cards, etc.).

But, unlike a musical box (whose music can seldom be changed), a musician is free to modify any command of the MIDI interface.

We'd like to mention that one immutable MIDI rule is the serial transmission of all types of commands. Even a chord — whose notes are played simultaneously — is transmitted and handled like a sequential MIDI event. Due to the high speed of data transmission, no delay can be heard.

For users' convenience, and for the so-called "humanization" of the MIDI language, the programmers invented various kinds of notation or translation of the machine language for human musicians. In Cubasis VST and Cubasis Notation, these are the List Edit, Key Edit, and Score Edit editors.

These editors have their own features, as each of them is intended for certain types of operations. But some of their functions overlap, since the same musical material is presented in all editors from different standpoints.

The List Edit editor shows all MIDI events of the application. In this, the most comprehensive editor, you can introduce miniscule changes in the musical material. But, since all the commands are shown successively in a general list, it is not very convenient to correct them, and it must be done in special cases only, when no other editor can be used.

In the Key Edit editor, the notes are shown accurately and graphically as horizontal lines (key imprints) and vertical lines (MIDI events in the field of the controllers). In this editor, the musician can not only see the natural parameters of the sound — its length, pitch, rhythmic position, volume, and panorama — but also graphically correct them.

The Score Edit editor is intended for mapping the notation of the material and working with it on a higher level. This notation can be presented in one of two types: *non-adapted* or *adapted* (depending on the settings).

 ### Note

If the musician introduces some rhythmical deviations when playing a MIDI instrument, the software may write them down differently. In the first case, submitting to the will of the performer by default, the software minutely records his or her interpretation in notes (and the notation becomes overloaded with symbols and is often illegible). In the second case, the software may ignore the rhythmical deviations and make the notation more standardized.

Even if the Key Edit or Score Edit editors are more to your liking, it is important to understand the List Edit editor, since in certain cases you just might need to use it.

2.2. The List Edit Editor.
Types of MIDI Events

There's no doubt that for musicians that don't know very much about programming, note recording in the List Edit editor may seem unintelligible. Moreover, you will likely never need this editor when the music is being created. However, if there are errors, or if the application starts behaving strangely, etc., you can always "look under the hood" to find where the misunderstanding took place.

Below we will briefly outline this editor, and then we will turn to the details of its performance.

Fig. 2.1 shows the List Edit editor. On the left, there is a list of all the MIDI events. Note that all of them (despite their diversity) are positioned consecutively — according to the time of their creation. Even the three notes of the chord at the beginning of the second bar, which are *pressed simultaneously*, are recorded consecutively (the arrow in Fig. 2.1).

Here you can add, remove, or edit any commands (items of the list). Removing a selected line is done with the <Delete> or <Backspace> keys. To add a new line, press the <Insert> key. The new line appears *before* the selected line, with the status of the created MIDI event corresponding to the value in the Insert pop-up menu's field (see Fig. 2.2 and the comments).

Here, *all* numeric and alphanumeric values can be modified: just double-click on the value and enter a new one in the window that appears (see Fig. 2.1). All the resulting changes will affect the musical material and, consequently, its representation in the other editors.

In the middle part of the editor — Event Display (the MIDI event section) — you can graphically edit the events.

On the right, there is the List Edit Controller Display (the controller section), where the *parameters* of the events are visually displayed (these may also be edited graphically).

The vertical border between the List and Event Display sections can be moved. To do this, click the left mouse button on it, and when the hand appears, drag it to the new place.

You can navigate through these sections with the help of the scrollbars in the bottom and on the right side of the screen.

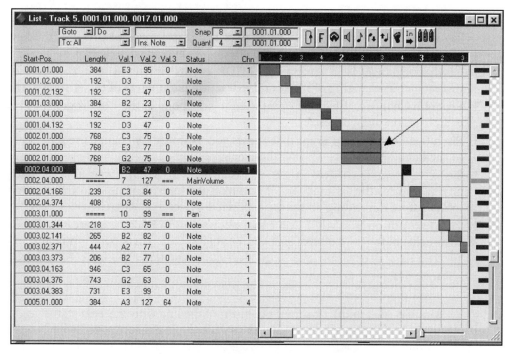

Fig. 2.1. The List Edit editor's window

At the top of the editor (on the **Status Bar**) there is the **Insert** pop-up menu's field. In the pop-up menu here you may select a MIDI event to paste and to do other operations with (Fig. 2.2).

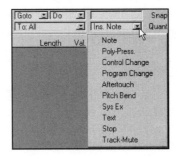

Fig. 2.2. The **Insert** pop-up menu

Now let's briefly look at the events, and then, using the example of the Note — one of the most common MIDI events — the way the List Edit editor operates):

❑ The Poly-Press and Aftertouch buttons, on some "extremely sensitive" synthesizer keyboards, allow you to apply extra pressure (extra force of pressing the key) in order to get, for example, the vibrato effect.

❑ Control Change is a group of MIDI events intended for continuous or instantaneous changing of the sound extraction parameters of the synthesizer.

❑ Program Change is the MIDI event used to select one of the 128 Programs, Presets, or Patches on the synthesizer.

❑ Pitch Bend is the MIDI event that allows you to smoothly change the pitch (similar to the Pitch Bend wheel on a synthesizer).

❑ SysEx (System Exclusive) is an exclusive system MIDI event that is partially normalized for the synthesizers of one manufacturer. It is used to transfer service information, depending on the type of MIDI device.

❑ The Text button is a MIDI event that allows you to make a recording of the text comments in the last column — Comment (Fig. 2.3). This operation is simple:

1. You have to select the line in the list before which the line with the comment is to appear.

2. Press the <Insert> key.

3. Double-click in the Comment column of the line with the Text status, and type in the text in the window that appears (the typing is completed when you press <Enter>).

❑ Stop is duplicated by the Stop button on the Transport bar.

❑ Track-Mute is duplicated by the Mute button in the Arrange window.

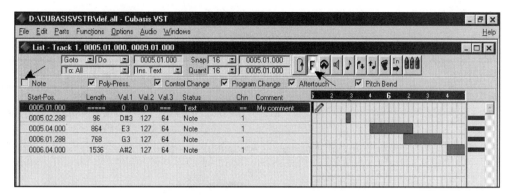

Fig. 2.3. Text comments

Pay attention to the useful event filtration function in the List Edit editor. If the F button (List Edit **Filters**) is pressed, then only the events on the top panel that are not checked are shown in the list (the arrows in Fig. 2.3). The rest of the MIDI events (those whose checkboxes are activated) are hidden.

Now let's go back to the primary MIDI event — Note — and take a look at the values in the columns of the **List** field.

❏ The start position is shown in the **Start-Pos.** column — the start of the command's execution. The illustration shows the number of the bar, the number of beat of this bar, and the number of the tick.

> ### Note
>
> The first note in Fig. 2.1 is on the *first* beat of the *first* bar — 0001.01.000. (This is easily seen from the marks on the upper **Ruler** in the middle of the **Event Display** section.)

❏ The second column shows the length of the note. (A quarter note is equal to 384 ticks, and so a whole note is equal to four quarters, or 1,536 ticks.)

❏ The Val 1 column shows the name of the note. *E3* corresponds to the *E* note of the three-line octave in MIDI numbering (see more on note designation in *Sections 2.8.2* and *2.8.3*).

❏ The Val 2 and Val 3 columns show the speed of pressing and releasing the key, respectively. This essential parameter of note "extraction", called Velocity, is extremely important, as it affects the volume and patch of the note (in "advanced" synthesizers). The majority of synthesizers do not react to a key being released. Therefore, only the parameters of the Val 2 column need be edited.

❏ The Status column contains the type of MIDI event.

❏ The Chn. column (Channel) shows the number of the channel through which this MIDI event will be transmitted. (MIDI channels are described below.)

For the sake of convenience, the parameters of the MIDI events are shown in Table 2.1.

Table 2.1. Parameters of MIDI Events

Status	Val 1	Val 2	Val 3
Note	**Pitch**	Note On Vel (the speed of pressing the key)	Note Off Vel. (the speed of releasing the key)
Poly-Press	**Pitch (key)** (the name of the note)	Amount (pressure)	—
Control Change	**Contr. Type**	Controller Value	—
Program Change	**Prog. Number**	—	—
Aftertouch	**Amount**	—	—
Pitch Bend	**Fine Value**	Coarse Value	—
SysEx	*Entered in the* **Comment** *column*	—	—
Text	* *Entered in the* **Comment** *column*	—	—
Stop	—	—	—
Track-Mute	*Track №* *In the* **Comment** *column the track name is shown.*	0–Unmute (switch on) 1–Mute	—

There are several ways to modify the parameters of the MIDI events:

- ❑ By clicking with the right (increase by 1) or left (reduce by 1) mouse button in the field of the modified parameter.
- ❑ By holding the left or right mouse button pressed for step-by-step scrolling of the list of values. (Clicking with <Shift> key pressed accelerates the scrolling.)
- ❑ By dragging the mouse cursor with the left mouse button, which is done as follows: click, hold + <Ctrl> — which drags up or down.
- ❑ By entering from the keyboard. This is done as follows: double-click, enter from the keyboard, and press <Enter>.

 Note

The above rules are common for the numeric fields of the Cubasis interface.

From the point of view of the practical use of the List Edit editor, the following can be mentioned. You can perform all the basic operations with the musical material here, e.g., recording from the MIDI keyboard, auditioning and cycle editing, rhythmical quantization of notes, and editing controllers (all these operations are described in corresponding sections of this chapter). And we are sure that those who have mastered the technique of using the Key Edit editor will encounter no problems with this editor either.

We must stress, however, that the List Edit editor is most suitable for making amendments and additions in the musical material on a "low level". Therefore, we're going to cover the methods of doing this.

2.2.1. Methods of Editing in the List Edit Editor

If you need to "check the program's engine" when working in the **Arrange** window of the Key Edit or Score Edit editors, set the cursor of the multitrack over the musical part's problem area, and then activate the List Edit editor, either via the **List** option in the **Edit** menu, or by using the key combination <Ctrl>+<G>.

The track area where the cursor was at the moment of opening will be what is shown in the editor. Errors are identified by looking through the commands or, if necessary, by listening to the fragment repeatedly, making the necessary real-time corrections. For loop editing — "with the sound" — the following needs to be done.

1. Select a small area (a mini-loop) on the Ruler. To do this, drag the mouse along the ruler holding the left mouse button pressed. The selected area will change color (see Fig. 2.4).

▶ *Tip*

   In order to remove a mini-loop, press and hold the left mouse button for a while on the selected area of the **Ruler**. After the mouse button is released, the selected area is removed.

2. Press the Play button on the Transport bar. The looped playback of the fragment will start.

▶ *Tip*

   If the tempo is too high for editing, it can be temporarily slowed down. This is done using any of the traditional methods: e.g., press and hold the left mouse button, or enter the required tempo from the keyboard (shown with an arrow in Fig. 2.4).

Any values in the List field can be edited (within or without a loop). To do this, first select the line (click on it), and then change any of its numeric values, observing the general editing rules mentioned above.

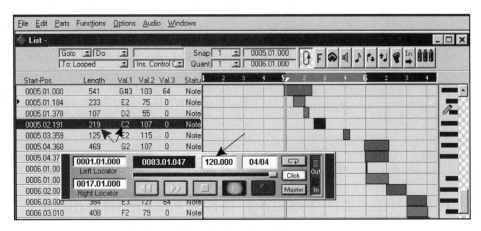

Fig. 2.4. Loop editing

Thus you can change the start of the note (the Start-Pos. column), the length of the note or its pitch (shown with arrows in Fig. 2.4), and the velocity (the Val 2 column). The changes to the parameter will be graphically shown in the List Edit Controller Display controller section.

Event editing can be done graphically in the Event Display and List Edit Controller Display sections. This is done using the toolbar called by the right mouse button.

Now, that you have finished getting acquainted with the List Edit editor, where you can obtain "competent help" for your musical project, we can turn to the *basic ideas* inherent in working with MIDI, using examples in Cubasis VST and Cubasis Notation.

▶ *Note*

The graphical interfaces of Cubasis VST and Cubasis Notation differ, but only slightly. The exception is the Score Edit editor, which is better implemented in Cubasis Notation.

2.3. MIDI Ports. Channels. Instruments. Tracks

So that the basic notions of the MIDI interface are not troublesome to the musician, we will try to present this material in the least complicated way, by means of some images familiar to everyone.

▼ *The MIDI Track*

This chapter deals with *MIDI tracks* — tracks containing MIDI information. Remember that there are two classes of tracks in Cubasis VST: MIDI tracks and Audio tracks. The selection of a track's class is done in the **C** column (Class) after clicking on the icon (indicated by the arrow in Fig. 2.5). A MIDI track is marked by the symbol for a note.

So, MIDI events are transmitted via MIDI ports by the MIDI channels. Each MIDI port cannot have more than 16 channels. One instrument is assigned to one channel.

Imagine two hotels with 16 *single* rooms in each. Let's say that some musicians are staying there. Despite the fact that the room numbers in both hotels coincide — from № 1 to № 16 — the guests in the single rooms of the two hotels are *different*. And these hotels are not always full, either.

In this example, the hotel is the MIDI port, the rooms are MIDI channels, and the musicians are the instruments (or to be more precise, they are patches (programs) of the synthesizers). Remember this simple example, since we will use it again below.

We will take a look at the work of MIDI using an example of the most popular sound card among beginners, which is also quite inexpensive — SB Live.

 Note

There are three MIDI ports in our example — two internal and one external — used for controlling external devices (e.g., another synthesizer).

Fig. 2.5. shows how to select the port. You need to click the left mouse button on the selected track in the Output column, and select the required port from the list that appears.

Note

For the SB Live soundcard, the ports **A: SB Live! MIDI Synth** and **B: SB Live! MIDI Synth** are internal, and the third port in the list is external.

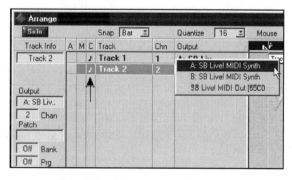

Fig. 2.5. Selecting the MIDI port

MIDI channels are marked in the Chn column (Channel). These channels are assigned the instruments which will perform the musical parts.

Note

To stay with our hotel example, various musicians can stay in the rooms of either hotel A or B: pianists, violinists, trumpet players, etc.

It is quite possible, however, that the saxophonists will occupy rooms with the same number in different hotels. Suppose that a saxophonist occupied room 15 in each hotel. Then there will be two saxophones in the MIDI orchestra — both with MIDI channel 15, but connected via *different MIDI ports*: one via MIDI port A, and the other via MIDI port B.

When two MIDI ports are used (in our case, A and B), the maximum number of patches that can sound *simultaneously* in the arrangement can be 32 (16 in each).

In addition, "MIDI musicians" can "read the notes" from several MIDI tracks *at the same time*, which enables them to distribute a complicated part of one MIDI instrument among several tracks.

Now, let's study the theory with an example, and then turn to some actual practice — track renaming, instrument selection, channel assignment methods, etc.

There are 6 tracks shown in the left part in Fig. 2.6. Each track has the name of an instrument. The tracks contain recorded instrument parts. These are on the right, in the Part Display section of the arrangement window.

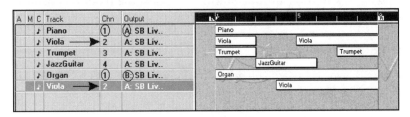

Fig. 2.6. MIDI channels and MIDI ports

The various ports of the sound card are selected in the **Output** column (A: SB Live! MIDI Synth and B: SB Live! MIDI Synth).

Note an important moment in Fig. 2.6. As we already mentioned, the "carrying capacity" of a MIDI port is 16 channels. Of course, it is more prudent (but not necessary) to first use all the resources of one port and then move to another one. For the sake of example, we have shown that the musician is free to use *the same "rooms"* in different MIDI ports. In Fig. 2.6, the *first* channels of two *different* ports are assigned the Piano and Organ patches.

Note

Of course, for SB Live, the patches are defined by the content and structure of the loaded banks, so this example is somewhat artificial. In practice, the external MIDI port may be used, for example, to gain access to special sounds of the external MIDI module, and in this case the use of another MIDI port becomes necessary.

Fig. 2.6 shows that the instruments of four channels are assigned via the A: SB Live! MIDI Synth port: 1 — Piano, 2 — Viola, 3 — Trumpet, and 4 — Jazz Guitar. The example deliberately demonstrates that the viola part can be distributed among *different* tracks of *the same MIDI channel and MIDI port* (indicated by arrows).

> ### ▼ *There Can Be More Tracks than Channels*
>
> This example shows that *the same MIDI channel can be simultaneously used by several tracks*. The number of MIDI tracks *does not depend* on the number of MIDI channels.

2.3.1. Duplicating Parts of Various Instruments. Ghost Copies

Suppose the saxophonist is "obliged" to play the part of the pianist at the same time as his own part. In reality this is nonsense, but in virtual reality the musicians always do what you tell them to.

Consider the following example.

There are three tracks created (Fig. 2.7). The first one contains the part of the piano. (The Piano patch is assigned to MIDI channel 1.) The second has the part of the sax. (The Sax patch is assigned to MIDI channel 2.) The third track has no part as of yet. But the patch has already been selected — this is the same sax as in the previous track, and is assigned to the same MIDI channel.

Now, perform a simple operation: with the <Ctrl> key pressed, drag the Piano part down (opposite the third track). As a result, a new part will be created (which we will call Piano = Sax), and the "pianist's" notes will be played by the sax.

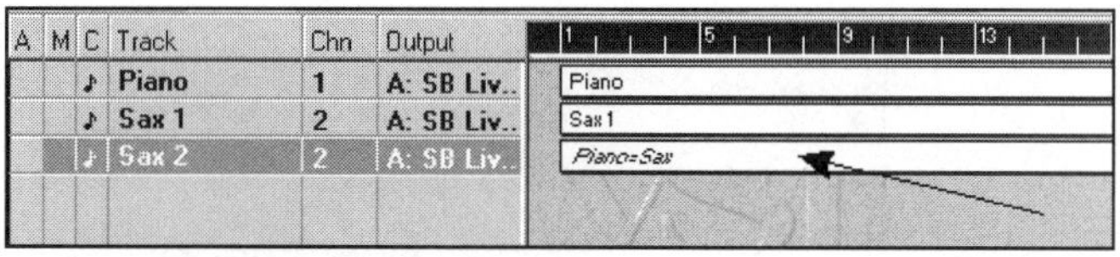

Fig. 2.7. Reassigning a part to another instrument

In the example in Fig. 2.7, a *ghost copy* of the Piano part was created, since the dragging was done with the <Ctrl> key pressed. The name of the ghost copy is written in italics. A ghost copy is a simple reference to the original part, and contains the information as to where the original part should be reproduced. Editing the original part entails the automatic and synchronous editing of all ghost copies. After the ghost copy is edited, you must correctly respond to the **Convert Ghost to Normal Part?** inquiry of the software. A **Yes** converts the ghost copy into a regular part, leaving all the rest of the ghost copies and the original unchanged. An answer of **No** means that the changes will be applied both to the original part and all its ghost copies.

This method allows you to easily add variations to the repeated part (or group of parts).

For example, let's repeat the selected part using the special **Parts Repeat** command (<Ctrl>+<K>). Enter the required value from the keyboard in the **Repeat selected parts** dialog box in the **Number of Copies** field, and check the **Ghost Copies** checkbox. A sequence of the attached ghost copies of the selected part will be created. Then, when editing each ghost copy, you should answer **Yes** to the software's inquiry. Then the variation will be introduced into the edited parts only. On the other hand, to introduce general changes, it is sufficient to edit the original just once.

Dragging a part with the <Alt> key pressed creates a regular copy.

2.3.2. Virtual MIDI Ports

After we have explained the interaction of the MIDI ports, MIDI channels, and patches, to the make our readers happy, we are going to tell you how to *increase* the number of ports and channels, regardless of the sound card's resources.

This is done by connecting virtual MIDI ports, which also have 16 virtual channels each. The virtual instruments are connected to them. Moreover, the virtual transmission of the MIDI commands is quicker, and no delays occur.

Thus, the capabilities of the "sound paints" used to create music on the computer are considerably expanded.

Strictly speaking, virtual MIDI ports are the attributes of the VST instruments connected via the VST **Instruments** command in the **Audio** menu. This virtual technology is called the virtual studio — VST — which is a huge technological step ahead of the Cubase system software. Fig. 2.8 shows that, apart from physical ports, there are three virtual ports connected (**Lm-9, Neon,** and **VB-1**).

See the details on the VST instruments options in *Chapter 5*.

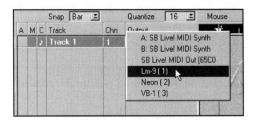

Fig. 2.8. Virtual MIDI ports

2.3.3. Renaming Tracks and Parts

The musician may name the tracks and parts as he or she wishes. If this is not done, the software will automatically number them: Track 1, Track 2, Track 3, etc. But it is more convenient if the names of the instruments are shown in the names of the tracks and parts.

The procedure of naming and renaming parts and tracks is simple. To name a track, double-click on it in the track column and type in the name from the keyboard. To name the part, double-click on it with the <Alt> key pressed and type in the name from the keyboard.

Pay attention to some characteristic features (see Fig. 2.8).

❏ By default, the tracks are assigned names consisting of the word "Track" and a number.

❏ If the track was named *before* the part was created, this name will *automatically* be assigned to all parts of this track.

It should be mentioned that names allow you to avoid "impersonality" of the musical material, enhancing the convenience of work with it.

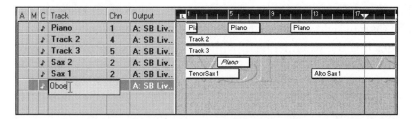

Fig. 2.9. Naming tracks and parts

In the end of the section, a few words should be said about "non-obvious" features of the software: parts played by *different* patches (instruments) can be placed on one track.

This will be described in the next section, after we cover the Inspector panel.

2.4. The *Inspector* Panel. Patch Selection

There is some basic information on the Inspector panel in the first chapter. The issue then, however, concerned work with audio parts, and the appearance of the panel corresponded to this type of part.

Be reminded that the Inspector panel is in the left part of the Arrange window, showing the virtual properties of the selected MIDI or audio part. This is a very useful function of the software — sort of the captain's bridge of the MIDI ship. It can be shown or hidden by means of the ▓ button located in the bottom left corner of the Arrange window.

Let's look at the options of the Inspector panel while working with MIDI material.

The Inspector panel allows us to edit the virtual properties of the selected tracks or parts. Depending on what is selected — a part or a track — the name at the top of the

Inspector panel window changes to Part Info or Track Info, respectively. The selected part *always* has priority (even if it is *outside* of the selected track). This means that if there is at least one part selected, all of the virtual editing done from the Inspector panel will be applied to this part.

 Note

The interface of the **Arrange** window was already covered in *Chapter 1*. Remember that selecting a part or track is done by clicking with the mouse. In order to select a group of parts, click on each part holding the <Shift> key pressed, or frame them. Unselecting is done by clicking on any blank area of the **Part Display** section.

The structure of the Inspector panel is always the same (no matter what is edited: a track or a part); it is shown in Fig. 2.10.

❒ The upper **Track/Part Name** field shows the name of the track or part.

❒ The Output field shows the MIDI port of a track or part.

❒ Under it is the **Channel** field, with the corresponding number of the channel for the track (or part).

❒ Next is the **Patch** (program, instrument) field. Here you'll see the name of the instrument assigned to the channel.

❒ Below it there are two fields — **Bank** and **Prg** (Program) — showing the number of the instrument bank and the patch number, respectively.

❒ You can control the volume of a track or part in the Volume field. The range of the volume values is from 0 to 127.

❒ The **Veloc** Velocity (field) is intended for shifting the velocity by adding values within a range from –127 to 127. A "0" value shows that the velocity *was not edited* (do not confuse with "zero volume").

❒ The **Transp** (Transpose) field enables you to transpose the musical material, shifting it by semitones (see "*Transposition*" in *Section 2.1.12*).

You can change the values in all fields in the usual way: either scroll by clicking the mouse buttons or holding them pressed, or type the values in from the keyboard in the dialog opened after double-clicking with the left mouse button.

Now that we have gone over the Inspector panel, let us turn to a very important topic — selecting the timbre of the musical instruments, called the "patch" in the program.

Below we will look at Sound Font instrument banks intended for the SB Live sound card.

There is a special service in Cubasis — SoundFont Bank Manager — for work with these banks.

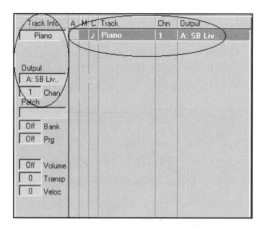

Fig. 2.10. The **Inspector** panel for the track

After clicking on the **Bank** field of the Inspector panel, a list of all the loaded banks is opened. For clarity, we have limited the selection to one standard bank — General MIDI — shown in Fig. 2.11.

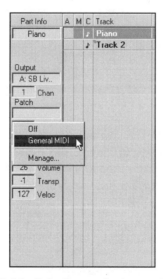

Fig. 2.11. Selecting an instrument bank

There is also the **Manage** command in the drop-down list of the **Bank** field (Fig. 2.11). It opens the SoundFont Bank Manager dialog, where, if necessary, you can edit the bank configuration. The SoundFont Bank Manager window consists of two lists: **Banks** and **Patches**. The loaded banks are shown in the left list. To gain access to the patches, you need to select a bank from the **Banks** list. The contents of the bank will then be shown in the right part of the **Patches** list window.

The **Load Bank** button invokes the **Load Soundfont Bank** dialog box, where you must select a sound bank file with the SF2 extension (Fig. 2.12). The **Clear Bank** button deletes the bank selected in the list.

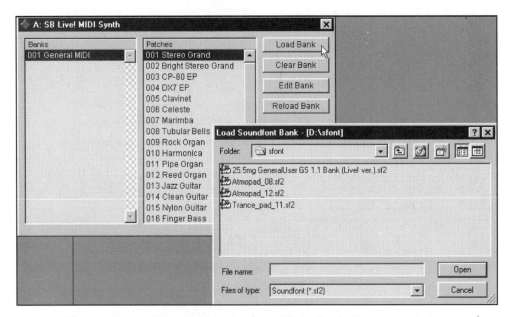

Fig. 2.12. Loading a bank in the **SoundFont Bank Manager** window

The **Edit Bank** button allows you to edit the bank without exiting Cubasis.

To do this, the Vienna SoundFont Studio software from Creative Technology Ltd. must be installed on the computer. The **Edit Bank** button automatically loads the selected bank in the Vienna SoundFont Studio application. After editing, the bank must be saved on the hard disk and reloaded into the memory with the **Reload Bank** button.

Note

It is recommended that you save SoundFont banks in separate folders on the hard disk.

Each project created in Cubasis can have its own bank configuration. In order not to be required to restore the working configuration of the banks manually, there are **Save Set** and **Load Set** buttons. The **Save Set** button saves the online configuration in a SoundFont Set file with the SFS extension, which may be easily restored later with the **Load Set** button.

The subsequent actions refer to the **Inspector** panel. Open the list of the loaded banks and select the necessary one by clicking on the **Bank** field.

After the bank is selected, you have to select the instrument (patch): click on the **Patch** field (Fig. 2.13). The list may consist of one or more patches. This depends on the internal structure of the bank.

Depending on the message in the upper part of the Inspector panel, the patch selected will be applied either to the whole track (**Track Info**), or to the selected part only (**Part Info**).

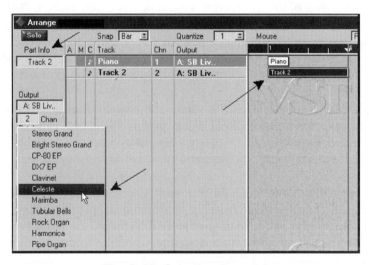

Fig. 2.13. Selecting the patch

The example in Fig. 2.13 shows that the info on the panel relates to the *selected part* (consequently, the Inspector panel is called **Part Info**). Therefore, it is the *selected part* (not the material on the selected *Piano* track) that will have the Celeste patch.

Changing the Patch for Several Selected Parts

Virtual editing with the **Inspector** panel allows you to locate parts with *different* patches on one track (irrespective of the track settings). Here is the explanation of this deviation from the rules: in the **Inspector** panel, you can assign an instrument for one or for *several* selected parts (which can be located in different places on the multitrack — i.e., on different tracks).

Keep in mind that selectively choosing parts is done by clicking the mouse button with the <Shift> key pressed. Then, to simultaneously change patches, you need just select the instrument from the drop-down list of the **Patch** field and click **Yes** when asked "**Copy value to all selected parts?**".

Changing the patch can be done at any stage of work. This is a special advantage of MIDI. For example, you cannot make a violin out of a saxophone in Audio — you will have to rewrite the track. However, there are no strict limitations on patch use — everything is governed by the sense of proportion, musical taste, and general competence of the composer.

We still want to warn beginner musicians of some common errors:

☐ If the patch is intended to reproduce the sound of an instrument playing live, then the actual range of the "prototype" should be taken into account. This will guard you from any "incomprehensibility" of familiar instruments (guitar, trumpet, violin, etc.).

☐ It is not worthwhile to change the musical idea of the composition just to show off some "pretty sounds". It should be remembered that sounds are just the "paints" of the musician, and there is no sense in exhibiting cans of expensive paint instead of the picture.

☐ It also should be noted that the world of the synthesized sounds is extremely rich and diverse. You can create unique worlds of sound with the help of newly synthesized sounds. And there are very many unexplored areas that may await you, dear reader, in the course of your creative development.

Thus, virtually changing the patch is easy: you select the part that is to be assigned the new patch. Then select the required value from the list of patches (Fig. 2.14). If for some reason you have to move to another MIDI channel or MIDI port, then you need to make the necessary amendments in the **Chn** or **Output** columns in the **Track Columns** section, or on the **Inspector** panel (indicated by the arrows in Fig. 2.14).

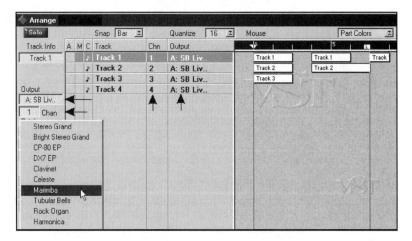

Fig. 2.14. Selecting the patch

Note

Non-destructive (virtual) MIDI editing is done with the **Inspector** panel. This means that you cannot see the results of the editing in, for example, the **List Edit** editor. Of course, Cubasis does generate the MIDI events that correspond to the **Inspector** panel settings, but these events remain "off screen". In order to "destructively" lock the virtual settings in the list of the MIDI events, there is a special **Freeze Play Parameter** command in the **Functions** menu.

It should be mentioned that when Channel 10 is selected, the instrument bank looks different (Fig. 2.15). This is because Channel 10 is intended for percussion instruments.

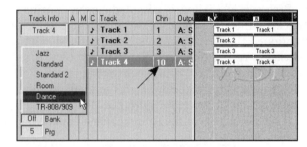

Fig. 2.15. The instrument bank in Channel 10

The note's pitch in the percussion group is defined by a separate instrument (sound). For example, *C1* — Bass Drum 1, *C#1* — Side Stick, etc.

2.5. MIDI Recording in the *Arrange* Window

This section provides the reader with algorithms of music recording from the MIDI keyboard in real time in the Arrange window.

Note

All the musical notions related to time and rhythm will be explained in detail later in this chapter.

The **Arrange** window interface was described in detail in *Chapter 1*.

First, let's consider some preliminary operations and recording techniques.

2.5.1. Preparing to Record. Setting up the Metronome

First, make sure that the MIDI keyboard is connected correctly. When a key of the MIDI instrument is pressed, it must sound, and the In and Out indicators on the Transport bar must respond (their columns oscillate).

Then, specify the tempo and time of the future composition. By default, the tempo is 120 beats per minute, and the meter is four-four. Amendments are made using the right or left mouse button in the corresponding fields on the **Transport bar**.

Then, set the metronome (if it will be used during the recording) as required. Open the metronome setup window with the **Metronome** option in the **Options** menu, or by double-clicking the **Click** button on the **Transport bar** (Fig. 2.16).

The sound of the metronome is switched on by pressing the **Click** button on the **Transport bar**. The metronome can start counting either right at the beginning of the recording, or several bars prior to it. This parameter is set in the left part of the window. If the **Precount** checkbox is disabled, the recording begins simultaneously with the first click of the metronome. The maximum number of intro bars is 32. It should be mentioned that a recording is being made during these bars as well. This method may be used to record, for example, an incomplete first bar.

In the right part of the window, you can change the pitch of the note and the volume of the clicking: for strong beats you do this in the **High Note** and **High Velocity** fields, and for weak beats in the **Low Note** and **Low Velocity** fields. The sound of the metronome can also be changed (in the **Audio Click** or **Channel** and **Output** fields).

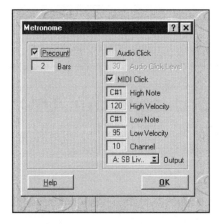

Fig. 2.16. The metronome setup window

It may be convenient to use various percussion sounds of Channel 10 for strong and weak beats. To do this, just change the note pitch in the **High Note** and **Low Note** fields.

2.5.2. Recording Techniques

As is commonly known, the majority of operations in a computer application can be performed in several ways. When recording, you can use either the mouse or the hotkeys. The second method seems more convenient to us.

Below are the main functions of the Cubasis VST and Cubasis Notation software that make the process of recording in the **Arrange** window much more convenient (they are described in detail in *Chapter 1*).

The following hotkeys are found on the *additional keyboard*:

- ❏ <*> — starts/stops recording
- ❏ <Enter> — starts playback
- ❏ <0> — stops recording or stops playback
- ❏ <1>, <2> — moves the multitrack cursor to the exact positions of the locators (markers) (L and R)
- ❏ <+>, <–> — increases or slows down the tempo
- ❏ </> — duplicates the **Cycle** button of the **Transport bar**

The following hotkeys are found on the main keyboard:

- ❏ <G>, <H> — zooms the horizontal scale in and out
- ❏ <Shift>+<G>, <Shift>+<H> — zooms the vertical scale in and out
- ❏ <Ctrl>+<T> — creates a track
- ❏ <Ctrl>+<P> — creates a part
- ❏ <Delete> — deletes the selected track or part (parts)
- ❏ <Page Up>, <Page Down> — moves the cursor
- ❏ <8> — duplicates the **Cycle** button of the **Transport bar**
- ❏ <9> — starts/stops recording
- ❏ <Home> — returns the cursor to the beginning of the multitrack

The main functions of the software in the **Arrange** window are the following:

- ❏ The **Solo** button (<S>) leaves the selected track playing, temporarily switching off all the rest of the tracks.
- ❏ A click in the **M** (**Mute**) column temporarily mutes the track (clicking again unmutes the track).
- ❏ You can change the track's volume in the Volume field of the Inspector panel.
- ❏ You can change the tempo on the Transport bar.

▶ *Note*

See *Section 2.19* for details on locally changing the tempo in the **List Mastertrack** window.

2.5.3. Sequential Track Recording

This is the simplest method of recording. All the operations here are sequential: first, the track is created, then the recording is created on the track, etc.

1. Create a MIDI track (using the **Create Track** option in the **Parts** menu, using the <Ctrl>+<T> key combination, or by double-clicking in the **Track** column in the **Track Columns** track section).

2. Select the instrument bank and patch in the drop-down lists of the **Bank** and **Patch** fields. If necessary, you can name the track, for example, according to the patch selected.

3. Mark the area where the part will be recorded. To do this, position the L and R locators. The recording starts from the left locator, L. When the cursor crosses the right locator, R, recording will be automatically stopped without interrupting the playback.

 Note

This method of recording is called *Auto Punch*, or recording in paste mode into the area limited by the two locators — **L** and **R**.

Note that the locators are set by clicking the left and right mouse buttons on the **Ruler** above the multitrack. The left locator must be always set before the right one (and never vice versa).

There is another method of recording implemented in Cubasis — *Punch on the fly*. Without interrupting the playback, you can start and stop recording in any area of the multitrack using the <*> key (on the additional keyboard).

4. If there are several tracks created, select the one where the recording will be performed (click on it in the **Track** column).

5. Start the metronome (press the **Click** button on the **Transport** bar).

6. Start the recording (with the **Rec** button on the **Transport** bar, or with the <*> key on the additional keyboard).

7. Play the part on the MIDI instrument and stop the recording (with the **Stop** button of the **Transport** bar or the <0> key on the additional keyboard). If some of the musical part turns out to be outside the official part (after the right locator), it *will not* be recorded. Therefore, it is advisable to set the R locator with some margin left.

8. Return the cursor to the beginning of the next part (using the buttons on the **Transport** bar or the <1> key of the additional keyboard).

9. Record the other parts of the composition, repeating steps 1–8 (if necessary, the previous tracks can be selectively muted in the **Mute** column).

If a part is overwritten, the new MIDI data will appear instead of the previous data.

 ### *Note*

See *Chapter 1* for details on general methods of the part editing in the **Arrange** window (cutting, pasting, etc).

In order to "look inside" the recorded part and edit the MIDI material, call the Editor (from the Edit menu).

2.5.4. Cycle Recording

This method of recording not only enables you to quickly create the composition, but also to make changes in the created material in the cycle mode. We think it is very interesting to look for new ways of expressing yourself "on the spot": to change the patches of the instruments, increase or slow down the tempo, add parts, listen to the compatibility of the parts (muting them selectively), transpose the material, etc. This is the cycle recording algorithm:

1. Create several tracks and assign instruments to them.
2. Name the tracks.
3. Set the locators (limit the recording area).
4. Put the multitrack cursor at the position of the left locator (the <1> key on the additional keyboard).
5. Start the cycle recording mode (with the Cycle button ([⟲]) on the Transport bar) and the metronome (the Click button on the Transport bar).
6. Select the first track where the recording will be take place (click on it in the Track column).

Tip

If there is percussion in your composition, it is best to start with it. Then, when the rest of the parts are recorded, you can switch off rhythmic support of the "monotonous" metronome.

7. Start the recording (for instance, with the <*> key on the additional keyboard) and record the part *without interrupting* the playback.
8. Listen to the part and, if necessary, write additions to it over top of it during the next repetition of the cycle.
9. Select another track and play the next part *without interrupting* the playback.
10. Continue recording the other parts, repeating steps 8 and 9 (you can create new tracks in the track section without interrupting the cycle recording).

Despite the fact that the Cubasis VST and Cubasis Notation software are simplified versions of the professional Cubase software, they have inherited some extra editing features in the cycle recording mode.

You can edit the recording using hotkeys *without interrupting* the cycle process:

❏ <V> removes the last recording of the cycle. All the previous recordings remain. The command works in the reverse direction — with each pressing of the <V> key, the recordings are sequentially removed, from last to first.

❏ <B> removes all the recordings of the cycle. This command clears the *subtrack* — the "invisible" track where all the MIDI events in the cycle are recorded.

❏ <K> removes notes of the same name (with respect to the octave) from the cycle. For example, to remove all the *C3* notes, you have to press and hold the key (in this case, the *C* note of the three-line octave) on the MIDI keyboard, and then press the <K> key.

❏ <N> rhythmically quantizes the last recording in the cycle according to the **Quantize** parameter selected in the **Arrange** window. Quantization can be cancelled with the <U> key. *(See Section 2.20.)*

Fig. 2.17 shows the process of cycle recording. For the sake of example, there are two percussion tracks created — **Drum 1** and **Drum 2** — and the **Organ** track is muted.

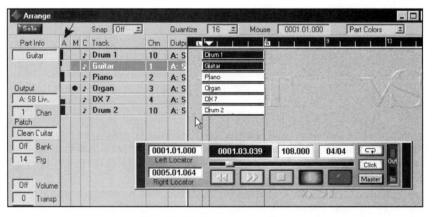

Fig. 2.17. Cycle recording

These algorithms are sufficient to record technically complicated parts. For example, you can sequentially record a live complicated percussion part in a cycle on one or, better yet, several tracks, using *rhythmical quantization* when necessary. Below is a simple method of mixing the recorded material.

2.6. Mixing the Composition.
The MIDI Mixer in Cubasis VST

You can use the MIDI mixer of the software for the simplest way of mixing the composition and setting the volume balance among the MIDI channels. The mixer is invoked by the MIDI Mixer command in the **Edit** menu. Since the MIDI interface has several specifications, the MIDI mixer in Cubasis VST can function in various modes.

 Note

> In order to determine what mode you should use, check the manual for your synthesizer (or sound card, or external synthesizer, etc.). The following should be taken into account when the mode is selected: the GM specification (General MIDI) is compatible with any MIDI device, while the other two (GS and XG) were manufactured by two big companies (Roland and Yamaha, respectively) for their products in particular.
>
> The MIDI mixer in Cubasis Notation is implemented as the GM/GS/XG Editor.

Fig. 2.18 shows the MIDI Mixer in the GM specification mode.

Using the MIDI mixer, you can quickly and easily balance the MIDI channels. The MIDI mixer is actually a programmatic superstructure that generates MIDI events of the Control Change and Program Change type. These events enable you to change the volume level and provide control over the panorama and the Send level of the reverberation and chorus effects. Also, the MIDI mixer can change the patch for the channels "on the fly". You could say that it partially duplicates the functions of the Inspector panel (where you can also change the volume and select the instrument (patch)), but for the synthesizers of the standard MIDI specifications.

Let's take a look at the structure of the mixer shown in Fig. 2.18. The larger section consists of 16 vertical blocks where the indicators of the MIDI channels are located with the volume and panorama sliders, as well as the **Reverb** and **Chorus** controllers. On the right is the general MASTER section.

Instrum and **Bank** sections are located at the bottom for each MIDI channel (0 means that the GM bank is selected). If you click on the **Instrum.** field of any channel, any other instrument can be selected from the list that opens (Fig. 2.19).

When the mode is changed in the MASTER section (e.g., to the XG specification), the appearance of the mixer changes: additional rows of **Mute** and **Solo** buttons appear (Fig. 2.20), and so do additional widgets in the MASTER section.

At the end of this brief overview of the MIDI mixer in Cubasis VST, let's turn to the Key Edit editor.

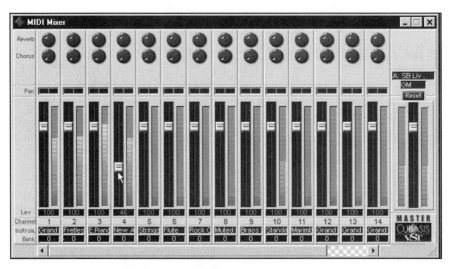

Fig. 2.18. The MIDI mixer in GM mode

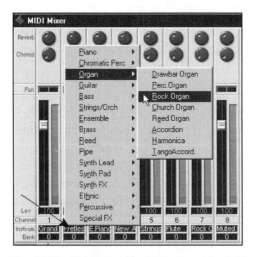

Fig. 2.19. Changing the instrument (patch)
in the MIDI mixer

Here the music is presented visually — in the form of key imprints. This not only lets you easily correct any inaccuracies in the performance and make the necessary additions to the parts, but also to graphically draw the music. This feature can surely not be overestimated for beginners.

Fig. 2.20. Changing the mode of the MIDI mixer

2.7. The Key Edit Editor.
A General Overview

There are three types of editors in the Cubasis VST and Cubasis Notation software — Key Edit, List Edit, and Score Edit. Undoubtedly, each of them has its own advantages and drawbacks, since they are intended for different operations.

In our opinion, the Key Edit editor is ideal for an initial acquaintance with Cubasis VST, since it acquaints you with the basics of the graphical interface of the software and music theory all at once.

 Note

If you know musical notation, but are quite a lame duck in the Cubase computer software, we recommend that you become acquainted with the methods of working in Key Edit before working with the note editor. First of all, the understanding of the basic principles of notation will remove many subsequent problems (e.g., with the Score Edit note editor), and, secondly, the options of the Key Edit editor in the area of rhythmical editing are much more powerful than those in notation.

The Key Edit editor is extremely illustrative. Here, all the main parameters of the MIDI events are presented graphically in two sections: the upper — Note Display, and the lower — Controller Display (Fig. 2.21).

The MIDI events — **Note events** (from here on out referred to as "*notes*") are shown as bars of varying length (key imprints) in the Note Display section.

Thanks to the virtual keyboards and the ordered structure of the note display, notes become familiar both to users who never were competent in musical notation, and to the professional musician accustomed to traditional musical notation:

❏ The length of the line corresponds to the note length.
❏ The height of the key imprint corresponds to the note's pitch (its name).

All the additional parameters of sound extraction are controlled in the Controller Display section. Here, the various parameters of sound, such as smooth change of volume or pitch, panorama, etc., are graphically shown.

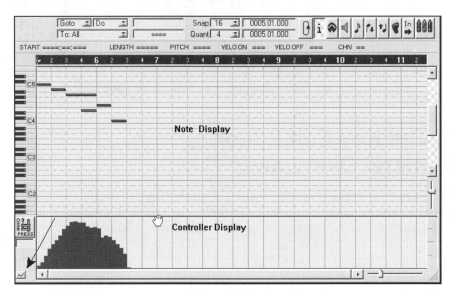

Fig. 2.21. The Key Edit window

You can move the vertical border that divides the two sections by placing the mouse cursor over it and dragging the border vertically until the "hand" appears (Fig. 2.21). Thus you have the option to maximally extend the lower section, for example, when working with the controllers.

If necessary, you can leave only the top section on the screen (this is convenient when working with the note material only). There are two ways of doing this:

❏ Press the <~> button (marked in the figure with an arrow) (pressing it again returns you to the previous view)
❏ Use the <Alt>+<Ctrl>+<C> key combination (using it again cancels this operation)

In the Key Edit editor, you can enter and edit MIDI events (on the note screen or controller screen) in several ways: enter the commands from the MIDI instrument with the mouse, use key combinations, or enter the data from the keyboard (e.g., the name of the note).

Some of the methods allow you to introduce changes that cannot be reproduced in the notes (including "irregular" note lengths).

With the help of the Key Edit editor, the various "errors" made while playing the MIDI instrument can be easily corrected; it is easy to add certain elements of the musical parts, introduce the slightest rhythmical changes, etc.

One important detail: the principles of operation of Key Edit are the same in all applications of the Cubase system. After this editor is mastered in one application, the knowledge that you have gained can be used in other applications, too.

To end, we will repeat that in our opinion, the main advantage of the Key Edit editor for the beginner is the "illustrative" presentation of the note parameters — its correspondence to the key (pitch) and length.

Therefore, with the help of the Key Edit editor, it is easy to learn the basics of musical "science", which are necessary for moving to the next level — including work in Cubasis Notation.

2.8. The Key Edit Interface.
Notes and Key Imprints

This section deals with basic information on the Key Edit interface; the features of the editor will be considered below in detail.

First of all, this is done to present to readers a general idea of the possibilities when working with this editor. Second, we do this for advanced users who lack the information needed to start work. And third, the brief information in this section might be used by readers later on, for recalling the main features of the Key Edit editor.

Before we take a look at the Key Edit interface, let's consider its launching algorithm. (Note that this sequence of operations is the same for both Cubasis VST and Cubasis Notation.)

The launching algorithm of the Key Edit editor is the following:

1. Launch Cubasis VST.
2. In the **Arrange** window opened by default (Fig. 2.22), create a part on the MIDI track using one of the following methods:
   1) Select a track and check the **Create Part** option in the **Parts** menu.
   2) Select a track and use the <Ctrl>+<P> hotkey combination.
   3) Double-click the left mouse button at the level of the selected MIDI track in the **Part** section between the L and R locators.
   4) Click or drag the **Pencil** tool to the selected area of the **Part** section.

Note

If you can not create a part, the reason is probably the position of the locators. **L** *MUST be to the left of* **R**. You can "draw" the parts with the **Pencil** instrument, regardless of the position of the locators.

Remember that the locators are set by clicking the mouse buttons (left and right) on the ruler above the multitrack.

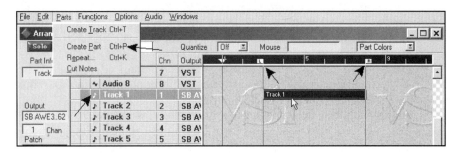

Fig. 2.22. Creating a blank part on a MIDI track for opening the editor

3. Open the Key Edit editor for the created (and selected) part using one of these methods:

- By selecting the Edit option from the Edit menu
- With the <Ctrl>+<E> key combination
- By double-clicking with the left mouse button on the part

Note

Double-clicking on the part can open any of the editors: Key Edit, List Edit, or Score Edit. Which one depends on the option selected in the **Options/Double click opens** menu. By default, the **Key** option is checked (Fig. 2.23).

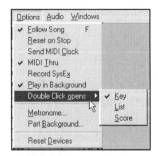

Fig. 2.23. Setting which editor opens upon a double click

After such a sequence, a blank editor window — one without MIDI events — will appear (see Fig. 2.21).

Tip

Unlike with the **Inspector** panel, all the changes made in the Key Edit editor are kept in the list of MIDI events. In the Cubase system software, you can only undo the last operation. However, if you exit the editor by pressing the <Esc> key, the question **"Do you want to keep the edits?"** will appear. If you answer **Keep**, all the changes made *from the moment of the last call of the editor* will be accepted. Answering **No** means that the changes will not be accepted. Thus, you may escape the limitation of one undo level (<Ctrl>+<Z>).

We have conditionally divided the upper part of the Key Edit editor window (Fig. 2.24) into several parts: the sections of the Status Bar panel are numbered 1–5, and the Info Line panel is number 6.

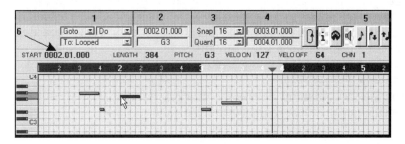

Fig. 2.24. The upper part of the Key Edit editor window

There are three fields in the section marked 1. Clicking the left mouse button on any of them opens a drop-down list.

The bottom field — To:. Here the area in which all the operations selected in the top field (Do) will be applied is specified. This area may cover:

❐ All MIDI events of the track being edited (All Events)

❐ MIDI events selected in the editor (Selected Events)

❐ Cycles or their fragments: Looped Events (all MIDI events of the loop in the editor), Cycled Events (all MIDI events of the cycle between the locators), Looped Sel. Ev. (MIDI events selected within the loop), Cycled Sel. Ev (MIDI events selected within the cycle between the locators)

Cycle and Loop

There are two types of cycles in the software. One of them is the area between the **L** and **R** locators in the **Arrange** window, called a **Cycle**. The other is determined by the area specified *in the editor only*, called a **Loop**.

Besides which, the command selected in the To: field specifies the area in which to apply rhythmical quantization (the Over Quantize command in the Functions menu).

❏ The Goto field moves the editor window to one of nine positions: Song Position (the multitrack cursor position), First Event (the first MIDI event), Last Event (the last MIDI event), First Selected (the first selected MIDI event), Next Selected (the next selected MIDI event), Last Selected (the last selected MIDI event), Prev Selected (the previous selected MIDI event), Next Part (the beginning of the next part, if several parts are edited simultaneously), Prev Part (the beginning of the previous part, if several parts are edited simultaneously).

❏ The Do field is intended for two operations that considerably accelerate the creation and removal of key imprints.

❏ The Fill operation immediately creates a series of key imprints of the same pitch and length in the area specified in the To: field. The length of the note and the rest between the notes is set by the user in the Snap and Quant fields. In order to select the pitch of the note, you need to click on the virtual keyboard. The Fill option frees the musician from the monotonous "drawing" of notes. You can move the notes set by the software up or down (with the mouse or MIDI keyboard) to the required pitch positions.

❏ The Delete command deletes the musical material. The area to be deleted is also specified by the value in the bottom To: field.

► Note

Be careful with the **Delete** command: if the **All Events** option is set in the **To:** field, then *all* the edited information will be deleted.

❏ There are two indicators in the section marked with the number 2, representing the mouse cursor position in the field of the key imprints (or the note parameters when it is moved).

❏ The upper Position Box display shows the horizontal coordinates of the mouse cursor: the number of the bar, the number of the beat, and the part of the beat (in ticks).

► Note

In the example, the figures 0002.01.000 mean that the cursor is in the second bar (0002), in its first beat (01), at the beginning of the first beat (000).

❏ The lower Transpose/Pitch Box display can show two parameters:

- The mouse cursor position (in the example in Fig. 2.24, the cursor is on the G note of the three-line octave — G3)

- The value of the note's transposition when it is moved. In this case, instead of the name of the note, the display shows the word *Transpose* and the number representing the number of the semitones that the note has been transposed by (if the number is negative, then the note is transposed down).

There are two windows with similar drop-down lists in the section marked as number 3:

❑ The value of the upper **Snap** field specifies the permissible positions for entering MIDI events:

- In the **Note Display** section, this is the "invisible" grid used for setting the key imprints.

- In the **Controller Display** section, this is the "density" of the MIDI events of the controller (or rather, the smoothness of the line drawing "increment" of the controllers).

❑ The value of the lower **Quant** field (quantize) specifies the following:

- The size of the grid visible on the screen

- The length of the visible note when clicked with the Pencil tool

- The length of each key imprint in the note sequence set when the **Paint Brush** tool is used or the **Fill** command is executed

- The length of the note during step recording from the MIDI instrument — in the **Step** mode

- The rhythmic positions to which the notes will be moved without changing their lengths (when the **Over Quantize** command in the **Functions** menu is used)

`0008.01.000` `0009.01.000`   The section marked in Fig. 2.24 as number 4 is intended for work with the loop created in the Key Edit editor.

Here you'll find the **Loop** button and two fields that show the borders of the colored area on the Ruler (Fig. 2.24).

When the **Loop** button is pressed, the loop is activated (its area is colored blue on the Ruler).

When the Loop button is not pressed, the loop is switched off. It may be restored, however, since the previous borders are saved (they are in gray on the Ruler). Pressing the Loop button again restores the loop.

▶ *Note*

The **Loop** button is duplicated on the keyboard by the key combination <Alt>+<Ctrl>+<O>, which can also be used to activate and deactivate the loop.

▶ *Tip*

Use the mouse to remove the selected area from the **Ruler**: click and hold the left mouse button on the selected area of the **Ruler**.

The Loop Start and Loop End fields are active: here, you can set either the borders of the loop or its size.

There are several ways to change the loop borders in the Loop Start and Loop End fields:

❑ Click on the value to be changed (clicking the left mouse button reduces the value by 1; clicking the right mouse button increases the value by 1). If the mouse button is held, the value is increased or reduced until you release the button.

❑ Enter the required coordinates from the keyboard. The field is opened in one of the following ways:

● Double-click the left mouse button

● Use the <Alt>+<Ctrl>+<L> key combination for the upper display, and <Alt>+<Ctrl>+<R> for the lower display

See *Section 1.6* for details on entering new values.

In addition to the methods mentioned above, a loop can be created by simply dragging the mouse cursor (with the left button pressed) along the Ruler in any direction. The accuracy of selection depends on the Snap parameter.

The section marked in Fig. 2.24 with the number 5 combines nine buttons.

 The first one, with the letter i (information), is used to activate the Info Line panel (marked in Fig. 2.24 with the number 6).

 The Speaker button allows you to switch the sound on when the notes are drawn and edited in the Note Display section.

 The following four buttons — MIDI Input — are used for step editing of the note parameters with of the MIDI keyboard. The MIDI connector button (with the picture of the five-pin connector of the MIDI keyboard) switches on the connection mode with the MIDI keyboard, which allows you to change the note parameters (when the buttons with the note symbols are pressed).

There are three parameters that can be changed with the help of the MIDI instrument:

❑ Pitch (the pitch of the note). In order to do this, the Note Pitch button (with the picture of a note) must be pressed.

❑ On-velocity (the velocity of pressing the key). In this case, press the Note On-velocity button (the note with the down arrow).

❑ Off-velocity (the velocity of releasing the key). The Note Off-velocity button (the note with the up arrow) must be pressed.

If all buttons are pressed simultaneously, editing from the MIDI keyboard is done by three parameters: the pitch of the note is changed in the Note Display field, and, depending on the key pressed, the velocity lines increase or decrease in the Controller Display field.

 The Step button switches on the Step Recording mode, allowing you to enter the notes and chords at the specified rhythmic positions without following the tempo and the beat when playing. The notes are set to the positions specified in the Snap field, their lengths being equal to the value specified in the Quant field.

 The Insert button inserts notes into the created musical material. And when the inserting is done, the material following is moved to the right, whether it be a step recording from the MIDI keyboard or a note "drawing" with the Pencil or Paint Brush tools.

 The Edit Colors button allows you to select colors for MIDI events in the Note Display and Controller Display fields. The list that opens when the button is pressed contains 6 options:

❑ Default — no color is used to highlight the MIDI events.

❑ Channel colors — MIDI events are colored according to their affiliation to the channels.

❑ Pitch colors — a color corresponds to the name of the note (e.g., all C notes, no matter what octave they are in, will be shown in one color).

❑ Velocity colors — the color of the key imprints and objects in the controller area depends on the value of the Velocity parameter. The color range in the Controller Display section is shown in 16 tints (each corresponding to 7 gradations of velocity).

❑ Colorize by Parts — when this option is selected, the MIDI events have the same color as the part they belong to.

Turning back to Fig. 2.24, let's take a look at the section marked with the number 6. This is the Info Line panel, where the information on the selected note is shown. (If several notes are selected, the Info Line panel is inactive).

It is called in one of two ways: with the "i" button in the upper row, or by using the <Alt>+<Ctrl>+<I> key combination (and is hidden if you repeat either of these operations).

All the values here are subject to traditional editing: either with the mouse or by entering values from the keyboard.

The following parameters can be changed in the Info Line panel:

❑ Start Position — the position of a note's start in bars/beats/ticks.

❑ Length — the length of a note in ticks.

❑ Pitch — the name of a note with respect to the octave.

❑ Velo-On — the velocity of pressing the key.

❑ Velo-Off — the velocity of releasing the key.

❑ MIDI Channel — the MIDI channel transmitting this note. This parameter is often edited in the track settings, and not on the Info Line panel. If required, you can change the patch for one or more notes in the part. After this, you will have to set the any value in the track section (**Arrange** window) of the **Chn** column corresponding to this track.

In finishing the overview of the Key Edit editor interface's features, we will briefly mention some other aspects:

❑ The toolbar is invoked by the right mouse button. To select a tool, go to its icon holding the right mouse button pressed.

❑ There are two ways to change the scale in the Note Display section: with the sliders next to the scroll bars, and from the keyboard:

  ● <G> — reduces the scale horizontally

  ● <H> — increases the scale horizontally

  ● <Shift>+<G> — reduces the scale vertically

  ● <Shift>+<H> — increases the scale vertically

❑ The scale in the Controller Display section is changed as follows:

  ● Horizontally — the <G> and <H> keys and the sliders.

  ● Vertically — you can increase/reduce the size of this section by dragging the border up/down.

❑ You can navigate the virtual keyboard using the horizontal scroll bar in the right part of the screen.

Now, let us turn to the detailed description of the Key Edit editor features and, at the same time, to the basics of musical notation. We have done our best to state them in the simplest way, since these basics are necessary for a full understanding of the program's operations, as well as for a thorough understanding of the examples and methods of work that will gradually become more and more complicated.

2.8.1. The *Note Display* Section. Key Imprints

The note recordings in the Key Edit editor are presented as bars of various length located at various heights. These are the imprints of the pressed keys (Fig. 2.25).

 Note

Recording notes on the staff (the five lines) — and indicating their pitch — is dealt with in *Chapter 3*.

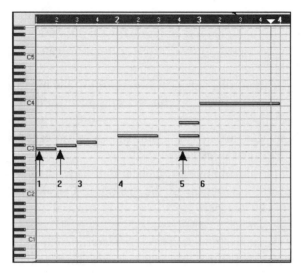

Fig. 2.25. Notes in the Key Edit editor

The horizontal level of each line of the note corresponds to a certain key — it reflects the pitch of the note.

The vertical borders of the note correspond to its start and end.

Thanks to such a clear presentation, the user can *visually* define the ratio of the pitch and length of sound, which helps, in the beginning, to work according to your intuition when you have no idea of how to use notation (or have never even given it a thought).

Moreover, such visualization allows you to easily correct the positions of the notes — to move them (horizontally or vertically) to new positions using the mouse.

It is worth mentioning that the pitch of the key imprint is clearly recorded by the program — you cannot draw a note that will turn out to be between keys.

If a white key is pressed, its imprint is *between* the horizontal lines, whereas the imprint of a black key is located *on* the horizontal line. Compare (Fig. 2.25) the notes corresponding to white keys (marked with the numbers 1 and 3) and the imprint of a black key (2).

As for the horizontal location of the key imprints — setting the note length — absolute freedom is possible here: you can create notes of whatever length you desire and place them randomly; if necessary, you needn't even pay attention to the grid.

The ratio of the notes is clearly seen in this editor. From Fig. 2.25, we can see that the majority of the notes in the example are played one by one, and the three notes marked with the number 5 sound simultaneously — i.e., this is a chord.

We can also see that the vertical lines divide the musical material into parts. Note that this division is done not in traditional units of time (seconds, minutes, etc.), but strictly adheres to equal parts of the *bar*.

A little digression is necessary here to explain some of the notions related to the rhythmic basis of music to readers unfamiliar with notation.

People who have never studied musical notation can easily tell a march from a waltz by ear.

This is because the sounds in music are rhythmically organized. The alternation of sounds by beats equal in time produces a smooth motion in music (which is also called pulsation).

Some of these beats are *accented*, and therefore are called *strong beats*. Beats that have no accents are called *weak beats*.

A *bar* is the interval from one strong beat to the next strong beat.

It is the uniform alternation of the strong and weak beats (called the *meter* in music) which enables listeners to differentiate musical compositions with different rhythms.

In a march, the alternation takes place every other beat, whereas in a waltz, the strong beat is every third (the meter of a march is double time, and the waltz meter is triple time), and it is easily discernible by ear.

In Fig. 2.25, the interval between the strong beats is equal to four beats. Therefore, each bar is divided into 4 parts.

Note how the bar borders are marked: the beginning of the bar is shown by the more prominent vertical lines, and has a number assigned. The beats within the bars are also divided by vertical lines and numbered (Fig. 2.25).

The vertical grid of the editor is very useful. It:

❐ Visually represents the rhythmic ratio of sounds: in Fig. 2.25, you can clearly see that note 2 corresponds to one beat in length, note 4 to two beats, and note 6 lasts for four beats (here this means, for the length of the entire bar).

❐ Accurately defines the note position. This definition includes the number of the bar and the number of the beat in the bar: chord 5 is positioned at the fourth beat of the second bar (Fig. 2.25).

The numbering of the bar has its own peculiarities: it is continuous, sequential (despite possible big breaks in the recording of some of the tracks), and synchronous (vertically) for *all* the tracks.

Despite the fact that the interface of this editor is quite obvious, its advantages are revealed in full only to users with a basic knowledge of the keys and rhythmical division of the lengths.

Therefore, let us now move on to the two main parameters of a note — pitch and length.

2.8.2. Names of Keys and Notes (Syllabic and Alphabetic)

The virtual keyboard, which is vertically positioned in the left part of the Key Edit window, exactly replicates the keyboard of the MIDI instrument (the so-called MIDI keyboard) and looks very much like standard keyboards of acoustic instruments: piano, grand piano, accordion, harpsichord, etc. But is has its own distinctions.

The main similarity of all keyboards lies in the names of the keys (notes).

Despite the fact that, to an uninformed person, the keyboard is "terra incognita" consisting of many keys that look the same, its structure is very simple.

A keyboard consists of *repeated groups* of 12 keys: seven white and five black.

It can be clearly seen on any keyboard that the black keys are positioned in strict alternation: by pairs and triplets (see Fig. 2.25).

It is this "peculiar" positioning of the black keys that helps musicians easily navigate the keyboard, even without looking at it. Thus, any white key is easily identified in respect to a group of black keys (two or three).

Each white key has *one* (individual) name. The names of the black keys, however, (*two* for each) are derived from the two nearest white keys.

Fig. 2.26 shows the names of the white keys: *C, D, E, F, G, A, B.*

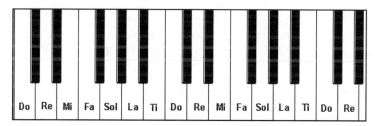

Fig. 2.26. Names of white keys

Readers who have just started to master notation should keep in mind the fixed position of *each* white key relative to the black keys: you can see in Fig. 2.26 that the *C* key is always *before* the group of *two* black keys, the *D* key is between the group of *two* black keys, the *B* key is after the group of *three* black keys, etc.

So, *any* keyboard consists of these groups of white and black keys. The name of each *eighth* note repeats. The interval between keys *of the same name* is called an *octave* (from the Latin *octava* — "the eighth").

▼ The Octave in Measuring Keyboards

The size of a *keyboard* is measured in octaves, *beginning with the C key.*

The names of the keys (notes, steps of the musical scale) are varied: they can be presented in a number of different ways.

There are names of notes that consist of syllables, and there are those that correspond to letters.

These letter names are international, and used very often. They are commonly used for the names of the keys and the chords, as well as for the "official" names of the notes in musical software. Thus it is important that you know them when working in Cubasis.

The alphabetic names harbor some intrigue, which is rooted in the past and expressed in the double designation of the *B* note. To avoid confusion, let us consider it in more detail, mostly for those who have only a basic idea of notation (Table 2.2).

Table 2.2. Names of Scale Steps in Music

Alphabetic designation in Cubasis	Classical alphabetic designation	Notes
A	A	La
B	H	Ti (or Si)
C	C	Do
D	D	Re
E	E	Mi
F	F	Fa
G	G	Sol
	B (*H*-flat)	

At first, a person unfamiliar with the alphabetic names of the notes may be stricken by the lack of logic. Everything becomes clear, though, with a little historical digression.

▼ The Double Standard in the "TI" Note's Designation: the Letters B and H

In the early Middle Ages, the musical scale consisted of two singing octaves built from the "La" (*A*) note (this is why the first letter of the alphabet corresponds to "La", and not "Do" (*C*)). The second step was of two varieties: the sound "Ti" and the sound "Ti-flat". Both notes used the letter *B* in their name (but written differently). Later, to avoid misunderstanding, "Ti-flat" became *B*, and "Ti" became *H*, after the next "free" letter of the alphabet. These designations existed for quite a long time. In the twentieth century, however, historical justice was partially restored, and the white key "Ti" (between the notes designated with the letters *A* and *C*) was logically designated by the letter *B*. But this did not happen everywhere. Nowadays, the "Ti" note is designated differently in different parts of the world: *B* in America, and *H* in Europe.

Now let's consider the principle of naming the black keys, which are also important to know for work in the Key Edit editor.

As we already mentioned, the black keys do not have independent names — their names are derived from one of the two neighboring white keys. In other words, the name of a black key consists of the name of the main note and the corresponding symbol or verbal designation of this symbol: *sharp* — ♯ or *flat* — ♭.

Sharp means that the root note is raised by a semitone, and flat means that the root note is lowered by a semitone (see *Chapter 3* for details on accidentals — alteration symbols).

The principle by which black keys are named is very simple: if the name of a black key comes from the diminished sound of a white one, then the flat symbol is added; if the black key is named by the augmentation of the sound of a white one, then the sharp symbol is added.

The most important thing is to take into account the direction of the shift — up or down. Diminishing on the traditional horizontal keyboard always means a shift to the left (to the basses), and augmenting means a shift to the right (Fig. 2.27).

Everything is logical in the virtual (vertical) keyboard — up and down mean up and down.

Thus, each black key can have two names (Fig. 2.27).

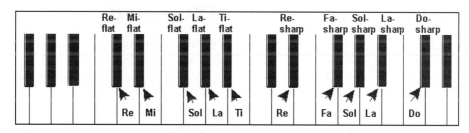

Fig. 2.27. Names of black keys

There is very convenient function in the Key Edit editor that enables you to learn the names of the keys upon your first acquaintance with the keyboard.

The coordinates of the mouse cursor (or any tool on the Toolbox panel) are automatically fixed both on the keyboard and on the **Position Box** display (Fig. 2.28):

❑ The key on the level of the cursor changes color.

❑ The name of this key appears on the display in alphanumeric designation (shown by an arrow).

❑ Fig. 2.28 shows that the name of the black key on the display includes three parameters: the alphabetical designation of the *C* note, sharp, and the number of the octave — *C#3* (see the details on octave numbering in Table 2.3).

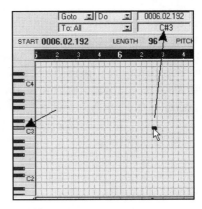

Fig. 2.28. Names of notes on the display

Note that when the black keys are named in the Key Edit editor, the sharp symbol is *always* used. This is because there is a symbol on the standard English keyboard similar to the sharp symbol — # (<Shift>+<3>).

Knowing the names of the notes on the virtual keyboard considerably accelerates working in the Key Edit editor.

2.8.3. Features of the Virtual Keyboard

The features of the virtual keyboard are the following: its vertical position, its enhanced range, and its special way of designating the octaves.

Indeed, the virtual keyboard is considerably larger — in its range and thus in its number of keys — than the standard keyboard of an acoustic piano. The difference is considerable: 88 keys on the piano and 128 on the virtual keyboard. By the way, 128 keys is the standard for all MIDI keyboards. The additional keys are necessary to introduce the parts of those instruments with a range that exceeds that of the acoustic piano. But note that in most cases, the actual size of the MIDI keyboard is much smaller — the range is achieved by switching the registers.

Another important feature that beginners must be aware of is that there is *always* only a part of the virtual keyboard shown on the screen. The hidden octaves may be seen traditionally — using the vertical scrollbar on the right side of the screen.

For user convenience, all the *C* notes are marked with the Latin letter *C* and the number of the octave (Fig. 2.29).

For musicians' reference: the octave designations deviate from the traditional ones, and correspond rather to the virtual keyboard (Table 2.3).

**Table 2.3. Keyboard Correspondence: Acoustic Piano
and MIDI Keyboard — the Name of the *C* Note**

Traditional designation of octaves (piano)	Traditional name of the *C* note in different octaves	MIDI keyboard standard name of the C note in different octaves
Non-existent	—	C8
Broken octave (short: only one note (*C*))	c5	C7
Four-line octave	c4	C6
Three-line octave	c3	C5
Two-line octave	c2	C4
One-line octave	c1	C3
Small	c	C2
Great	C	C1
Contra-octave	C_1	C0
Subcontra-octave (short: three notes — *H*, *B*, A)	A_2 (no *C* note)	c–1
(Non-existent)	—	c–2

▶ *Note*

The octave designations in the table are presented from the highest registers to the lowest (basses).

Now let's move from the first acquaintance with the pitch of the notes and their names to the second important parameter of sound — length.

2.8.4. Note Length, Time Signature, Tempo, and Means of Presentation in Key Edit

Beginners should pay attention to two details: first, the symbols of length in the musical software are the same as in traditional notation, and second, they are absolutely clear, since the majority of symbols are based on a number sequence, each number being *twice* as much as the previous one (1, 2, 4, 8, 16, 32, 64, 128). These are called *straight notes* (regular notes).

In music, lengths are used to express the ratio of sounds in the composition.

Now let's draw a parallel with the scale of an image. When the scale is reduced (or increased), the ratio of the image's details remains. In just this way, the ratios between the lengths are changed, despite the tempo of the composition.

Among the almost ten main straight notes, only half are actively used: the whole note, the half note, the quarter note, the eighth note, and the sixteenth note.

▶ *Note*

Later in this chapter, irregular notes will be considered. This material is deliberately omitted here in order to give musically inexperienced users the opportunity to master working with notes in the Key Edit editor using simple examples.

One of the lengths — *quarter* — occupies a significant position in the world of music. It is traditionally considered to be a sort of standard. There are several reasons for this. First, the quarter is the average among the lengths most often used, and second, in most cases bars are measured in quarters.

Indeed, it is also very easy to calculate other lengths in quarters, since:

- ❏ A *whole* note is four times longer than a quarter note.
- ❏ A *half note* is equal to two quarter notes.
- ❏ An *eighth note* is half of a quarter note.
- ❏ A *sixteenth note* is one quarter of a quarter note.

It is not particularly difficult to remember the names of the lengths, since they are related to the division of the longest length (a whole) into equal parts.

Fig. 2.29 graphically shows the ratio of the five most common lengths and their names.

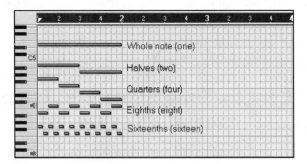

Fig. 2.29. Lengths in the Key Edit editor

You can see from the example that it is easy to define the length of the note using points of the meter grid. But first you must understand the concepts of time, tempo, and bar length.

It is up to the composer to select the time, according to his or her creative aspirations.

So, theoretically, the bar length can be of any value. In practice, however, the choice is reasonably limited (we will come back to this topic later, in *Sections 2.14* and *2.15*).

▼ Meter. Bar

Remember that *meter* is the uniform alteration of strong and weak beats. The interval between equal strong beats is called a *bar (or measure)*.

Understanding the main principle is important here. The time is shown as two values: the length (quarters, eighth notes, half notes, etc.) and the number of these lengths in the bar.

For example, if the beat pulsation goes by quarters, and the strong beat is every third quarter, then this time is called *three-four*.

The time signature is written as two numbers (in the form of a fraction), where the numerator denotes the number of beats in the bar, and the denominator gives the size of the beat:

◻ On the Transport bar (in Cubasis) `03/04`

◻ On the clef (in notation)

So, bars can have any size, according to the composer's desires. It is specified for the whole composition before work starts. For example, if the time is 2/4, the bar length is two quarters; if the time is 6/8, it is six eighth notes.

The time is shown in the meter grid visible on the screen. The cells of the grid depend on the user's preferences. They can be wide (to mark the metric beats only) or fine, dividing each beat into even smaller ones.

By default, the software always offers the following standard: four-four time with a grid step of sixteenth notes, as shown in Fig. 2.29.

▼ Attention Beginners

The total number of notes that consequently sound in the bar can not exceed its time.

▶ Note

If you need to increase or decrease the "size" of the bars (even one of them) somewhere in the composition, you should "officially" change the time in this bar (see *Section 2.15.3*).

This is illustrated with an example. It is shown in Fig. 2.29 that with *four-four* time, the bar can contain a strictly limited number of *sequentially identical* lengths (not exceeding four quarters):

- One whole note
- Two half notes
- Four quarter notes
- Eight eighth notes
- Sixteen sixteenth notes

We know that the overwhelming majority of musical compositions contain alterations of notes that differ in length: long notes alternate with short ones, and there are pauses between them called rests.

Fig. 2.30 shows that here there are notes of different length in one bar. The blank spaces between them are rests. But the bar remains unchanged, since the total length of the notes and the rests (positioned sequentially in time) must strictly correspond to the *meter of the bar.*

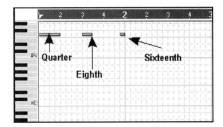

Fig. 2.30. Lengths of notes

We're glad to say that rests are not marked with special symbols in the Key Edit editor (unlike in traditional notation). They are just blank cells. This circumstance considerably simplifies mastering musical laws.

Often, a person taking the first steps towards learning the mysteries of the musical art will ask a perfectly logical question: how is the tempo of my composition to be defined?

Here is a brief account (we will return to it later).

The tempo of the composition — as well as the time signature — is specified by the creator. In order to provide performers with an exact idea of the tempo, the author correlates this tempo with universal and constant units of time: minutes.

Thus, the tempo is determined by the number of clicks per minute, where each click is a beat of a certain value.

In musical notation, the tempo is shown above the first bar of the composition. It is represented graphically: the length and (after an equals sign) the number of such lengths per minute. The illustration shows that the time at the clef is four-four. This is why tempo symbols contain the quarter note sign.

 There is a special device for beating out the tempo — the metronome.

Tip

If there are no devices for accurate tempo measurement at hand (e.g., just before an impromptu concert), you can always guide yourself by the second hand of a clock: it makes 60 strokes per minute, exactly. You can accurately identify the tempo in this case: two beats per second (i.e., 120 quarters per minute).

There is a metronome integrated into the computer software, so, the "old-fashioned" method will not likely be necessary.

The tempo in Cubasis is shown on the **Transport bar** next to the time signature.

`120.000  04/04` Note that, as in the previous example, the time here is four-four, and the tempo is 120 beats per minute.

But the designations here are somewhat different: here we can see some additional features (determined by the number of zeros). Indeed, the Cubasis software allows you to specify the tempo with utmost precision — up to a thousandth part of the length.

Now let's go back to the note positions in the **Note Display** field and pay attention to another important detail. In the previous illustration, all the key imprints were positioned exactly on the points of the grid: the beginning and the end of the note coincided with the lines. We deliberately gave simple examples here in first stage of your acquaintance with rhythm.

In practice, this exact "computerized" rhythmic positioning is by no means obligatory (which will be shown in the next example).

Moreover, during a live performance on the MIDI keyboard, slight rhythmical deviations are inevitable, which end up giving the composition the necessary "liveliness" (of, course, with a certain sense of proportion).

It is not recommended, however, that you abuse deviating from the rhythmical grid, as this may produce the impression of an uneven performance.

We will return to the peculiarities of rhythm — one of the most important topics in the book.

2.8.5. Securing Performance Features in the Key Edit Editor

Before we turn to practical operations in the Key Edit editor — becoming familiar with the rhythmical grid and the options of the instruments — here are some essential additions to the aforesaid.

If necessary, you can freely change the length of the note in this editor, as well as start and end the note at any place (without associating it with the bar grid). Thus, you can use notes with lengths that are several times longer or shorter than normal (e.g., a "super-long" note with a length of several bars).

► Note

For the sake of convenience, the pitch of the grid can be changed — in Fig. 2.31, it is equal to a thirty-second length (the principle of dividing the grid is described in *Section 2.9*).

Fig. 2.31 shows the example of some "wrong" notes: the lengths are wrong and positioned without rhythmic compliance to one another.

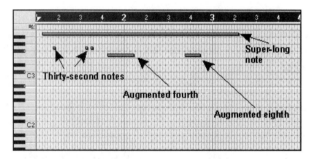

Fig. 2.31. Irregular lengths

Now we are going to anticipate some of your questions about the functions of "irregular" notes.

To do this, a little digression is necessary to explain the fundamental difference between traditional musical notation and that in the Key Edit editor.

Certainly, many (but not all) such rhythmical deviations can be written in traditional notation. This, however, is not necessary.

Musical notation is information communicated by one person to many people — i.e., the composer's message to the musicians and, via them, to the listeners.

The computer musician also addresses his or her compositions to people, but scores them with the help of a machine, which can only repeat the entered commands. Unlike a human being, the machine can not expand or interpret the composer's concept. And, if there are no commands to define various shades, the machine will emasculate the creative ideas of the composer, rendering them futile by its "soulless" performance.

Like in texts with words, part of the message in musical notation is written "between the lines", but the shades of the interpretation communicated by such a "secret" method can be identified by humans *only*. It is not up to the machine (as of yet) to perceive and communicate such information.

For example, the mark "*ad libitum*" ("as you wish") in the notation will be properly interpreted by a pianist, but not by musical software.

The communication between the machine and the human takes place during work with the software.

It is very important to understand that the composer must be able to "explain" to the new type of musician — the "electronic performer" — all the shades of the composition. If this task is solved, the user can "teach" the computer to play not mechanically, but rather to masterly perform live music for people, not machines.

It is important to remember that if *only* the notation is entered into the computer — without the nuances of the performance — the computer's music will always be played "correctly", but rather stiffly and with no emotion, similar to the way a robot would pronounce words.

Here is an example explaining the methods of communicating the musical information from a composer to different performers: the human musician and the computer software.

Suppose the composer needs to solve a simple task: notes are to be played shortly (staccato).

These traditional marks will be made for the musician in the notation:

❏ The word "staccato"
❏ A dot under or above the note

In both cases, the musician will play shortly. But the composer *cannot* define the level of "shortness" of these notes. This is up to the performer.

With the software, the algorithm communicating the method of performance must be absolutely different.

In order for the machine to play staccato, the length of the produced sound must be *defined by the composer* (instead of the "electronic performer"). This is due to the *inability* of the software to independently interpret the idea of a human being.

Similarly detailed instruction of the software must take place in all other cases as well: it is the musician who specifies the value of the rhythmic offset in swing, the volume of the sound, etc.

In other words, it is the composer (or in our example — the computer musician) who must take on part of the role of the performer. He or she must introduce *all* nuances for the performance of the machine — i.e., "enliven" it.

For a person to be able to make such changes with the least work, a special interface in the form of the Key Edit editor was created. Figuratively speaking, it is a form of notation that is clear to the machine and acceptable to the humans, too. (Note that some operations can be done in the Score Edit editor.)

The functions of the Key Edit editor enable the musician to introduce the slightest shades, which can be expressed by "wrong" (from the point of view of traditional notation) notes.

Changes can be made in this editor both manually (using the tools) and automatically, such as with rhythmic quantization (see the section below).

The features of the two types of notation can be briefly defined as follows:

❏ Notation intended for a musician must be maximally readable to a human: not overloaded with symbols, but informative (this topic is dealt with in *Chapter 3*).

❏ Notation for a "computer performer" (notes as key imprints in the Key Edit editor) must be maximally detailed, best reflect the composer's idea.

In light of the above, you should pay attention to some of the advantages of the Key Edit editor.

The distinguishing feature of the Key Edit editor is that it gives the user absolute freedom:

❏ Key Edit *does not impose* its terms in the form of rhythmic limitations. Its true worth can only be estimated after practical work with it, when the musician's tasks become more complicated, and the software easily copes with them.

❏ Key Edit impartially records whatever notes are created by the user, even if they were drawn freehand with the mouse or entered from the MIDI keyboard with no observance of any rules whatsoever.

Because of the wide range of abilities of rhythmic representation, this editor allows truly meticulous operations when changing the note's position horizontally. And, if you need to correct rhythmic faults — set notes to the correct rhythmic positions — this operation can be done immediately in the Key Edit editor. The user can correct nuances of the sound's extraction, etc. in the **Controller Display** field.

Another advantage of the Key Edit editor is the unique opportunities of working with loop fragments.

However, along with unreserved admiration for the options of the Key Edit editor, you should also understand that, just as any editor of the Cubasis software, it has its own strictly limited area for satisfying users' needs. For example, the majority of operations that are quite common for the Score Edit editor (where notation is primary), are beyond the scope of the Key Edit editor.

▶ *Note*

Since musical competence is a sort of "pass" into a professional level of work with the Cubase software, a large portion of this book is allotted to basic ideas of music theory.

Now let's continue our description of the Key Edit editor, where, in the course of mastering the main operations, the reader will become acquainted with the laws of the musical language.

2.9. Metric Grid (*Snap* and *Quant*)

Often, when you first try to record notes in the Key Edit editor (and in the Score Edit editor), some questions emerge: why do the notes sometimes not "obey" — refuse to be set to the right places, fail to change their length, automatically become shorter or longer, etc.?

Before answering these questions, we would like to draw our readers' attention to the fact that an understanding of the basic logical principles of the software's performance is extremely important for successful and comfortable work with the Cubasis VST and Cubasis Notation software.

You see, the user is the one who specifies the rhythmical parameters of the software. And the musician is guided by the features of the future composition: prevailing lengths, the frequency and length of the rests, etc.

The values in the Quant and Snap fields are specified in accordance with these goals (Fig. 2.24, Section 3).

Now we will try to digress a bit from the rules, and, before the functions of these fields are explained, briefly convey their essence (in our opinion, the names of the fields do not quite express their purpose accurately enough).

The value specified in the lower Quant field corresponds to the points of the grid that are *visible on the screen.*

▶ Note

The length value in the **Quant** field also shows the length of the note (notes) set in various ways: by clicking on the **Pencil** tool, by dragging with the **Paint Brush** tool, or by executing the **Fill** command from the **Do** menu.

The changes to a certain grid — which cannot be seen on the screen, but are very important — are made in the upper Snap field. Its pitch determines those "authorized" vertical borders from which the notes may begin.

In other words:

❑ The values in the Quant field are the pitch of the grid on the screen and the "standard" length of the notes in the key imprints field.

❑ The values in the Snap field are the rhythmic positions where these notes are permitted to be placed.

❑ By assigning the appropriate parameters in the Quant and Snap fields, you can easily alternate notes and rests without intently scrutinizing the screen.

▶ Tip

If you fail to set a note in a position, you have to change the value in the **Snap** field (in most cases — you'll have to specify a lower one).

❏ Now we'll consider the parameters of the Quant (Quantize) and Snap (binding) fields in a few examples.

2.9.1. Note Length. The *Quant* Field

A note created by one click of the mouse button is equal to one point of the grid visible on the screen.

If a value of 16 is specified in the Quant field, then by clicking the left mouse button, you will "draw" a sixteenth note in the key imprints field; if the value is 4, you'll draw a quarter note, etc.

Values are selected in the Quant drop-down list (Fig. 2.32).

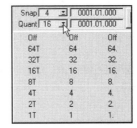

Fig. 2.32. Grid pitch selection in the **Quant** drop-down list

The "common" lengths (straight notes) mentioned above are positioned in the middle of this list.

 ### Note

The middle column contains the straight notes, the left one contains triplets (each divided into three equal parts), and the right column contains the lengths of dotted notes (corresponding to a sesquialteral length). Examples of their use will be considered below.

If Off is selected, then any fixed note length is cancelled, allowing you to set *any* length.

2.9.2. Note Position. The *Snap* Field

Note positioning depends on the value in the Snap drop-down list.

In other words, the value selected here determines the *authorized grid division* (with no impact on the length) — the vertical borders from which notes may *start*.

There is a set of values similar to these in the Quant list (Fig. 2.33). The difference is the availability of highly accurate positions: from 2pp to 7pp. These are needed to position the notes not only on the borders of the beats, but also near the borders — with an offset of a few ticks.

If the Off option is selected, notes may be set without the grid — *anywhere*.

The principles of dividing the **Quant** and **Snap** grids are the same (see Figs. 2.32 and 2.33). Therefore, you can show the "invisible" grid — i.e., the positions at which notes can be set — in the following way: switch the value of the grid in the **Quant** drop-down list for a while to make it equal to the **Snap** value (at the moment of comparison).

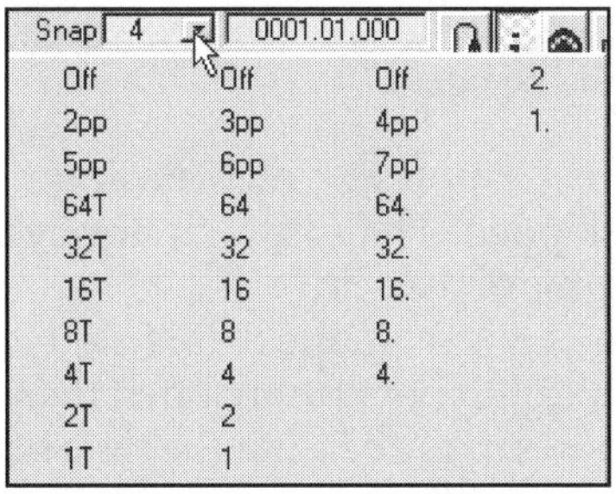

Fig. 2.33. Selecting the length in the **Snap** drop-down list

▼ *Moving the Editor Cursor*

The vertical line crossing the key imprints field is the cursor of the editor. Its position determines the position in the song: you can place a note here, have this place be where playback starts, or make it so that the material from the clipboard will be pasted from here, etc.

Attention: The editor cursor can *only* be set in positions authorized by the **Snap** field value.

You can move the cursor a number of ways: with the buttons on the **Transport bar**, with the <Page Up> and <Page Down> keys, or by clicking the left mouse button on the **Ruler** — the strip with the bar numbers.

► *Tip*

We should note that sometimes it is convenient to change the values in both windows simultaneously. This is done with keys <1>–<8>, and for triplets and dotted notes with <T> and <.>.

Since a basic understanding of the **Snap** and **Quant** fields is extremely important when working with the software, detailed illustrations of their settings are shown in Figs. 2.34—2.37.

In the first three examples, one parameter — note length — remains unchanged. The repeating sixteenth notes are shown for clarity.

But in each of these examples, the positions at which the notes can be placed are different: 4, 8, 16 (quarter, eighth, and sixteenth).

Example One. A value of 4 is set in the **Snap** field — i.e., the "authorized" positions are quarter notes. Therefore, notes of *any length* (including the shortest) can only start at positions where the quarters are "officially" started. And it is extremely important to realize that positioning notes *between* the points of the invisible grid is *impossible.*

As a result of the positioning shown in the example, you may get a common rhythmic figure — short notes marking the beginning of each fourth beat.

Note

In addition to the example in *Section 2.8.6*, remember that this is yet another way to designate staccato for the computer.

It is not obligatory to set notes at each position (as shown in the example) — authorized beats can be skipped. The software, however, forbids you to set notes *more often* than the grid step in the Snap field.

Example Two. A value of 8 is set in the Snap field (Fig. 2.35), and so the notes can be placed at positions of each eighth note (more often than in the first example). Therefore, there are more sixteenth notes in the bar, but the rests between them are shorter.

Fig. 2.34. Sixteenth note positioning with a quarter grid step

Fig. 2.35. Sixteenth note positioning with an eighth grid step

Example Three. Fig. 2.36 shows that the values in the Snap and Quant fields are the same: 16. This means that the points of the "invisible" grid are equal to the points shown on the screen. Therefore, the notes may be placed anywhere on the visible grid: the upper row of sixteenth notes are set close to one another.

This condition, however, is not obligatory: in the example in the lower rows, the key imprints are set randomly.

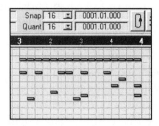

Fig. 2.36. Sixteenth note positioning with a sixteenth grid step

In practice, using various combinations of the Quant and Snap parameters lets you set notes with fixed rests, and considerably simplifies the process of note positioning (the user does not have to scrutinize the screen, counting the small grid divisions).

Example Four. Here we show the option of positioning notes *between the grid divisions*. This is possible when the value in the Quant field exceeds the value in the Snap field.

Fig. 2.37 shows a ratio of values that is the reverse of what we considered in the three examples above: the step of the visible grid is big (Quant = 4), and the allowed positions for such lengths are small (Snap = 16).

Therefore, quarter notes can *start from any* (invisible) "official" sixteenth positions, which is shown in the illustration.

With such Snap and Quant values, the limitations related to the visible grid are removed, and the musician can set notes between the points of the grid.

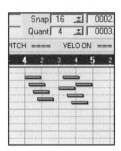

Fig. 2.37. Note positioning
between the grid divisions

The Key Edit editor allows you to shorten or lengthen the notes, as well as shift them not only by the musical beats, but by their parts — ticks — too.

2.10. The Key Edit Editor Toolbar

Let's consider the tools of the Key Edit editor: Arrow, Eraser, Line, Magnifying Glass, Pencil, and Paint Brush.

Its main working principles and appearance (Fig. 2.38) are similar to the toolbar in the Arrange window, considered in *Chapter 1*.

Fig. 2.38. The Key Edit editor toolbar

The toolbar is opened by clicking the right mouse button in the Note Display section (the key imprint area) or in the lower Controller Display section.

Four of six tools are functioning in the Controller Display section: Arrow, Eraser, Line, and Pencil.

To select a tool, move the cursor along the panel to the required icon (*with the right mouse button pressed*).

One of the six instruments — Arrow — is used more often than all the rest, and is, in fact, the mouse cursor. This is why moving to the Arrow tool can be done with a simple click of the right mouse button, if any other tool is selected.

Using the tools, you can edit not only the key imprints, but also graphic objects in the controller section.

Now let's take a look at each of the tools and dwell on their main operations — selecting, moving, copying, and deleting — in the Note Display and Controller Display sections.

2.10.1. *Arrow*

The main purpose of the Arrow tool is to select MIDI events (and also move, copy, or delete them) in the Note Display and Controller Display sections:

❐   To select a MIDI event, click on it with the left mouse button.
❐   There are two methods for selecting several MIDI events at once: you can drag the Arrow diagonally (select a frame) holding the left mouse button pressed, or you can click on several MIDI events holding the key <Shift> pressed.

MIDI events can be moved and copied: to move them, you only need to move the events to a new place holding the left mouse button pressed; to copy them, do the same operation with the <Alt> key pressed.

 Note

With any kind of movement, the new positions of the events are correlated to the authorized positions (**Snap**).

2.10.2. *Eraser*

The appearance of this tool leaves no doubt as to its purpose. The Eraser tool "erases" key imprints. It is very easy to use: to delete one note, just click on it; to delete a group of notes, drag the eraser across the key imprints (erase them) holding the left mouse button pressed.

Note

The key imprint is erased when the **Eraser** touches its *top left* corner.

If the Eraser is used in the paste mode (the In button), the material will be moved to the left.

2.10.3. *Line*

The illustration shows the Line tool in the form of a cross, denoting that this tool may work both horizontally and vertically. (The Line tool is used horizontally when editing controllers.)

You can perform the following operations with the Line tool in the Controller Display section:

❏ You can align (cut) the line for changing a MIDI controller parameter. To do this, drag the Line in the required direction (horizontally or diagonally) holding the left mouse button pressed.

❏ You can create new MIDI events in the controller section. Drag the Line to the controller field holding the <Alt> key pressed.

Using the Line tool, you can shorten individual notes or groups of notes *by any value* (independently of the grid). It is in this that it differs from the Pencil tool, which "obeys" the grid divisions.

Moreover, the Line tool can cut the note from *any* end. It is very easy to use: drag it to the place where you would like it to be cut. The material to the right of the cut line will be deleted. If you press and hold the <Alt> key during this operation, the left part will be deleted.

Fig. 2.39 shows quarter notes "cut" from different ends by an arbitrary value with the help of the Line tool. The appearance of the lower quarter note after cutting will depend on whether the <Alt> key is pressed.

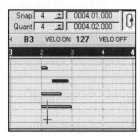

Fig. 2.39. Shortening a note with the **Line** tool

You may change the length of a group of notes with the **Line** tool (Fig. 2.40). To do this, drag the tool vertically or diagonally, holding the left mouse button pressed. In this example, the lower part of the chord will be deleted, or if the <Alt> key is pressed, the upper part of the chord will be deleted.

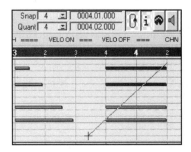

Fig. 2.40. Shortening a group of notes with the **Line** tool

2.10.4. *Magnifying Glass*

The icon of the Magnifying Glass tool fully represents its purpose. This "magnifying glass of sound" enables you hear individual notes or note groups better.

If you bring the Magnifying Glass to the key imprint and click, the sound will be heard (if speakers or headphones are connected, and the settings of the sound card are correct).

The sound will correspond to the pitch and length of the note "drawn". But you must take into account the fact that sometimes the note being played may turn out to be shorter than the length shown. This depends on the instrument: for example, unlike percussion, the organ may sustain a note for quite a long time.

In order to listen to several notes, you must drag the **Magnifying Glass** tool across the key imprints in either direction, holding the left mouse button pressed.

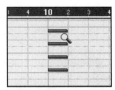

Fig. 2.41. The **Magnifying Glass** tool

Here, the notes affected by the Magnifying Glass will sound one by one. Therefore, the chord may not be heard as a whole, but rather in a "disjointed" way — performed in the *arpeggiato* style.

Apart from the **Magnifying Glass**, you can hear the notes by means of the <←> or <→> keys. (For this, the **Speaker** button must be pressed).

This method has a peculiar feature: the notes are moved in the order in which they were created.

2.10.5. *Pencil*

Let's now consider the option of "drawing" the notes with the Pencil tool. Keep in mind that it this is related to the settings in the **Snap** and **Quant** fields.

There are two simple methods of creating a note with the Pencil tool.

❐ Click the left mouse button in the key imprints field, and separate notes of a strictly fixed length equal to the value in the **Quant** field — will be created (Fig. 2.42, indicated by the number 1).

❐ You can create a lengthened key imprint as follows: hold the left mouse button pressed and draw a line from left to the right (Fig. 2.42, indicated by the number 2). The end of the note, however, will correspond to the beats specified in the **Snap** field.

Besides drawing notes, the Pencil tool allows you to perform two more operations: shorten or lengthen a note.

There are two ways to shorten a note: either by clicking on it twice (closer to the beginning), or by "counter-drawing" — holding the left mouse button pressed, move along the key imprint in the reverse direction, from right to left (Fig. 2.42, indicated by the number 3).

▶ **Tip**

If the length of the note is to be changed, press and hold the <Alt> key to avoid accidental creation of an unnecessary note.

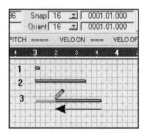

Fig. 2.42. Drawing a note with the **Pencil** tool

You can lengthen a short imprint by additional drawing. Drag the Pencil to the right holding the left mouse button pressed.

Using the Pencil tool, you can also change the length of the notes in the group — *simultaneously* lengthen or shorten them.

For this, do the following:

1. Select the group of notes (there are four notes (marked by numbers) combined in the group in Fig. 2.43).
2. Select the Pencil tool.
3. Grab any note of the group and drag it to the left or to the right (in the illustration, notes are shortened).

 Note

The changes in length will correspond to the points of the grid. This function can be cancelled by switching the grid off by selecting **Off** in the **Snap** field.

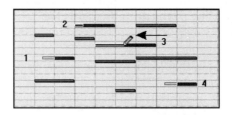

Fig. 2.43. Changing the length of notes in a group

In
➡

If the notes are entered in the Insert mode, then the subsequent material will be moved to the right. (You can move it back to the left with the Eraser tool: "erase" the key imprints with the In button pressed.)

► *Tip*

After editing, double notes (one superimposed on another) may be found. In this case, it is recommended that you finish editing with a command that will delete them — **Delete Doubles** in the **Function** menu. If this is not done, some strange double tones may be left in the score.

The Pencil tool may be used in the Controller Display section to draw "continuous" MIDI events (those with no spaces between them). To do this, you need to drag it with the <Alt> key pressed.

If you simply click with the Pencil tool on a graphic object in the Controller Display section, its size will be changed: it will be enlarged or reduced to the point indicated by the Pencil tool. (The use of the Pencil tool in the controller section is described below.)

2.10.6. *Paint Brush*

This tool is intended for quick creation of a note sequence (both horizontally and vertically).

The procedure is extremely simple: drag the **Paint Brush** tool horizontally or — with the pressed <Alt> key — in any direction (diagonally, in circles, etc).

As when drawing with the **Pencil** tool, the "laws of note positioning" will be strictly observed: their lengths will correspond to the **Quant** field value, and the interval between two key imprints will correspond to the value of the **Snap** field (Fig. 2.44).

 Note

If **Paint Brush** is used in the paste mode (the **In** button pressed), then all the subsequent material will be moved to the right. You can return it by deleting with the **Eraser** tool (with the **In** button pressed).

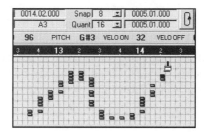

Fig. 2.44. Drawing a note sequence with the **Paint Brush** tool

The Paint Brush tool can be used when recording rhythmical sequences built upon the repetition of a sound of one pitch, as well as for special effects.

Now let's turn to the main operations with tools, function keys, and commands in the Note Display section.

2.11. Key Imprints. Main Operations
2.11.1. Note Selection

Selecting a note is done in order to edit, copy, delete, and quantize it.

Note separation. There are two methods of selecting one note:

❑ Click on it with the Arrow tool (or select the note in a frame)

❑ Press the <←> or <→> key

The selection is cancelled by clicking on the blank area of the imprint section, or by selecting another note (or group of notes) using any method.

Groups of notes. There are several methods of selecting a group of notes:

❏ Frame the notes with the Arrow tool by dragging the arrow diagonally holding the left mouse button pressed (Fig. 2.45).

Note that the group includes even partially framed notes. In the example in Fig. 2.45, all the notes will be selected as soon as the left mouse button is released.

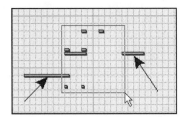

Fig. 2.45. Selecting a group
of notes with the **Arrow** tool

❏ Move among the notes with the <←> and <→> keys, holding the <Shift> key pressed. *Only* consecutively positioned notes will be selected.

❏ Click on the notes selectively with the Arrow tool, holding the <Shift> key pressed. You can form *any* groups with this method, including groups made of notes that are not positioned consecutively (Fig. 2.46).

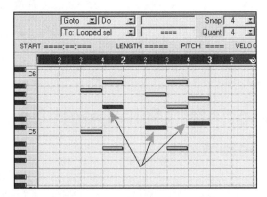

Fig. 2.46. Selectively combining notes into a group

❏ Selecting all of the musical material is done traditionally, either with the Select All command from the Edit menu, or using the <Ctrl>+<A> key combination.

❏ Obscure selection. This method uses the commands in the To: drop-down list (Fig. 2.47).

Note

This one stands out, since first of all, the selection is not made graphically, and second, it is intended for quantization (the **Functions** menu) and the **Fill** and **Delete** commands of the **Do** drop-down list (Fig. 2.47). Keep in mind that the **Fill** command forms a chain of identical notes, and the **Delete** command deletes them from the selected area.

Fig. 2.47. Selecting events using the **To:** list

Changing the composition of a group. In order to remove one *or more* notes from a group without breaking it up, click with the arrow on the note (notes) that you want to remove holding the <Shift> key pressed.

The procedure of returning a note to a group is similar: click twice on the key imprint with the left mouse button, the <Shift> key pressed.

To break up a group, just click on a blank area of the imprint section (between the selected notes).

Any kind of note selection is a preliminary step necessary for performing further operations: moving, copying, deleting, quantizing, etc.

2.11.2. Moving Notes

You can move notes or groups of notes in any direction. Keep in mind that any rhythmic move is possible only by the beat authorized in the Snap field.

Tip

If the **Speaker** button is pressed (Fig. 2.48), the pitch of the note can be heard when you use the mouse to move the note.

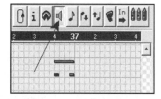

Fig. 2.48. The **Speaker** button

There are several ways to move a note.

The first method (and the most universal one) of moving individual notes is by dragging them with the mouse. For the user's convenience, moving the note is accompanied by a change in the color of the key on the keyboard, and is shown on the Position Box and Transpose/Pitch Box displays (Fig. 2.49).

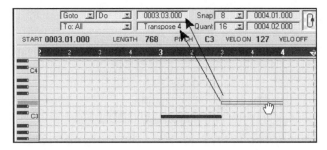

Fig. 2.49. Indicating the note position during a move

Let's look at the example in Fig. 2.49. The figures on the Position Box panel (0003. 03.000) show that after the move, the note will be in the third bar (0003) at the *beginning* of the third beat (03) (the last three zeros denote ticks).

The lower display, where the name of the note was previously shown, now shows the number of semitones by which the note has been shifted: Transpose 4.

▼ *Transpose*

A *semitone* is the interval between adjacent keys — between a black and a white one, as a rule. There are two exceptions — when there is no black key between the white keys (between *B* and *C*, and *E* and *F*) — in these cases the interval is also equal to a semitone.

Transposition — changing the note's pitch.

In the example, the *C* note indicated on the keyboard as C3 is moved to a new position — i.e., becomes the *E* note. There is an interval of four semitones between the *C* and *E* keys. Therefore, the value of the transposition is expressed by the number 4. Since the new position of the note is *higher* than the previous one, the **Transpose** value is expressed by a positive number.

Here is an example of diminishing a note. In Fig. 2.50, the *C* note is moved down by one octave. The value of the move is expressed by a negative number: Transpose — –12.

▶ *Tip*

It is recommended that you memorize this number, since it indicates the number of the *semitones* by which the octave is measured (in the Cubasis VST and Cubasis Notation software).

The interval of an octave is constant — the interval between the nearest keys of the same name is *always* equal to 6 tones, or 12 semitones.

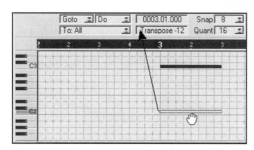

Fig. 2.50. The note's position after a move lower

If you plan on moving the note *strictly horizontally or vertically*, you'll need to use the <Shift> key. And it is important to observe the following sequence of operations:

1. Click on the key imprint and *hold the mouse button pressed* until the "hand" appears (see Fig. 2.50).
2. Press the <Shift> key.
3. Start moving in the required direction.

When you use this algorithm, you are safeguarded against the note moving perpendicularly, and thus making an error.

The second method consists of using the **Info Line** panel. It enables you to move a note both vertically and horizontally.

Moving the note vertically is done by changing its pitch. To do this, you need to:

1. Select the note (click on it with the **Arrow** tool).

 Note

All the values on the **Info Line** panel appear when the note is selected.

2. Change the pitch of the note:
   - Click with the *right* or *left* mouse button on the name of the note in the Pitch field on the **Info Line** panel (Fig. 2.51). The pitch of the note will be changed by semitones: it will be augmented or diminished, respectively.
   - The pitch of the note is changed continuously if one of the mouse buttons is held pressed.
   - Type in the name of the note from the keyboard. To do this, double-click on the name of the note in the **Pitch** field on the **Info Line** panel, in which the name of the note is entered from the keyboard (Fig. 2.52). After typing in the name of the note, press <Enter>, or click the mouse button outside of this field.

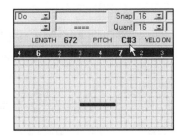

Fig. 2.51. Moving a note on the **Info Line** panel

▼ *Entering the Note's Name during Transposition*

The name of the note can be entered as an uppercase or lowercase letter, and the sharp symbol can be added using the <Shift>+<3> key combination. You can see in the example in Fig. 2.52 that the *C* note of the four-line octave (*C4*) will be diminished, and become the *D* sharp of the contra-octave (D#–2).

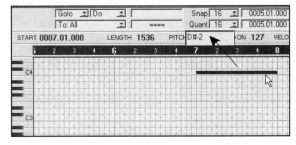

Fig. 2.52. Moving a note with the **Info Line** panel

The convenience of this type of transposition is that moving the rhythmic position of the note is impossible — i.e., the note is moved *strictly* vertically.

Horizontally moving the note is done in the same manner. The rhythmical coordinates of the note on the START display of the Info Line panel (Fig. 2.53) are changed either by clicking on the corresponding categories (bars, beats, ticks) with the right or left mouse button, or by typing in the new values from the keyboard in the same way as you did when changing the Pitch parameter.

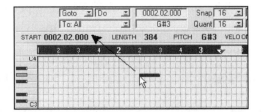

Fig. 2.53. Changing the start position of a note

Moving groups of notes. There are certain features of working with groups.

After a group is selected, *grab* the key imprint of this group with the cursor (if the arrow is on a blank area, the group is *automatically* broken up).

First method. You can move a group of selected notes without limiting the direction or interval. To do this, drag the group to a new position holding the left mouse button pressed (Fig. 2.54).

The example shows that, when the group was moved, the **Arrow** tool was on the C note, which was on the third beat of the sixth bar before the move. This note was moved up by three semitones (which is confirmed by the "Transpose 3" message on the Transpose/Pitch Box display), and now is on the first beat of the seventh bar (shown by the numbers 0007.01.000 in the **Position Box** display).

Despite the fact that the position change of only one note (the one held with the mouse) is fixed when the group is moved, the value of the move is the same for all notes of the group.

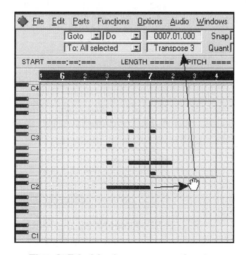

Fig. 2.54. Moving groups of notes

Second method. If *only* a horizontal or vertical move is planned, you need to *strictly* observe the following sequence of operations (as when moving one note):

1. Select a group using one of the methods.
2. Click and *hold the mouse button pressed* on the imprint of one of the keys included in the group (before the "hand" appears).
3. Press the <Shift> key.
4. Start moving the group in the required direction.

Note that after the group is moved to new position *by any method*, it is not broken, which means that it can be moved again if necessary. This is convenient, as you can always correct the position later.

2.11.3. Copying and Deleting Notes

The principles of copying and deleting notes in Key Edit are similar to those in any text editor.

 Note

All copying and deleting operations are done with selected material.

Copying and deleting can also be done using various methods.
To delete something in the Key Edit editor, we have the special **Delete** command in the Do drop-down list (Fig. 2.55). You can delete selected groups of notes, loop objects, and all of the material in the Key Edit editor.

! *Attention*

The working area is specified in the **To:** drop-down list, and the MIDI events thus selected are *not* highlighted in color.

If the **All** command is selected in the **To:** drop-down list, then all of the material in Key Edit will be deleted.

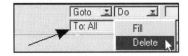

Fig. 2.55. Deleting all the material

Deleting is also possible using the <Delete> or <Backspace> keys. In this way, you can delete both individual notes and groups.
After the deletion is completed, the note adjacent to the deleted one is automatically selected. Therefore, you can delete subsequent notes by repeatedly pressing of one of these keys.

 Tip

When selective deletion is done, it is convenient to delete unnecessary notes with the <Delete> or <Backspace> keys, moving around the notes using the <Right arrow> and <Left Arrow> keys.

Copying single notes. This operation can be done using several methods. With the Arrow tool, it is done as follows:

❑ Press and hold the <Alt> key and move the note in *any* direction.
❑ If the note must be moved *strictly* vertically or horizontally when copying, then the following operations must be done (the sequence is important):
1. Press the <Alt> key.
2. Press and hold the note with the Arrow tool (the "hand" will appear).
3. Press the <Shift> key.
4. Move the note vertically or horizontally.

▶ *Note*

If you reverse points 1 and 2 (first select the note and then press the <Alt> and <Shift> keys), the note is not copied but rather moved.

Another method of copying and deleting is the traditional (clipboard) method — using the **Edit** menu or hotkeys (Fig. 2.56):

❑ Cut (<Ctrl>+<X>) cuts the selected events into the clipboard.
❑ Copy (<Ctrl>+<C>) copies the selected events into the clipboard.
❑ Paste (<Ctrl>+<V>) pastes the selected events from the clipboard.
❑ Delete Events deletes events (the selected material).
❑ Select All (<Ctrl>+<A>) selects all the events.

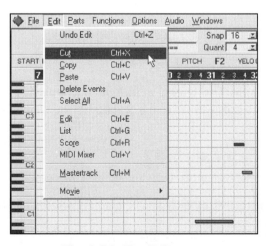

Fig. 2.56. The **Edit** menu

When copied in the usual way (using the clipboard), the note must be selected, copied into the clipboard, and then inserted at one (or several) new positions. The procedure is the following:

❐ Select the note and copy it into the clipboard using the Copy command in the Edit menu (or the <Ctrl>+<C> key combination).

❐ Click with the right mouse button on the ruler bar (Ruler) — i.e., set the cursor to the place where the note is supposed to be inserted (Fig. 2.57). The beginning of the note will coincide with the cursor's position.

❐ Press the <Ctrl>+<V> key combination, or select the Paste command from the Edit menu.

You can insert a note only into the rhythmical positions authorized by the Snap field value.

In the example in Fig. 2.57, we can see that the C note (C5) was placed, when copied, on different quarter beats of the bars (with the value in the Snap window = 4).

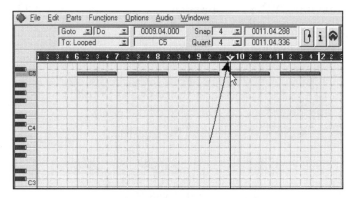

Fig. 2.57. Inserting deleted notes

Copying note groups. This operation is done much the same as with a single note. But, since operations with groups are quite frequent, let's briefly consider each one of them.

Note

You can form a group from adjacent notes (using a frame), as well as by selectively including the notes into a group (with the <Shift> key pressed).

A group can be copied by dragging it to a new position with the Arrow tool:

❐ With the <Alt> key pressed, the group, when copied, can be moved in any direction (including diagonally).

❑ If you want to move the group strictly vertically or horizontally, then repeat the same sequence of operations as with a single note: press the <Alt> key, select the group, grab one of the notes of the group, and when the "hand" appears, press the <Shift> key and move the group.

The group copying method can be used, for example, for creating chord sequences or repetitions in the form of sequences.

The following is the algorithm for creating a chord sequence by means of copying:

1. Create a chord (using the mouse, or entering it from a MIDI instrument).
2. Press the <Alt> key.
3. Select the chord (e.g., frame it with the **Arrow** tool).
4. Grab, for example, the upper note (the "hand" appears).
5. Press the <Shift> key.
6. Move the chord vertically (you may follow the interval on the **Transpose/Pitch Box** display, or with the key highlighted in color on the keyboard). You can see from Fig. 2.58 that the chord is transposed down by 10 semitones. Its upper *C* note (C5) has become the *D* note (D4).

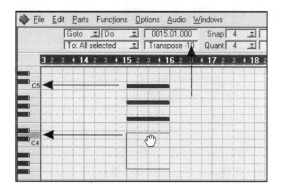

Fig. 2.58. Transposing a chord (moving down)

7. When the chord is set to the required vertical position, release the <Shift> key for a moment, then press it again and hold.
8. Move the chord horizontally (checking, if necessary, the rhythmical position on the **Position Box** display) (Fig. 2.59).
9. Release the mouse button (thus fixing the chord).
10. To set other chords, *hold the <Alt> key pressed after step 9*, release the <Shift> key, and repeat the sequence of operations in steps 4–9 for the selected chord.

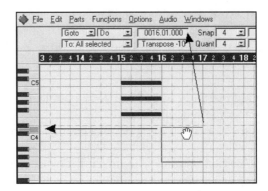

Fig. 2.59. Moving the chord strictly along the rhythmic grid

Thus, keeping in mind the artistic appropriateness of course, you can not only create chains of chords, but also easily repeat the same melody fragments starting from different notes (Fig. 2.60). It is important that the chord retain the interval between the notes during the move (e.g., a major triad will not be changed to a minor one, etc.).

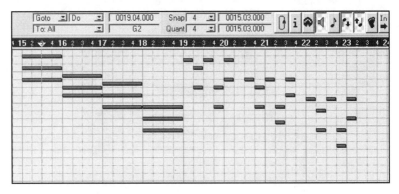

Fig. 2.60. The results of using the copying algorithm

If it is necessary to repeat a group in a large interval, it is more convenient to use clipboard copying:

1. Select the group, copy it in the clipboard (e.g., using the key combination <Ctrl>+<C>).
2. Place the editor cursor on the required rhythmic position:
   - By clicking with the left mouse button on the **Ruler** bar (Fig. 2.61)
   - With the <Page Up> and <Page Down> keys
   - With the **Transport bar** buttons

Note

The editor cursor also "yields to the grid": it is not possible to place it on beats shorter than those specified in the **Snap** field.

If you can not move the editor cursor to the right, it means that you have come to the end of the part. You can enlarge it in the **Arrange** window. To do this, you will need to temporarily exit the **Key Edit** editor.

3. Paste the group from the clipboard (e.g., using the key combination <Ctrl>+<V>).

 Note

In the example in Fig. 2.61, the notes begin from different beats. When moved to a new place in the position of the editor cursor, there always be a note whose starting border is *before* all the rest. In our example, this is the upper note: it will be started from the fourth beat of the second bar (according to the position of the vertical line (editor cursor)).

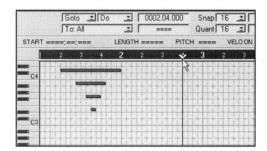

Fig. 2.61. Moving the editor cursor when copying

This method only allows you to move a group horizontally. If you need to transpose the notes, then the moving is done in two steps. In the second step, the group is dragged either up or down with the mouse.

2.12. The *Controller Display* Section of the Key Edit Editor

In previous sections, we examined operations with notes (or rather, with key imprints) in the upper section — Note Display. Now we'll take a look at the Controller Display section of the Key Edit editor.

As we mentioned above, the Controller Display section enables the musician to graphically (even in real-time mode — during recording or playback) edit events that are generally known as Non-Note Events (non-notes).

Non-Note Events in the Controller Display *Section*

The oddity of this name is explained by the fact that the **Controller Display** section contains not only controllers (Fig. 2.63). Strictly speaking, the only controllers are the last three items in the list: **Modulation**, **MainVolume**, and **Pan**. In the beginning of this list, you'll find MIDI events: **Pitch Bend** and **Aftertouch**. **Velocity** is in the middle, which is a parameter of the most common MIDI event, called Note. This explains why the **Velocity** "controller" is different (for example, it cannot be created apart from a note).

However, despite the variety of Non-Note Events in the lower section, the software developers decided to call it **Controller Display**. This is because, apart from the events that appear in the drop-down list, you can graphically edit all 127 controllers offered by the software in this section. They are selected via the List Edit editor. We will skip their detailed description here, since the principles of their operation are similar to those described below.

From now on, the lower section will be called — in accordance with the program manual — the controller section, and all the Non-Note Events that it contains will in general be called "controllers".

The basic information on the Controller Display section is the following:

❑ Calling the controller section is done using the **Controller** button in the bottom left part of the Key Edit editor, which is marked with the "~" character. Pressing the button again hides this field.

❑ In order to see the graphic image of any controller in the Controller Display section, select it from the list (see Fig. 2.62). By default, all the controllers (except for Velocity) are set to zero.

❑ Only *one* of six types of the Non-Note Events can be shown on the screen. Therefore, you cannot edit them all simultaneously.

❑ You can enlarge the visible part of the Controller Display section (Fig. 2.62). To do this, drag the line dividing the two sections up or down (grabbing it with the mouse cursor).

❑ You can also change the horizontal scale in the controller field (which is convenient when editing). This is done with the methods used for this operation in the Note Display section — with sliders or the <G> or <H> keys.

❑ In order for the musician to be able to easily define a controller's value during editing, the position of the mouse cursor is shown as a number in the special Value field. It is positioned under the controller selection button (indicated with an arrow in Fig. 2.62).

► Note

For five of the controllers, the range of values is 0–127; the **Pitch Bend**'s range is wider: 16,383 gradations.

❒ There is one toolbar for both sections: it is called in the same way (with the right mouse button), and when the field borders are crossed, the tool remains. The exceptions are the **Magnifying Glass** and the **Paint Brush**. They are disabled in the Controller Display section.

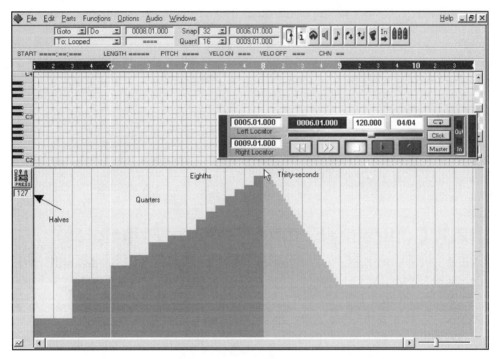

Fig. 2.62. The **Controller Display** field

Now we should probably say a few words about visible and invisible grids of the Controller Display section.

The design of the lower section differs from the upper one: first of all, it is divided by vertical lines only, and second, these lines are quite widely spaced, since they *always* show only the beats of the bar.

For example, if the time is four beats (if the second figure is 4), then each bar will be divided *into only four parts*, no matter what length the beats (the first figure of the time signature) are: quarters (as in the example in Fig. 2.62), eighths, sixteenths, or some other length. Moreover, even if the beats in the upper section are divided into parts, this will not affect the lower section.

Despite the fact that the visible grid in the Controller Display section is "sparse" (corresponding to the beats), the musician can edit the controllers with any level of precision or gradation, including by parts of beats.

We should probably explain this thesis. You can see from in Fig. 2.62 that the line may be of different "smoothness". For the sake of clarity, it changes in each bar. These changes are introduced by the change of values in the **Snap** field. The values in the example were chosen as follows: 2, 4, 8, 32. Therefore, the line is first changed by half lengths, then by quarters, then eighths, and finally by thirty-second lengths.

Generally, we can say the following: the **Snap** field sets the invisible grid for both fields, and sets the authorized positions. The difference is that in the upper field, this relates to notes, while in the lower field it relates to controllers. Thus the smoothness of the line when drawing or editing the controller line in the **Controller Display** section depends on the value specified in the **Snap** field.

▼ *Warning*

The simplicity of graphic editing comes about due to the fact that it is based on many MIDI events, since each (even the slightest) change is an authorized and independent command (this is clearly seen in the List Edit editor). Since too many commands may overflow the channel's carrying capacity, which would lead to failures, we do not recommend that you try for maximum smoothness of the controller lines unless this is absolutely necessary.

2.12.1. Controller Editing (General Principles)

Selecting controllers in the Key Edit editor is done from the drop-down list that opens when the Event Type Selector button is pressed (indicated with an arrow in Fig. 2.63).

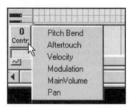

Fig. 2.63. The list of controllers

If a controller is not selected, then you will see the "0 Control" message on the Event Type Selector button (Fig. 2.63). If one of the six Non-Note Events is selected from the drop-down list, the icon on the button changes accordingly (no more than one controller can appear on the screen).

 Pitch Bend. The range of values is from –8192 to +8191. Using this controller, you can create smooth passages from one note to another (produce sounds "between notes").

 Aftertouch. Shows the force of pressing a key. Range: from 0 to 127.

Velocity. Shows the *volume* (and timbre, if a synthesizer is supported) of the *beginning* of the note. Range: from 0 to 127.

▶ *Note*

> **Velocity** is a parameter of a Note MIDI event, so it is created automatically (together with the note); you can not "draw" it separately in the controller section.

Modulation. This controller specifies the depth of the frequency modulation in the channel. Figuratively speaking, the modulation shows the frequency of the sound's vibration relative to the main tone. By default, this controller is deactivated (a value of zero is set); the maximum value is 127.

MainVolume. Defines the main volume of the note sequence (or one sound). Range: from 0 to 127.

▶ *Note*

> Using the **MainVolume** button, you can vary the volume in the course of the note (or several notes), and correct the time of the sound fade.

Pan (Panorama). Specifies the position of the sounds in a panorama (between the left and right channels). By default, the middle position is specified (64). The 0 value corresponds to a full move to the left stereo channel, and 127 corresponds to a full move to the right stereo channel.

Now let's consider some methods of creating and editing Non-Note Events.

"Drawing" a controller in a blank section is possible only if you have pressed the <Alt> key *previously.*

The smoothness of the line indicating the controller's change (except for Velocity) depends on the value in the Snap field.

If the controller does not "obey" while being drawn, one possible reason is that you may have gone beyond the borders of the created part. (If this is the case, lengthen the Part in the Arrange window).

The basic editing approach is the following:

❑ In order to create MIDI events, select a controller, and then, holding the <Alt> key:
  1. Click on the Pencil tool.
  2. Drag the Pencil tool (in any direction) or the Line tool (from left to right).
❑ You can select MIDI events in the same way as you would key imprints:
  1. Click on the Arrow tool — a single MIDI event will be selected (its size depends on the value in the Snap field — Fig. 2.64).
  2. Select several neighboring events, or those placed far from each other by holding the <Shift> key pressed (Fig. 2.64).

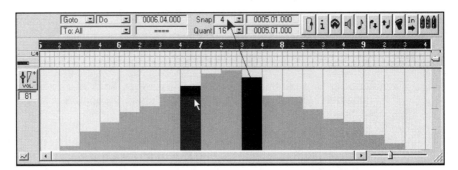

Fig. 2.64. Selecting an object in the **Controller Display** field

3. Frame MIDI events by dragging the **Arrow** tool across them.

❒ There are several methods of editing MIDI events:
   - Click with the **Pencil** tool in the proper place
   - Drag the **Pencil** tool in the required direction
   - Drag the **Line** tool in any direction
   - Erase the MIDI event with the **Eraser** tool (not applicable to **Velocity**)

► *Tip*

It is more convenient to edit controllers if one color corresponds to the same levels. This is possible when the **Velocity colors** option is selected from the drop-down list of the **Editor colors** button (the colored pencils icon) (Fig. 2.65). Despite the name, this option changes the color of all the controllers, not only **Velocity**.

❒ MIDI events are deleted as follows:
   - Drag the **Eraser** tool across the events, or
   - Select the controllers (in any manner), and press the <Backspace> or <Delete> key

▼ *"Turn out the Lights when You Leave"*

Note that controllers operate on a trigger principle. In other words, they have a common switch: if the light is on, it will be on until switched off; if the light is off — there is no chance it will be switched on by itself.

This principle, when applied to the controllers, means the following: the controller remains in its last position, and can not be changed on its own. Therefore, the user must remember to perform these operations.

We need to keep this in mind because, when you begin editing another controller, the former settings become invisible, and you can easily forget about them. Fig. 2.66 shows that a controller switched on, for example, for one note, is valid for all subsequent notes unless it is switched off.

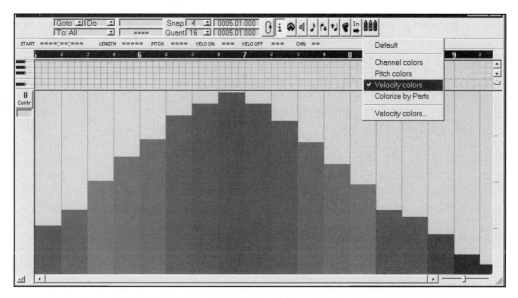

Fig. 2.65. Color gradation while marking controllers

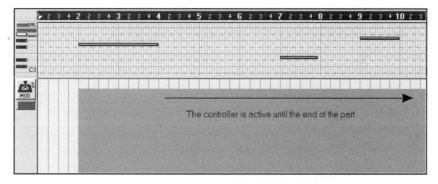

Fig. 2.66. The trigger principle of controller switching

2.12.2. *Velocity* Editing

Now let us dwell a bit on describing the features of the most frequently used parameter — Velocity.

 Note

As we already mentioned in the beginning of the section, velocity is an integral part of a Note MIDI event. To simplify the understanding of the material, we will generally call this

parameter a "controller", since the developers of Cubasis placed this parameter into the **Controller Display** section for graphic editing.

Velocity is shown on the screen in the form of vertical lines placed in positions at the beginning of the note (Fig. 2.67). The height of the line denotes the initial level of the note's volume. The fading of the volume depends on the timbre of a certain synthesizer, and is not set by this controller.

By entering new numeric values on the **Info Line** panel, you can edit two parameters related to velocity: the key pressing velocity (**Velo on**) and the key releasing velocity (**Velo off**). We should mention that sound card synthesizers ignore the **Velo off** parameter.

Velocity appears automatically when the note is created. (You can not "draw" it separately.)

❐ If notes are entered from the MIDI keyboard, their volume level depends on the *velocity* of key pressing.
❐ If notes are created using the **Fill** command of the **Do** menu, then the velocity level is always the highest (127).
❐ When the notes are "drawn" with the mouse, different levels of **Velocity** can be set (Fig. 2.67):

- Level 127 (the first note in the illustration) is created by default (without using key combinations from the computer keyboard).

- Level 96 (the second note in the illustration) is used when the <Shift> key is pressed while the notes are created.

- Level 64 (the third note in the illustration) is used if the notes are created with the <Ctrl> key pressed.

- Level 32 (the fourth note in the illustration) is used when the <Shift>+<Ctrl> key combination is pressed.

- The **Velocity** for a chord looks the same as for one note (Fig. 2.67) (if the notes of a chord are of the same volume).

Note selection and velocity are interconnected: when you select a note, you automatically select the velocity (and vice versa). This is particularly convenient when MIDI events are dense (Fig. 2.68).

Velocity is selected in the same way as a note:

❐ Click with the **Arrow** tool on **Velocity** (or on the key imprint)
❐ Click on the events holding the <Shift> key pressed, or drag the Arrow tool to frame the necessary objects
❐ Use the Select All command in the Edit menu (<Ctrl>+<A>); all MIDI events will be selected

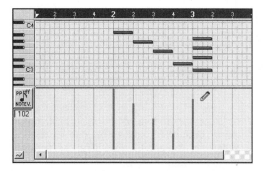

Fig. 2.67. A different velocity level
from using hotkeys

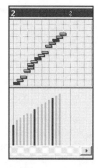

Fig. 2.68. The interconnected
selection of notes and velocity

► *Tip*

It is convenient when editing to color the velocity differently. If the **Pitch Colors** command is used (Fig. 2.65), the color of velocity will depend on the pitch of the note. If the **Velocity Colors** option is selected, then the relation will be different: the velocity level will affect the color of the note.

You can edit velocity with the Pencil or Line tools:

❏ Click with the Pencil or Line tool on the new level along velocity or nearby (in the range up until the next MIDI event) (Fig. 2.67)
❏ To edit one MIDI event, drag the Pencil tool vertically along velocity or nearby
❏ To edit several MIDI events, drag the Pencil or Line tool horizontally in the required direction

You can delete velocity in several ways:

❏ Delete the note in the Note Display field — velocity will be automatically deleted too
❏ Select Velocity, then delete it with one of the following methods:
 1. With the <Delete> or <Backspace> keys
 2. Using the Delete option in the Do drop-down list (for the area selected in the To: drop-down list)
❏ The Delete Events command in the Edit menu deletes all MIDI events (after they are selected with the Select All command of this menu)

► *Note*

You can not erase the velocity with the **Eraser** tool. But you can delete notes, and then the velocity will be deleted automatically.

See details on the step recording of the velocity in *Section 2.17*.

2.12.3. Selecting Controllers (the Key Edit and List Edit Editors)

Now a few words must be said about controller selection in the List Edit editor.

◤ *Note*

By default, there is a limited set of controllers for editing in the Key Edit editor. If the controller is selected in the List Edit editor, then the number or icon of the controller appears on the **Event Type Selector** button in the Key Edit editor (while that part is edited). This method, however, has its disadvantages. For example, after the controller is changed in the Key Edit editor, you cannot edit the previous controller (also selected in List Edit) anymore.

The sequence of selecting a controller is the following:

1. Invoke the List Edit editor (with the <Ctrl>+<G> key combination or the List option of the Edit menu).
2. Select the **Control Change** command in the **Insert** drop-down list (change the controller) (Fig. 2.69).

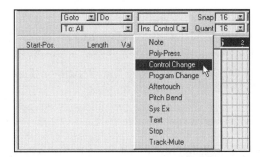

Fig. 2.69. Controller selection commands in the List Edit editor

3. Click with the Pencil tool in the Event Display section (Fig. 2.70).

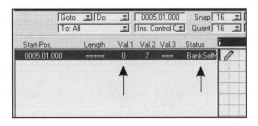

Fig. 2.70. Changing the controller in the List Edit editor

4. Change the type of the controller in the Status or Val. 1 columns (Fig. 2.70).
5. Return to Key Edit, and if necessary, graphically edit the selected controller using the methods described above.

2.13. Step Recording on the MIDI Keyboard

It is generally known that entering notes from the MIDI keyboard considerably accelerates the work of the musician. However, to be fair, we should mention that we personally are acquainted with some musicians whose assiduousness is astounding: they create huge musical canvases "manually" — without a MIDI instrument, using the mouse only.

We will begin with a simple mode — Step Recording — which is pretty much self-explanatory: notes are entered in steps.

Technically this goes as follows: the musician presses keys one by one, and the notes are recorded on the specified rhythmical positions. Such recording does not at all require a correspondence to the rhythm or tempo of the composition, since the notes are placed at previously specified positions.

Due to its slowness, the Step Recording mode lets a beginner record parts of any complexity level.

In the Cubasis Notation and Cubasis VST software, the step mode is available in all three editors. This chapter deals with the general working principles of the Step Recording mode for the Key Edit editor.

Here we will list the most characteristic features of the Step Recording mode.

☐ With step recording, you can add notes to an existing part or create a new one.
☐ The lengths of the entered notes depend on the value in the Quant field, while the rhythmical positions at which they are fixed depend on the value in the Snap field.
☐ Notes are entered at the rhythmic position at which the editor cursor is placed (remember that the cursor is moved by the beats authorized in the Snap field). After entry is completed, the cursor automatically moves to the next position specified in the Snap field.
☐ If chords are recorded in step mode, sounds included in chords must be pressed all at once, otherwise they will appear at different rhythmic positions.
☐ When you enter any note from the MIDI keyboard in step recording as well — the Velocity is recorded together with the note.

▶ *Tip*

It is necessary that you follow the melodiousness of the performance during step recording: this will save you time when editing velocity.

❏ You can listen to the material at any stage of the performance. To do this, move the cursor to the required position and switch on the **Play** mode from the **Transport bar.**

Later, material entered in step mode can be edited using *any* method (with tools, commands, etc.).

We'd like to note that, despite its "military accuracy", the Step Recording mode allows deviations: it lets you change the step's dimension, make insertions, skip steps, add notes to previous positions, etc.

Now we'll consider the features of the Step Recording mode in more detail.

The Step Recording mode is switched on and off in the **Status Bar** panel with the **Step** button (indicated by an arrow in Fig. 2.71). The **MIDI connector** button is automatically switched on, informing you of the fact that the mode of the editor's connection with the MIDI keyboard is on.

Fig. 2.71. Switching on the Step Recording mode

The step recording mode is switched off with one of two buttons:

❏ **Step.** The connection with the MIDI keyboard is retained.
❏ **MIDI connector.** The connection with the MIDI keyboard is broken, and consequently, the Step Recording mode becomes unavailable.

Below is an example of entering notes in Step mode (Fig. 2.72). The **Snap** field has a value of 4, and so the beginning of each next note is located a quarter away from the previous one. You can see that the cursor is ready for the next entry, waiting at the second beat of the sixth bar, which is illustrated in the **Step Position** display (indicated by an arrow).

As we said, to change the step dimension, you need to select a new value in the Snap field's drop-down list.

Before we give the step recording algorithm, here is a brief review of some methods of working in Step mode.

❏ You can move the cursor traditionally:
  • With the <Page Up> and <Page Down> keys
  • By clicking on the Ruler
  • With Transport bar buttons
  • By clicking on the Step Position display

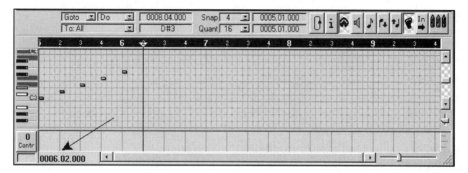

Fig. 2.72. The **Step Position** display

! *Warning*

If the cursor disappears from the editor window, it means that you are beyond the borders of the part. You'll have to lengthen the **Part** in the **Arrange** window.

In order to insert a rest (skip one step of the grid), press the <Tab> key instead of a note.

▶ *Tip*

There are other methods of inserting rests when recording, such as moving the cursor by changing the values of the **Step Position** display. To do this, click and hold the mouse button on the corresponding number of the display. Here the rest may be of any length — for example, one not equal to the step dimension.

❏ Inserting notes with a shift of the material to the right is done in Insert mode. Press the In button, set the cursor to the required position, and then play the notes.

▶ *Note*

In the Insert mode, you can enter notes using the **Pencil** and **Paint Brush** tools.

❏ The Eraser tool erases notes in the Insert mode, *moving* the subsequent material to the beginning.

❏ If the last step was a mistake, you can delete it with the <Backspace> key. Repeatedly pressing this key deletes the previous notes (or chords).

❏ You can delete unnecessary notes in any way you prefer, e.g., select the notes and press the <Delete> key.

2.13.1. Step Recording Algorithm

1. Make all the necessary connections (MIDI keyboard, speakers or earphones, etc.).
2. If necessary, change the time set by default on the **Transport bar** — four-four (04/04).
3. Set the length of the entered notes (select the value in the **Quant** field).
4. Set the authorized positions for the notes — the interval between the "steps" (select the value in the **Snap** field).
5. Set the cursor to the beginning of the recording.
6. Press the **Step** button.
7. Play the part (the tempo and the rhythm do not matter).
8. The notes of chords must be pressed simultaneously. In order to skip a position (insert a rest), press the <Tab> key.
9. Listen to the entered material:

   - Outside of rhythm — lay the **Magnifying Glass** tool on the key imprints or move the **Note Display** field using the <→> and <←> keys

   - In real time — set the cursor to the beginning of the recording and activate Play mode

► ***Tip***

It is convenient to listen to the part in a loop.

10. Edit the part, if necessary.

2.13.2. How to Rhythmically Enliven Computer Music During Step Recording

The step recording mode has one huge advantage over entering musical material with the mouse in the Key Edit editor. You can enter the notes in steps not only at precise positions determined by the grid in the **Snap** field, but also with a slight shift away from them, which allows you to *considerably* enliven the computer's "performance". We strongly recommend that you follow the instructions below and employ "creativity" when working in this mode — make use of features shown on the **Step Position** display which you may not have noticed at first.

The Step Position display is very convenient during step recording:

☐ It reflects the cursor position.
☐ It enables you to fix notes with a shift along the grid (in ticks). In this case, the notes are not set precisely on the rhythmic beats, but with a slight offset, which noticeably enlivens the computer performance.

You can use the following algorithm for step recording with added "enlivening":

1. Set the cursor to the beginning of the recording.
2. In the **Snap** and **Quant** fields, select values that show the general rhythmical structure of the musical fragment.
3. Switch on step recording: press the **Step** button.
4. Play the first note (or chord).
5. Hold the right (left) mouse button for a moment in the tick part of the display to increase (reduce) their number a little, e.g., by 3-7 ticks (Fig. 2.73).
6. Enter the next note (or take several steps in the Step Recording mode without changing the previous rhythmical shift on the display).
7. Change the number of ticks (left mouse button to reduce, right mouse button to increase).
8. Continue step recording.

► *Tip*

The shift from the grid lines must not be large (it is almost invisible in Fig. 2.73). You *must* know when to stop; deviations that are too obvious may produce the impression of an uneven performance.

Thanks to this "little ruse", the MIDI sound will be closer to a live performance. You may even swing in such a way. If necessary, this material can be edited in the controller field (add the speakers with the **MainVolume** controller, and accents using **Velocity**). With certain skill, however, you may be able to enter a part in the Step Recording mode that hardly differs from one played live. This would be because live **Velocity** values are recorded during step recording.

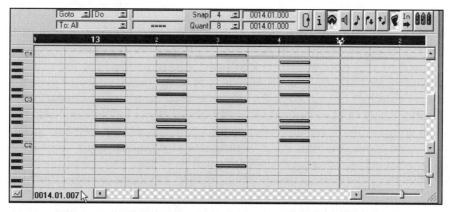

Fig. 2.73. "Enlivening" a computer performance during step recording

Now, after we have mastered two stages of complexity in the Key Edit editor (positioning notes with the mouse and the Step Recording mode), it is time for some theoretical training before recording in real time.

It is not a great exaggeration to say that MIDI recording in the Key Edit editor holds *unique* opportunities for creating rhythmic patterns of the highest complexity. Even a beginner can create complex rhythmical patterns that would be difficult to deal with for a live performer. But in order to understand the principles of rhythmic modeling offered by the software, you have to understand the diversity of meters and rhythms that exists in music.

2.14. Recording Note Length. Rhythm Basics

In *Sections 2.8* and *2.9*, we introduced basic concepts related to the rhythmic foundation of music, and showed examples of ratios of the most common lengths.

Now let's think about what the more complex rhythmic patterns are made of and how they are recorded (both in traditional notation and in the Key Edit editor).

Traditional notation will be the basis for the description of the Score Edit editor, and will help us to illustrate the material.

Readers unfamiliar with musical notation who assume that it is difficult and that "I can do without it" should not be so worried.

First, notwithstanding the common opinion, notation in music is *much easier* than is usually thought. Second, once you have mastered it, you can use the options of the software fully to create various rhythmic and melodic patterns.

To make things easier, let's go back to some theoretical points.

The length of notes is a relative value. Its main and only purpose is to show the *ratio* of sound duration in the composition. The ratio of the lengths among themselves is always constant and *does not depend* on the tempo of the composition (just like the details on a drawing when the scale is changed).

The entire flow of musical information, consisting of notes of various lengths, is divided into *equal* parts called "bars". In most cases, the borders of the bars are easily identified by ear, since they begin with the strong metric beat. In writing, they are divided by a vertical line (a bar line). The size of the bars is specified by the composer. He or she decides on what lengths are to be used to express the idea, and how often the strong beats will be repeated. After the choice is made, the composer sets the *time* of the composition. The time is shown as two figures, the first one meaning "*how many*", and the second indicating "*what*": how many metric beats there are in the bar, and by what lengths these beats are expressed.

After these basic ideas are grasped, further "rhythmic complexities" will also be clear.

Up until now, we have only looked at the main lengths — those that are divided evenly. Their essence is that each length is expressed in arithmetical fractions based on division by 2: whole, half, quarter, eighth, sixteenth, etc. The names of the lengths come from this division *(see Section 2.8 for details on the length ratio)*.

We noted in previous sections that the lengths of the notes are presented visually in the Key Edit editor: the longer the key imprint, the longer the note. Now we'll consider how the lengths are presented in notation.

The note components used in contemporary notation are the following:

❑ A note head (round or oval), and hatched (the so-called "black note") or unhatched (white note)

❑ The stem or "cauda", going up from the right side of the head or down from its left side

❑ The tail or beam attached to the end of the stem

▶ *Note*

If small lengths are positioned side by side, for the sake of readability they are connected into groups — the tails are combined, becoming "beams".

The shorter the length, the more marks — tails or beams — it needs.

Thus, notes look as shown in Table 2.4.

Table 2.4. Straight Notes

Note	Note designation	Part of whole note
Whole	○	1
Half	♩ (half)	1/2
Quarter	♩	1/4
Eighth	♪ ♫ (one tail or beam)	1/8
Sixteenth	(two tails or beams)	1/16
Thirty second	(three tails or beams)	1/32
Sixty fourth	(four tails or beams)	1/64

Note

First of all, musicians need to master lengths up to sixteenth. Shorter lengths are rare (outside the sphere of professional scores).

The one hundred twenty eighth length — 1/128 of a whole note (five tails or beams) — is practically not used. There are no such lengths in Cubasis VST and Cubasis Notation.

Now let's consider what kind of rhythmic pattern can be made from straight notes. Keep in mind a main rule: the sum of all the notes sounding one after the other within one bar *must not exceed its meter*.

Example 1. The time of the bar is four-four (this time is set by default). Having this time, the bar cannot contain more than four quarters (i.e., a whole note, see Table 2.4). But the "bar items" (the lengths) can be different. It is this variety that produces the various rhythmic patterns. Here are several variants (Example 2.1).

 Note

In the examples, the sum of the lengths is *always strictly equal* to the time (four-four).

Example 2.1.

Whole note

Half and quarter notes

Quarter and eighth notes

Eighth and sixteenth notes

Quarter, eighth, and sixteenth notes

Quarter, eighth, sixteenth, thirty-second, sixty-fourth notes

 Note

The last bar is shown as a theoretical illustration — in notation intended for a live performer, you will rarely encounter such short lengths. If the composer needs to express this rhythmical sequence, he or she is more likely to choose longer lengths (for the musician's convenience), specifying a faster tempo.

Unlike a human being, the machine has nothing against "small notes". So, such notation can be present in "computer notes" — sounds to be reproduced by the software (both in Key Edit and in Score Edit).

Example 2. Consider six-eight time (6/8). The bar's "capacity" is equal to six eighth notes (or three quarters of a whole note — see Table 2.4). Consequently, the bar can not contain more lengths than this "total ".

Note

To anticipate the question: "Aren't the time signatures 6/8 and 3/4 the same?" we may say, that, despite their equal "mathematical" capacity, they "musically" differ in the number of strong beats (see details below).

Compare rhythm recording in notation with that in the Key Edit editor. For the sake of clarity, the grid in all of the examples is set by eighths (the Quant field value is 8) (Example 2.2).

! Warning

In all further examples in this chapter, the pitch of the note does not matter, and the key imprints are positioned at *different heights* for clarity.

Example 2.2.

Half and quarter notes

Quarter and eighth notes

Two eighths and sixteenths

Now we'll take a look at how rests are shown in notation.

You know that rests have no special marks in the Key Edit editor: if there is no note, then the cell is empty.

There are special symbols for rests in the notation.

! Rest

A *rest* is a break in the sound for a strictly determined period of time in one or more and sometimes in all parts of a musical composition.

In the Cubasis Notation and Cubasis VST note editors, the rests are set into the blank spaces of the bar, according to the rules of notation. This is done *automatically*. Despite this, the rules of rest positioning are important — they enable you to easily find your way around length positioning.

Table 2.5. Rests: Designation and Correspondence to Lengths

Name of length (note and rest)	Rest	Note
Whole*		
Half*		
Quarter		
Eighth		
Sixteenth		
Thirty-second		
Sixty-fourth		

* Whole and half notes are equal in form; they differ in the way they are attached to the staff line: from the top or from the bottom. (Staves and rests for several bars are considered in *Chapter 4*).

► *Tip*

It is very easy to memorize marks for short rests: their number is equal to the number of the tails of the short notes that correspond to them in length (see Table 2.5).

With rests present, rhythmic sequences can become much more diverse. Below are some examples of bars with rests.

Example 3. The time signature is 4/4. Note that even if there are rests in the bar, the main rule remains unchanged: the *sum of notes and rests* must be equal to the meter of the bar (Example 2.3).

Example 2.3

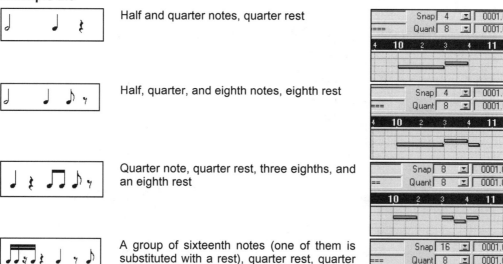

Example 4. Below are several variants of bars with three-four time (3/4). There are two variants of recording: notes and key imprints. (Pay attention to the grid in the examples from the Key Edit editor — the values in the **Quant** field.) Remember that the sum of notes and rests here is equal to three quarters (Example 2.4).

Example 2.4.

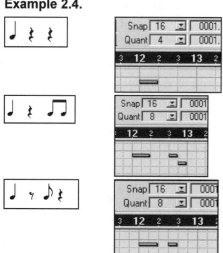

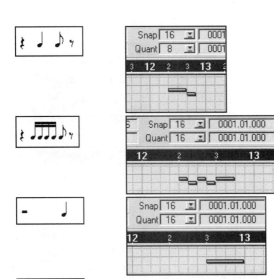

Note that in the notation, a *blank bar* of *any* meter (e.g., 7/8 or 3/4) is marked as a **whole rest** (its inscription coincides with a one-bar rest).

By combining straight notes or alternating them with rests, you can create many interesting rhythmic sequences.

▶ *Note*

We deliberately do not show lengths shorter than a sixteenth, since they are quite rare, and if you understand the general concept, then they should not cause you any trouble.

Later on, leaning on the basic concepts that we have gone over in this section, we will consider complex rhythmic sequences.

2.14.1. Dotted Notes

Much variety in rhythmic sequences can be introduced by increasing the length by half. In traditional notation, an increase in the length is marked by a dot *beside* the note. The dot increases the note by half as much: a whole dotted note sounds like three half notes, a half dotted note is equal to three quarters, an eighth dotted note is equal to three sixteenth notes, etc.

▶ *Note*

The dot increases rests in the same way as it does notes. Dotted rests, however, are not frequently used. This is due to the principles of note grouping (which will be described in *Chapter 3*). Double-dotted lengths are also considered in *Chapter 3*.

Below is an example of increasing a quarter note and a rest with a dot (Example 2.5).

Example 2.5

A dotted quarter note is equal to a quarter and an eighth note

A dotted quarter rest is equal to a quarter and an eighth rest

$$\text{♩.} = \text{♩} + \text{♪}$$

$$\text{𝄽.} = \text{𝄽} + \text{𝄾}$$

Dotted notes are used to create rhythmic sequences where short and long sounds are alternated.

▼ *Dotted Rhythm*

Dotted rhythm is based on the alternation of the strong and the shorter (weak) beat (for example, three or more times). The name is understandable, since in notation, the strong beat is usually shown as a dotted note. This type of rhythm is often used in dance music, marches, solemn compositions, etc.

The "formula" for dotted rhythm is simple. Figuratively speaking, the redistribution of the sounding period takes place from two adjacent beats of the same length. As a result, one note becomes longer by half as much (becomes dotted), and another note becomes shorter (its length becomes half as short).

In a dotted rhythm, a dotted note usually goes first (falls at the strong beat of the bar), but the reverse sequence is also possible (e.g., when a syncope is formed).

Compare the same recording of a dotted rhythm in the Key Edit editor and in notation (Example 2.6).

Example 2.6

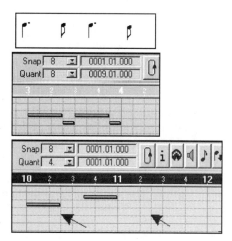

In notation, a dot beside a quarter lengthens it by half as much.

A dotted note occupies three cells, whereas an eighth note occupies only one. (The field is divided into parts equal to eighth beats.)

If you select a number with a dot in the Quant drop-down list, an additional line will appear in the grid (indicated with an arrow). It divides only one beat in half — always the second. This is a kind of reminder of the dotted rhythm, where the dotted note occupies one and a half beats (according to the value in the Quant field).

Dotted notes may alternate within a bar with all types of notes — both straight and irregular (which will be dealt with in the next section) — creating combinations of rhythmic patterns. Below are some examples with elements of dotted rhythm. The time signature is 4/4, and for clarity, the grid was set for sixteenth beats (not by dotted notes). Compare the correspondence of the notation with the recording in the Key Edit editor (Example 2.7).

Example 2.7

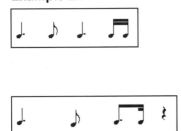
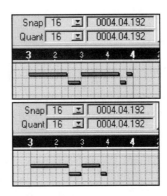

2.14.2. Triplets

Up to now, we have only looked at straight notes (each note was simply divided into two smaller notes). These notes are the main ones used in music. Apart from them, there are other notes — *irregular* ones — formed by dividing main notes into more than two parts.

Any musical beat can be divided not only into two, but three, four, five, and more parts, with the sounding time of the beat remaining *unchanged*. Lengths included in this beat, accordingly, sound shorter.

All irregular notes are recorded with the traditional musical symbols specially marked above with the corresponding numbers: 3 (triplet), 4 (quartlet), 5 (quintole), etc.

The most common irregular notes used are triplets. Among all the irregular notes, you can only work with triplets in the Key Edit editor.

 Note

Triplet — from the Latin *tres* — three — is a special rhythmic pattern of three notes, equal in length to two common notes of the same designation.

Let's consider some examples of the triplet's correspondence to commonly used notes (Example 2.8).

Example 2.8

The triplet consisting of quarters is equal to a half note (or two regular quarters).

An eighth triplet is equal to one quarter note (or two eighths).

A sixteenth triplet is equal to one eighth note (or two regular sixteenth notes).

To set triple lengths in the Key Edit editor, select a value with the letter T from the Quant drop-down list. The grid of the Note Display section will be changed accordingly: it will divide the bar into parts corresponding to triplets. Now let's take a look at some types of triplet groups in an example using 2/4 time: both in traditional notation and in the Note Display section.

► *Tip*

The values in the **Snap** and **Quant** fields can be simultaneously changed using the <1> — <7> keys. If these keys are pressed in combination with the <.> and <T> keys , the values are changed to dotted notes or triplets, respectively.

Note that when a triplet appears, the *lengths of the beats of the bar and the time for which they sound remain unchanged*: it's just that more notes are at one beat, and these notes are shorter (Example 2.9).

Example 2.9

There are two quarters in the bar (grid by quarters).

There is a triplet in the bar (grid 4T — extra lines appear).

There are four eighth notes in the bar (grid by eighths).

There are eighth triplets in the bar (grid 8T).

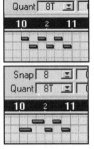

One quarter in the bar is divided into two eighths, another is divided into triplets (the grid was changed: first it was 8, then it was changed to 8T).

The note and rest symbols in the triplets are the same as with straight notes. The only graphic difference with the triplet is the number 3 above or below it.

Below are examples of more complicated rhythmic patterns, where triplets are used with 2/4 time (Example 2.10).

Example 2.10

Notes in the triplets may be skipped. If they are, they are replaced by corresponding rests.

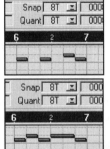

Triple notes may be united into one big length. In the example, two triplet eighths have become one triple quarter.

Triple notes may be divided into smaller triple lengths. In the example, two groups of triple sixteenth notes replace one group of triple eighth notes.

If you are a beginner, keep in mind that triplets are much more complicated theoretically than they are in practice. All you need to do is create and listen to a few triplets in order to dispel the "mystique" of their origin.

If you find it difficult to play triplets in real time, you can use step recording, set triplet notes using the instruments, or use the Fill command from the Do menu.

Below are a few additions to the above information.

❐ Triplets allow you to considerably vary the rhythmic texture.

> ► *Tip*
>
> *Simultaneous* combination of the rhythmic patterns of straight and irregular notes may produce interesting results.

❏ In order to correct triplets played unevenly, you will have to quantize on the corresponding triplet grid.

2.15. Times and Meters

It's no secret that modern computer music is notorious for its monotony. Moreover, there is a widely held opinion that it is "the machine's fault". However, we can say with absolute certainty that this is not true.

The reason for this is not that there are no sufficiently powerful computers, but that many computer "musicians" *have no idea* of the rhythmic structure of music.

Unfortunately, even those who have attended a music school in childhood are liable to sin against the metering rules, which are the *basis* of any rhythm. However, even though they are very important, schemes of accenting the metric beats remain beyond any kind of designation in notation. Therefore, they could be thought of as an implicit but extremely important feature of the rhythmic construction in music; you might say that meter is "the secret knowledge of the real musician".

If a computer musician has mastered the distribution of the metric accents and started making use of the rich options of the musical software to specify them, then his or her music is *no longer monotonous.*

This section deals with the performance of compositions of *all* musical genres, and parts of *any* instrument, not only percussion.

Now we will turn to these very important concepts. Before we start, however, recall the main ideas that have to do with meter and rhythm.

When you hear the metronome clicking (e.g., in Cubasis), you can easily tell the strong clicks from the weak ones.

> ► *Note*
>
> A *metronome* is a device used for counting metric beats.
>
> *Meter* is the even alternation of strong and weak beats in music.
>
> *Accents* are stresses that emphasize the metric beats.
>
> A *bar* is the alternation of time periods within the metric chain — from the *strongest* beat to the next beat of *the same* force. (Variants of accenting strong beats will be considered below.)
>
> The strongest metric beat is the beginning of a new bar.

When you listen to the metronome, you can tell *how many* beats there are in the bar, even if you have no idea *what* these beats are (quarters, eighths, etc.).

If the *meter* is expressed in certain lengths, then it is called the time. Knowing the time, we can tell *what* beat falls at each click of the metronome.

It is up to the composer to set the time. The meter of the beat is shown as two figures: the first is the number of beats in a bar, and the second is the length of these beats.

▶ *Note*

Suppose that the metronome alternates one strong beat and one weak. That would mean that the meter (and time) is called *duple*. If we know that each click corresponds to a quarter, then the time is 2/4, if the clicks count eighths, then the time is 2/8, etc.

Times are divided into simple and compound. The latter are just a combination of several simple times.

2.15.1. Simple Times

There are two types of simple times: duple and triple (ternary). Only *one* beat is accented in a simple time. It is called the *strong beat.*

Two beats are alternated in *duple* time: strong and weak beats. The metric formula for duple time is: > —.

In *triple* time the strong beat is repeated, but next come *two* weak beats. The metric formula for triple time is: > — —.

Since beats can be expressed by various lengths, you can specify four types of each time in Cubasis VST and Cubasis Notation (Table. 2.6).

Table 2.6. Simple Times

	Halves	Quarters	Eighths	Sixteenths
Two beats	2/2 ¢ *	2/4	2/8	2/16
Three beats	3/2	3/4	3/8	3/16

* 2/2 meter will be considered in the next section.

Irrespective of lengths that show simple duple or triple time (Table. 2.6), its metric base — the periodic repetition of the strong beats — remains unchanged.

Rhythm (from Greek *rhythmos* — slow flow) — is the alternation and ratio of the musical lengths and accents. Figuratively speaking, this is the structure over time. In the overwhelming majority of cases, the strong beats of the time and the accents in the rhythmic patterns coincide with each other. But exceptions are possible. For example, if the metric accent does not coincide with the rhythmical one, a so called *syncope* is formed (which we will look at below).

Before we turn to examples, we'd like to get back to the main idea: sounds *must* be accented during the performance. This is particularly applicable to a computer performance: even if you are unaware that there are any accent rules at all, a human musician *cannot* play several notes in exactly the same manner — unlike a computer, which can play the whole composition *in the same exact way*!

Example 1. Fig. 2.74 shows the correspondence of meter (lower line) and the rhythm (upper line) with two-four time. The strong beats are marked with an accent symbol.

Note that in the rhythm, a note *of the same length* as that of the strong metric beat is marked with an accent.

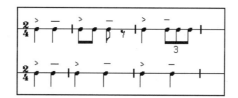

Fig. 2.74. The time and rhythm ratio (time signature 2/4)

This rule — to stress the strong beats — is not shown in the notation. But it is observed by *all* musically competent performers.

If the music is composed on the computer, then the accents can disappear due to technical reasons. This happens, for example, when notes are "drawn" with the mouse, or when a part is formed using the Fill command in the Do menu. The default Velocity of *absolutely all* notes is the maximum — 127. This is one of the reasons for a dull performance, which can be concealed neither by fine timbres, nor by sophisticated rhythmic patterns of percussion, nor even professional vocals.

So if the volume of the notes is initially the same, it *must* be edited — e.g., you have to set the accents in the **Controller Display** section.

Fig. 2.75 illustrates setting the velocity for the rhythmic group shown in the previous example (Fig. 2.74). Note that the velocities of the lengths on the metrically strong beats are at the maximum.

Of course, if you enter the music from the MIDI instrument, then the velocity depends on the key pressing. But sometimes it too needs editing.

(See the details on **Velocity** in *Section 2.12.2*; step recording of velocity is dealt with in *Section 2.17*.)

Example 2. Fig. 2.76 shows an example of accent distribution in simple triple time — with a 3/4 time signature. Note that in this example, different lengths fall at the strong beats in all three bars: eighth, dotted quarter, and first eighth in the triplet. It is these lengths that must be accented during the performance (compare the upper and lower lines).

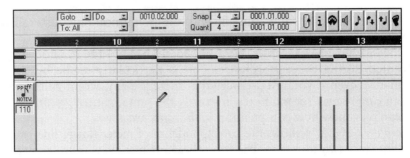

Fig. 2.75. The velocity with a 2/4 time signature

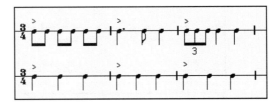

Fig. 2.76. The time and rhythm ratio (3/4 time signature)

Rhythm is one of the main expressive means in music. We can add that accents are "the heart of rhythm". Unless beats are accented, the music will always be flat and uninteresting to listeners.

2.15.2. Compound Times

Compound meters (and, consequently, compound times) are combined from two or more simple times. Their main difference from simple ones is the appearance of the *weak* beats.

Compound symmetrical times are those that come from joining two of the same simple times — either duple or triple.

For example, when the simple times 3/8 and 3/8 are joined, the compound time 6/8 appears. The 4/4 time appears as a result of joining the simple duple times 2/4 and 2/4.

Compound asymmetrical times combine *different* simple times. For example, 5/4 is the result of joining 2/4 and 3/4, or 3/4 and 2/4. And the shifting of items in music does matter (unlike in mathematics) — it affects the distribution of the *relatively strong beats* in the bar.

Relatively strong beats are those with weaker accents than those on the first beat of the compound time.

Note

Joining simple times is possible only if they have a common denominator: you can not make a compound time by joining, say, 3/8 and 2/4.

Consider 9/4 time. It is the result of joining three simple triple times: 3/4, 3/4, and 3/4.

The metric formula for the 9/4 time is the following:

```
 >
 >       >
 > — > — — > — —
```

You can see that the accents are repeated in two beats, but they are of *different* force.

If you put three bars with 3/4 time, the accents will be repeated in two beats, but they will be of the *same* force.

The difference between one 9/4 time and three 3/4 times lies in the *force* of the accents.

Compare the velocity of the relatively strong beats of bars 2, 3, 4 (time signature 3/4) with the weak beats in bar 5 (time signature 9/4) in Fig. 2.77.

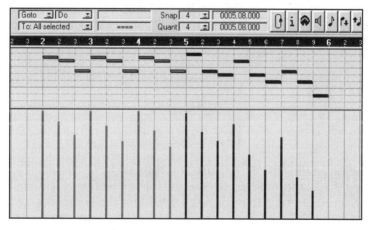

Fig. 2.77. The velocity at 3/4 and 9/4 time

Of course, there is no need to measure the velocity in millimeters. The construction of a musical phrase is subject to the general idea of the composition, and therefore it has many shades and deviations from the metrical scheme. Even so, it is still necessary to understand the distribution of strong beats.

The level of your performance may be enhanced by several times if you make competent use of the options of the Cubase system software. Professional musicians spend many long hours at an instrument, learning to express their thoughts and mood in music. Musical mastery is the sum of two items: musical thinking and its technical implementation during the performance.

Of course, a person who never studied music may still possess musical thinking. Such people often want to express their musical fantasies, but lack of a performing technique prevents them from doing it.

We can say for sure that level of modern computer music not only lets you imitate the main techniques of the musician, but to considerably enhance them as well.

▶ Note

Of course, it must be remembered that a live performance will *always* differ from *any* computer performance, since the mutually enriching energetic interchange — that precious sacrament between musician and listener — takes place in real-time only.

As for the topic of this section, we'd like to add that an "acoustic" musician masters his or her skills for many years (including the skill of producing sounds of various volume). The computer musician, in order to stress notes by various accents, must be able to edit in the controller section in compliance with the artistic concept of the composition and the rules of meter and rhythm.

Of course, this will require some time, but it will take just a moment compared to the years a person needs to professionally master an acoustic instrument.

Below is an example of a compound mixed meter (5/4). With this meter, the time is asymmetric: its relatively strong beat may fall at the third as well as at the fourth beat. Compare:

❑   5/4 (3/4 + 2/4)

❑   5/4 (2/4 + 3/4)

Depending on this, the music pulsation will vary.

It is up to the composer to specify the sequence of simple times within a compound time. In order to inform the musician, the composer "encrypt" the meter in the notation. It looks like: 7/4 (3/4+2/4+2/4). You must understand that in notation, this explanation is addressed to the musician; the computer software can not place the accents on its own!

Theoretically, there are many compound times due to the many choices that we have as to their composition.

Table 2.7. Compound Times

	Halves	Quarters	Eighths	Sixteenths
Four beats	4/2	4/4 c	4/8	4/16
Five beats	5/2	5/4	5/8	5/16

continues

Table 2.7 Continued

	Halves	Quarters	Eighths	Sixteenths
Six beats	6/2	6/4	6/8	6/16
Seven beats	7/2	7/4	7/8	7/16
Eight beats	8/2	8/4	8/8	8/16
Nine beats	9/2	9/4	9/8	9/16
Ten beats	10/2	10/4	10/8	10/16
Eleven beats	11/2	11/4	11/8	11/16
Twelve beats	12/2	12/4	12/8	12/16
Thirteen beats	13/2	13/4	13/8	13/16
Fourteen beats	14/2	14/4	14/8	14/16
Fifteen beats	15/2	15/4	15/8	15/16
Sixteen beats	16/2	16/4	16/8	16/16

The 4/4 and 2/2 Times (Meters)

These are the only times that can be designated with a letter instead of numbers. (A crossed or not crossed letter "C" — compare Tables 2.6 and 2.7). The time 2/2 is called "alla breve", designating that the count in the 4/4 bar goes not by quarter beats but by half beats. Thus, in 2/2 time, the third beat is not relatively strong (as it is in 4/4) and consequently, there is no second accent in 2/2 time.

The most commonly used times are:

- ❑ Simple: 2/2, 2/4, 3/4, 3/8
- ❑ Compound symmetrical: 4/4, 6/4, 4/8, 6/8, 9/8, 12/8
- ❑ Compound asymmetrical: 5/4 (3/4+2/4 or 2/4+3/4), 7/4 (3/4+2/4+2/4 or 2/4+3/4+2/4), 7/8 (3/4+2/4+2/4 or 2/4+3/4+2/4)

2.15.3. Variable Times. Changing the Time in the *List Mastertrack* Window

If the meter is changed in the course of one composition, it is called *variable*.

Frequent change of time is typical for folk dance and "song" music, as well as for compositions of contemporary authors.

Bars of various meters are alternated in the composition with a variable meter. This alternation may take place either randomly or in a certain order (e.g., every other bar, or 3 bars of one meter and 5 bars of another in the course of the whole composition).

If the variable meter is alternated in every other bar, then you might wonder how it is different from a compound meter. For example, what is the difference between the variable meters 3/4 and 4/4 and the compound 7/4? The difference can be found in the force of accenting the beats. Let's go a bit into depth on this.

Consider three bars: two of variable meters (3/4 and 4/4) and one of a compound meter 7/4 (Fig. 2.78). You can see from the example that a different number of "loudest notes" will fall at the same period of time (two small bars or one big one): two in the first case and one in the second.

Such a difference may play the key role in reproducing the artistic concept of the composition! Let's draw an analogy to human speech: the meaning of it often depends on *which* words are *stressed* and how often (or which *words* are stressed and *how often*).

Note that there are *two* maximally strong beats in the variable meter (see bars 2 and 3). There is only *one* strong beat in the compound meter, the second beat being *relatively strong* (see bar 4).

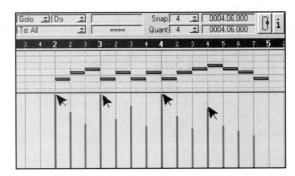

Fig. 2.78. The difference between variable and compound times

Let's consider a method of changing the time for one or several bars in Cubasis VST. Suppose the general meter of the composition is 3/4. You need to change it in the 4th and 5th bars to 7/8 time.

The algorithm of change is the following:

1. Place the editor cursor in the beginning of the bar where the meter will be changed (in our example, this is bar 4 — see Fig. 2.79).

2. Double-click on the **Master** button (or select the **Mastertrack** command from the **Edit** menu) on the **Transport bar** (indicated with an arrow in Fig. 2.79).

3. The List **Mastertrack** window will be opened (Fig. 2.80). Here you need to:

   1) Select the time change command from the **Timesigns** drop-down list (indicated by arrow 1).

2) Click on the Insert button (arrow 2).

3) In the line that appears (arrow 3) you can change the numbers in the time by clicking the left or right mouse button (or enter the time from the keyboard after double-clicking). The time on the Transport bar will be changed accordingly (Fig. 2.80).

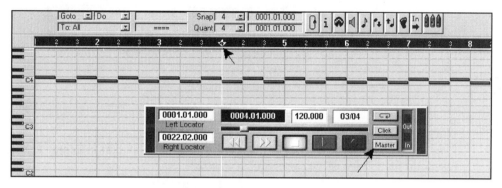

Fig. 2.79. Preparation for a time change

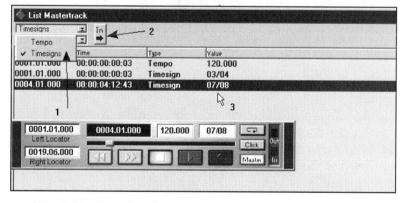

Fig. 2.80. Changing the time in the **List Mastertrack** window

4. Close or minimize the List Mastertrack window, return to the Key Edit editor, and place the cursor at the beginning of the bar, where the previous value should be specified (in our example, it is the 6th bar).

5. Repeat the operations in item 3, but only after changing the meter from 7/8 to what it was previously — 3/4.

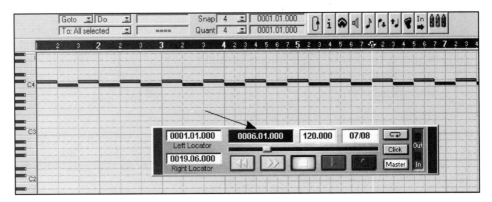

Fig. 2.81. The intermediate result of changing the time

▶ *Tip*

If you need to set the cursor very accurately, do it in the **Position Indicator** field of the **Transport bar** (shown with an arrow in Fig. 2.81).

2.16. Syncopation. Swing

The essence of syncopation is that the weak beat of the bar becomes the strong one — a new accent is formed within the bar.

Syncopation (from Greek *syncope* — cutting, reduction) is the shift of the rhythmically strong note from the strong (or relatively strong) beat of the bar to the weaker one.

In music, the syncopation phenomenon is quite frequent: it supplements the rhythm with elements of unexpectedness and wittiness. Below are schemes of forming syncopes (the lower line is the meter and the upper is the rhythm; the syncopated notes are circled or shown with arrows).

You get a syncopated rhythm if (Example 2.11):

Example 2.11

☐ The sound of the weak beat continues without a break to the following strong beat.

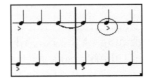

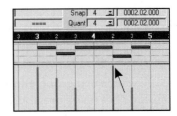

❏ The sound of the weak beat is much longer than that of the previous strong beat.

❏ There is a rest in place of the strong beat.

❏ There are periodic accents on weak beats (set by the composer).

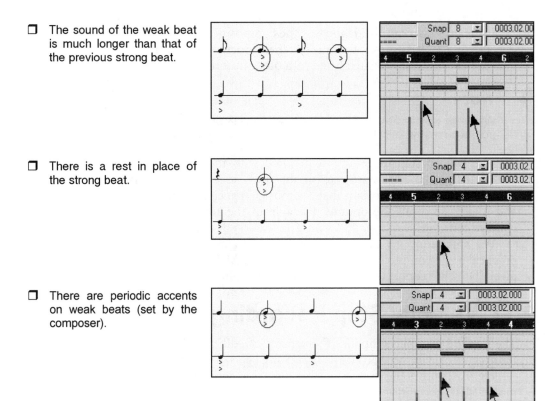

If syncopated beats are not stressed by volume, then listeners may "fail to understand" the rhythmical structure of the composition and come to the conclusion that the performance was uneven.

Despite the rules, however, there is a "free zone" for music performers. It is called swing.

Swing is a typical element of a jazz performance that appears to be in constant and continuous rhythmical pulsation.

▶ *Note*

This term also is the name of a jazz style developed in the mid-1930s, which was the transitional period from traditional to modern jazz.

The essence of swing is that the musician "breaks the rules" during the performance: he or she plays with a rhythmic swing — plays notes ahead of time or later, shifts the accents, etc.

Of course, it is much easier to swing when you play live. But swing is not something that is impossible for the software that we are describing.

If the musician can "hear" the way the composition should be performed, he or she can move the key imprints and set the velocity in accordance with his or her interpretation, stress accented beats with other timbres, etc.

 Note

When the <Shift> key is pressed, you can selectively highlight notes and then shift them from precise rhythmical positions (the value in the **Snap** field must be **Off, 2pp — 7pp**).

The second step in getting acquainted with the notion of "time" being almost completed, let us once again repeat the main idea. When music is created on the computer, it is very important that the musician keep in mind the main "musical laws" and make use of all the options available in the software to implement his or her creative concept.

We will return to discussing rhythm again in *Chapter 3*. Now consider some practical advice on recording the accent using a MIDI instrument and the methods of diversifying the computer's performance using volume and tempo.

2.17. Velocity Step Recording

The method we offer simplifies the process of editing velocity. It is convenient to set the accents or, vice versa, mitigate the strong beats using this method.

Fig. 2.82 shows the button combination that activates the Velocity Step Recording mode: MIDI connector and Note On-velocity.

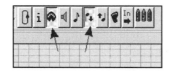

Fig. 2.82. Turning on the Velocity
Step Recording mode

Let's take a closer look at this mode in an example.

Let's suppose that a part was created with the Pencil and Paint Brush tools, or with the Fill command. As a result, the volume of all the notes is the same — the maximum (Velocity = 127) (Fig. 2.83).

 Note

When a note is entered using tools, different velocity levels can be specified with he <Shift> and <Ctrl> keys or their combination (<Shift>+<Ctrl>). (See the details on velocity editing in *Section 2.12.*)

Fig. 2.83. A part before velocity editing

In order to edit the volume of the selected notes in Step Recording mode, do the following:

1. Press the MIDI connector and Note On-velocity buttons (Fig. 2.82).
2. Select the first note to be edited.
3. Press *any* keys on the MIDI keyboard with the required volume. The Velocity of each subsequent note will be changed in accordance with the velocity of the key pressing.

▶ *Note*

If a chord is pressed, then the velocity of several notes positioned in a row will be changed.

4. If a note doesn't need to be edited, it can be skipped by pressing the <→> key. You can go back to the previous note to change its volume in exactly the same way — with the <←> key.
5. During editing, the new Velocity value is graphically laid over the previous value and is colored in (to make it easier to see the result of the change). You can remove "graphic double values" by clicking on the controller selection button (Event Type Selector) and selecting the velocity anew.

▶ *Tips*

We do not recommend that you edit the notes of a chord with the step method, since all of them must be played with the same volume (unless the accents of certain notes are part of the composer's idea). Therefore, it is better to first select the chord, and then *simultaneously* edit the velocity of all the notes of the chord with the **Pencil** tool (Fig. 2.84).

The results of editing the velocity will be more visual if they are in color. Press the **Editor Colors** button (indicated by an arrow in Fig. 2.84) and check the **Velocity colors** option in the drop-down list.

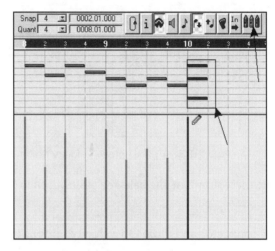

Fig. 2.84. A part after editing

2.18. Dynamic Nuances (Increasing and Decreasing Volume)

The Cubasis VST and Cubasis Notation software allow you to introduce dynamic nuances and tempo changes, which considerably brighten up the composition.

Dynamics (from the Greek *dynamicos* — forceful) are a set of phenomena related to the volume (force) of the music's sound.

Dynamics are based on the combination of various nuances of sound, as well as on their sudden or gradual change, the stressing of certain sounds, etc. The accents considered above are also dynamic nuances. But since accenting can be introduced not only by the force of the sound but also with other means of musical expressiveness, we'll give you a fuller definition.

 Note

Accent (from Latin *accentus* — stress) — accenting or emphasizing a sound or chord mainly by strengthening it, as well as by rhythmic lengthening, changing the harmony, timbre, direction of the pitch, etc.

The palette of dynamic nuances is quite broad. Below are some of them (Table 2.8).

Table 2.8. Main Types of Dynamic Nuances

Name	Symbol in notation	Meaning
Piano	p	Quiet, weak
Pianissimo	pp	Very quiet
Piano-pianissimo (three pianos)	ppp	Extremely quiet
Forte	f	Loud, heavy
Fortissimo	ff	Very loud
Forte-fortissimo (three fortes)	fff	Extremely loud
Crescendo	——————◁	Increasing force
Diminuendo	▷——————	Reducing force
Mezzo piano	mp	Quiet, but not too quiet
Mezzo forte	mf	Loud, but not too loud
Sforzando	sf sfz sff	Stressing, emphasizing with force

Any of the above dynamic nuances can be easily applied in the Key Edit editor. This is done in the Controller Display section by editing the Velocity or the MainVolume controller.

▼ *Warning*

If the issue of dynamic nuances is solved by velocity editing by *dragging* the **Line** and **Pencil** tools, then all the accents that result after playing the MIDI instrument will be removed. This is because the general velocity will be lined up, and the difference between the strong and weak beats will disappear. As a result, the rhythmical basis of the composition will be lost.

To avoid this, you must enter the dynamic nuances in some other manner, e.g., by editing the **MainVolume** controller.

If dynamic nuances are used, then "intricate" times are unnecessary. Here is a simple example. If you *gradually reduce the volume* in three successive 3/4 bars (i.e., introduce diminuendo with the MainVolume controller), then the strong beats of the second and third bars will be reduced and will become equal in volume to the *weak* beats of a 9/4 bar (see Fig. 2.77).

Unfortunately, this can not be illustrated, since the controllers appear on the screen one by one only. It can definitely be heard, however, when you reduce the volume on the Controller Display section while editing the MainVolume controller (drag the Pencil holding the <Alt> key pressed).

Below is an example of dynamic shades appearing in the Controller Display field after the volume was edited with the MainVolume controller (the example is deliberately exaggerated).

The figures in Fig. 2.85 have the following marked: 1 — crescendo, 2 — diminuendo, 3 — accent, 4—10 — various grades of volume: from pianissimo to fortissimo.

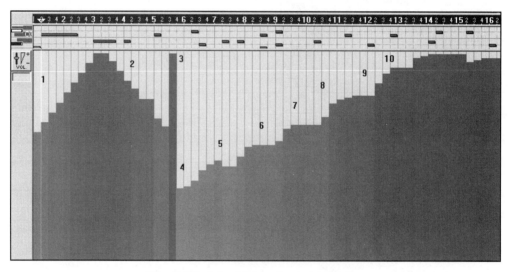

Fig. 2.85. Introducing dynamic shades

2.19. Tempo. Changing the Tempo

Tempo (from Latin *tempus* — time) is the speed at which the beats of the meter move.

The tempo is measured by the number of clicks per minute, where one metric beat corresponds to one click. For example, with a time of 3/4, the tempo will be expressed as the number of *quarter* beats that sound in one minute.

In notation, the tempo is indicated in words and/or by precisely counting the bar beats with the metronome. The metronome is integrated into the computer software, and the tempo for the whole composition is specified on the Transport bar.

The accuracy and steadiness of the tempo plays an important part in creating a musical picture. For greater expressiveness, however, deviations from the main tempo are frequently required in certain musical phrases, passages, etc.

Below are the main indications of tempo, their correspondence to the metronome, and some additional indications (Table 2.9). Then we will spend some time on changing the tempo locally in Cubasis.

Table 2.9. Main Ways of Designating Tempo

Name, metronome clicks	Translation
Slow tempos	
Largo 40–60	Very slow
Lento 60–66	Lingering
Adagio 66–76	Slow, leisurely
Grave	Significant, solemn, heavy
Moderate tempos	
Andante 76–108	Moving with a moderate tempo
Andantino	Faster than andante
Moderato	Moderate
Sostenuto	Sustained
Allegretto	A little slower than allegro
Allegro moderato	Moderately fast
Fast tempos	
Allegro 120–168	Quite fast
Vivo, Vivace	Lively, animated, brisk
Presto 168–208	Fast, rapid
Prestissimo	Very fast
Specifying the nuance when the tempo is deviated	
Molto	Very
Assai	Quite, very
Con moto	With agility
Commodo	Comfortably

continues

Table 2.9 Continued

Name, metronome clicks	Translation
Specifying the nuance when the tempo is deviated	
Non troppo	Not too much
Non tanto	Not so much
Sempre	Always
Meno mosso	Less agile
Piu mosso	More agile
To slow down	
Ritenuto	Restraining
Ritardando	Lagging
Allargando	Expanding
Rallentanto	Slowing down
To speed up	
Accelerando	Accelerating
Animando	Inspiring
Stringendo	Speeding up
Stretto	Briefly
To return to the primary tempo	
A tempo	With the original tempo
Tempo primo	Primary tempo
Tempo I	Primary tempo

You can see from the table that there are a wide variety of tempos and deviations in music. Therefore, the tempo can be easily varied, depending on your musical idea. When the tempo is selected, you must remember that it always depends on the content and character of the composition.

In the Cubasis VST and Cubasis Notation software, a tempo can be specified of anywhere from 30 to 250 beats per minute. Setting and changing the tempo for the whole composition is done on the Transport bar by clicking the mouse button or entering the new value.

Tip

If you find it difficult to play fast, then the tempo can be slowed down during the recording and accelerated up to the required value later.

As we mentioned above, tempo diversification allows you to communicate the artistic idea of the musical composition in full.

You can introduce a local change in the tempo in the Cubasis software — speed it up or slow it down for one or several beats (or bars).

The sequence of operations is the same as when changing the time. But since tempo changes are more frequent than time changes, we'll consider the algorithm of tempo change in more detail.

Suppose you need to slow down the end of a musical phrase (Fig. 2.86).

Slow it down according to the values shown in Fig. 2.86: the general tempo is 180, but in the ninth bar the tempo will be slowed at each beat, and then returned to its primary value (180) — Tempo I.

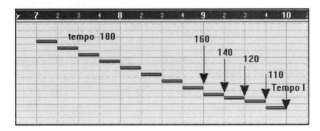

Fig. 2.86. Scheme for future changes to the tempo

2.19.1. The Tempo Change Algorithm (Speeding up or Slowing down)

1. Place the editor cursor on the beat of the bar at which you plan to introduce the deceleration (bar 9, beat 1).

2. Double-click the Master button (<Ctrl>+<M>) on the Transport bar. The List Mastertrack window will be opened.

3. Here you must do the following (Fig. 2.87):

    1) Select the Tempo command for changing the tempo in the drop-down list of the upper field.

    2) Press the Insert button. A new line will appear (here in the beginning, the number of the bar and the beat where the tempo change command is to be inserted are indicated).

3) Change the tempo by clicking the right or left mouse button, or enter the new value after double-clicking the left mouse button (Fig. 2.87).

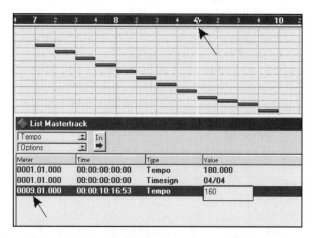

Fig. 2.87. Changing the tempo at the first beat of bar 9

4. Close or minimize the **List Mastertrack** window. Return to the Key Edit editor, set the cursor to the next beat (bar 9, beat 2), and set the new tempo — 140, repeating item 3.

5. Similarly, after the cursor is set to the third and fourth beats of this bar, change the tempo to 120 and 110 (Fig. 2.87).

6. Do not forget to return to the primary tempo after deceleration: set the cursor to the first beat of the next (10th) bar and select a value of 180. As a result, messages will appear in the List Mastertrack window, as in Fig. 2.88, and after the required deceleration, the music will continue with the original tempo.

▼ *Working Randomly in the* List Mastertrack *Window*

You can delete lines in the **List Mastertrack** window (<Delete> key). Tempo values can be repeatedly changed in any lines. You can also make insertions in any order you wish to in this window.

▼ *Attention*

To be able to trace the tempo changes during playback, press the **Master** button on the **Transport bar**.

It is quite possible that some users may find it more convenient to change the tempo prior to recording — on a blank track. Then they can play "with emotion" along with the slowing click of the metronome on another track. In this case, the sequence of the tempo change operations will be the same as in the algorithm above, since tempo changing is controlled by the special Mastertrack track.

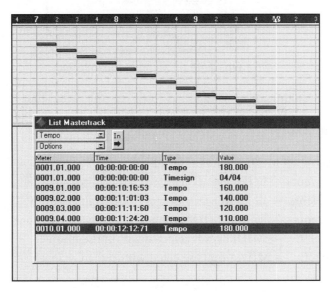

Fig. 2.88. The result of changing the tempo in the **List Mastertrack** window

2.20. Rhythmic Quantize

Rhythmic quantization is the function of the software that allows you to move notes to new *rhythmic* positions. Its principle of operation reminds one of musical chairs — those notes outside of the rhythmic frame quickly occupy the *nearest* authorized rhythmic positions when they hear the "Quantize!" command.

Its main function is to correct rhythmic errors made during recording from a MIDI instrument.

Despite the fact that quantization is a "remedy", a means of eliminating rhythmical faults, it may produce some very interesting results if you use it in some musical experiments.

There are special options in the Functions menu for working with quantization: Over Quantize and Undo Quantize. Both are duplicated by the <Q> and <U> keys (Fig. 2.89).

▼ *Warning*

Remember that the quantize operation can only be *undone once*.

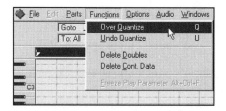

Fig. 2.89. Turning on quantization

Rhythmic quantization is applied *only* to the area that at the moment of quantization was selected in the **To:** field. Remember the commands of the **To:** drop-down list (Fig. 2.90):

❑ All Events — all MIDI events of the edited track
❑ Selected Events — MIDI events selected in the editor
❑ Looped Events — all Loop MIDI events (loop in the editor)
❑ Cycled Events — all Cycle MIDI events (cycle between the locators)
❑ Looped Sel. Ev. — MIDI events selected within the Loop
❑ Cycled Sel. Ev. — MIDI events selected within the Cycle

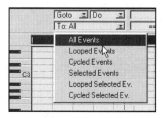

Fig. 2.90. The area in which quantization will be applied

First we'll consider the traditional method of using rhythmic quantization. Let's suppose that some eighth notes were played out of rhythm (in Fig. 2.91, the deviation is exaggerated for clarity).

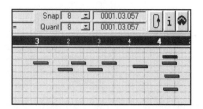

Fig. 2.91. Eighth notes before quantization

In order to place them at precise positions, the Over Quantize command must be selected. As a result, the *beginning* of each note will be snapped to the nearest grid line.

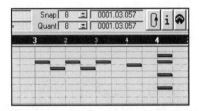

Fig. 2.92. Eighth notes after quantization

Such correction of rhythmic faults has its advantages and drawbacks. The advantages are that you can correct the rhythm without overplaying and tedious editing with the tools. The main drawback, however, is the loss of a lifelike performance together with the deviations from the rhythm.

Below is some good advice when using rhythmic quantization.

❏ It is not recommended that you apply it to the material as a whole. It is better to select the notes that are *especially* inaccurate in the rhythm and select the Over Quantize command.

❏ If there are a lot of rhythmic deviations, it is better to replay the part, since it is possible that the notes that have shifted from the "correct" positions may be shifted even more and "snapped" to the wrong points of the grid.

❏ When different lengths are corrected, you should specify the value in the Quant field according to their value (make the corresponding grid).

❏ If there are different lengths in the part (e.g., dotted quarters and "common" quarters), then quantization must done in steps. Each time you need to change the grid in the Quant field in compliance with the changed length, select these notes and apply the Over Quantize command.

❏ If the results of quantization do not suit you, undo it with the Undo Quantize command, correct the notes that overstep the limits of the rhythm manually (or exclude them from the group of notes being quantized), and then repeat quantization.

Now we'll move on to some experiments with rhythmic quantization.

During quantization, notes are moved to the *nearest* grid divisions. Logic suggests that, in order to correct unevenly played eighth notes, it is necessary to specify a value of 8 in the Quant field.

You can quantize length using other grids, as well as notes that were entered not from the MIDI instrument, but, for example, using the Pencil tool. If the rules are "expanded", then you can gain some quite interesting rhythmic combinations.

For example, Fig. 2.93 shows 4 rows of the same length. For comparison, the upper row will remain unchanged, while the rest of the rows will be quantized by various grids.

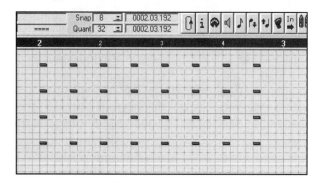

Fig. 2.93. Before quantization

Select the second row of notes, change the grid into dotted eighth (Quant field = 8) and press the <Q> key. Fig. 2.94 shows that the notes of the second row have changed their positions.

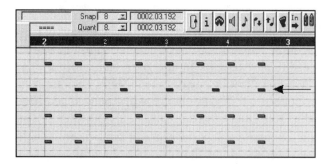

Fig. 2.94. The second row after quantization (by dotted eighths)

Now repeat this operation with the third row of notes: select them, select the triplet halves value in the field (**Quant = 2T**) and apply quantization (Fig. 2.95).

The last row will be quantized by simple quarters (**Quant = 4**).

Quantization has one important feature. Pay attention to the fact that now there are fewer notes in the 2nd, 3rd, and 4th rows. They did not disappear, though, but were laid on top of one another. This is because the nearest points of the grid turned out to be the same for different notes. You can remove double notes with the Delete Doubles command of the Functions menu.

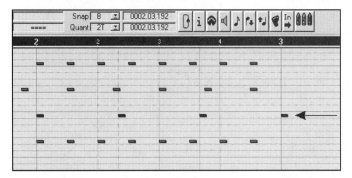

Fig. 2.95. The third row after quantization (by dotted half notes)

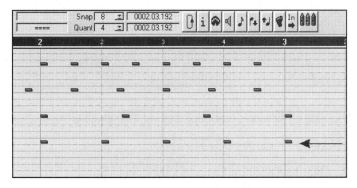

Fig. 2.96. The fourth row after quantization (by quarters)

Warning

Fig. 2.96 shows a way of modifying a rhythmic sequence using rhythmic quantization. Of course, this example should not be taken as a guide to action — the rhythmic structure here is superfluous, and presented for the sake of clarity only; moreover, the pitch of the notes was not taken into consideration.

It is quite possible to use rhythmical quantization for creative purposes.

2.21. Polymetry and Complex Rhythms

Polymetry (from Greek *poly* — many and *metron* — measure) means the *simultaneous* combination of two or more meters (bars of different meters).

Polymetry varies the rhythmical pattern, due to the constant shifting in time of the ratio of the accented beats. Fig. 2.97 shows the combination of two meters: 4/4 and 5/4. You can clearly see that each strong beat of the 4/4 meter falls at *different* beats of the 5/4 meter: the first falls at the strong beat (the first), and then the weakest beat (the fifth), then a weak beat (the fourth), etc.

 Note

Remember that polymetry is useless unless the metric beats are accented.

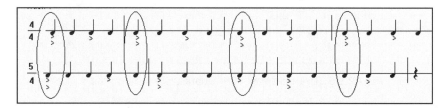

Fig. 2.97. Polymetry

Only highly skilled professionals can play live in several times simultaneously, but the Key Edit editor makes it possible even for beginners who have mastered the method of cycle recording.

2.22. Cycle Recording in the Key Edit Editor as a Method of Creating Complex Rhythms

A *cycle* is the repetition of a musical fragment during recording or playback multiple times.

As we mentioned above, there are two types of cycles in the Cubasis VST software: one is found in the Arrange window (between the L and R locators). It is called Cycle. Another can be found in the editor (List Edit, Score Edit or Key Edit), and in the terms of the software, this mini-cycle is called a Loop.

Keep in mind the main principles of how cycles work in the Key Edit editor.

Select the area for a future cycle by holding the left mouse button pressed and dragging it along the Ruler. The selected area on the ruler will change its color, and the Loop On/Off button 🔟 will be activated (Fig. 2.98).

When the Loop button is pressed, the loop is in operational status (its area is highlighted on the Ruler in blue).

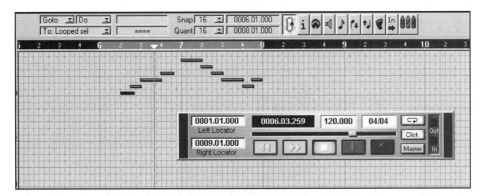

Fig. 2.98. Recording a loop recording

If the **Loop** button is released, the loop is switched off. It can be restored, however, since the primary borders are retained (colored in gray on the Ruler). Pressing the Loop button again restores the loop.

 ## Note

The **Loop** button is duplicated on the keyboard by the <Alt>+<Ctrl>+<O> key combination; you can activate or deactivate the loop using this key combination

You can delete the loop with the mouse: hold for a moment the left mouse button pressed on the highlighted area of the Ruler. When the loop is deleted, the readings on the digital displays beside the Loop button are automatically cleared.

The Loop Start and Loop End displays are active; here the borders of the loop are shown, and you can change its size or specify new values.

Precisely Changing the Loop's Borders

You can change the **Loop**'s borders in the **Loop Start** and **Loop End** fields either by clicking the left or right mouse buttons or entering new values from the keyboard into the fields of the displays. They are opened by double-clicking the left mouse button or using the <Alt>+<Ctrl>+<L> key combination for the upper display and <Alt>+<Ctrl>+<R> for the lower display.

Once you have entered the new values, certain rules, such as those concerning the sequence of the coordinates (bar, beat, tick) and the period between numbers, must be observed.

After the Loop for one part is created, you can perform cycle recording. This allows you to add on to fragments by overlaying new material or to correct material using tools and commands in the *continuous* playback mode.

2.22.1. Sequential Cycle Recording

Thanks to its clarity, this method of recording is especially convenient for beginners. The key imprints of different parts are shown in one window of the Key Edit editor.

1. Create the part in the **Arrange** window between the locators (in our example they span the length of one bar).
2. Press the Cycle button on the **Transport bar**. (If necessary, activate the metronome with the Click button).
3. Open the Key Edit editor for the created part (<Ctrl>+<E>).
4. Activate the recording mode (with the <*> key on the additional keyboard or with the Rec. button on the Transport bar).
5. Record the material.

Note

You can supplement the part or otherwise change it (e.g., remove a wrong note, etc.) *without interrupting* the process of the cycle's playback.

6. Stop the recording (using the <0> key on the additional keyboard or the **Stop** button on the **Transport bar**), and exit the editor.
7. Create a part of the same duration on another track (Track 2 in our case).
8. Select two parts in the **Arrange** window and invoke the Key Edit editor to jointly edit *two* parts (with the **Edit** option in the menu of the same name, or using the <Ctrl>+<E> key combination).
9. Switch on the recording (<*>) and start performing the second part, recording it on the active track (selected in the **Arrange** window); in our case, this is Track 2 (Fig. 2.98).
10. Without stopping recording, you can navigate the tracks and edit the material in one window of the Key Edit editor — i.e., work with the arrangement in real time.

You can see from Fig. 2.98 that the key imprints of the track selected in the Arrange window are brighter in the   editor. This means that this part is ready for editing. If you need to move to another track, click one of its notes — a "blank imprint" — and another part will be brought to the forefront.

Advice

It is more convenient to work with parts if they are differently colored. To do this, when the tracks are created, "paint" them, selecting the colors from the **Part Colors** drop-down list, and select the **Colorize by Parts** option in the Key Edit editor.

11. Deactivate the recording (playback) mode with the <0> key or the Stop button of the Transport bar.

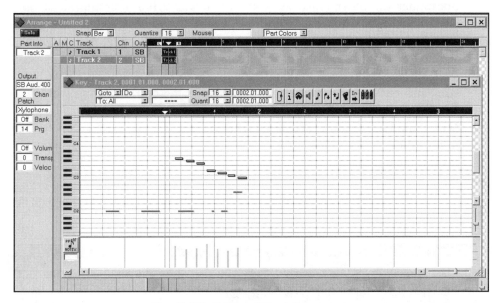

Fig. 2.99. Cycle editing of two parts

This way of recording allows you to graphically reveal and easily correct faults in the performance, such as dissonant intervals or the same notes played asynchronously.

If you make this algorithm more complicated, then it is easy to get polymetry and complex rhythms.

Here we offer such a method in an example using two tracks (there can also be more tracks).

The idea is that loops of *different* duration will be created on different tracks in the Key Edit editor. During simultaneous playback, the loop fragments will be gradually moved relative to one another. As a result, the rhythmic patterns change as if they were in a kaleidoscope. As in the previous case, the material is available for editing. After you are satisfied with the result of this "rhythmical impromptu" of the software, it can be re-recorded on the audio track for later use (see the details on MIDI transformation into audio in *Chapter 5*).

2.22.2. Creating Polymetry Using Loops

1. Create two parts on different tracks in the **Arrange** window.
2. Open a separate window of the Key Edit editor for each part.

3. Without minimizing the window, select one of the options of the Windows menu — Stack, Tile, or Cascade — in order to position the windows beside each other or one under the other (such as is shown in Fig. 2.100 after the Stack option is checked).

4. Select a loop of *different* duration for each (in our example, there are *four* beats selected in one part, and *five* in the other).

5. Switch the recording mode (with the <*> key or the Rec button on the **Transport bar**), and record the part for the first track in the corresponding window of the Key Edit editor.

6. Make another window active by clicking the mouse button on it, without interrupting the recording.

7. Record the next part.

8. Stop the recording.

9. Re-record the MIDI on the audio track without closing the windows of the Key Edit editor.

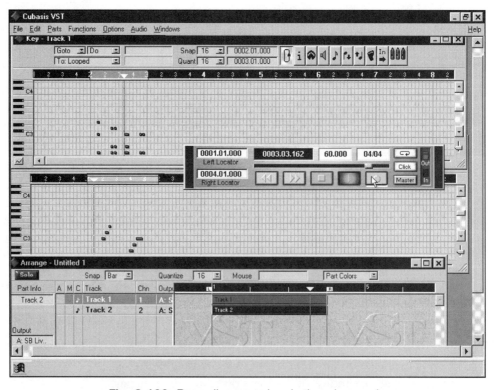

Fig. 2.100. Recording complex rhythms in a cycle

This method can be used for editing parts recorded earlier (during cycle playback).

Now that you have mastered the Key Edit editor, let's turn to another no less interesting editor — Score Edit, which enables you to work with musical material on a more advanced level.

If you are not familiar with musical notation, we still recommend that you read the material on the Score Edit editor, since the most difficult issue — the rhythmic structure of music — has already been described in this chapter in an example using key imprints.

2.23. A Brief Overview of Some Operations in the Key Edit Editor

Table 2.10. Basic Operations in Key Edit

Operation	Brief description	Comments
Open the Key Edit editor	☐ <Ctrl>+<E> ☐ **Edit** option in the **Edit** menu ☐ Double-click on the **Part** option in the **Arrange** window (if the **Key** option is checked)	
Open or show/hide the Key Edit window	Icons in the top right corner of the window	To save the results of editing, press the **Save** button before you close the editor
	Open another editor	Key Edit is closed automatically, and the results of editing are saved
	1. Click on the window icon. 2. Select the required option from the drop-down list.	The ▨ (**Keep**) command saves the results of editing when Key Edit is closed
Open the toolbar	Press and hold the right mouse button on the **Note Display** or **Controller Display** field	
Select (change) the tool on the toolbar	Move to the required tool holding the right mouse button pressed	The **Arrow** is invoked by clicking the right mouse button

continues

Table 2.10 Continued

Operation	Brief description	Comments
Move or hide the toolbar	The <F12> key or the option in the **Windows** menu (show or hide the toolbar) Grab at an area free from buttons and drag the toolbar while holding any mouse button pressed	

Change the meter, tempo	❑ Enter the new values on the **Transport bar**:
	
	   ● Click or hold the left or right mouse button on the figure to be changed
	
	   ● Enter the new value after double-clicking in the tempo or meter field
	
	❑ The tempo is changed with the pressing of the <–> or <+> key on the additional keyboard
		![120.000 04/04]
		Temporarily changing the meter and tempo is done in the **List Mastertrack** window (see *Sections 2.15.3* and *2.19.1*)

Change the scale in the **Note Display** field	❑ Horizontally: the sliders at the bottom of the window or the <G> and <H> keys ❑ Vertically: the sliders on the right or the <Shift>+<G> and <Shift>+<H> key combinations	
Change the size of the **Note Display** or **Controller Display** fields	❑ The **Controller** button at the bottom on the left hides (shows) the **Controller Display** sections ❑ With the mouse button pressed, grab at the section border and drag it up or down	
Keyboard navigation (up, down)	❑ Vertical scrollbar (on the right)	
Navigate the composition (**Part**) forward, backward	❑ Horizontal scrollbar (at the bottom) ❑ The <–→> and <←–> keys ❑ Slider and the buttons on the **Transport bar** ❑ Selecting the required option in the **Goto:** drop-down list (at the top on the left)	See also: methods of moving the cursor

continues

Table 2.10 Continued

Operation	Brief description	Comments
Moving the editor cursor (only to the positions specified in the **Snap** field)	☐ Click with the left mouse button on the **Ruler**	If a loop is switched on, the cursor can only be moved within it.
	☐ With the <Page Up> and <Page Down> keys	Attention: the cursor is invisible if there is no **Part** being edited in the **Arrange** window.
	☐ On the **Transport bar** (rewind buttons or changes of the **Position Indicator**)	
	☐ The <1> and <2> keys (the **L** and **R** locators)	
Audition	1. Set the cursor to the start of the fragment to be listened to.	
	2. Press the **Play** button on the **Transport bar** (or the <0> key on the *main* keyboard or <Enter> on the additional keyboard).	
	3. After the audition is finished, press the **Stop** button on the **Transport bar** (or the <0> key on the *additional* keyboard).	
	☐ When the **Speaker** button is pressed, click on the note with the **Magnifying Glass** tool, or move along the notes using the <→> and <←> keys	

Table 2.11. Methods of Entering Notes and Grouping Them for Further Editing

Operation	Brief description	Comments
Select the length	1. Click in the **Quant** field. 2. Select the required value from the drop-down list.	1 — whole, 2 — half, 4 — quarter, 8 — eighth, etc. (T — triple; dotted numbers — dotted notes) (see *Sections 2.8, 2.9, 2.14*)
Set the permitted positions	1. Click in the **Snap** field. 2. Select the required value from the drop-down list.	If the lengths in the **Snap** field are longer than those in the **Quant** field, rests appear between the notes (see *Section 2.9*)

continues

Table 2.11 Continued

Operation	Brief description	Comments
Allow entry of notes of any length	Set the **Off** value in the **Quant** field.	
Allow many positions for the note start and end	❏ Set the minimum values in ticks: 2pp — 7pp ❏ Cancel restriction — select the **Off** value in the **Snap** field	
Create notes using the tools	❏ Click or drag the **Pencil** tool ❏ Click or drag the **Paint Brush** tool	
Create a note sequence using the commands of the **To:** and **Do:** drop-down lists	1. Select values in the **Quant** and **Snap** fields (except for **Off**). 2. Press a key on the virtual keyboard. 3. Select the area in the **To:** drop-down list. 4. Apply the **Fill** command from the **Do:** drop-down list.	
Create notes using the MIDI instrument (step mode)	1. If necessary, change the values in the **Quant** and **Snap** fields. 2. Set the editor cursor to the starting point of the recording. 3. Press the **Step** recording button. 4. Play the notes or chords (with any tempo and rhythm).	
Enter notes using a MIDI instrument (in real-time mode)	1. Set the tempo and meter (on the **Transport bar**). 2. Start the recording on the **Transport bar** (or using the <*> key on the additional keyboard). 3. Play the musical part. 4. Stop the recording on the **Transport bar** (or using the <*> key on the additional keyboard).	See *Section 2.5* for details on recording in the **Arrange** window. See *Section 2.22* for details on the loop recording mode.

continues

Table 2.11 Continued

Operation	Brief description	Comments
Select notes (grouping)	❐ Drag the **Arrow** tool to make a frame	Adjacent notes are selected.
	❐ Press the <→> or <←> keys holding the <Shift> key pressed	Notes are selected one after the other.
	❐ Click with the **Arrow** tool on the key imprints holding the <Shift> key pressed	Notes far away from each other can be selected.
	❐ Select an area in the **To:** drop-down list	The selected notes do not change their color
Exclude notes from a group	❐ Click on one or several notes of a highlighted group holding the <Shift> key pressed	
Ungrouping	❐ Click on a free area	

Table 2.12. Editing the Selected Notes

Operation	Brief description	Comments
Cut out notes (from the end to the beginning)	Drag the **Pencil** tool over the key imprint	Limited by the value in the **Snap** field
Cut notes from either side	1. Drag the **Line** tool (delete what is to the right of the "cut"). 2. Drag the **Line** tool with the pressed <Alt> key (delete what is to the left of the "cut").	
Rhythmic quantize	1. Select a group of notes. 2. Select the quantizing step (in the **Snap** field). 3. Select the **All Selected** option from the **To:** drop-down list (with the cycle mode switched off).	If a group of notes is selected within one of the cycles (Loop, Cycle), select the required option from the **To:** drop-down list.

continues

Table 2.12 Continued

Operation	Brief description	Comments
	4. Apply the **Over Quantize** command from the **Functions** menu (or press the \<**Q**\> key).	
Copy using the mouse	1. Select the note (notes). 2. Holding the \<Alt\> key, drag them to a new place with the **Arrow** tool.	When copying the group, grab at a key imprint with the mouse.
Copy using commands	1. Select the note (notes). 2. Place them in the clipboard (\<Ctrl\>+\<C\>). 3. Set the editor cursor to the required position. 4. Paste from the clipboard (\<Ctrl\>+\<V\>)	
Move	1. Select the note (notes). 2. Holding the \<Ctrl\> key, drag them to a new place with the **Arrow** tool.	When moving the group, grab at a key imprint with the mouse.
Move strictly horizontally or vertically (Transpose)	1. Select the note (group of notes). 2. Grab the note until the "hand" appears. 3. Press the \<Shift\> key. 4. Move the notes.	
Delete	❏ Click on the key imprint with the **Eraser** tool ❏ Drag the **Eraser** tool across the key imprints (delete them)	
Delete all the events in the selected area	1. Select the deletion area in the **To:** field. 2. Apply the **Delete** command in the **Do** field	
Add and remove notes in the insert mode	With the pressed **Insert** button, using the **Pencil**, **Eraser**, or **Paint Brush** tools, or entering from the MIDI instrument	

continues

Table 2.12 Continued

Operation	Brief description	Comments
Change the instrument (patch) for one note	1. Select the note. 2. On the **Info Line** panel, select the channel with another instrument (Patch).	For the track being edited, the **any** channel should be set in the **Arrange** window. (See the details on the instrument (Patch) change in *Sections 2.3* and *2.4.*)

Table 2.13. Methods of Working in the Controller Display Section

Operation	Brief description	Comments
Choosing and switching controllers in the Key Edit editor	Select from the **Event Type Selector** drop-down list	 See the details on switching controllers via the List Edit editor in *Section 2.12.3.*
Change the rule for selecting the controller's color (for editing convenience)	Select the required option from the **Editor colors** drop-down list	
Create a controller in the **Controller Display** section	1. Press the <Alt> key. 2. Click or drag the **Pencil** or **Line** tool.	❐ The **Velocity** is created together with the note (automatically). ❐ If you cannot create a controller, it is possible that you need to increase the **Part** in the **Arrange** window.
Change the "smoothness" of a controller's curve (except for **Velocity**)	Change the value in the **Snap** field before the controller is created.	*Attention*: the smoother the curve, the heavier the load on the MIDI channel.

continues

Table 2.13 Continued

Operation	Brief description	Comments
Select controllers in the **Controller Display** section	❏ Click on them with the **Arrow** tool	The selection of the note and its **Velocity** is inseparable
	❏ Click on them with the **Arrow** tool holding the <Shift> key pressed (to select several events)	
	❏ Frame them by dragging the **Arrow** tool	
	❏ Use the commands in the **To**: drop-down list (not highlighted in color)	
Edit **Velocity**	❏ Click or drag the **Pencil** or **Line** tool along one **Velocity**	See details on the accents in *Sections 2.15, 2.16,* and *2.21*
	❏ Drag the **Pencil** or **Line** tool along several **Velocities** (all the previously created accents will be *smoothed*)	See *Section 2.17*
	❏ Record the **Velocity** in step mode	
Specify the **Velocity** level when the note is created	❏ Default level is 127	Can be used as a way of creating accents
	❏ With the <Shift> key pressed, the level is 96	
	❏ With the <Ctrl> key pressed, the level is 64	
	❏ With the <Shift>+<Ctrl> keys pressed, the level is 32	
Delete **Velocity** (along with deleting notes)	❏ Delete the note (notes)	Note and Velocity deletion is inseparable
	❏ Select and delete the note using any method (e.g., with the <Delete> key)	
Edit controllers (except for **Velocity**)	❏ Click with the **Pencil** or **Line** tool on the required level	See details on dynamic shade creation using the controllers in *Section 2.18*
	❏ Drag the **Pencil** or **Line** tool	
	❏ Click or drag the **Eraser** tool	

continues

Table 2.13 Continued

Operation	Brief description	Comments
Delete controllers (except for **Velocity**)	❑ Drag the **Eraser** tool ❑ Select and delete identical notes: with the <Backspace> or <Delete> keys ❑ Select via the option in the **To:** drop-down list and delete with the **Delete** command in the **Do** drop-down list	The **Velocity** is deleted together with the notes

Table 2.14. Lengths in Ticks in Cubasis VST and Cubasis Notation

Length	Length in ticks	Symbol in the Snap and Quant fields
Whole note	1536	1
Half note	768	2
Quarter note	384	4
Eighth note	192	8
Sixteenth note	96	16
Thirty-second note	48	32
Sixty-fourth note	24	64
	1	Off
Dotted whole note	2304	1.
Dotted half note	1152	2.
Dotted quarter note	576	4.
Dotted eighth note	288	8.
Dotted sixteenth note	144	16.
Dotted thirty-second note	72	32.
Dotted sixty-fourth note	36	64.
	1	Off

continues

Table 2.14 Continued

Length	Length in ticks	Symbol in the Snap and Quant fields
Whole note (triple)	1024	1T
Half note (triple)	512	2T
Quarter note (triple)	256	4T
Eighth note (triple)	128	8T
Sixteenth note (triple)	64	16T
Thirty-second note (triple)	32	32T
Sixty-fourth note (triple)	16	64T
	1	Off

CHAPTER 3

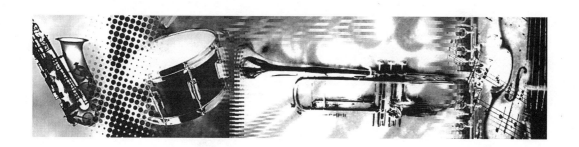

Creating a Score
in Cubasis Notation

3.1. The Score Edit Editor.
General Information

Basically, the note editors in all the Cubase system applications are similar. Therefore, after you understand the Score Edit editor in Cubasis Notation, we hope you will be able to grasp the basic concept of working in any note editor in Cubase system software.

The note editors of the Cubase system are *intended for efficient work with musical projects.* They are an integral part of the Cubase system, and should not be seen as just a means of printing notes.

The Score Edit editor of the Cubasis Notation software is a tool that can be used by a very wide range of musicians, including beginners.

3.1.1. Score Edit and Knowing Notation

It is not only professionals who need to be competent in musical notation. It is hard to challenge the fact that a literate person has many advantages concerning the perception of the world as compared to an illiterate one. It is written language that makes it possible to hand over knowledge from one person to another with *completeness* and *accuracy.*

Imagine the following situation: a poet writes a beautiful poem on five pages and gives it to an actor to read on stage. This should be no big deal: the actor takes the text, learns it, and then meets the author to more accurately define the shades of meaning. But the situation is completely different if either one of them is illiterate.

Musical notation is the written language of musicians. In conformance with the topic of this chapter, we can say that knowing notation reveals not only the knowledge "encrypted" in the notes, but enables you to communicate with professional musicians on equal terms.

Nowadays, a "devolutionary" return to live music is gradually taking shape. Musicians of the classical school are more often enlisted in various projects, and electronic sound is being supplemented and enriched by acoustic instruments. But when such a musician is recruited into a project, he or she needs to be explained the task: figuratively speaking, to be given the "text of the poem". Of course, you could give a lengthy clarification of the artistic character of your composition, hum the part, begging the musician to play it "by ear", or learn this part jointly, with the composer playing and the musician repeating and memorizing, etc.

It makes much more sense to write this part down with the generally accepted symbols — notes — making all the necessary remarks as to the character of the performance: changes in the tempo, repetitions, dynamic shades, ad lib zones, etc. A professional will be able to play the composition on the spot. Moreover, in the course of time (when some of the material is forgotten), there will be no need for him or her to learn everything anew — it will be sufficient to refresh their memory by just looking at the notes.

If before writing down music could only be tackled by professionals, the Cubase system software now enables you to "translate" your music "in both directions".

Figuratively speaking, the Score Edit editor is a "musical translator": it allows you to record *sounds* as notes and play musical *notation* as sound.

The Score Edit editor makes it possible to represent a part both in adapted and non-adapted form. This is its crucial difference from the Key Edit and List Edit editors, where the sound is almost the same as what is written.

Cubasis Notation allows you to accurately reproduce a part played by a MIDI instrument in notes. Humans, however, may find it difficult to understand such notation visually. Therefore, in most cases, a score intended for a musician must be simplified.

Score adaptation makes the notation simplified and "readable" thanks to certain special settings, reproducing the material *without distortion.*

When you have the notation in front of you, it is easy to become acquainted with a project, make amendments and addenda, produce an accompaniment to the melody displayed in the notation on the screen, etc.

You can also work with dynamic nuances and the tempo, and add some "performer's touches" in the Score Edit editor.

For the score to be readable, you may set some distinguishing marks in the form of symbols, curtail the notation using abbreviations, etc.

The changes to the notation made in the Score Edit editor may lead to various results: they can either affect just the notation or they can affect the actual sound (be complete MIDI events).

The latter is a very precious capability, since it helps us to retain the performer's special touches in a live MIDI recording without overloading the score with tiny notes, ties, unnecessary rests, etc.

Now let's turn to a no less important issue. The note editors of the Cubase system let the musician work with the material at a new, more advanced level. The notes in the Key Edit and List Edit editors are "understood" as separate, uncoordinated commands. The Score Edit editor can "interpret" a note as a component of a modal system, which helps (like rhythmic quantization) to perform scale correction — to change both the melodic and harmonic basis of the composition. This, in turn, is one of the ways of finding a new means of artistic expression.

Some people are of the opinion that a real musical composition is a sort of revelation, information "from on high", which was heard and interpreted in sounds by the composer. Without refuting this statement, we'd like to remind you that in ancient times, the word "composer" meant anyone involved in *composition* in *any* art form. The Latin word "composito" means "creation, composition", and can be used even in describing the art of flower arrangement.

If we look at the creative process through a microscope, we are bound to notice that the composer also "composes" music: from his or her ideas, sounds found in the world at large, etc.

The latest achievements in the area of music software allow the composer to pick up interesting ideas for his or her compositions while experimenting with musical material. Therefore, we think that musical compositions created with a computer have a bright future.

You can fully use the capabilities of the Score Edit editor only if you know the basics of music theory. Therefore, in describing this editor, we will give you some information on the main "laws" of musical language.

The different types of Cubase system software are meant for users of different levels of competence. In these applications, you can also work in other editors (ones that don't use notation). But we can state with confidence that knowing notation is a sort of "pass" to a higher level of work with musical material.

In our opinion, "musicians" who believe that you needn't have any knowledge of notation to create music are similar to cyclists who are unwilling to admit the advantages of a car.

3.1.2. Designating the Pitch of Notes

Upon your first acquaintance with Score Edit, you might get the feeling that the software does not "obey" the user: notes refuse to stay in the positions you assign, and many strange rests, tied notes, ledger lines, etc. occur. Sometimes such "intimidating" notation can perplex even professional musicians, to say nothing of those who have only picked up a smattering of musical knowledge.

However, once you study Score Edit closer and have actually tried it, you begin to perceive the farsightedness of its developers. The programmers did their best to take into account the needs of musicians.

In order for examples to be clear to all readers (including those who have never encountered notes before), let us dwell for a while on the main elements of notation.

In *Chapter 2*, we spoke about how to show note lengths using notation symbols. Now our subject is a bit simpler: the symbols for pitch in notation.

In order to visually identify the pitch of a sound, symbols are positioned on a *staff*, consisting of five parallel lines. The lines are counted from the bottom (Fig. 3.1). The notes are positioned either on the lines or in the spaces between them, as well as above the fifth line and below the first line. Thus, the staff can hold 11 notes.

Fig 3.1. Notes on the staff

In order to write more notes on the staff, short *ledger lines* (*help lines* in the software) are added above or below the main staff (one for each separate note) (see Fig. 3.10).

Note

To make the pitch more precise, alteration symbols are used (sharp, flat, etc.).

The names of the notes written on the staff and the fact that they belong to a certain octave is shown by the *clef* at the beginning of the staff. This is an absolutely necessary attribute of *each* staff, as it is impossible to identify the pitch of a note without a clef.

The clef shows the position on the staff of *one of the notes* of a certain pitch (and thus the rest of the notes). There are several clefs. The most common are treble clef and bass clef. The former is used for recording high-pitched parts and instruments with a high register, and the latter is for low-pitched parts and instruments with a low register.

The treble clef (*G* clef) shows the position of the *G* note of the first octave on the staff (in MIDI numbering. this is the *G3* note, or the *G* of the three-line octave). (See *Section 2.8.3* for details on the correspondence of the octave names.) The inscription of this clef is simply a distorted letter *G*. Fig. 3.2 shows that the *G* note and the treble clef are *on the same line* — the second.

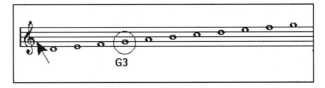

Fig 3.2. The treble clef

Thus, the treble clef informs the musician that the notes correspond to certain sounds (Fig. 3.3). (*C3* and *C4* are the symbols for the *C* notes using MIDI numbering.)

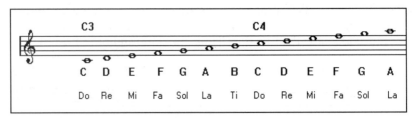

Fig 3.3. Names of the notes in the treble clef

The bass clef (the *F* clef) shows the position of the F note of the small octave (in MIDI numbering, this is the *F* note of the two-line octave — *F2*). The bass clef (just as the F note) is written on the fourth line (Fig 3.4). This illustration shows the names of the bass clef notes (*C2* and *C3* are symbols of the *C* notes in MIDI numbering).

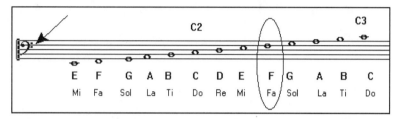

Fig 3.4. Names of the notes in the bass clef

The ledger lines allow you to widen the range of the notes shown on the staff.

For example, if you add one *lower* ledger line to the treble clef and one upper ledger line to the bass clef, then the note on them both is *the same C* note (Fig. 3.5). Figuratively speaking, this note is "neutral", since it is positioned on neither staff, being the "link" between them.

With this note present, the correspondence of the two staves becomes clear: the notes are positioned *one after another*.

To illustrate this, we'll employ a small ruse — draw another line for the C note between the staves (Fig. 3.5). It will correspond to the first *lower* ledger line in the treble clef and, simultaneously, to the first *upper* ledger line in the bass clef.

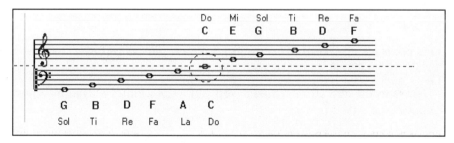

Fig. 3.5. Notes on the staff lines

Now the staves are "combined", and *all* the notes on them are set as a continuous chain.

The notes *on* the lines denote the keys shown in Fig. 3.6 (compare with Fig. 3.5).

Knowing the names of these keys, and that they are written *on the lines*, it is very easy to define the rest of the white keys. They are written *between* the lines of the staff, and are between the lettered keys in Fig. 3.6.

As for the black keys — there turned out to be no "room" for them on the staff. This was not the result of an injustice, but rather just the simplification of notation.

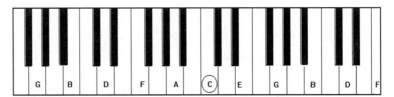

Fig. 3.6. Key correspondence to the notes on the staves

Remember that *each* black key can be named in two ways, depending on which white key it is counted from (see *Section 2.82*, Fig. 2.27).

Figuratively speaking, in order to say if a half-filled glass of water is already a lot or not as much, you need to know the tendency: if the water in the glass is being poured in or out. The same thing can be said of the black keys: the same key can be called *C* sharp or *D* flat, depending on whether its name came from augmenting the previous note (white key) or diminishing the next one.

In order to show a black key in notation, the same principle is used as in their names: an augmenting symbol — *sharp*, or a diminishing symbol — *flat* is added.

Thus, the sound corresponding to the black key on the piano keyboard may be written as the note either *on the line* or *between the lines*, but *always* with the "warning" alteration symbol.

This symbol warns the pianist: press the black key instead of the white one!

Thus, the black key between *G* and *A* may be shown in the notation as *G* sharp or A-flat (Fig. 3.7).

 Note

For beginners: the name of the symbol is always *pronounced after* the note, but always *preceeds* the note in the notation.

Thanks to the alteration symbols, you can write a notes played by any key on the five lines of the staff.

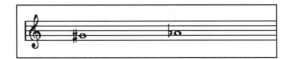

Fig. 3.7. Sharp and flat symbols

Now let's go back to the ledger lines. You can considerably expand the capacity of the staff and show notes of another register using ledger lines (Fig. 3.8). The ledger lines, however, should not be used excessively, since they are harder to understand. There are special methods that enable you to move the notes of the neighboring register to the staff. For example, one of these is the Octave symbol, considered in *Section 3.11.1*.

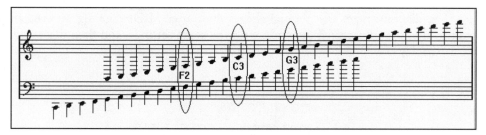

Fig. 3.8. Note correspondence in the treble and bass clefs

If you take a closer look at the notes written on the ledger lines in Fig. 3.8, you will see that they duplicate the notes of the neighboring staff. This means that you can write *the same notes* on different clefs.

Certainly you will require some practice to be able to identify notes in different clefs, but it is not as difficult as it may seem.

Note that ledger lines are nothing but "fragments" of the neighboring staff; in other words — they are an "abbreviated" form (including the "personal" line of the *C* note shown in Fig. 3.9).

▶ *Note*

Fig. 3.9 shows the notes of the treble clef with their stems up, and those of the bass clef with their stems down.

Fig. 3.9. Additional ledger lines and staves

You are given a hint as to what the selected note is in the Score Edit editor — its name is shown in the **Info Line** panel (the same function is available in the Key Edit editor).

In some cases, it is sufficient to recognize the notes in the treble clef (e.g., to be able to read the melody), but knowing the lengths is also absolutely necessary (see *Chapter 2*).

3.1.3. Notation: History and Future

The Score Edit editor is a sort of superstructure above the MIDI data of the application. It translates them from the "zero-one" language into a language understandable to musicians — notation.

The diagram from the manual shows that, after MIDI data are entered into the editor, they are interpreted depending on the score settings, and then displayed in the score display (Fig. 3.10).

Fig. 3.10. The principle of **Score Edit**'s operation

This is why the same musical material — if the user so desires — can be presented differently in the score.

Note

Remember that in the editors described earlier (**Key Edit** and **List Edit**) *all* changes were displayed with *utter precision*, and *affected* the sound.

In order to understand some functions of the software that may at first seem redundant, we will now take a small historical digression.

Notation has changed throughout the centuries, as if it were catching up with growing human potential.

In ancient times, notation was extremely primitive, with no indication of rhythm, and you could only approximate the pitch of the sound.

The "notes" were letters of the alphabet and *neumes*. The lettering of notes is still used nowadays, such as when indicating the chords in figuring.

Neumes consisted of various symbols (hyphens, dots, commas, etc.) and their combinations. Neumatic notation was used for writing vocal music only, and was only useful for reminding a singer of a melody that he or she already knew: it showed its motion — ascending or descending — as well as certain melodic turns, ornamentation, etc.

While polyphonic music was being developed, when a more *accurate* and *coordinated* performance was needed, notation underwent some modifications.

During these reforms, in order to accurately identify the pitch, the neumes were underlined with one, and later with several, horizontal lines. These lines were multicolored and preceded by the letters denoting the sound. So the first line that appeared was red, with the letter "f" in the beginning, which meant that all the neumes on this line corresponded to the *F* note. A little bit later, lines with letters *C* and *G* appeared, denoting the *C* and *G* notes (later these letters formed clefs). By the eleventh century, the number of lines had already reached four.

> The "four line" invention belongs to an Italian musician, choral singing teacher, musical theorist, and monk — Guido d'Arezzo.

By the fourteenth century, there were five lines, called a "staff". Despite the huge progress — the fixed pitch of the sound — the length of the notes was still not indicated in the medieval system of notation *at all*.

Due to the development of polyphony during the period from the twelfth to the sixteenth centuries, it became necessary to coordinate the parts of a polyphonic composition that differed in their *rhythm*. This led to the introduction of a rhythmic measure of sounds, which set different values for the length of the notes — mensuration (from the Latin *"mensura"* — measure).

So, the cradle of contemporary notation lengths in notation can be found in mensural notation. The "ancestors" of contemporary notes looked almost the same: longa (a half note), semi-minima (a quarter), fusa (an eighth), and semifusa (a sixteenth) (Fig. 3.11). Rather insignificant evolution for five hundred years, isn't it?

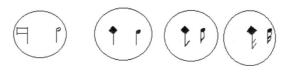

Fig. 3.11. The correspondence of medieval
and contemporary notes

It is worth mentioning that all the achievements in notation are present in contemporary notes: by the appearance of a note, a musician can identify its length and see the motion of the melody (up, down, bound, smooth, etc.).

Not only has notation changed; the search for the optimal scale has gone along much the same path.

Scale is the position of the pitch and the ratio of the sound range.

One of the ancestors of the contemporary scale was created in Italy in the sixteenth century, and was called an open-ended, or *clean* scale. The sounds here were differentiated by a hardly audible value — 1/8 to 1/10 of a tone. Due to this, an octave consisted of 85(!) notes. Of course, this made tuning an instrument extremely difficult, and was practically unacceptable for performance.

Later, this scale was simplified, and the tempered scale appeared, where the pitch ratio of two neighboring sounds was the same *in all cases*, and equal to a half tone.

Thanks to its conciseness and simplicity of use, this scale became very widely spread everywhere, beginning in the eighteenth century. Each octave of this scale is divided into 12 equal parts (semitones). This makes it possible to play a melody from *any* note with a transition to different octaves, and the pitch correlation *between* the notes will always be retained.

Contemporary notation, reflecting the existing tempered scale, is no doubt more informative than those previous versions of notation with written symbols (neumes, etc.). But is still retains drawbacks that impel scholars to attempt to reform notation (not a single attempt, however, has given positive results *thus far*).

All of us are contemporaries of new computer technologies in the area of music. Historically, the fact that a "machine brain" enables software to play notation of *any* level of complexity at any tempo immediately is a big step ahead.

Moreover, it is no big deal for the computer to write "by ear" a score for the most complicated polyphonic composition, and then perform it, for example, as an orchestra would. Before, this required much time and effort, both the composer's and the musician's.

You need to remember, however, that despite its flawless "virtuosity", the computer can not *interpret* the composition by itself.

Surely, the development of computer technologies related to music will lead to a reform in notation.

Until recently, "notes" were intended for a human performer *only*. For convenience of writing and understanding, people have been trying to make notation as simple and concise as possible, and all the shades of the performance were taken outside the symbol of the note itself. A person playing a composition is always the unacknowledged "co-author" of the composer, since they willy-nilly introduce their own interpretation and different nuances into the music.

When computer applications appeared, the situation changed. The new technological possibilities broadened the horizons of notation.

Now the "ideal electronic performer" can play music of *any* complexity. Moreover, the composer may program this "performer": introduce *all* the nuances into the "computer notes".

The computer musician must clearly understand that notation for the human musician and notation for the computer are definitely *different*.

Computer music would remind you of a modernized street organ if the computer just reproduces notation intended for a *human being*, without being supplemented with special commands for the computer, indicating the "human touches" of the performance.

And vice versa: if notation is made by the computer and not adapted for a human musician, the latter may not understand it, since it will be overloaded with information.

The "machine" is not the rival of man, it is his "instrument". So, the efforts that you put out when mastering the Cubase software are paid back with interest when the music is created.

Before, in order to start on the path to become a musical master, one needed to get over the hump known as "technique". Many are those who dropped out of the race.

But music beckons, for it is universal language, employed to communicate the slightest shades of emotion, mood, and feelings. And the language of music is clear to all, regardless of their sex, education, age, etc.

Nowadays, the "helicopter of modern technology" can easily raise a beginner musician to a cherished peak, past the thorns and straight to the stars.

This became possible due to the division of labor between the machine and the man: the computer and the musician.

New technologies in musical education. In our opinion, computer technologies must pay some dividends for mankind in the musical area. The new capabilities of computer software can be actively used in musical education.

The computer can be used as a simulator for teaching notation, or as a basis for a new strategy of musical education — creating interpretations of musical compositions that are very difficult technically for the student to perform, but useful for helping him or her gain an artistic understanding using the computer. We think that the development of such programs is a very interesting area of activity.

This method by no means minimizes the advantages of traditional education. It should exist parallel to the mastering of the acoustic instrument. But the emotional, artistic, and sound enrichment of a composition is not only enthralling, but very useful too.

The introduction of various slight meanings into a composition (using different touches, dynamic shades, new sounds, etc.) is nothing but the highest level of the skill of creating music. Such achievements before were possible only *after* the difficult mastering of the performance technique, but now the work of artistic creation has become available to a wide range of people interested in the world of sound.

And the last, but not the least important conclusion. Notation obtained on a computer as a result of a human performance may become a historical milestone in changing recording standards, and a new branch of notation may well be developed: "detailed notation for the electronic performer".

Now we'll move on to a few examples of the software's operation. Suppose a musician runs through a musical phrase from the song "Happy Birthday to You" in Cubasis Notation. The style is simple: a one-part melody and chords on the strong beats.

Then, in Score Edit (depending on the settings) the musician may see either a horrifying passage (Fig. 3.12), or the clearly written "international birthday anthem" (Fig. 3.13). Note that both will sound the same, since the MIDI events entered were not changed due to the score settings of the Score Edit editor.

▶ *Note*

In the example in Fig. 3.13, *only* the line with the text was added manually, while the rest of the simplifications were made using a few very simple commands.

Of course, the editor settings in the example in Fig. 3.12 are not suitable for recording a simple melody.

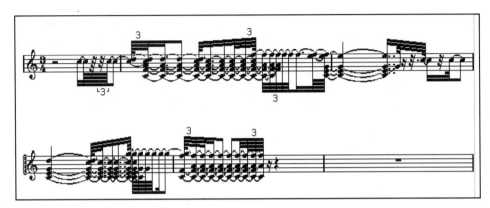

Fig. 3. 12. Non-adapted score of the song "Happy Birthday to You"

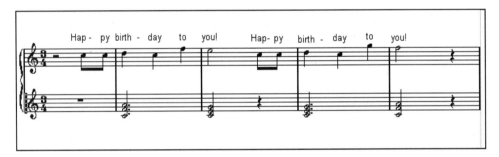

Fig. 3.13. Adapted score of the song "Happy Birthday to You"

You can see from the example, however, that Score Edit can record and play back a style of any complexity.

Before we dwell on the principles of working in the Score Edit editor, note that the application makes it very easy to simplify the notation.

The clarity of the score can be clearly seen (compare Figs. 3.12 and 3.13), and it is easy to select the settings you need. The software will record your selection in compliance with the rules, since it never "makes mistakes". The note editor of the Cubasis Notation software *automatically* follows *all* the rules of the notation, including insertion of rests into blank spaces of the bar. This considerably simplifies the musician's task of creating the score.

3.1.4. The *Score* Window:
Interface Capabilities

This section deals with the capabilities of the Score Edit editor that are presented as interface elements in the Score window.

Note

Many ways of working in the **Score Edit** editor coincide with those of the **Key Edit** editor described in the previous chapter. Thus we will emphasize the features peculiar to **Score Edit**, and when the features of the two windows are the same, we will refer to *Chapter 2* in order not to tire the reader with repetitions.

The Score Edit editor is called in the **Arrange** window using one of the traditional methods: the Score option from the Edit menu, the <Ctrl>+<R> key combination, or a double-click on the part (if the Score option is checked in the Double Click opens submenu of the Options menu).

 Note

Here, **Score Edit** is no different from the **Key Edit** editor (see *Section 2.8*).

After the Score Edit editor is invoked, the Score window appears on the screen (Fig. 3.14). Its appearance corresponds to the default settings offered by the developers. You can see in Fig. 3.14 that if you keep the defaults, the recording will be done on one staff, in the treble clef, in 4/4 meter, with four bars on each staff, have a title and one part (indicated by the arrow), the scale of the score *on the screen* will be 100% (also indicated by an arrow), etc.

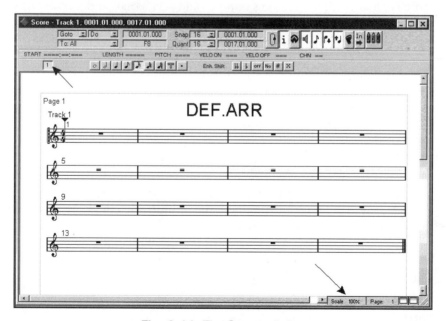

Fig. 3.14. The **Score** window

The interface of the window is very similar to that of the Key Edit editor. The interesting thing is the *complete* similarity of the widgets and the design of the upper part of the window — the Status Bar and Info Line panels. This similarity is not only visual: *all* the main principles of working with the musical material described in detail in *Chapter 2* are the same.

The major part of the window is taken up by the Score Edit Note Display section (from here on out referred to as Score Display).

You'll also see the Score Edit Toolbar (the toolbar of the Score Edit editor) between the score section and the Info Line panel. Here you may select notes of certain length (including dotted notes and triplets), select or change the accidentals for the note, and select a voice to work with.

There are four fields in the bottom left corner.

❐ The Window Zoom Factor field allows you to change the scale of the notation display anywhere from 35% to 200% (Fig. 3.14 uses a scale of 100%, which is the default value). You may use this option to conveniently position notes on the screen.

❐ The Page Indicator field displays the selected page of the score on the screen (if there is more than one page).

❐ The Show/Hide Toolbar field shows/hides one panel on the screen — the Score Edit Toolbar (with the symbols of notes and accidentals and number of voices).

❐ The Show/Hide Status Bar field (the rightmost one) shows/hides all the panels (Status Bar, Info Line, and Score Edit Toolbar).

The last two functions are very useful, as they allow you to free up the space of the screen for the score.

Below is a brief overview of how the Status Bar and Info Line panels operate and their features in the Score Edit editor.

There are three fields in the pop-up menu: Goto, Do, and To.

❐ The Goto field is intended for quick navigation through the material being edited. Selecting a command from the drop-down list moves the multitrack cursor to this area, and it appears on the screen

❐ The difference from the Key Edit editor is that two commands are missing here: Next Part and Prev Part.

❐ Song Position — the multitrack cursor position
❐ First Event — the first note
❐ Last Event — the last note

❑ First Selected — the first *selected* note

❑ Next Selected — the next *selected* note

❑ Last Selected — the last *selected* note

❑ Prev Selected — the previous *selected* note

The To: field is, figuratively speaking, the "administrative authority", deciding who will be affected by the new laws.

This field determines the track area that will be subject to: some of the commands from the Do list, transposition, and rhythmic or stop quantize (the Functions menu, the Over Quantize and Transpose/Velocity options).

❑ All Events — all notes

❑ Selected Events — all *selected* notes

❑ Looped Events — all notes within the *loop*

❑ Cycled Events — all notes of the *cycle*

❑ Looped Sel. Ev. — all *selected* notes within the *loop*

❑ Cycled Sel. Ev. — all *selected* notes within the *cycle*

 Note

A *cycle* is an area selected in the **Arrange** window (between the **L** and **R** locators). A *loop* is an area selected in the editor.

The Do list contains the nine most frequently used commands for work with the notes.

(In Key Edit, only the first two commands were in this list.)

❑ Fill creates a note sequence that corresponds to the settings (Fig. 3.15):

- The length of the note depends on the value in the **Quant** field.
- The rhythmic positions authorized for the note are specified in the **Snap** field.
- The area of note positioning is specified in the To: field.
- The notes of such a chain are *always* equal in pitch (*C3*).

▶ *Tip*

This option may be used as the basic material for creating notes, since in many cases it is much easier to edit notes that have already been written (to move them to new positions, change their lengths, etc.) than to "write" each of them manually. In our opinion, it is especially convenient to do so using step editing with the MIDI keyboard, described in *Section 3.10.2*.

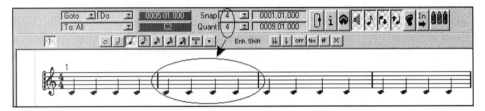

Fig. 3.15. Creating a sequence of notes

- Delete — deletes the material from the area specified in the **To:** field.

▼ *Warning*

Be careful with the **Delete** command, as it deletes *all* the notes of the track being edited if the **All Events** (all notes) option is checked in the **To:** field.

- Make Chords — automatically identifies chords from the created note material and positions them in figure form (Fig. 3.16). (The chords will be determined in the area specified in the **To:** field.)

This function is unavailable if there is only a one-voice melody, without sub-voices, accompaniment, etc.

Fig. 3.16. Positioning chords with the **Make Chords** command

☐ By double-clicking with the left mouse button on the name of the chord, you open a window in which the automatically set designation of the chord can be edited or changed completely (Fig. 3.17). See *Chapter 4* for information on chords.

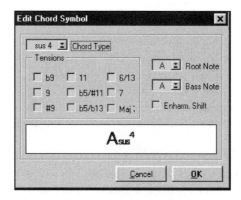

Fig. 3.17. Editing chords

- Flip Stems — flips the direction of the stems (Fig. 3.18).

  Available for selected notes *only* (one or more). The function is duplicated by the <Alt>+<Ctrl>+<X> key combination.

Fig. 3.18. Changing the direction of the stems
with the **Flip Stems** command

- Group — this option graphically groups notes (with one beam), or ungroups them (Fig. 3.19). It is available for selected notes *only*. The function is duplicated by the <Alt>+<Ctrl>+<G> key combination. See details on ungrouping methods in *Section 3.4.4.*

Warning

When notes are grouped, you need to select several notes; when you want to ungroup them, *only one* note need be selected.

Fig. 3.19. Grouping and ungrouping lengths
with the **Group** command

- Auto Grouping — automatically groups notes according to meter. This function is especially useful when compound or variable meters are recorded (see details on meters in *Chapter 2*).

Grouping is needed, for example, for the musician to visually identify the parts of the bar, and consequently, find the positions of the relatively strong beats.

Fig. 3.20 shows the difference between recording two variants of the compound time signature 5/4: as 3/4 + 2/4, and as 2/4 + 3/4. (See details on length in *Chapter 2*).

▼ *Removing Group Settings*

You can clear all the group settings of the score in the **Score/Format** menu of the **Clean Up Layout** window: check the **Grouping** option and press **OK**.

Fig. 3.20. Automatic grouping of length

The "configuration" of the compound time is specified in the Edit Time Signature window (Fig. 3.21), activated by double-clicking on the time signature or in the Score/Symbol Palettes/Clef etc. menu. If the For Grouping Only option is checked, then the upper number of the 5/4 time signature is written as one number — 5, and not 3+2 (as in Fig. 3.21). However, the note group image remains unchanged.

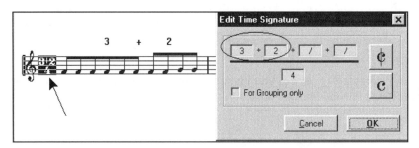

Fig. 3.21. Compound time configuration

- Hide — this option enables you to hide score elements: rests, the time signature, the clef, notes, text, the number of the bars, the bar line, titles of the tracks, shades, etc. (Figs. 3.22, 3.23). It is duplicated by the key combination <Alt>+<Ctrl>+<B>. Using this option, for example, you can easily create an upbeat (compare examples A and B in Fig. 3.22).

See *Section 3.4.4* for details on how to make visible *some* of the score elements and *partially* restore note grouping, stem lengths, and beam positions.

Upbeat

An upbeat often begins a musical composition (or a part of one). It features rests before the *first note* that are not written.

In most compositions that begin with an upbeat, the last bar is also upbeat, and these outermost bars make up an entire bar, thus balancing the musical form.

If the last bar is complete, then the first bar is not truncated either — it is written with rests. This explains the fact that music beginning with an offbeat can be written in different ways — beginning with either a complete or incomplete bar.

To make an upbeat, select a rest and hide it with the **Hide** option (Fig. 3.22). The same method is used when the last incomplete bar is written.

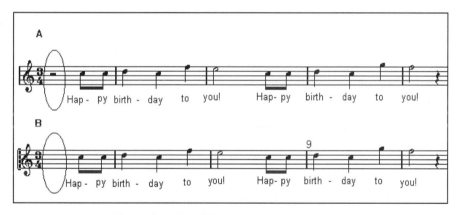

Fig. 3.22. The **Hide** option and the upbeat

- Show — this option *simultaneously* shows *all* the hidden objects. Fig. 3.23 illustrates how you can change the appearance of the score using the Hide and Show options. Examples A and B sound the same, but the rests, clefs, time signature, symbols of the dynamic shades, signatures of the chords, text, accompaniment, and accolades are hidden in Example B.

Note

An *accolade* is a bracket combining several staves. It means that the notes on them are to be played simultaneously.

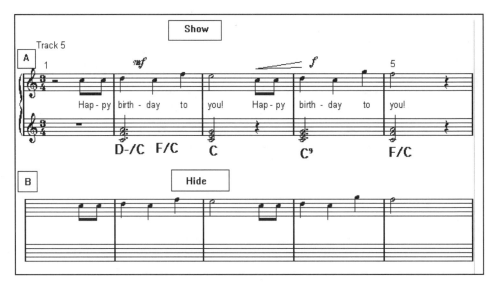

Fig. 3.23. The **Hide** and **Show** options

- Multi Insert — this option enables you to add some of the note symbols from the Note Symbols toolbar to several notes *simultaneously*. Fig. 3.24 shows that the staccato symbol is added to the first six notes, and the last two are accented. Inserting note symbols will be considered in detail in *Section 3.11.3*.

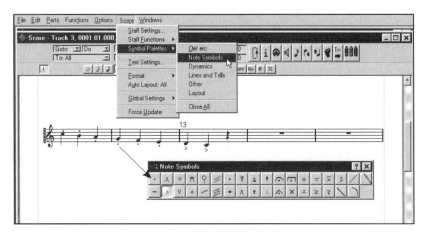

Fig. 3.24. Positioning note symbols

Now that you are familiar with the Goto, Do, and To: fields, we'll move on to the main operations of the Score Edit editor.

There are two fields on the Status Bar panel: Position Box and Transpose/Pitch Box, for showing the mouse cursor position. It is very convenient to set and move notes using these fields.

The upper field shows the rhythmic position of the note, and the lower indicates its pitch — i.e. the name of the note in MIDI numbering. Note that they are used the same here as in the Key Edit editor.

The lower field has two names, and therefore performs two functions. In normal mode, it shows the pitch of the note.

When the note is moved, the word "Transpose" appears in this field, as well as the figure showing the number of *semitones* the note is moved by. Fig. 3.25 shows that the C note (when moved up 4 semitones) becomes the E note.

(For beginners: unlike the keyboard, semitones are not shown on the staff.)

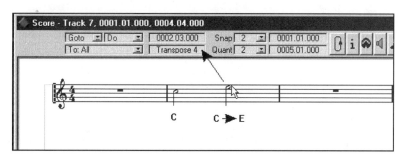

Fig. 3.25. The **Pitch/Transpose** field during transposition

In the upper Position Box field, the note coordinates are shown as three numbers: bar, beat, and tick.

In the Score Edit editor, you can't *graphically* change the value of the note symbol by a few ticks, just as you can't increase or reduce the value of a dollar bill by a few cents. But you can control the actual length of the note's sound from the note editor: it can be changed either on the Info Line panel or using special symbols (see below).

The ticks also show the cursor position in the Position Box field, and consequently, the "authorized" positions for the notes on the staff.

(Remember that the notes cannot be placed *between* these positions.)

 ## Note

We should mention that in most cases, the musician doesn't really need such accuracy (in ticks), since he or she is sufficiently guided by the lengths.

Here is brief overview of the note positions in the Position Box field:

The note pointed to with the arrow on Fig. 3.26 has the following coordinates: 0001.01.192. This means that it is in the first bar (0001), within the first beat (01), on the second half of this beat — 192 ticks (i.e., one eighth note) from the beginning of this beat.

A value of 8 is set in the Snap field, and so notes can *only* be placed on *eighth* note positions (i.e., no more often than every 192 ticks — an eighth note).

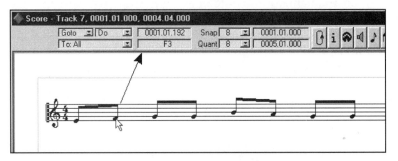

Fig. 3.26. Note coordinates

When we described the Key Edit editor, *Section 2.9.2* covered the ways of positioning the key imprints *in detail*. When note symbols are set in the Score Edit editor, *the main principles are the same*.

There is also the "invisible grid" in Score Edit, in which you may place notes. It is specified in the **Snap** field.

The **Quant** field is intended for selecting the length.

Length selection is done in the **Quant** field by clicking on the note symbol on the Score Edit **Toolbar** panel or with the <1>—<7> keys of the main keyboard. And when the length is changed in the **Quant** field, the length on the Score Edit **Toolbar** panel is also automatically changed (and vice versa) (Fig. 3.27).

Fig. 3.27 shows that the lengths are eighths and that the "authorized positions" are quarters (Snap = 8, Quant = 4). When the notes are positioned and these values are selected, the rests are set automatically among the notes.

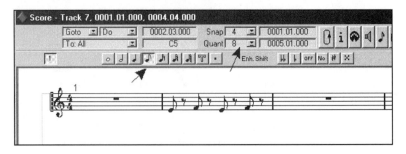

Fig. 3.27. Selecting the length

The application automatically sets not only rests, but ties, too. This is because *any* length can be set at the "authorized" positions of the bar, and in some cases, the length may go beyond the border of the beat or bar — cross the bar line or the border of the beat.

In such a case, the application will *automatically* record the note in compliance with the rules — as tied notes of the *same* pitch (Figs. 3.28, 3.29).

Tied notes that appear when the notes are set are often a nuisance to the beginner: of course, the "strange independence" of the software is liable to get on your nerves when, instead of a quarter note, shorter tied notes are "somehow" set.

The reasons for such dislike seem even more justified, since in other applications (e.g., text editors), "incorrect" words are not replaced automatically.

In the initial stage, the attitude toward the note editor is typical: until it is mastered, it seems easier to just use a pen and paper. After you learn the application, it is clear that Cubasis Notation is not "self-willed" at all, but *silently* and *implicitly* fulfills all the wishes of the user. So you really shouldn't reject the score editor from the Cubase system out of hand — it is actually amazingly convenient!

The ties that join notes of the same pitch within a bar are needed for the reader to be able to easily understand the notation: it is thanks to the ties that the musician can see the borders of the beats.

Ties as a Means of Increasing the Length

A *tie* is an arched line that connects adjacent notes. The tie symbol can take on several meanings. In the examples we give, notes of the *same pitch* are joined. This means that only the *first* note is played, and all the rest simply prolong its length, and are not played separately.

A "long" note that occurs at the border of a beat or bar is divided into two shorter notes of the *same pitch* (equal or unequal), which are tied.

Fig. 3.28 shows two half notes. The first is within the bar (A), the second goes outside the border of the bar (B). Therefore, this half note is shown as *two tied quarter notes*.

Fig 3.30 shows two quarter notes. One of them — *C* — is within the metric beat, while the other — *D* — crosses its border.

Fig. 3.29 shows that, due to the *sixteenth* rest, the quarter note was moved by this value, and its part that was "forced out" of the border of the metric beat is designated as a *sixteenth* note.

The border of the metric beat is shown as a dotted line. The application "becomes aware" of it by the time signature: if the time signature is 2/4, than the bar line falls between *quarters*.

We will consider note positioning in more detail later. Now, we'll continue with our overview of the main functions of the **Status Bar** panel.

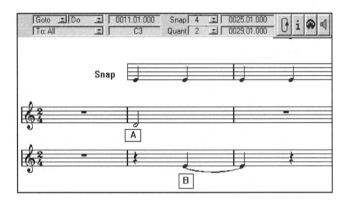

Fig. 3.28. Recording a length that crosses the border of a bar

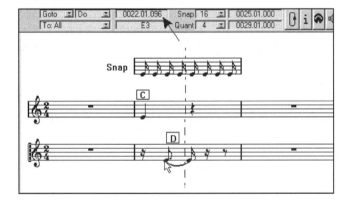

Fig. 3.29. Recording a length that crosses the border of a beat

The **Loop On** and **Loop Off** fields determine the borders of the loop; the **Loop Start/End** button is used to activate/deactivate it. (A loop is an area selected in the editor.)

We'd like to mention that in the Score Edit editor, you can specify the borders of the loop only in the **Loop On** and **Loop Off** fields.

This is done in the traditional manner. Click the left or right mouse button on the figures to be changed, or, after double-clicking the left mouse button, enter a new value in the field that opens.

There is also the "i" button (information), shown in Fig. 3.30, which opens/hides the **Info Line** panel. As in the Key Edit editor, this panel shows information on the selected note: its beginning (START), its length in ticks (LENGTH), its pitch (PITCH), the velocity of pressing and releasing (VELO ON, VELO OFF), and the channel (CHN).

You can edit all the parameters on this panel in the same way as in the Key Edit editor (see *Sections 2.8* and *2.11.2*).

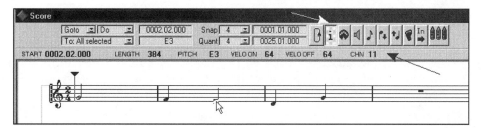

Fig. 3.30. The **Info Line** panel

 These 5 buttons are used for step recording from the MIDI keyboard (a MIDI instrument). They work in the same way as in the Key Edit editor (see *Section 2.13*).

Briefly, their main functions are:

☐ The **MIDI connector** button (a five-contact socket symbol) activates the connection with the MIDI keyboard, which makes the step recording mode and step editing possible. Step editing consists of changing the pitch and the velocity of the key pressing, which affects the volume of the note (On Velocity and Off Velocity).

☐ The **Step** button (the footprint) activates the step recording mode, in which you can "write" notes on the staff by pressing the keys of the MIDI keyboard.

☐ In **Step Recording** mode, notes and chords are set independent of the performance (tempo, rhythm): their rhythmical positions are equal to the values of the **Snap** field, and the lengths to those in the **Quant** field.

☐ The three buttons with the note symbols are intended for notation editing (they work when the **MIDI connector** button is pressed).

☐ The **Note Pitch** button (the note without the arrow) allows you to move the selected notes to new *pitch* positions.

This is done as follows: a note that was played wrongly is selected, and the correct key is pressed on the MIDI keyboard. The selected note is moved to the new place. The next note, which you can move in the same way, will be automatically selected.

► *Tip*

To select notes, you can use the arrow keys: <←> and <→>.

If you need to make some notes louder or quieter using the MIDI keyboard, you can use the button with the "arrow down" symbol (Note On-velocity).

For example, if you need to make some of the notes quieter, press the Note On-velocity and MIDI connector buttons and edit the volume (velocity) according to the force you use to press *any* note on the keyboard.

The button with the **Speaker** symbol allows you to make the note sound. To do this, click the button with the mouse cursor.

If this button is pressed, the notes will sound when set and edited.

When the **Insert** button is pressed, any editing operation affects the subsequent material: when notes or rests are removed, they are moved to the beginning, and when a note or rest is added, it is put at the end.

Insertion works in all modes: step recording, with the Pencil and Eraser tools, etc.

The drop-down list of the **Editor Colors** button offers the option of "painting" a note. Its **Edit** option allows you to change the colors and designations.

Now that we have finished with the interface's capabilities, we'll turn to the "alter ego" of the Cubasis Notation software's note editor. Literally, Score Edit has a dual character, a "second bottom". This editor can change its guise: it can "be" one thing and "seem" another.

3.1.5. Lengths: Recording and Listening

The Score Edit note editor lets you show MIDI Note events in the score as different lengths. This is a very useful function of Cubasis Notation: here you can reform the score's appearance *without affecting the sound*.

The software automatically records all the peculiarities of the performance. But it does not know when the actual MIDI events are to be shown with maximum accuracy in the notation, and when they are to be "approximated" to bigger notes so that a musician is able to read it.

Using the **Score** menu settings, *any* notation is easily reformed in the software: both those needing simplification, and those to which you want to add the maximum detail of all rhythmic nuances.

For the notation to look as you want it to, you need to make the correct settings in the Display Quantize section (the Staff Settings window of the Score menu).

Below is an example of how *the same* MIDI events may be shown differently in the score.

Fig 3.31 illustrates 4 key imprints that are 24 ticks long (or a 64th note). In Score Edit, they can be presented as *different* lengths: from a 64th to a quarter (Fig. 3.31). This depends on the settings in the Auto Quantize: section, the option selected, and the values in the Notes and Rests fields.

We can see in the illustration that, depending on these values, *the same key imprints* are shown as *different* lengths in the score (A, B, C, D).

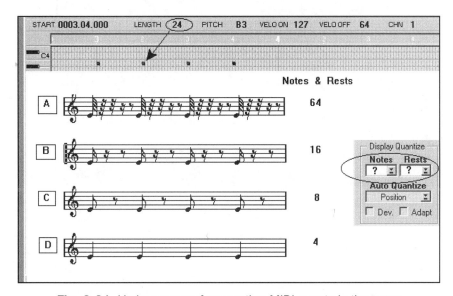

Fig. 3.31. Various ways of presenting MIDI events in the score

The following is very important: *the settings of the* Score *menu affect only the notation and not the sound* — i.e., the MIDI information *is not affected*, and consequently, the parameters of the sound — the length, the rhythmic position, and the pitch — are not changed either.

But the task of the Score Edit editor is not only to keep track of the appearance of the score. If the commands are executed *directly* in the editor (and not from the Score menu), then they affect the MIDI information, i.e., they change the pitch.

Fig. 3.32 shows some "source material": three *G* notes with a length of a sixteenth.

Then we processed these notes *in the score*: the pitch, the length, and the rhythmic position were changed. Fig. 3.33 shows that these changes affected the key imprints, and thus the *sound*. This can be seen from the key imprints (compare Figs. 3.32 and 3.33).

So, to draw a conclusion, we can say that editing the notation may have various results: it can either affect the pitch, or simply the graphic presentation of MIDI events in the Score Edit editor.

Now we'll take a look at the settings that *only change the score*, without affecting the *sound of the part*.

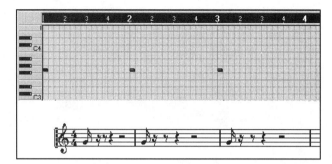

Fig. 3.32. Notes before editing in the **Score Edit** editor

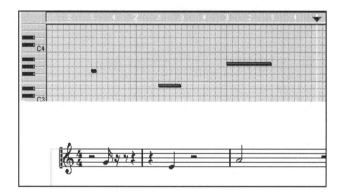

Fig. 3.33. Notes after editing in the **Score Edit** editor

3.2. The *Staff Settings* and *Staff Options* Windows

The settings in these windows are basic for *any* type of score. A user who neglects these settings may find all the operations in the Score Edit editor strange and illogical, including setting notes with the mouse.

Actually, these settings are for making the musician's work as automated as possible, and for *considerably* simplifying the score design process.

3.2.1. The Score's Dependence on the Settings

We already mentioned that the score is intended for a human being, since it doesn't matter to the software which notes to play. In any case, for the software, notes are *simply a superstructure over the MIDI commands.*

The score's appearance is of greater importance for the musician, since it is very informative. The wrong time signature, for example, can "shift the accents" entirely, distorting the idea of the composition, while a very detailed recording may make the score "unreadable", etc.

Below are examples of the importance of *some* of the score settings.

Time signature. Fig. 3.34 shows that the C note that fell at the *fourth* click of the metronome may appear on different beats of the measure, depending on the time signature. If the time signature is 4/4, then it is on the fourth beat of the measure (A), whereas if the time signature is 3/4, the fourth click of the metronome goes into the next measure, and the note turns out to be on the first beat of the second bar (B).

This is one of the very important moments in notation, since the inflection stress of the note depends on its position in the bar. From this point of view, examples A and B must be played differently, since the first beat is always stronger than the last one (see *Chapter 2* for the details on downbeats).

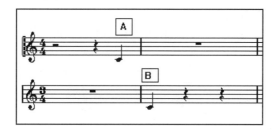

Fig. 3.34. Note designation depending on the time

Clef. Fig. 3.35 shows that the same *C* note may "look" different in the treble and the bass clefs (Examples C and D). The wrong choice of clef may considerably complicate reading the notation (e.g., many ledger lines will appear, or the musician may not be able to read the notation as easily due to the "*basso profundo*" clef set instead of the common bass clef).

Fig. 3.35. Note designation depending on the clef

Key. The designation of black keys also needs setting, since the computer has no idea how the black key is to be designated: by augmenting the previous key or by diminishing the following one — what symbol is to be used: sharp or flat? If the musician sets the *accidentals* (specifies the key), then the notes will be designated in compliance with them. Correctly setting the key is extremely important (e.g., for transposing tools).

▼ *Alteration Symbols: Clef and Accidental*

Alteration symbols (from Latin *"alterate"* — change) indicate the augmentation or diminishing of a note by a semitone without changing its name.

The clef symbols — flats or sharps (accidentals) — are positioned in the beginning of the staff beside the clef. They are valid for the notes of these names *in all octaves* up to the end of the composition (or until the symbols are changed).

The alteration symbols may be set right before the note. They are valid only within the bar and for one octave. These symbols are called *accidental*. (See details in *Section 3.10.6*).

Fig. 3.36 shows that the same black key (between the *A* key and the *B* key) can be written differently in the score. In a flat key, it is designated as *B* flat, and in a sharp key it is designated as *A* sharp.

In the majority of cases, it is easier for a musician to play with *fewer* key accidentals.

Fig. 3.36. Note designation depending on the key

Types of staves. Fig. 3.37 shows that the material can be positioned on one or two staves, depending on the musician's preferences.

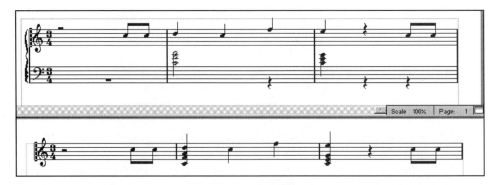

Fig. 3.37. Note designation depending on the staff settings

Lengths. The correct settings are extremely important when working with the software, since excessive minuteness may make the score "unreadable" (Fig. 3.38, the upper line), whereas excessive simplification may deprive the score of very important details.

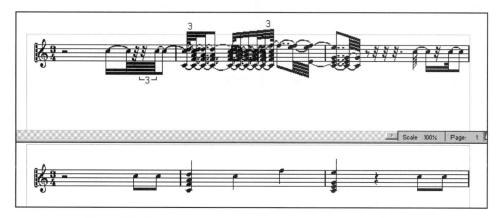

Fig. 3.38. Note designation depending on the length settings

Fig. 3.39 shows the Score menu, which combines commands used to make the score settings. All the settings of this menu are valid for *all types of scores* (recorded from the MIDI keyboard, entered with the mouse, etc.)

Fig. 3.39. The **Score** menu

This section deals only with the first option — Staff Settings.

This option is used to open two important windows: Staff Settings and the nested Staff Options window, which opens with the Staff Options button (Fig. 3.40).

You may call these windows from the score — by double-clicking at the beginning of the staff in the Score window (shown with an arrow in Fig. 3.40).

The Staff Settings and Staff Options windows are intended for the main settings of the score. In order for the selected settings to affect the score, press OK (if the changes were made in the Staff Options window, press the Exit button followed by OK).

If you need to apply the changes *simultaneously* to all tracks opened in the editor, hold the <Alt> key pressed (when pressing the OK button).

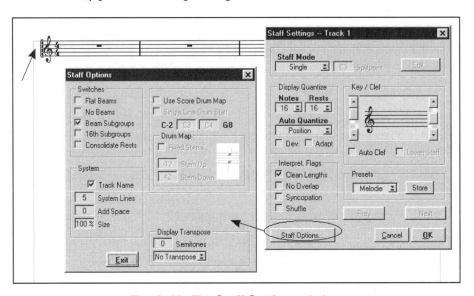

Fig. 3.40. The **Staff Settings** window

Fig. 3.40 shows the windows with their default settings.

3.2.2. Clefs. Keys. Time Signature

This section allows you to set (or change) the key and the clef. The selection is made with sliders. The default settings are the treble clef and a key without key signatures (*C* major or *A* minor).

Key setting (KEY). When moved up, the right slider increases the number of flats, and when moved downward the number of sharps are increased (from 1 to 7). In this way you can set the symbols for any of the existing keys (Fig. 3.41).

❗ *Changing the Key Signatures*

In order to change the key signatures in the course of the composition, click on any sharp or flat beside the clef, and then select the required symbols with the slider in the window that opens (Fig. 3.42). To change symbols in the middle of the staff, the **Clef ...** window is used (see Fig. 3.44).

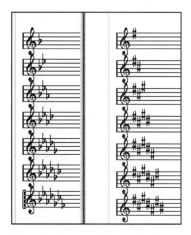

Fig. 3.41. Accidentals in keys

Fig. 3.42. The window for changing key signatures

Clef setting (Clef). The left slider allows you to select clefs. Keep in mind that there are various clefs in the notation so that the notes of the selected register can be positioned on the staff and thus avoid using a lot of ledger lines.

Information on the "special" clefs is for a limited circle of readers. Since operations with these clefs are the same as with the rest of the clefs, we will concentrate on the most common clefs: treble and bass.

Warning

You should not confuse similar clefs. The common bass clef is on the *fourth* line (example E in Fig. 3.43).

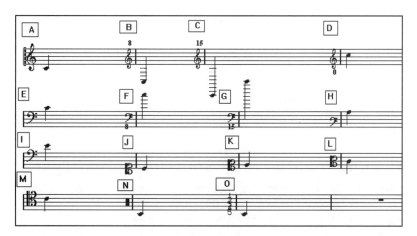

Fig. 3.43. The *C3* note in various clefs

You can clearly see from Fig. 3.43 how the same note is shown in each clef: the *C* of the one-line octave (*C3* in MIDI numbering).

☐ There are several variants of the treble and bass clefs illustrated (marked A, B, C, D, E, F, G).

❗ *Transposition by Octave*

The numbers 8 and 15 above or below the clef indicate the transposition of the staff by one or two octaves up or down, respectively. They may be used to avoid using many ledger lines when the register is moved.

In traditional notation, the symbols "8----" or "15 ---" are used. See *Section 3.11*.

Octave transport — the transition of the sounds by an octave up or down is used for recording some instrumental parts. For example, the piccolo plays an octave higher than the notes are **written**. The bass viol and the contra bassoon play an octave lower (if their parts are written in the treble clef), just as a singing tenor sings his part an octave lower if written in treble clef.

☐ The clefs of the C system are marked with the letters J–M. The alto clef, marked with the letter L, is used for the viola and trombone. The tenor clef (M) for the cello, bassoon, and trombone (with a lower range).

☐ The soprano (J) and mezzo-soprano (K) clefs are somewhat old-fashioned (they were used in vocal music, so their names correspond to the ranges of the human voice).

☐ There are two types of F system clefs: (H) — baritone and (I) — basso profundo, which are out of use now.

☐ The clef marked with the letter N is the one used in percussion scores and those of ancient music.

☐ Line numbering is used for a tablature (O) recording, but can be used for other purposes, such as educational ones. This numbering is changed according to the change of the line numbers (from 1 to 127).

Changing the key is the same as changing the key symbols. After double-clicking on the clef, the Edit Key window is opened, where the required clef is selected with the slider (Fig. 3.44).

❗ *Changing the Clef, Key Signatures, and Time Signature*

In order to change the clef, key signatures, or time signature *in any bar*, call the **Clef etc...** panel via the **Score/Symbol Palettes** menu (Fig. 3.44). Click on it and select the parameter to be changed. Then click with the **Pencil** tool on the required place of the staff and make the necessary changes in the window that opens (**Edit Clef** or **Edit Time Signature**). Then press **OK**.

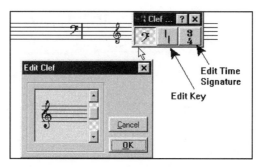

Fig. 3.44. Changing the clef, key signatures, and time signature

The Auto Clef option automatically determines the register and sets the corresponding clef on the staff: treble or bass.

Fig. 3.45 shows that the notes recorded in the *treble* clef (A) will be shown in the *bass* clef (B) after this option is applied. So the ledger lines disappear.

This option is switched off by default, so that all the notes are shown in the treble clef. The Auto Clef option works only when a *single-part* melody is set (Single).

▼ *Warning*

If the **Auto Clef** option is activated, then you can not change the clef "manually".

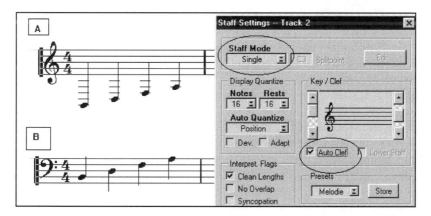

Fig. 3.45. Automatic clef setting with a single-voice melody

The Lower Staff option lets you select the *clef* and/or *key* separately for the lower staff (Fig. 3.46). It works only if there are *two* staves in the score.

This option may be used for creating multi-key music (where different parts are played in different keys).

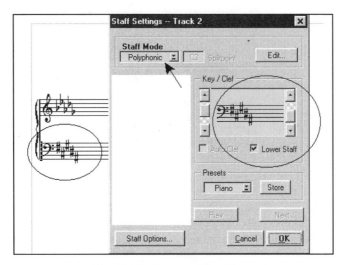

Fig. 3.46. Bass staff settings

3.2.3. Staff Mode. Polyphony

This section distributes the material along the staves — one or two — when one or several parts are recorded.

Fig. 3.47 shows the difference between recording one part and several parts. In the upper staff (A), there is a single-part recording, and notes that sound simultaneously have one stem. In the lower staff (B), there is a polyphonic recording, so that the stems of the different parts are reversed. The last note has two stems, which means that it is performed by *both* parts.

Remember that one part of each of the voices may consist of both single notes, and of intervals, chords, etc.

The options of this section will modify *any* recording to comply with the settings: **Single.** The material is presented as a single part on one staff.

Split writes a single part on two staves. The split of the part is mechanical — by the note shown in the **Splitpoint** field. All the material below this note is automatically placed on the lower staff (*always* in bass clef, regardless of the note in the **Splitpoint** field).

Fig. 3.48 shows a *single-part* melody (A), which is now written on two staves (B), as a result of applying this option.

Polyphonic allows you to present the material as a double-part score written on one or two staves. When this option is selected, the **Edit** button becomes active, which opens the **Polyphonic Settings** window intended for making the settings for a polyphonic score.

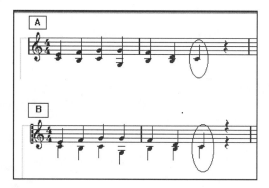

Fig. 3.47. Single and polyphonic recording

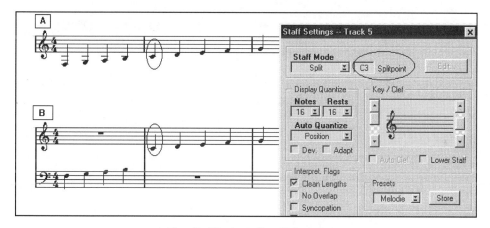

Fig. 3.48. A staff split in two

Fig. 3.49 shows this window with the default settings and the fragment of the score made after these settings were applied. You can see that the default setting is a one-staff recording.

The Polyphonic Settings window:

❐ ON indicates the number of enabled voices (max — 4). In order to enable a voice, check it by double-clicking the left mouse button. Clicking again disables the check — deactivates the voice. If you need to put the score on two staves, then you need to activate the voices of the different staves (Upper and Lower) in the SYSTEM column.

❐ VOICE shows the number of voices. In the example, voices 1 and 2 are active. It is duplicated in the score in the Score Edit Toolbar panel (shown by the arrow).

❐ SYSTEM shows the staff where the voice will be positioned (Upper, Lower).

❏ CHANNEL is the channel of the signal. The number of the channel can be changed, and the patch will be changed accordingly.

❏ RESTS shows or hides rests. These settings may be changed.

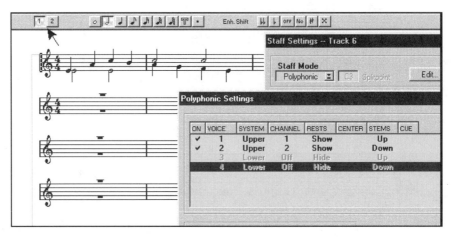

Fig. 3.49. Polyphonic default settings

▌ *Warning*

▎ Remember that the absence of rests (just as the absence of commas in a text) can make
● the notation unreadable. In some cases, however, such as when sub-voices are brought into a separate part, it make sense to hide the rests using this option.

❏ STEMS is the column in which you can change the direction of the stems for all the notes of this voice: turn them Up or Down.

❏ CUE makes the notes graphically smaller. Small notes are used for more dense note positioning in the bar, when, for example, there are many notes of short length in one of the voices (Fig. 3.50, upper voice).

Fig. 3.50. CUE (graphical reduction of the note size)

❏ CENTER shifts the rests to the center of the staff.

• You don't need to use it if the notes are not set far from the rests (Fig. 3.51, Example A).

- If the notes are shifted, then for the sake of "readability", the rests can be moved closer to the notes. To do this, check the checkbox for this part in the CENTER column (Fig. 3.51, Example B).
- If you shift the rests in both parts, then the rests will be combined into one (Fig. 3.52).

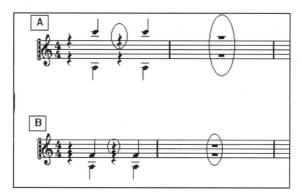

Fig. 3.51. The **Center** option: centering rests

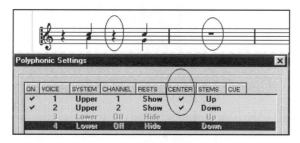

Fig. 3.52. The **Center** option leads to the combination of the rests in two voices

At the bottom of the Polyphonic Settings window, there is a section intended for distributing the notes among the voices. Fig. 3.53 shows its default settings.

Fig. 3.53. The default settings for automatic voice splitting

The settings in this section are valid only *when there is polyphony*: when the **Polyphonic** option is selected in the **Staff Mode** and two or more voices are activated in the Polyphonic Settings window. The results are noticeable only if there is a *sufficient* number of notes in the material for it to be split into voices.

The Lines to Voices and Bass to Lowest options let you select separate voices from the material: Lines to Voices — *upper*, Bass to Lowest — *lower*. (See details in *Section 3.3.4*).

3.2.4. *Display Quantize*. "Authorized" Lengths

The Display Quantize section specifies the *minimum* length of the notes and rests that are authorized to be shown in the score (Fig. 3.54).

This option is a sort of "power broker": its settings are not seen in the Score window, but it is exactly *these* settings that are the most important to the lengths of the score.

You can make the settings in the Display Quantize section *before* or *after* the score is created. They may be changed at any time, and these settings are related to scores created using *any* method.

Fig. 3.54. The **Display Quantize** section

We should mention that transforming the score using the settings of the Display Quantize section is very convenient.

Thanks to this function, notation entered, for example, from the MIDI keyboard can be made either extremely detailed or sparse (depending on the composer's idea).

The person playing the MIDI instrument will inevitably make at least slight rhythmic deviations from the computer grid. This is what differentiates a live performance from the mechanical production of sound.

In certain cases, deviation may be treated as an element of interpretation (e.g., swing), and there is no need to show it in the notation. But in others, the musician may need to have a complex rhythmical pattern shown in the notation.

There is, so to speak, a secret in the Cubasis Notation software in the Display Quantize section. Here its capabilities may be *temporarily* truncated down to the simplest note editors, or vice versa — expanded up to a professional level.

The Notes and Rests fields have the same drop-down lists (Fig. 3.55). Here you will find two columns of values, from a quarter to a sixty-fourth.

The main approaches are simple: the minimal lengths for this score are specified in the Notes and Rests fields. If "common" lengths are prevalent in the score, then you should select a number from the right column; if triplets prevail, select values with the letter T (Fig. 3.55).

▼ *Warning*

Selecting the length in the **Notes** and **Rests** fields means that notes (or rests) of the *shortest length* will *by no means* be shown in the score! The "norms" specified in the **Notes** and **Rests** fields are applicable to the *entirety* of the material being edited, and they *cannot be undone* in the **Score** window. But all the settings of this section may be changed at *any* stage of work.

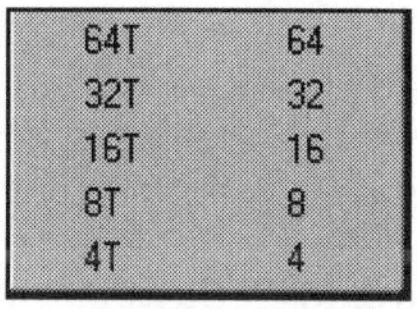

64T	64
32T	32
16T	16
8T	8
4T	4

Fig. 3.55. Drop-down lists
of the **Notes** and **Rest** fields

The selection you make in the Auto Quantize field is also important for all scores. When selecting a value for this option, keep in mind the following:

None — allows you to work with *homogeneous notation,* which contains *only* straight notes or *only* triplets.

If the score is uncomplicated — there are no triplets — check the None option and select the shortest length of the score in the Notes and Rests fields (without the letter T!).

▶ *Note*

It is this option that was used with a value of 4 in the **Notes** and **Rests** fields when the "Happy Birthday to You" score was adapted (see Fig. 3.13).

If there are *only* triplets in the score — which is almost impossible — this option is also applicable (select numbers with the letter T from the Notes and Rests fields).

Position — recognizes *mixed* notation and *takes into account the position of the note with utter precision.* You can check this option when there are both triplets and straight notes in the score. If the score is simple (without many triplets), this option can be used *without* the extra checks.

The Dev. checkbox (deviation) is checked for a *more accurate* identification of the note's position, and also the position of additional triplets that are not played exactly "in time".

The Adapt checkbox (adaptation) is used when the note position must be identified with absolute accuracy. The software developers recommend that you check this box *only* for a repeat examination of the notation (when not all of the triplets are found on the first try). If this checkbox is used in "mild cases", the software will find triplets where there are no triplets at all, since the slightest deviation from the "standard" will be subject to its "interpretation".

Distance — optimizes the notation, making it more readable due to a *slight prolongation of the lengths* and the *positional change of the notes on the offbeats*. This option is used when short notes in the score need to be slightly lengthened because the rests are set *after* the notes. Mind you, however, if the performance is *uneven*, this method is invalid, since the notes can be moved from the weak position to the next, strong one.

It is quite possible that these brief recommendations will be sufficient for score adaptation. When complicated situations arise, see *Section 3.3*, where these options will be described in more detail.

▼ *Warning*

If you enter the material from the MIDI keyboard in real time, then the performance must be as rhythmic as possible. Otherwise, the software may introduce considerable deviations in the notation, and the score will not look as you expected it to.

If the note of the selected length is *not shown* in the score, change the settings in the **Notes** and **Rests** fields and the **Display Quantize** section.

3.2.5. *Interpret. Flags*

The options of the Interpret. Flags section are mainly intended for interpreting the notation recorded while playing a MIDI instrument. Its settings are also valid for notation created by any method.

Fig. 3.56 shows the default settings.

Fig. 3.56. The **Interpret. Flags** section

The Clean Lengths option slightly "rounds" short notes — makes them longer (Fig. 3.57). If the application of this option does not bring you the desired result, lengthening the notes must be done manually.

Fig. 3.57. The **Clean Lengths** option

The No Overlap option removes tied notes. This option is applied only to notes recorded for *one* voice only.

Fig. 3.58 shows *four F* quarters and *one* whole *C* note recorded as four tied quarters (A).

After the No Overlap option is activated, the *C* note also becomes a quarter (B).

The important thing is that the pitch of the *C* note has *not changed — it did not become shorter* (this can be seen from the key imprints).

▶ *Note*

If you need to remove tied notes from the score without *shortening* the "appearance" of the length, split the notes into different voices.

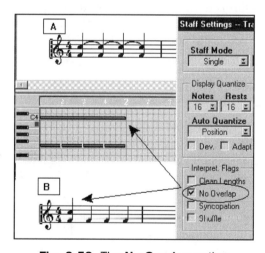

Fig. 3.58. The **No Overlap** option

Syncopation — the option intended for showing the notes as syncopes — without ties. See *Chapter 2* for the basic information on syncopes.

On the upper staff (A) in Fig. 3.59, there are notes crossing the borders of the beats, that are, therefore, tied.

The lower staff (B) shows that after the Syncopation option was applied, the ties were removed and the notes are shown as longer.

(The middle line in Fig. 3.59 is the one that shows the metric beats.)

Fig. 3.59. The **Syncopation** option

The Shuffle option is used for the software to recognize and show in the score the various notes: straight ones and triplets. Thanks to this option, the initial notation with the triplets (A) will be simplified (B) (Fig. 3.60).

Note

If such adaptation is not within the composer's idea, this option should be switched off.

The Shuffle option is common for jazz, where straight and irregular notes are used with equal frequency.

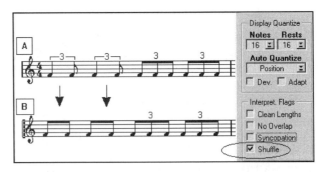

Fig. 3.60. The **Shuffle** option

Now we'll consider the Staff Options window, which is opened by pressing the button of the same name, and later we will go back to the last section in the Staff Settings window — Presets.

This section lets you save the configuration of the settings specified in *both* the Staff Settings and Staff Options windows as presets.

3.2.6. *Switches.* Note Grouping

The Switches section is for showing the note grouping.

Rules of grouping. Below is some brief information on why notes need to be grouped, and the principles of the procedure.

Note grouping is joining notes into groups according to the bar structure. When grouped, only short notes are joined with beams, which considerably enhances the readability of the score.

Fig. 3.61 shows two variants of notation: the wrong one (A), and the right one (B). In the upper staff, the notes are not grouped, so they are difficult to read: you need to scrutinize each to figure out its length by the tail.

When notes are grouped (B), short notes are joined by one beam, and the bar structure is clearly seen.

There are four beats that can be seen clearly on the lower staff (they are marked by a dotted line). You can easily find a note on the relatively strong beat, and you can see the number of notes for each click of the metronome, which marks the quarters.

Besides which, the beams make clear the position of the notes relative to each other, as if stressing the melody's motion: up, down, etc.

As a result of grouping, the notation becomes *considerably* more readable.

Fig. 3.61. The principle of grouping

Grouping notes is especially important in compound times. For example, when the compound time five-eight (5/8) is recorded, you can show it in one of two variants using grouping.

Fig. 3.62 shows that in the first case, three beats will be "beamed", whereas in the second case only two beats will be, and the musician can easily find the "relatively strong beat" (shown by the arrow).

Note

See *Chapter 2* for details on meters, downbeats, etc.

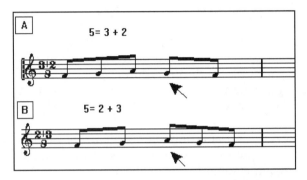

Fig. 3.62. Grouping notes in compound times

Grouping is different for notation for a *voice with text*, since the "law" here is not the meter, but the *syllabic structure of the language*.

Fig. 3.63 shows an example of wrong (A) and right (B) note grouping.

The lower staff (B) shows that only *two notes* are subject to grouping: those sung for one syllable (outlined). The rest of the notes are ungrouped, since a *separate* syllable corresponds to *each*.

Note

"Gaudeamus" (Latin *Gaudeamus igitur* — "Let's have fun") — the popular student song composed in the eighteenth century in Latin and sung to this day in many countries.

Fig. 3.63. Grouping in "Gaudeamus"

See *Section 3.4.4* for details on cancelling settings.

▶ *Tip*

If you need to write two parts *on one page* — one for the voice and one for the accompaniment — it is best to do so on different tracks, since different settings must be made in the **Switches** section for grouping lengths.

The procedure is the following. First, make the settings for each track. Then, after the parts are created, select *both* tracks in the **Arrange** window (with the <Shift> key pressed) and open the **Score** editor, e.g., with the <Ctrl>+<R> key combination. The result will be the correct grouping of notes for both parts — vocal and piano (Fig. 3.64).

Fig. 3.64. Note grouping in a voice-piano score

The change of the grouping in the score may be marked with special messages, enabling you to *locally* restore the grouping. See the details in *Section 3.4.4*.

Now we'll take a look at the options of the Switches section. All of them are intended to simplify notation as much as possible.

The Flat Beams option makes all the beams flat (horizontal) in the score, regardless of the pitch of the note (Fig. 3.65).

Sloping beams emphasize the note positions relative to one another, make the motion of the melody more clear and, therefore, considerably simplify the perception of the notation. Fig. 3.65 illustrates the various positioning of the beams: sloping (A) and flat (B).

If the Flat Beams option is deactivated, the slope is automatically selected. If *no* slope is needed, the beams remain flat.

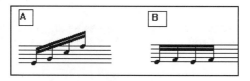

Fig. 3.65. Beam positioning

If the beam position is inappropriate *in only some cases*, you can change it manually (Fig. 3.66). Double click on the beam and, grabbing the square that appears with the mouse cursor, move it to the new place. You can change the length of the stems in the same way.

These changes can also may be marked in the score by special messages, and they can also return the beams and stems to the default position (see details in *Section 3.4.4*).

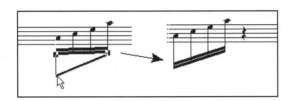

Fig. 3.66. Changing the beam's slope using the mouse

If there are many cases in the score where beams are crossed, e.g., due to the counter-motion of the voices, the Flat Beams option is recommended. This option is necessary when polyphony is created: in cases when sloped beams are to be rejected for the sake of the notation's readability (Fig. 3.67).

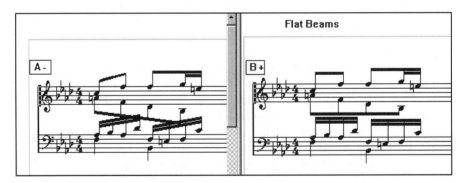

Fig. 3.67. The Flat Beams option

The No Beams option ungroups *all* the short notes: their beams are removed. This option is used when vocal parts are recorded.

► *Tip*

If you need to join some of the notes of the vocal part, select them by framing them with the mouse. Then use the **Group** option or the <Ctrl>+<Alt>+<G> key combination (Fig. 3.68).

The *Beam Subgroups and 16th Subgroups* options. The main rule for grouping short notes is the following: they are grouped *relative to the beats of the bar*. There are cases, however, when, for the sake of better visualization, another grouping is used: a finer or larger one. The **Beam Subgroups** and **16th Subgroups** options are intended for dividing the groups into smaller ones.

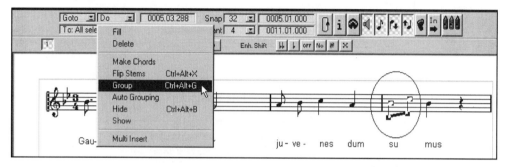

Fig. 3.68. Grouping notes manually in the vocal part

▶ *Tip*

It is not recommended that beginner musicians use these options. In the majority of cases, the automatic grouping done by the software when the **Beam Subgroups** and **16th Subgroups** options are *switched off* is sufficient.

Below are examples of how the **Beam Subgroups** and **16th Subgroups** options work.

If neither of the options is activated, then the notes are grouped automatically, according to the main rule — depending on the time signature. Fig. 3.69 shows that for *two*-two meter (A), notes are joined into *two* groups; when the meter is *four*-four (B), they are joined into *four* groups.

Fig. 3.69. The dependence of note grouping on the time signature

If the **Beam Subgroup** option is activated, then the groups within the beat are divided into subgroups (Example B in Fig. 3.70).

If the **16th Subgroups** option is activated, then the division is even finer (Fig. 3.71, Example B). The **16th Subgroups** option only works when the **Beam Subgroups** option is switched on.

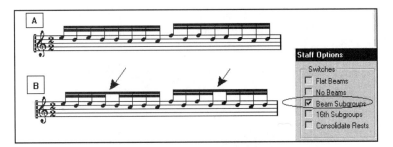

Fig. 3.70. Note subgrouping

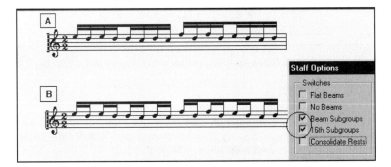

Fig. 3.71. 16th Subgroups note grouping

If you need to join several groups under one beam (Fig. 3.72, Example B), you need to frame the notes and apply either the **Group** option or the <Ctrl>+<Alt>+<G> key combination.

If, on the other hand, you need to select a note from *any* group (A), click on the note and apply either the Group option or the <Ctrl>+<Alt>+<G > key combination.

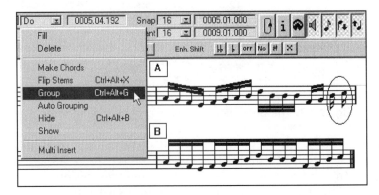

Fig. 3.72. Grouping and ungrouping notes

The **Consolidate Rests** option consolidates the rests. Fig. 3.73 (B) shows that when this option is checked, instead of two rests, only one is written, equal to them in length. This option may be used when dotted notes (and dotted rests) prevail in the score.

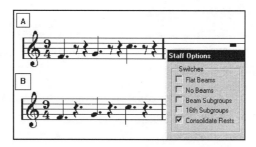

Fig. 3.73. Rest consolidation

3.2.7. *System*. The Staff

The System section of the Staff Options window is used for changing the appearance of the staff:

❑ The number of the lines from 0 to 127 can be changed in the System Lines field.
❑ The space between the lines (from –2 to 5) can be changed in the Add Space field.
❑ The score may be zoomed in the Size field — from 25% to 250%.
❑ The Track Name option is intended for showing or hiding the name of the track in the score. If it is unchecked, the name of the track is not shown in the score.

The names of the tracks are shown synchronously: when a change is made in the score (after a double-click), the name of the track is also changed in the Arrange window, and vice versa.

Fig. 3.74 shows the default settings of this section. For traditional notation, most likely you will not need to change these settings. But since the software is aimed at users of various levels of musical competence, changes in these settings may become necessary at some point.

▶ *Tip*

If you need to enlarge the scale of the score on the screen *only* for convenience when setting notes, do not change the settings in this section. You can change it in the drop-down list of the **Score** window, or enter a new value after double-clicking in the **Scale** field (Fig. 3.75).

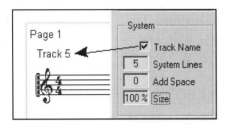

Fig. 3.74. Default settings
of the **System** section

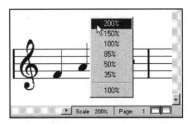

Fig. 3.75. Changing the scale
in the **Score** window

Fig. 3.76 illustrates *some* of the cases of changing the staff using the System section.

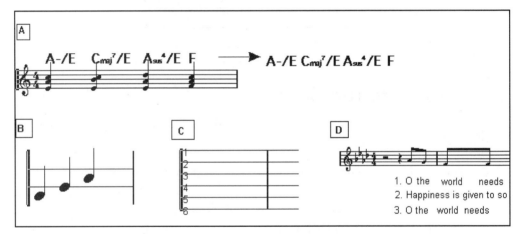

Fig. 3.76. Examples of using the **System** section

Consider these examples.

❑ *Example A.* When quick figuring is done, you can use the System Lines field. The figure shows that first the notes were played, then the Make Chords option of the Do menu was applied (the chords were lettered), and after that the notes were deleted with the Delete option in the Do menu and the lines were removed: there is a 0 in the System Lines field. As a result, the figuring of the score was done quickly.

❑ *Example B.* The initial stages of the music lessons with children sometimes requires an uncommon representation of the staff: enlarged notes and staves, a different number of lines on the staff — from 0 to 5, and sometimes even 11 (in the bass clef).

Music teachers can conveniently prepare educational materials using the software. The settings of this section allow you to enlarge the space between the notes (the Add

Space field), modify the scale (the Size field), and change the number of lines (the System Lines field).

❏ *Example C.* In order to create a tablature, where the lines represent strings, enlarge the number of the lines in the System Lines field, e.g., up to 6, and change the treble clef for special designation — line numeration.

❏ *Example D.* If the text in the score is more important than the staff (in songbooks), you can change the scale of the score in the Size field and add several verses of subscript text (Example D). The size may be varied by intervals of one percent — from 25% to 250%.

Of course, these are only general ideas for using the System section settings. Each user independently makes the settings that are necessary for his or her own situation. The main thing is to understand that there is a *huge variety* of staff settings in the Cubasis Notation software.

3.2.8. *Display Transpose*. Transposition

Transposition (from Latin *"transponere"* — move) is the shifting of sounds to another pitch. It is needed for:

❏ Changing the register (e.g., if you need a high-pitched voice to perform something lower)
❏ Changing the key to one more suitable for a certain instrument
❏ The readability of the notation (e.g., by moving the notes to a more customary octave or key)

All the relationships among the notes (alteration of the steps, chord structure) are retained during transposition, since every sound is kept at *the same* interval.

The variants of transposition in the Cubasis Notation software are many: changes in the notation and the pitch may be either interconnected or *independent* (Table. 3.1).

These types of transposition are capable of meeting *any* of a musician's demands. For example, you can:

❏ Print the score without changing the pitch
❏ Change the pitch in any way, leaving the most "convenient" key in the score
❏ Play the composition in a "simple" key, but get the score in a "complex" one — with many key accidentals, etc.

Table 3.1. Types of Transposition in Cubasis Notation

Type of transposition	Pitch	Notation
Using the mouse in the **Score Edit** editor	Jointly moved	
The **Transpose/Velocity** option (**Functions** menu)	Jointly moved	
The **Inspector** panel in the **Arrange** window	Shifted	Remains the same
The **Display Transpose** section (**Score/ Staff Settings/ Staff Options**)	Remains the same	Shifted

The Display Transpose section enables you to transpose the material "on paper": to represent the notation in different keys *without changing the real pitch* of the part.

The Display Transpose section is mainly intended for the parts of the *transposing instruments,* so that the parts of these instruments in the score can be written in compliance with the orchestral rules (in different keys), but so that they are played in a single key on the computer (as in a real orchestra).

The Display Transpose section can be used in other cases when you need to change the key *in the notation only* (without changing the actual sound of the part).

 Transposing Instruments

Transposing instruments are the "irregular" representatives of an instrument family. Their size is different, so with the same fingering, they sound either higher or lower. In order not to overload the score, the notation of their parts is the same as that of the main instrument.

If you produce the *C* note on a transposing instrument, the sound will correspond to another note, and it is this note that determines the *pitch* of this instrument.

For example, the clarinet in *A*, when playing the *C* note, gives an *A* note — i.e., sounds three semitones lower than it is written in the score.

For a trumpet tuned to *B*, the *C* note will be the *B* sound that is two semitones lower than the "regular" *C* note. (In Europe, the *B*-flat note is designated with the letter *H*, see *Section 2.8.2*).

In an orchestral score, the part of the trumpet is written in "its own" key (the part is marked: "Trumpet in *B*"). In order for the trumpet player to produce the *C* note (C3), a note two semitones higher should be written in the score — the *D* note.

There is a rule in "classical orchestral notation": the parts of transposing instruments are written with a deviation for the interval that corresponds to the pitch of the instrument.

In the *majority of cases*, however, small scores have the wind instrument parts written in the *real* pitch. Such notation is called *"C key score"* or *direction*.

Figuratively speaking, this function "serves two masters". It enables you to combine in one score the parts of trumpets, saxophones, etc., written in different keys, and what is more important, to *listen* to them in *one* key (common for all).

Below are some examples of the work of this section (Fig. 3.77).

Fig. 3.77. The **Display Transpose** section

In the upper field — Semitones — you can specify the number of semitones by which the score must be shifted. You can either enter these values from the keyboard, or select them by scrolling with the mouse buttons.

The range of changes is from −48 to 48. Remember that there are 12 semitones in the octave, so this option allows you to shift the notation up by 3 octaves or down by the same interval (if a negative value is selected).

The lower field offers several standard settings for 4 wind instruments (Fig. 3.78).

When one of these settings is selected, the notation is *shifted up* by the number of semitones necessary for the score of the same instruments:

❐   Trumpet — by 2 semitones
❐   Alto Sax — by 9 semitones
❐   Tenor Sax — by 14 semitones
❐   Baritone Sax — by 21 semitones

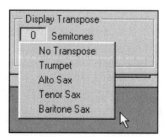

Fig. 3.78. The standard settings
for some wind instruments

For example, if the **Trumpet** option is selected, then the score will be shifted by 2 semitones *without changing the actual sound of the note* (Fig. 3.79).

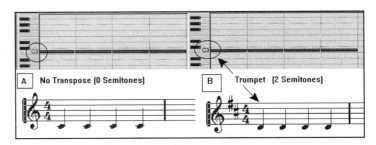

Fig. 3.79. Transposition "on paper" in the **Display Transpose** section

3.2.9. *Score Drum Map.* Percussion

This section is intended for creating a percussion part. Remember that in the General MIDI specification, Channel 10 is allotted for the percussion. So, if you need your arrangement to be compatible with a certain synthesizer or sound card, you first need to appoint the track for it in the **Arrange** window. Other channels, however, may also be used for the percussion (see *Section 2.3* for details on instrument selection).

The creation of the percussion part is subject to the *standard rules of work with the score*: the "limitations" in the Display Quantize section and the settings in the Snap and Quant fields.

As with any notation in the Score Edit editor, the percussion part can be an adaptation of a recording made in the Key Edit editor or played on the MIDI keyboard. But it can also be created directly in the Score Edit editor, and if it is, you will need to enliven the notation, or it will sound too mechanical. The procedures for this are given in *Section 3.12*.

There are several standards for writing parts of a percussion instrument. For example, the notes here are written on a so called *thread* — one horizontal line, which is justified: if the pitch of the instrument is *undefined*, only the rhythm is important in the notation.

You can convert the staff into a line with the **Single Line Drum Staff** option. The appearance is restored by adding lines in the **System Line** field (of the System section).

Fig. 3.80 shows parts of *different* tracks in one score. In order to open several tracks in one score, select the necessary parts in the **Arrange** window with the <Shift> key pressed, and then call the editor (<Ctrl>+<R>). The parts will be named automatically — according to the name of the track. You may change the names in the score, however (by double-clicking on the name), and the name of the track in the Arrange window will be changed synchronously.

► *Tip*

In order to apply the settings of the **Staff Options** window *synchronously* to all the tracks being edited, press the **Exit** button, and then, holding the <Alt> key, press the **OK** button in the **Staff Settings** window. Thus you may convert the staff for several tracks at one go.

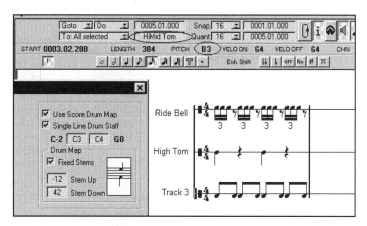

Fig. 3.80. The **Score Drum Map** section

The percussion parts may be written on a regular staff: this is offered in the standard Drums preset.

The five lines are more visual in terms of simultaneously showing the rhythm of *several* instruments on one staff, since each percussion instrument has a different pitch.

Professional percussionists can read such notation very easily if the "right" (regular) notes are chosen to designate the instruments. Putting the cart before the horse, we will say that the percussion part can be easily "rewritten" in the software; you just need to show the regular notes for the timbres in the drum map.

When the Fixed Stems option is checked, the length and direction of all the stems are specified in the Stem Up and Stem Down fields. The range of change is from – 99 (up) to 99 (down).

If the Use Score Drum Map option is checked, then the name of the timbre is shown in the Transpose/Pitch Box field (circled in Fig. 3.80). In traditional notation, this field shows the name of the note. The *real* pitch of the percussion note can always be seen in the PITCH field on the Info Line panel (circled).

If the part is written on one line (a thread), then there are three positions in which you can set the note: on the line, under the line, and above the line. This is controlled in the fields between the names of the outermost notes of the MIDI keyboard: C-2 and G8. The note (or notes) of the range specified here will be *on the line*. The rest of the notes will be set either above or below the line.

Actually, any sounds can be *simultaneously* written on the one-line staff, but we don't think this is very convenient. The length of the percussion sound, actually, does *not depend* on the percussionist. You cannot lengthen the sound of the drum beat (unlike that of the violin), and it is always expressed as a short note. But notation with an excessive number of rests is difficult to read, so it is necessary to look for a reasonable compromise when the lengths are chosen in the notation.

A percussion part often needs to have timbres "assigned" to notes of *different* registers. If the notation is done on five lines, it becomes much more complicated (Fig. 3.81).

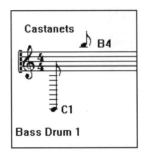

Fig. 3.81. Displaying percussion notes
without using **Drum Map**

This problem is easily solved: assign the "convenient" notes to be shown in the score to the timbres used.

Drum Map is used for this purpose. This is a very useful function, which allows you to choose only the percussion timbres that will be needed, and show them in the score as "convenient" notes — those that are easily readable and "writeable" on a staff.

The settings of the drum map are made in the **Drum Settings** window called from the Score/Global Settings menu with the **Drum Map** option.

The names of *all* the notes of the MIDI keyboard can be found in the **Pitch** column: from the lowest — C-2 — to the highest — G8. You can navigate through them using the scrollbar (on the right). The **Name** column contains the names of the timbers corresponding to the notes. If the name is missing, it means that the note is not used in this bank. You can not change the values in the **Pitch** and **Name** fields.

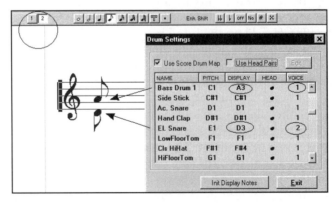

Fig. 3.82. Drum Map. The **Drum Settings** window

In order to show the sound in the score as a "convenient" note, enter the new name of the note in the corresponding line in the DISPLAY column. In this case, the timbre will be shown in the score as a note of the pitch selected by the user.

Fig. 3.82 shows that the more common *A3* note is selected in the DISPLAY column for the Bass Drum 1 timbre, and the *D3* note is used for the El Snare timbre. This is the way they will be shown in the score.

In order to clear these settings, press the Init Display Notes and Exit button, and all the notes will be written in the DISPLAY column and the score in accordance with their natural pitch.

If you need to split the percussion part into different voices, enter the numbers of the voices in the VOICE column. This service is available only when the settings of the Polyphonic Settings window allow you to show polyphony (see the Score Edit Toolbar panel, circled in Fig. 3.82).

Methods of changing the note head. In the notation, the percussion notes differ in their heads. There are several methods of changing the form of the note head.

After double-clicking on the note, the Note Info window will be opened. Click the Note Head field and select a new note head from the drop-down list (Fig. 3.83). This method can be used for *one note only* — the command is invalid for the rest of the notes of the same pitch.

You can clear all the settings of the Note Info window via the Score/Format menu in the Clean Up Layout window: check the Note Info option and press OK. All the note heads will be restored.

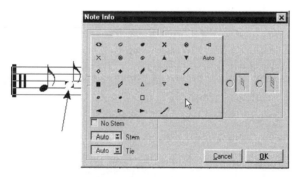

Fig. 3.83. Changing one note head

Changing the head of all the notes of one pitch is done in the Drum Settings window. Double-click the note symbol in the Head column, and make the selection in the field that opens (Fig. 3.84). *All* the notes of *this pitch* in the score will have the selected head form (the Use Score Drum Map option must be checked).

You can assign different heads for notes of one pitch: a "white" note will have a head of one design, and a "black" one will have another (Fig. 3.85, compare Examples A and B).

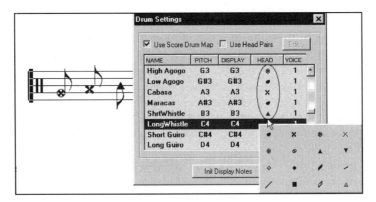

Fig. 3.84. Assigning a head to a note

Check the Use Head Pairs option, and click on the HEAD column. Select the head for the "white" note in the list that opens (the same as in Fig. 3.84). The head of the "black" note will be set automatically.

If the variant offered is not suitable, select the note head on your own. Click the Edit button, then click on one of the columns in the Head Pairs window that opens: WHOLE/HALF for a "white" note, FULL for a "black" note. Make the selection in the window that opens.

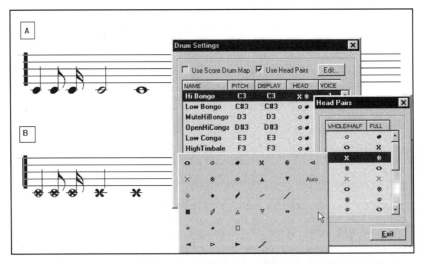

Fig. 3.85. Assigning various note heads in accordance with the lengths

Musicians who have never dealt with percussion parts may find it easier to write them "for private use" as notes of a regular part.

To do this, uncheck the Use Score Drum Map option of the Staff Options window, and set the notes as you would for typical polyphony (on two staves using the settings in the Polyphonic Settings window).

Of course, this will prevent you from using some capabilities, such as seeing the names of the timbres in the Transpose/Pitch Box field and programming the drum map. But on the other hand, the notes can be written immediately: you will not have to set them by pitch and voice in the Drum Map beforehand.

To conveniently show the "outermost" notes, you can use "clefs with eighths" (Fig. 3.86). Remember that such notation can always be transformed if it needs to be made understandable for the "live" drummer.

Fig. 3.86. The notation of a percussion part on four lines

In the Score Edit editor, you can use the same methods as you did in Key Edit for working with percussion parts (see *Section 3.13*).

3.2.10. *Presets*. Saving Settings

The settings made in the Staff Settings and Staff Options windows can be applied to one track only, to several tracks, or can be made a preset for later use.

> ## ❗ Warning
>
> If you need to apply the settings, the windows must be closed using the **Exit** and **OK** buttons, and not by clicking on icons.

The settings for one track are made as follows: open the Score Edit editor, open the Staff Options window from the Score menu (using the Staff Settings option), and make the necessary settings. Press Exit and OK.

If there are several tracks opened in the editor, you can make the settings for all of them *simultaneously*. The sequence of operations is the same as when setting one track, but you must press and hold the <Alt> key before pressing the OK button.

The Presets section is intended for using the presets offered in the software, or to create material of your own. The Melodie preset is the default one. Its settings are very simple and shown in Fig. 3.87: a one-part melody, no key signatures, limitation to sixteenth notes, treble clef, etc.

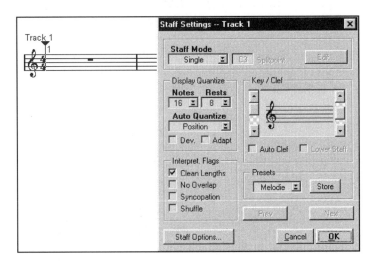

Fig. 3.87. The default **Melodie** preset

If you click on the Presets field, a list appears in which you can select the preset.

Fig. 3.88 shows the score of the **Piano** preset: here are two staves, different clefs (treble and bass), and polyphony (**Polyphonic**) is specified in the **Staff Mode** field. However, if you click on the Edit button — to see the polyphony settings — you might see that only two voices out of four are active (1 and 3), and rests are hidden in the lower voice.

The seven offered presets are examples — basic settings, and of course cannot be used in all cases.

If you want to change certain settings of an existing preset, select it in the list, make the necessary settings, press the Store button, and complete the operation by pressing the OK button.

It is very easy to rename the preset: select it from the list, enter the new name after a double-click, and press OK.

Empty is the basis for a new preset, and it is always at the bottom of the list. To create a new preset:

1. Select the **Empty** command from the drop-down list.
2. Make the necessary settings in the **Staff Settings** and **Staff Options** fields.

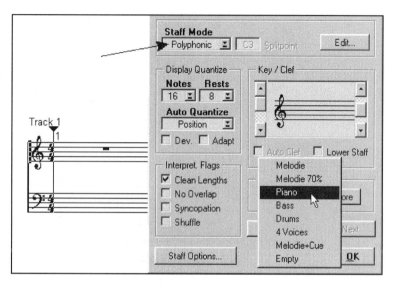

Fig. 3.88. The **Piano** preset

3. Double-click in the Presets field and enter the new name. Complete the operation by pressing the <Enter> key (or click outside of this field).

4. Press the **Store** button (a dotted line must appear). After performing such a sequence of operations, the name of the newly created preset will appear in the list, and the name **Empty** will be returned to the field, meaning that the software is ready to create another preset.

5. If the created settings are to be applied to the open file, then press OK; if you just wanted to create the preset for now, then the **Staff Settings** window must be closed by clicking on the x in the upper right-hand corner.

You can fix a frequently used key to a preset, as well as the space between the staves and the scale (the **System** section), note groups, clefs, voice distribution everything except for the time signature.

Remember that the meter of the score is changed in the **Edit Time Signature** window, invoked with a click on the time signature beside the clef, or, if the time signature is to be changed in the composition, via the **Score/Symbol Palettes/Clef ...** menu (See *Section 3.2.2* for details on changing the time signature).

Fig. 3.90 shows the purpose of the **Prev.** and **Next** buttons. They enable you to navigate the tracks in the score (up and down). The active track is marked with a black line at the beginning of the staff (shown with an arrow). The **Staff Settings** window shows the settings for this track. If necessary, they can be modified using the methods described above.

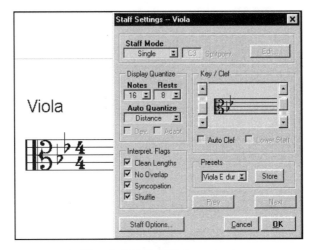

Fig. 3.89. The **Viola** preset

Remember that you can open several tracks at the same time if they are selected in the Arrange window with the <Shift> key pressed.

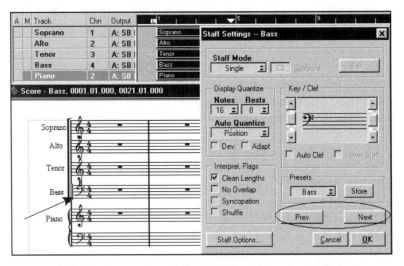

Fig. 3.90. Track navigation while making the settings

The presets are described below (*Section 3.3.1*).

The developers of Cubasis Notation give you a few variants of scores: for a choir, the piano, and a string quartet.

Now let's get in a little practice. We'll adapt a score entered from the MIDI keyboard.

3.3. Score Adaptation.
Recommendations and Examples

Score adaptation is a transformation of the notation to attain *maximum* readability for the musician.

In Cubasis Notation, this operation is done via the settings of the **Staff Settings** and **Staff Options** windows, which were described at the beginning of the chapter. Here are some practical methods.

As we already mentioned, notation is information addressed to a person. In order for the software to make a correct notation from the entered musical material, it is necessary to take into consideration certain issues: the score will look as expected only if the notes are distinctly dictated.

First. It is very important to perform the composition strictly observing the meter and rhythm — the downbeat must fall at the beginning of the bar, legato must be very accurate, etc.

If staccato is played, the score will be overloaded: there will be many rests and short notes. You should remember this if you plan to make a notation of the performed material.

When the tempo and rhythm are treated *ad libitum,* the software will interpret the part in a way different from expected, and much "manual" work will be needed to finish the notation if, for example, you'd like to print the score out.

Note

If you need to temporarily slow down or speed up the performance, you can make the preliminary settings in **Mastertrack**, but it would be better to make the recording in one tempo. With small rhythmical deviations, you can preliminarily quantize the part using the **Over Quantize** command from the **Functions** menu (*Section 2.20*).

To minimize rhythmical deviations, the material must be performed in a moderate or slow tempo kept by the metronome. The metronome is switched on (and off) with the Click button on the Transport bar. The tempo is specified in the field beside it (the default tempo is quite fast — 120).

It is extremely important to specify the correct time signature and perform the composition accordingly. Of course, notation will be created in any case, but due to the beat shifts, it may have a completely different feeling when performed by a musician later: imagine a march performed in waltz rhythm. Basic information on meters and time signatures is given in *Chapter 2.*

Experienced musicians can easily identify the time by ear. Below, we give a few methods for beginners.

The most important thing is to determine in how many beats the downbeat is repeated. To do this, you can count (to yourself of aloud), tap out the metric pulsation, wave your right hand (imitating a conductor's gestures), or switch on the metronome and perform the composition in various meters (you can also use the metronome variants on the CD (PRT files) for different meters).

Fig. 3.91 illustrates simple conductor patterns for three main meters: double (A), triple (B), and quadruple (C). The downbeat is always shown with a downward motion.

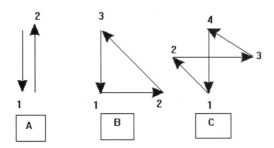

Fig. 3.91. Conductor patterns

▶ *Tip*

If the time was wrongly set, or you find that the score was shifted (e.g., all the downbeats fall at an upbeat), then this can be corrected. Shift the score back by inserting several rests at the beginning. Of course, you can change the time in a complete score, but it is better to specify the correct one at the start and perform the composition accordingly.

Second. It is important to specify the correct key. If you press the black keys, the software will record them all, but too "obtrusively": *every* note will have an alteration symbol. Such a notation with warnings at every turn — "Watch out for the sharp!" or "All clear" — is extremely difficult and sometimes impossible to read.

▶ *Note*

Natural is a symbol that cancels note augmenting or diminishing (see the details on setting symbols in *Section 3.10.6*).

This is why the alteration symbols are to be specified at the clef: once they are set at the beginning of the staff, they are valid for all notes with the corresponding name.

There is a simple method of identifying the key.

As a rule, a composition ends with the key note — the first and the most steady step of the key. So you can identify the key by the last note. (If the last note is not steady, it must be sung/played up until you do not want to continue the melodic motion any more.)

Knowing the key note, you can identify the key: whether the music was in major or minor. These two components — the name of the note and the tonality — make up the name of the key, and consequently, you can figure out how many accidentals are to be specified at the clef (see the details on keys in *Chapter 4*). Note that this method of key identification is *not suitable* in complex cases (when the key is changed in the course of the composition). Remember that when the key is changed, the key signatures at the clef also must be changed. The procedure is described in *Section 3.2.2*.

Table 3.2 shows the most common major and minor keys, as well as their corresponding signatures.

Table 3.2. Key Signatures and Tonalities

Major tonalities	Key signatures	Minor tonalities
C–dur	–	A–moll
Des–dur	5 flats	Bes–moll
D–dur	2 sharps	B–moll
Es–dur	3 flats	C–moll
E–dur	4 sharps	C#–moll
F–dur	1 flat	D–moll
Ges–dur	6 flats	Es–moll
G–dur	1 sharp	E–moll
Aes–dur	4 flats	F–moll
A–dur	3 sharps	F#–moll
Bes–dur	2 flats	G–moll
B–dur	5 sharps	G#–moll

Third. When the clef is selected, be guided by the register, and remember that ledger lines make the score more complicated (for more information on clefs, see *Section 3.2.2*).

3.3.1. Preset Description

Below are 15 presets with a description of their settings and visual examples of the score.

Presets 1–7 (original, factory presets) are in the def.all file. They are loaded to the song by default when the software is launched.

Presets 8–15 were created by the authors.

To help beginners, we created a separate song file for each preset (they cannot be saved otherwise in the software). All the presets are either saved in files of the same name as one additional preset to each original one.

In order to use the presets, copy the files from the Settings folder to the hard disk. Then select the required preset, save it as a new file, and start working.

The detailed list of settings is given to show how to select them for certain tasks and to provide examples of the setting variations.

We recommend the following:

❐ If you play a simple, one-part melody with one hand, select Preset 1 (Melodie), 4 (Bass), or 8 (Simple)

❐ If you play a melody with accompaniment with both hands, choose 3 (Piano), 6 (4 Voices), 9 (Song + Piano), or 10 (Normal All Presets)

❐ If you create a vocal part, choose 2 (Melodie 70%) or 12 (Vocal 2 voices)

❐ If rhythmically complicated music is to be written, pick 15 (Jazz), and if you have a complex polyphony, use 11 (Polyphonic)

❐ If you want to have all the offered presets available, load the Normal All Presets.all file

❐ If none of the offered settings are suitable for your score, amend them or create your own

Remember that if the settings are changed in the Staff Settings window and you *don't press* the Store button afterwards, the change will affect *only this score* — so you are free to make any "current" settings in this window (they will not change the preset).

▼ *Warning*

You will need to control the **Auto Move to Voice** option. After recording, in order for the software to distribute the material to two staves, open the **Staff Settings** window, press the **Edit** button, and *check* the **Auto Move to Voice** option in the **Polyphonic Settings** window. Then close both windows with the **OK** buttons. (This is applicable to presets with the **Polyphonic** option checked in the **Staff Mode** section).

The Melodie preset is loaded by default. Its settings are described in detail at the beginning of the table. The Settings column of both tables (3.3 and 3.4) contains *only the settings that differ* from this "standard". If there are no changes in the Settings column, it means that they coincide with the Melodie preset.

Table 3.3. Original Presets

Name of preset and ways of use	Score example	Settings
Melodie One-voice instrumental melody in treble clef. Notation is on one staff, *only* straight notes (no triplets), minimal length — sixteenth note. Attention: the sixteenth notes may be "rounded" to eighths due to rest removal (see the details on Note — 16, Rests — 8 in *Section 3.3.3*, Example 7).		Staff Mode: *Single* Key/Clef: *treble, C-dur, or A-moll* Auto Quant: *Position*, Note — *16*, Rests — *8* Interpret. Flags: *Clean Length* Switches: *Beam Subgroups* System: *Track Name, 5 System Lines, 0 Add Space, 100% Size* Display Transpose: *0 Semitones, No Transpose*
Melodie 70% Exactly the same as the **Melodie** preset except for the scale. Convenient for inserting lyrics.		System: *70%* Size
Piano Two-voice recording — 1st and 3rd on two staves. Rests are hidden in the 3rd voice. The melody may be recorded with the chords.		Staff Mode — *Polyphonic: activated voice 1 and 3, Rests — Hide — in 3rd voice;* *Split Note — C3, Lines to Voices, Bass to Lowest*
Bass One-voice part in bass clef.		Key/Clef: *bass*
Drums Two-voice recording of the percussion part one the 5-line staff. **Score Drum Map** is activated, so the name Sound is shown in the **Transpose/Pitch Box** field in the **Score** window.		Staff Mode — *Polyphonic: activated voice 1 and 2;* *Split Note — C3, Lines to Voices, Bass to Lowest* Key/Clef: *percussion* Use Score Drum Map

continues

Table 3.3 Continued

Name of preset and ways of use	Score example	Settings
4 Voices Four-voice recording on two staves (treble and bass clef) *without rest designation* on the lower staff.		Staff Mode – *Polyphonic: 4 voices are activated; Rests – Hide in the 3rd and 4th voices;* *Split Note – C3, Lines to Voices, Bass to Lowest*
Melodie + Cue Two-voice recording on the 1st staff in treble clef. High voice (small notes), the rests in the low voice are shifted to the center.		Staff Mode – *Polyphonic: activated voice 1 and 2; 1st voice – flag in the Cue column, 3rd voice – flag in the Center column*

Table 3.4. Authors' Presets

Name of preset (file on the CD) and its use	Score example	Settings
Simple (Simple.all) One-voice instrumental melody in treble or bass clef (set automatically depending on the note register). Rhythmically simple, recorded on one staff, consisting only of straight notes (no triplets), minimal length — eighth note.		Staff Mode: *Single* Key/Clef: *Auto Clef* Auto Quant: *None*, Note – *8*, Rests – *8* Interpret. Flags: *No Overlap, Syncopation*
Song + Piano (Song + Piano.all) A melody with accompaniment recorded on two staves, lengths vary: straight notes and triplets, minimal length — sixteenth notes, rests in voices — activated. Automatic splitpoint C3, so the notes cannot be transferred to another staff.		Staff Mode: *Split, Splitpoint C3* Auto Quant: *Position*, Note – *16*, Rests – *8* Interpret. Flags: *No Overlap, Syncopation, Shuffle*

continues

Table 3.4 Continued

Name of preset (file on the CD) and its use	Score example	Settings
Normal All (Normal All presets.all) Two-voice melody with accompaniment.	Normal All	Staff Mode: *Polyphonic, On: 1, 2, 4. Lines to Voices, Bass to Lowest, Auto Move to Voice, Split Note – deactivated, Rests Show, Stems: 1 – Up, 2 – Down, 4 – Down.* Interpret. Flags: *No Overlap* Auto Quant: Position. Note – 16, Rests – 16.
Polyphonic (Polyphonic.all) Four-voice polyphonic instrumental music: the 1st and the 2nd voices on the upper staff, the 3rd and the 4th on the lower staff (rests are present in both). Straight notes and triplets, minimal lengths and rests — 16; beams — flat. May be used for percussion.	 Polyphonic	Staff Mode: *Polyphonic, On: 1, 2, 3, 4. Lines to Voices, Bass to Lowest, Auto Move to Voice, Split Note – deactivated, Rests (1-4) – Show, Stems: 1 – Up, 2 – Down, 3 – Up, 4 – Down* Auto Quant: *Position*, Note – 16, Rests – 16 Switches: *Flat Beams*
Vocal 2 voices (Vocal 2 voices.all) Two–voice vocal music recorded on the treble clef. (Change the clef for male voices). Straight notes and triplets, minimal lengths — 16. No beams.	Vocal 2 Voices	Staff Mode: *Polyphonic, On: 1, 2. Lines to Voices, Bass to Lowest, Auto Move to Voice, Split Note – deactivated* Auto Quant: *Position*, Note – 16, Rests – 16 Switches: *No Beams*
Alto Sax (Alto Sax.all) The part of a transposing instrument — Alto sax. The difference between the score and the sound — 9 semitones: sounds in C-dur, notation in A-dur. One-voice melody, lengths — up to 16 (straights and triplets).	 Alto Sax	Staff Mode: *Single* Auto Quant: *Position*, Note – 16, Rests – 16 Interpret. Flags: *No Overlap, Syncopation, Shuffle* Display Transpose: *9 Semitones*

continues

Table 3.4 Continued

Name of preset (file on the CD) and its use	Score example	Settings
Drums 1 line (Drums 1.all) Percussion part recording on one staff. Percussion clef, straight notes and triplets, minimal length — 16.	Drums 1 Line	Staff Mode: *Single* Key/Clef: *percussion* Auto Quant: *Position*, Note — *16*, Rests — *16* Interpret. Flags: *No Overlap, Syncopation, Shuffle* Use Score Drum Map, Single Line Drum Staff, Fixed Stems
Jazz (Jazz. all) Rhythmically complex music, three voices, 1st and 2nd on the upper staff, 4th on the lower. Straight notes and triplets, minimal length — 32, rests — 16 consolidated.	Jazz	Staff Mode: *Polyphonic, ON: 1,2,4; Lines to Voices, Bass to Lowest, Auto Move to Voice, Split Note – deactivated, Rests 1,2,4 – Show* Auto Quant: *Position, Dev., Note – 32, Rests – 16* Interpret. Flags: *No Overlap, Syncopation, Shuffle* Switches: *Consolidate Rests*

3.3.2. The Score Adaptation Algorithm

The score is usually adapted after it is created. So create the notation of the score either in the **Arrange** window or in any editor. The main condition is a rhythmic performance. Then open the Score Edit editor (if the recording was made there) and make the corresponding settings in the **Staff Settings** and **Staff Options** windows.

The score settings can be made before recording, and then the finished score will best meet your requirements. The main question is what settings are to be made.

Some of the setting combinations are fixed in the presets. There are twelve examples in the sections below, showing the guidelines for selecting the settings for both lengths and voices. The rest of the settings of the **Staff Settings** and **Staff Options** windows were described above.

Here are some examples of the sequence of operations to be completed during score adaptation. In the first example, it is created either in the **Arrange** window or in the Key Edit editor, and in the second it is done in the Score Edit editor.

Example I. Track recording.

1. Create the track in the **Arrange** window.
2. Set the time and tempo on the **Transport** bar (called from the Windows/Show **Transport** Bar menu). (Open the Key Edit editor if you plan to make the recording there). Set the cursor to the starting position of the recording.
3. Switch on the metronome on the **Transport** bar with the Click button, perform the part, and record the track (either in the **Arrange** window or in the Key Edit editor).
4. Open the Score Edit editor for the created track.
5. Select the **Staff Settings** option from the **Score** menu and select the required preset in the **Presets** section. Then, if necessary, specify the key in the **Key/Clef** section and press the OK button.

Make your own settings in the **Staff Settings** and **Staff Options** windows if none of the presets meets your requirements (in order to apply the settings, exit these windows pressing the **Exit** and **OK** buttons). If necessary, do the required editing with the mouse.

Example 2. Recording in the Score Edit editor.

1. Create a part in the **Arrange** window, or open the file from the **Presets** folder with the created part for 20 bars with all the necessary settings.
2. Open the Score Edit editor (<Ctrl>+<R>).
3. Open the **Staff Settings** window in the **Score** menu and make sure that the required preset is specified in the **Presets** section. Then press the OK button.

    If there is something wrong, change the settings. If necessary, change the key with the slider in the **Key/Clef** section of the **Staff Settings** window. In order for the selected key to be applied to the score, close the **Staff Settings** window with the OK button.

    The time can be changed in the **Edit Time Signature** window. It is invoked by double-clicking on the time signature beside the clef. If the window fails to open, then check the cursor — it may be set on the time signature. If it is, move it aside.

4. Call the **Transport** bar, set the tempo, and switch on the metronome with the Click button.

    Before the recording starts, the metronome clicks two bars of introduction. You can change this setting in the **Metronome** window (the **Options** menu, **Metronome** submenu).

5. Switch on the recording with the Rec button on the **Transport** bar, or with the <9> key on the main keyboard.

6. Perform the part with the proper rhythm. Note that the downbeat must fall strictly at the beginning of the bar (the loud click of the metronome). Maintain the legato during the performance — "hold" the proper lengths.

7. Stop the recording with the Stop button or the <0> key on the additional keyboard.

8. If necessary, do some additional editing using the mouse. If there are too many mistakes, you would be better off replaying the part.

Two methods of effective editing. In the majority of cases, after the "automatic" adaptation of the score, some operations need to be completed manually.

Below are examples of the two most common operations: moving a note from one voice to another, and changing the length.

Moving a note from one voice to another is done via the Score menu.

Highlight (select) the notes to be moved (click on them with the <Shift> key pressed or frame them with the mouse). Then select the Staff Functions option from the Score menu and the number of voice to which the note will be moved in the Move to Voice drop-down list.

Fig. 3.92 shows that the *A* and *B* notes recorded on the bass clef staff with five ledger lines for the left hand part were moved to the first (higher) voice.

If the voice in the Move to Voice submenu is dimmed, it means it is not active. You can activate different voices in the Polyphonic Settings window, which is opened with the Edit button in the Staff Settings window.

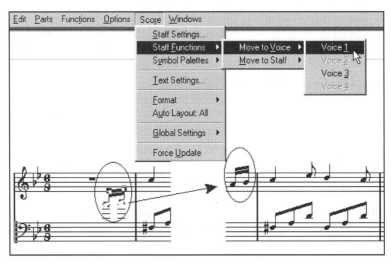

Fig. 3.92. The **Move to Voice** function

It is much more difficult to read a score with many tied notes. This may happen if (Fig. 3.93):

❏ The note failed to sound for the entirety of its length, since the keys were released earlier (Example A).
❏ The performance was rhythmically inaccurate — a key was pressed a little before or after the beat and, as a result, the note was somehow moved (Example B).

 Note

An inaccurate performance can be quantized with the **Over Quantize** function, but this operation should be used selectively (see *Section 2.20*). In more severe cases, it is easier to correct the score manually.

It is better to avoid ties when they are not absolutely necessary (as in polyphony), but only indicate the increase of the length. In order to remove unnecessary ties, you need either to increase the length or move the notes.

If the chord is tied (Example A), you should first remove (erase) its second tied part and then increase the length of each note of the main chord (Example C).

One of the methods of length change is the following: select the icon of the required length on the Score Edit **Toolbar** panel and click on each note of the chord, holding the <Alt> key pressed. (If you need to change the length into a triplet or dotted note, then, after clicking on the icon, click on the letter "T" or the dotted note icon.)

⚠ Warning

All operations with the notes done with the mouse (changing the length, position, etc.) affect the sound.

To move a note, grab it and move to another place. (As a result, Example B turned into Example D).

Fig. 3.93. Correcting the length

The length of the tied note may be shortened: erase its second part with the Eraser tool.

Simple recommendations are helpful in simple cases only. The variants of scores are many. Below are twelve examples, since the main problems occur when lengths and voice splitting need to be shown in the score adaptation. They demonstrate how the "main" sections — Display Quantize and Staff Mode — work, and help the musician make the proper settings in each case.

3.3.3. Length Settings

Examples 1–3 illustrate the operation of the None, Position, and Distance options in the Auto Quantize field. This section is mainly intended for automatic adaptation of notation recorded from the MIDI keyboard.

However, it also affects the appearance of *any* score, including those where the notes are positioned with the mouse. Briefly, these options are the following.

❒ None — the "straight" option. It shows either straight notes or triplets.

❒ Position — the most "precise" option, showing the "actual state of affairs" (unless there are restrictions in the Notes and Rests fields).

❒ Distance — the option "optimizing" the notation (including a mixed score) by "rounding up" short notes to sixteenth notes. It forbids short notes in the score (even if they are authorized in the Notes and Rests fields).

So if there are *only* straight notes in the score, or only triplets, then the None option should be checked. If the notation is "mixed", check the Position or Distance options, as they enable you to *simultaneously* show both straight notes and triplets.

Example 1. The None option — "no shades" — represents *any* notation in compliance with the settings in the Notes and Rests fields. If straight lengths are set in these fields, then the option "sees" only these, without the triplets. If there are figures with a T in these fields, the software finds only triplets, and *absolutely all* lengths are marked as triplets.

This option should be switched on only when the notation is "homogeneous" — contains only straight notes or triplets (the latter happens extremely rarely). Fig. 3.94 shows that "regular numbers" should be set in the Notes and Rests fields for a score containing only straight notes (example A). If values with a T are set, then the score will be distorted: the software will move all the notes, "looking for" the triplets (Example B).

Example 2. If the notation is mixed, check the Position option. Fig. 3.95 shows that when this option is switched on, you can set any notes in the bar: straights or triplets.

The Dev. and Adapt checkboxes are needed to more accurately identify the note positions and recognize triplets played "out of time".

The Adapt flag is used when not all of the triplets are found at first sight. The developers of the software recommend that you check this box for a *second revision only*. If it is used in simple cases, then the software will find triplets where there are no triplets at all, since the slightest deviation from the standard will be treated as a triplet.

Therefore, the Position option should be checked when short notes are *important* in the mixed score (the software does not "round them up"). And short lengths should be specified in the Notes and Rests field.

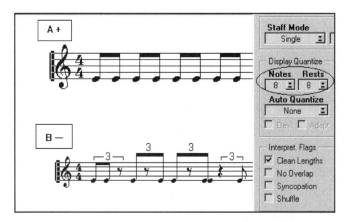

Fig. 3.94. The **None** option

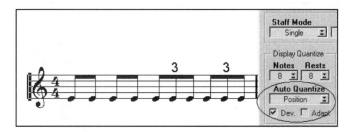

Fig. 3.95. The **Position** option: mixed score notation

Example 3. The Distance option simplifies the notation to sixteenth lengths (Fig. 3.96, Example B).

When the Distance option has values of 32 and 64, the lengths are "rounded" and sometimes moved to stronger positions. These shifts are not so large since the lengths are very short, so you can actively employ the Distance option. It also shows both straight notes and triplets (as in the Position option).

▼ *Attention!*

You cannot insert short lengths in the score when this option is checked.

Now let's consider the principles of specifying the lengths of notes and rests in the Notes and Rests fields. These settings are "restrictive" when working with the described options.

Example 4. If the lengths of the notes and rests in the Notes and Rests fields are *not shorter than those of the entered notes*, the notation will represent the sound with utter precision (the most accurate recording is with the Position option checked). But often, such notation is extremely detailed and visually difficult: there are many short rests and notes (Fig. 3.97).

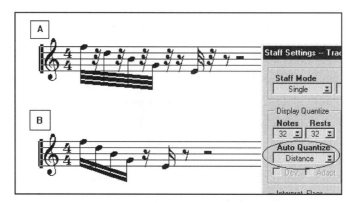

Fig. 3.96. Distance: score simplification

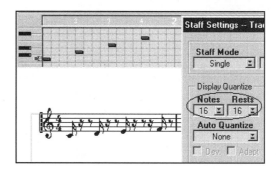

Fig. 3.97. Short notes and rests in a score

Example 5. The values in the Notes and Rests fields are "restrictive" — their length is longer than the length of the entered notes. In this case, the notes of the score are "forcedly" shown as longer notes.

Enter sixteenth notes (with the mouse or from the MIDI keyboard) and make some restrictions in the Notes and Rests fields. As a result, sixteenth notes in the score will be "rounded up" to those of longer length: eighth notes (Fig. 3.98) or quarter notes (Fig. 3.99).

When longer lengths are shown, the score looks simpler: there are no short notes and rests, but the meaning has not changed — the sound of the score remains the same (see the key imprints in the illustrations).

It is best not to overload a score intended for a musician with short notes and rests, but rather to record these notes as longer ones with a *staccato* symbol (compare Figs. 3.97 and 3.99).

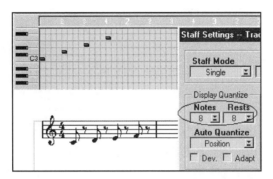

Fig. 3.98. Restricting notes and rests to an eighth in the score

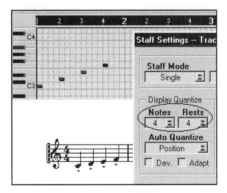

Fig. 3.99. Restricting notes and rests to a quarter in the score

Staccato and Legato

Staccato and legato are the two main methods of extracting sound (accents, shades). *Staccato* (broken, separate) is an instruction to play notes shortly, separating them with rests. Staccato is designated either with the word "staccato" or with dots *above* or *below* the heads of the notes (Fig. 3.99).

Legato (tied) is the smooth transition from one note to another without breaks. Designated either with the word "legato" or a tie (arched line) embracing the corresponding notes.

Example 6. The computer musician is the composer and the performer in one. He or she can solve various tasks when making the score, depending on the settings.

Case A. Suppose that during the performance, the composer *deliberately* presses a key later than it should have been played, and *wants to show this shift in the score.* The settings in the Display Quantize section make this possible: the values in the Notes and Rests fields must be quite small in order to show short notes and rests (with the None or Position options checked) (Fig. 3.100).

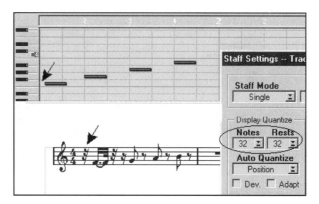

Fig. 3.100. Shades of a performance shown in the score

Case B. If the delay of the note *should not* be shown in the score (if it was a performer's touch, or just a mistake), then it would be best to specify bigger values in the Notes and Rests fields of the Display Quantize section so that this shift does not affect the score (Fig. 3.101).

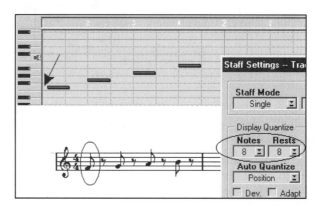

Fig. 3.101. Leveling the rhythmical deviations in the score

Example 7. You can remove unnecessary short rests from the score. This is done by making limits in the Rests field.

You can see from Fig. 3.102 that in the Rests field, the limitation was set *only* for the display of rests.

As a result of this operation, only *some* of the rests were removed from the score (Example B) — those in the weak positions — and their removal did not move the notes from their positions. The rests did not completely disappear, but increased the length of the preceding notes.

For clarity, some of the borders of eighth beats are shown by a dotted line. The *weak position* of the rest means that it is not at the *beginning of the beat* (they are circled in Example A).

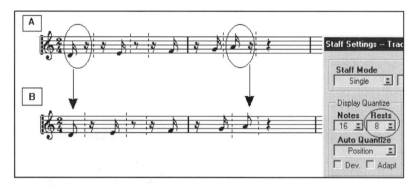

Fig. 3.102. Removing short rests from the score

Example 8. We do not recommend that you increase *only* the length of the notes in the Notes field, since the score will be distorted beyond recognition if there is even the slightest deviation from the rhythm.

Fig. 3.103 shows that the notes "willing" to be increased cross the permitted borders: they move to other beats and bars, "crawl" over each other, etc.

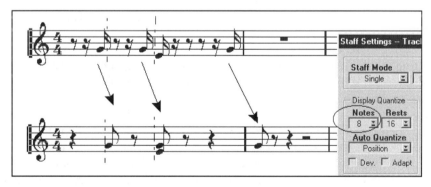

Fig. 3.103. Increasing the value in the **Note** field
(not applicable to an uneven performance)

3.3.4. Splitting into Voices

The options in the lower part of the **Polyphonic Settings** window (called with the **Edit** button in the **Staff Settings** window) enable you to quickly split the material into voices.

Example 9. The Split Note option shows the border where the notes will be split into parts (Fig. 3.104).

The *C* note and all those *above* it are moved to the higher voice, and the rest go to the lower voice.

► Note

The **Auto Move to Voice** option must be checked, and the **Lines to Voices** and **Bass to Lowest** options unchecked.

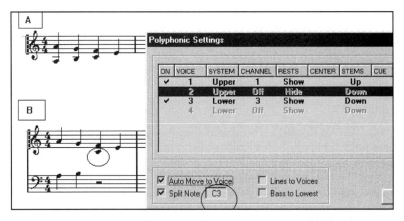

Fig. 3.104. Automatic voice splitting by the specified note

Example 10. The Lines to Voices and Bass to Lowest options are intended for splitting the entire material for one-voice parts. The Bass to Lowest option marks the *lower* voice, and the Lines to Voices option from 1 to 4 separate *high* voices (according to the number of checked options in the ON column). These options are useful only when there is a sufficient number of notes in the score for it to be split into voices.

If there are *two* voices checked in the ON column, then when the **Auto Move to Voice** and Lines to Voices options are checked, the highest notes go to the high voice, with the rest of the material remaining in the low voice (Fig. 3.105, Example B).

Example 11. If there are three checks in the ON column, then the material is split into three voices (Fig. 3.106, Example B).

Example 12. If there are four voices checked in the ON column, then the melody (A) is transformed into a four-voice melody, where *each* voice is emphasized (Fig. 3.107, Example B).

If there are more notes than voices in the material, they are always in the lower voice (circled on the illustration).

Example 13. The Bass to Lowest option allows you to emphasize the *low* voice (Fig. 3.108).

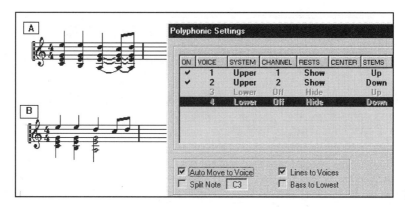

Fig. 3.105. Two voices (with the high voice emphasized)

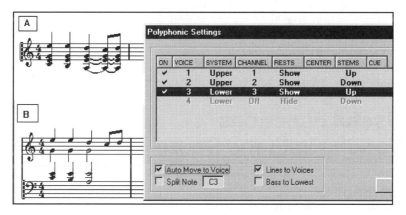

Fig. 3.106. Three voices (with the high and middle voices emphasized)

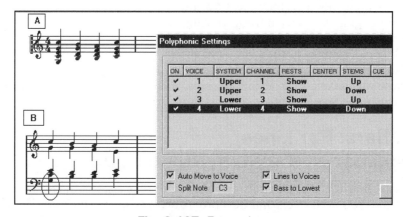

Fig. 3.107. Four voices

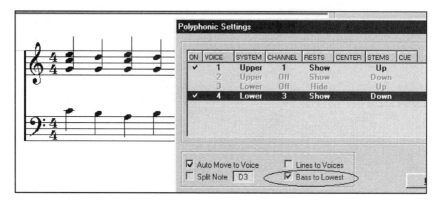

Fig. 3.108. Two voices (with the low voice emphasized)

To sum up, note that the Lines to Voices and Bass to Lowest options can be used for work with vocal parts too. But if the voice lines cross, then manual editing (described below) will be necessary.

You can specify any clefs on both the upper and lower staff of the score in the Score window (see *Section 3.2.2*).

3.4. Useful Functions for Working with the Score

This section describes the software settings that make the best score possible on the screen. We are deliberately considering this before describing the methods of handling notes with the mouse, since the preliminary settings may eliminate many questions beginners might have, such as how to make three bars instead of four on the staff, how to set a symbol closer to the note, how lines can be moved apart, etc. Such awareness saves the beginner musician from a feeling of helplessness every time he or she has to work with a "smart" machine.

The main settings of the score have already been made, and they are related to the notation (Score menu, Staff Settings submenu).

Now we'll take a look at the "decorative" settings, which affect the appearance of the score in the Score menu.

3.4.1. Bars: Bar Lines, the Number on the Staff, Numeration

Notes are positioned in a bar. By default, the graphic sizes of the bars are identical, but sometimes you need to expand the borders of a bar so that the notes do not crawl over each other.

If such cases are rare, you may do it manually, by clicking on the bar line and dragging it to a new place holding the left mouse button pressed (Fig. 3.109). The same method is used for shortening the line: move the first or the second bar line.

Fig. 3.109. Moving the bar line using the mouse

This method is simple, but sometimes it is not sufficient when you need to move bars to another staff. In this case, use the Scissors and Glue Tube tools.

If you click with the Scissors tool on the bar line, the notation on this staff will be distributed to two staves. Fig. 3.110 shows that, using the Scissors, the last bar of the upper staff (A) was "cut off" and moved to the next staff (B).

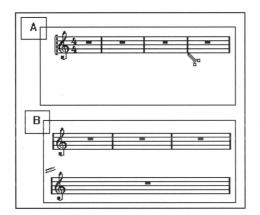

Fig. 3.110. Cutting the bar using the **Scissors**

The Glue Tube tool can be used at the end of the staff only. It "glues" *all* the bars of the next staff to the previous one. Fig. 3.111 shows that, after this tool is used, all the bars of two staves (A) were positioned on the upper one (B).

If there are many bars in the score that need to have their time changed, you can accelerate this process using the options of the Number of Bars window.

You can specify the number of the bars on the staff for this score using the **Bars across the Page** field of the **Page Mode Settings** window invoked in the Score/Format menu. Below are the three options this setting will be applied to:

❏ All Systems — for all staves on all pages.
❏ All following System — for the active staff and all subsequent ones.

❏ This System only — only for one active staff. Note that in order to activate the staff, you need to click on it: a black line then appears at the beginning of the staff.

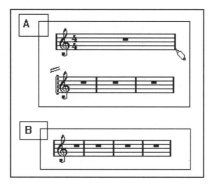

Fig. 3.111. Changing the number of bars using the **Glue Tube** tool

In order to change the number of bars, specify the required value in the **Bars across the Page** field, check the required option, and close the window with the **OK** button.

 Note

The default value in the **Bars across the Page** field (Fig. 3.112) can be changed; if it is, then when this window is opened, it will contain a new value (not the "standard" 4). The procedure is described below.

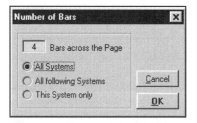

Fig. 3.112. The **Number of Bars** window

Fig. 3.113 illustrates an example of using the options of the Number of Bars window.

The initial All Systems setting was 4 bars, then the second staff was selected, and the value 7 was specified with the All following System option for all the *subsequent* staves (the previous staff excluded). After this, the change was made on one staff with the This System only option.

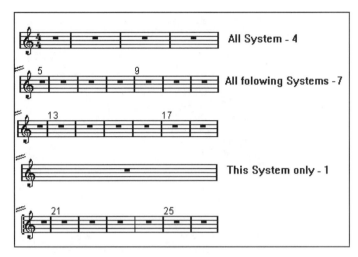

Fig. 3.113. The **Number of bars** option

When the bars are numbered, musicians feel that it is easier to work with a big score, or to print some of the parts. The procedure for this is the following.

The user can specify any period for bar numbering (or cancel the numbering altogether). This is done in the right part of the **Global Settings** window, when the **Bars** category is selected (Fig. 3.114).

Specify the number in the **Bar Numbers Every** field, which indicates the periodicity of the bar numbering: 1 — each bar, Off — no numbering, 4 — every fourth bar will be numbered, etc.

The **Default Bars across the page** field is used for changing the number of bars that will be placed on the staff by default (this value is for the **Bars across the Page** field (Fig. 3.112).

You can change the bar numbering by clicking on the number of the bar and specifying by how much the new number must differ in the **Barnum Offset** window (bar number settings) that opens. A positive number increases the number, while a negative one decreases it. Fig. 3.115 shows that the number 3 is changed to 13 in this way.

You can return the previous number either by setting 0 in this window for this bar, or via the **Clean Up Layout** window.

You can also change the appearance of the bar line by clicking on it and selecting the required variant in the **Bar Lines** window that opens (Fig. 3.116). The reprise symbol (a bar line with two dots) indicates the repetition of a fragment. If the **Hide** option is selected, then the bar line will be hidden.

You can either combine or separate the bar lines among several tracks.

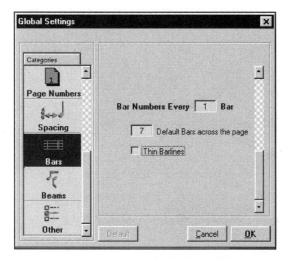

Fig. 3.114. The **Bars** option in the **Global Settings** menu

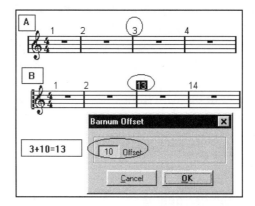

Fig. 3.115. Changing the bar numbering

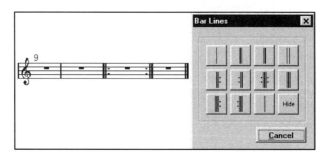

Fig. 3.116. Changing the bar line

By default, these bar lines of open tracks are combined into one. If you need to make them separate for each staff, click with the **Eraser** tool on the last bar line (Fig. 3.117, Example A). If a combination will be needed, click with the **Glue Tube** tool on one of the bar lines of the upper staff (except for the last one) (Example B).

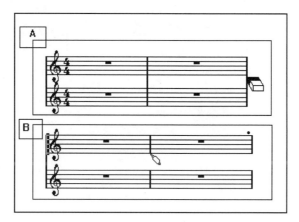

Fig. 3.117. Removal and restoration of single bar lines among several parts

3.4.2. Space between Score Elements

There is a function in the Cubasis Notation software that allows you to optimally position the score. This is done with the **Auto Layout** option in the **Score** menu. It distributes the notes of the score "at the discretion of the software". Of course, this method is quick and convenient, but there are two things to be taken into account. First, this method requires a lot of RAM (the operation will not be done unless the RAM is sufficient). Second, the distribution of the score concerns only the notes and *related symbols*, i.e., some of the symbols not related to the notes may remain unchanged. So, first apply this function and then set the symbols in the score.

❗ *Warning*

If the software does not "redraw the picture" of the score, check the **Force Update** option in the **Score** menu — the appearance will be updated, and another, correct variant will appear on the screen.

You can "adjust" the automatic distribution of the score by setting the required values in the Score/Global Settings menu.

The settings described below are applicable not only to bar positioning, but to all the rest of the elements of the score. Of course, in many cases the default values are sufficient, but sometimes changes are necessary.

Select the Spacing category from the Score/Global Settings menu in the Global Settings window, and in the list in the window on the right, change the settings controlling the space between the score elements (notes, rests, symbols, clefs, etc.). To do this, you can enter new values from 2047 to –2047 in the window that opens (Fig. 3.118).

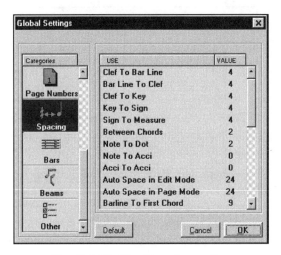

Fig. 3.118. The **Spacing** option
in the **Global Settings** menu

Note that these settings are the "basic" ones for the score: the space set here is minimal — you can not make it *less* when you manually edit the score.

Table 3.5. Space between Score Elements (*Global Settings/Spacing*)

Space between score elements	Example	Option
From the bar line to the clef (at the beginning of the staff).		**Bar Line To Clef**
From the clef to the bar line (when the clef is changed).		**Clef To Bar Line**
From the clef to the key signatures (at the beginning of the staff).		**Clef To Key**

continues

Table 3.5 Continued

Space between score elements	Example	Option
From the key signatures to the time signature.		**Key To Sign**
Between the key accidentals on *each* staff.		**Accidentals In Keys**
1st bar position on *each* staff.		**X Offset For First Bar Number (vertical)**
		Y Offset For First Bar Number (horizontal)
Number position of the rest of the bars on *each* staff.		**X Offset For Other Bar Number (vertical)**
		Y Offset For Other Bar Number (horizontal)
Space between the track name and the staff.		**X Offset Track Name (vertical)**
		Y Offset Track Name (horizontal)
Minimal space between the notes/chords.		**Between Chords**
From note to dot (for dotted notes).		**Note To Dot**
From the note to the accidental of the next note.		**Note To Acci**
From the accidentals to notes and between the accidentals in the chord.		**Acci To Acci**

continues

Table 3.5 Continued

Space between score elements	Example	Option
From the bar line to the first note (chord) in *each* bar.		**Barline To First Chord**
Tie form (for tied notes and legato symbol): curve, line thickness.		**Top Of Tie** **Tie Thickness** **Head Symbol Ties** **Slur Thickness**
Move line separator to the left (along the staff).		**Staff Separator X Distance**
Space between the grace notes.		**Behind Grace Notes**
Minimal space between the staves (valid after the **Auto Layout** option is checked).		**Min between Staves**
Minimal space between the text syllables under the notes. Valid after the **Auto Layout** option has been checked.		**Min Between Lyrics**
Minimal space between the bar elements (notes, rests). Valid after the **Auto Layout** option has been checked. The bigger the value, the fewer bars there are on the page.		**Auto Space in Page Mode**

If you select the Other category from the Score/Global Settings menu, then you can make settings related to the appearance of the score in the window that opens.

Table 3.6. Other Details on Positioning Score Elements (*Global Settings/Other*)

What the checked option does	Example	Option
The first bar in the score will be numbered as 0001, even if the score starts later.		**Start at Position 0**
The size of the clef when changed will be smaller.		**Small Change Clef**
Different rest designation for a few bars.		**Church Multi Rest**
Number *above* the rest.		**Multi Rest Number Up**
Automatic positioning of bar numbers.		**Auto Bar Number Space**
Triplets are *not marked* with brackets.		**No Triplet Bracket**
Triplets marked *above* the stems.		**Triplets above Stems**
Change of clef, key accidentals, and the time signature is *not marked* at the end of the staff, but before the next staff.		**No Change Clef/Keys at End**

Automatic note positioning within the bar. The Cubasis Notation software can automatically set the space between notes within the bar. This is done by selecting the option in the Spacing field in the **Page Mode Settings** window of the **Score/Format** menu (Fig. 3.119).

Fig. 3.119. The **Page Mode Settings** window

You can select one of three options from the drop-down list of the **Spacing** field, and set the most suitable variant of the note position within the bar for this score. It is recommended that you do this by trying the options out and seeing when the score looks best (the notes are set freely, the notation is readable, etc.). But the developers still provide you with a basis for choosing:

❑ Regular — the default setting. Recommended for melodic exposition, when the music is abundant with syncopes.

❑ Optimize — recommended for a chord part and syncope-free music.

❑ Equal — the note is positioned in compliance with its length (the "space" of one eighth note is occupied by two sixteenth notes).

3.4.3. Shortened Notation:
Rests for Several Bars, the *Real Book* Option

If there are many blank bars in the score, you can consolidate them into rests for several bars called **Multi Rests** in the software.

This method of rest consolidation enables you to *considerably* shorten, for example, the orchestra scores.

Rest settings for several bars are made in the **Multi Rests** field of the **Page Mode Settings** window. This means that if there are *more* rest bars set successively than the value specified, they will be consolidated into one. If Off is set, then no consolidation will take place — each blank bar will be shown in the score.

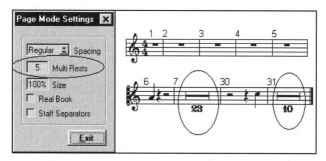

Fig. 3.120. Rest consolidation

Fig. 3.120 shows that the number 5 is specified in the **Multi Rests** field. So *more than* 5 bars are consolidated into one rest.

One blank bar with any meter is marked with a one-bar rest, which looks the same as a whole rest. Bars from 2 to 9 have a designation of their own. You need not memorize them, because the rest is always the number of "mute" bars in the software (as shown in Fig. 3.121). Besides which, all of them can be shown in the score in the same way (see Table. 3.6, the Church Multi Rest option).

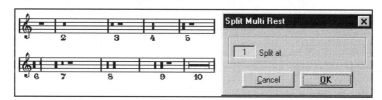

Fig. 3.121. Rests for several bars and splitting a long rest

If you need to "extract" bars from **Multi Rest**, double-click on it and specify the number of the bars you want to extract in the Split Multi Rest window that opens.

In order for you to see what rests are split in the score, you can set the "Split Rest" warning message (Fig. 3.122). Enter the Score/Global Settings menu, and click on the **Show Invisible** option. Then check the Split Rests option in the window that opens and press OK.

Fig. 3.122 shows that the rest in the upper staff was for 7 bars (A), and one bar was extracted from this rest in the lower staff (B). This is marked in the score, since the **Split Rests** option is checked.

If you want to consolidate blank bars into one rest, click on "Split Rests" and press the <Delete> key.

If this operation is to be done simultaneously for the whole score, do the following: enter the Score/Format menu and open the **Clean Up Layout** window, where you should check the Split Rests option and press OK. As a result, *all* the rests will be consolidated (Fig. 3.123, Example B).

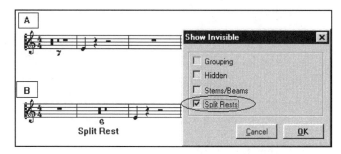

Fig. 3.122. The Multi Rest splitting message

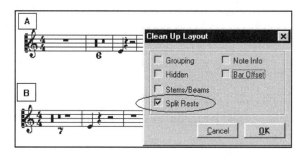

Fig. 3.123. Multi Rest consolidation after splitting

The consolidation of blank bars enables you to make the score more concise, and remove excess length.

The **Real Book** option in the same window can also be treated as an option promoting reasonable use of score space. If this option is checked, then each page of the score has the *clef on the first staff* (Fig. 3.124).

Of course, this frees up space for recording notes on the screen (or even saves printer ink when the score is printed). You must remember, however, that if this option is checked, you *cannot set the clef anywhere else in the score*. So it is recommended that you use this option only when *no register or clef change takes place in the part*. And be aware that such a simplification of the notation — the absence of a clef — is a deviation from the rules.

If the bars are repeated in the score, they may be replaced by special symbols — **Repeats**. The score will *not be changed*, but the notation will be shortened to "one symbol" (Fig. 3.125).

The **Repeats** symbols, circled in the illustration, indicate the repetition of one or two bars (by the number of slanted lines). They are set in case there are identical bars in the score. The first bar is written with the notes, and subsequent bars are marked with these repeat symbols.

In order to hide the notation, open the Other Symbols panel (Score/Symbol Palettes/Other menu) by clicking on the symbol holding the <Alt> key pressed, and then clicking in the bar area. In order to return the text to the score, delete this symbol with the Eraser tool.

If you need to hide two bars, click on the *first one.*

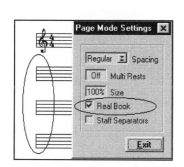

Fig. 3.124. The **Real Book** option: clef on the first staff only

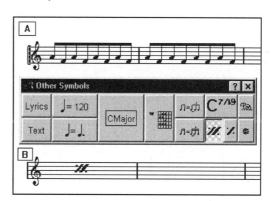

Fig. 3.125. Shortening the notation using a symbol

You can also shorten the notation using other abbreviations, such as reprise symbols and symbols for repeating a note group. These are described in the Symbol section.

3.4.4. Score Change Marks

The section describing the Score window interface dealt with methods of hiding unnecessary elements of the score in the Cubasis Notation software, changing the note grouping, correcting the length of the stems, and consolidating rests. These are very useful functions of the software. Below is a brief summary of these operations and how to control them in the Show Invisible and Clean Up Layout windows.

In order to hide an element, select it and click on the Hide option from the Do menu, or use the <Ctrl>+<Alt>+<B> key combination.

To change the length of the stem, click on the stem and move the marker that appears (the square).

Note regrouping is done with the Group option in the Do menu or the <Ctrl>+<Alt>+<G> key combination. To group notes, first frame them. To ungroup notes, select *only one note* in the group and press the <Ctrl>+<Alt>+<G> key combination.

Rest splitting was considered in the previous section.

The Show Invisible window in the Score/Global Settings menu is used for messages in the score where changes were made: objects hidden, length of stems and beam positioning changed, notes regrouped, multi rests split, etc.

Fig. 3.126 illustrates how this option works. Below are three variants of the score:

❏ On the top staff before the changes were made.

❏ On the middle staff where changes were made (the clef and the rest are hidden in the first bar, a rest for 7 bars was split into 6 and 1, the stem length of a note in the third bar was increased, and notes of the fourth bar were regrouped).

❏ On the bottom staff we have messages where changes were made, since all of these options are checked in the Show Invisible window (compare Examples A, B, and C).

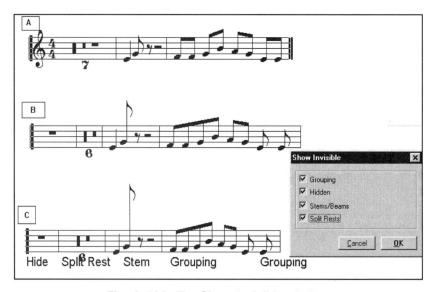

Fig. 3.126. The **Show Invisible** window

These messages are not only the "distinguishing marks" but also are very utilitarian. You can *locally undo changes* using these messages. Click on the message (it will be highlighted in black) and press either the <Backspace> or <Delete> key.

For example, if the Hide message denotes several hidden elements, then *each* such action returns *one* element to the score. Repeating this operation returns the next elements. If all the changes in this place of the score are undone, the message disappears.

Hidden notes can be returned to the score with the Show option in the Do menu.

The Clean Up Layout window in the Score/Format menu cancels all the changes made manually — restores the default settings.

The options checked in this window are valid *only for the area of the score* specified in the To: menu.

For example, if the Cycled Selected Ev. option is checked in the To: field, then only the notes selected in the editor will be affected; if the Cycled Events option is checked, the cycle selected within the editor will be affected, etc.

The checkboxes checked in the Clean Up Layout window mean that the changes of the score will be cancelled and the default settings will be restored:

- ❒ Grouping restores the previous note grouping.
- ❒ Hidden makes all hidden elements visible.
- ❒ Stem/Beams restores the initial length of stems/beams.
- ❒ Split Rests consolidates split rests into Multi Rests.
- ❒ Note Info clears all the settings in the Note Info window and restores the normal appearance of the notes.
- ❒ Bar Offset restores the bar numbering changed in the Barnum Offset option.

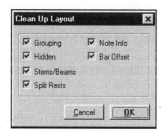

Fig. 3.127. The **Clean Up Layout** option

3.5. Principles of Working with the Score Manually

Below, operations with the notes using the mouse are described (as well as some of the options).

Previous sections dealt with the principles of adapting the score — methods of changing the score's appearance without affecting the sound.

Operations done with the mouse are different due to the fact that "touching" the note symbols affects their sound. If the note is drawn, it will sound; if it is moved, its pitch is changed; if it is removed, the corresponding MIDI event will also disappear.

We'd like to inform you of the following important aspects before beginning the description:

❐ All the operations described below are valid MIDI events: they affect both the sound and the appearance of the score.

❐ Most of the operations with notes (moving, copying, removing) are identical to those with key imprints, so users familiar with the Key Edit editor will find it easy to master these operations.

❐ Note positioning in the Score Edit editor is subject to the "grid laws" described in detail in the example of the Key Edit editor:

 • The length of the note being set corresponds to the value specified in the **Quant** field.

 • A note can be set *only* at the length position specified in the **Snap** field.

❐ The settings of the Score menu *affect the appearance of a score* created with the mouse.

▼ *Warning*

Before we list all the possible methods of note creation, be aware that the settings in the **Display Quantize** section of the **Staff Settings** window are "length limits" for the score: the notes of a length shorter than what is specified can not appear in the score.

So, for manual note positioning, it is best to set a value of 64 in the **Notes** and **Rests** fields and select **None** in the **Auto Quant** field if there are no triplets in the score, or **Position** if there are (see details in *Section 3.3*).

3.6. Score Edit Editing Tools

The toolbar of the Score Edit editor is invoked traditionally: by clicking the right mouse button.

There are eight tools used for working in the score (Fig. 3.128). To select a tool, hold the right mouse button pressed and move to the required icon. It is very convenient, since the tools are always on hand.

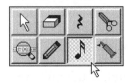

Fig. 3.128. The toolbar

The Arrow tool — which is the one most frequently used — is invoked by clicking the right mouse button. Using this tool, you can select, move, and copy notes and other elements of the score, select options and lengths, etc.

As we mentioned in *Chapter 1*, the mouse cursor and the Arrow tool are almost the same. If you have to click on a note (or another score element), use this tool (i.e., the mouse cursor).

The Eraser tool erases note symbols, rests, etc. To do this, click on the note, rest, or symbol with it, or drag it across several elements.

Notes are positioned in the score using the Note tool. You can also perform other operations using hotkeys <Alt>, <Shift>, and <Ctrl> (see below). The Rest tool adds a rest to the score and simultaneously shifts the material to the right. The length of the rest is selected in the same way as the length of a note is — on the Score Edit Toolbar panel or with keys from <1>–<7> (combined with <.> or <T> for dotted notes or triplets).

The Pencil tool is intended for positioning note symbols (some of which affect the sound, e.g., staccato, accent, etc.).

You can split two tied notes of *the same pitch* with the Scissors tool. The Scissors are also used for moving one bar to another staff — click with it on the bar line.

The Glue Tube tool is used for joining a neighboring note *of the same pitch*, as well as for joining bars into one line.

3.7. The *Snap* and *Quant* Fields

Based on the key imprints, *Section 2.9* dealt with the operating principles of the Snap and Quant fields. These principles are *the same* in the Score Edit editor.

The authorized positions for the notes are specified in the Snap field, and length of the notes is specified in the Quant field.

The Snap grid is for the musician's convenience only. It by no means should be considered an obstacle. First of all, if the grid is set correctly, you need not "catch microns" with the mouse cursor when positioning notes. Second, the user can change its pitch at any moment. When the pitch of the grid is set correctly, you can considerably simplify the note positioning process.

Be guided by the following when selecting values in the Snap field.

❏ The value must correspond to the *positions the notes will be set to*.

❏ For example, if you need to set quarter notes *at the beginning* of each beat, it is best to set a value of 4 in the Snap field, since a finer division of the grid will not be necessary. On the other hand, if you need to position syncopated quarters (shifted from the beginning of the beats), the grid divisions should be finer (8, 16).

❏ You can position a note of *any* value at any position authorized by the value in the Snap field.

If the length, however, crosses the border of the beat or bar, the notation will automatically feature tied notes (according to the rules of notation). You can partially avoid them by checking the Syncopation option in the Staff Settings window (the Score menu).

The value specified in the Quant field means the length of the note being positioned. It is this length which appears when the Note and Rest tools are selected.

▶ *Note*

> When the **Over Quantize** operation is performed, the value in the **Quant** field determines the grid towards which the lengths will be pulled (see *Section 2.20* for details on the quantize function).

Fig. 3.129 illustrates the difference in the note positioning with different values in the Snap and Quant fields.

For clarity, on the upper staff we showed as the lengths the cells of the invisible grid set in the Snap field (bars A, B, C).

On the left, you see the lengths of the set notes (according to the values in the Quant field).

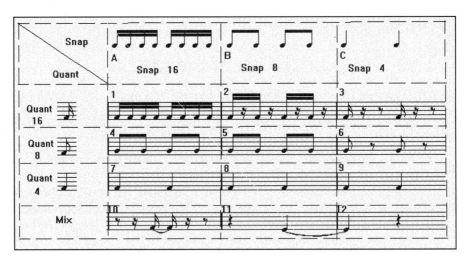

Fig. 3.129. The correspondence of the **Snap** and **Quant** fields

Bars 1—9 have the *maximum* number of the notes of the same length: sixteenths, eighths, quarters, and half notes.

The illustration shows that the bigger the value in the Snap field, the rarer are the authorized positions for a note in the bar (compare bars 1 and 3). The longer the length of the note being set, the less notes there are in the bar (compare bars 1 and 7).

The notes, however, can be set to any authorized position of the grid (bars 10—12). If the notes go outside of the borders of the beat or bar, the software automatically combines them using ties.

The main difference between notes and key imprints is that the note symbols can not be graphically shown to be several ticks longer or shorter, as is possible with key imprints; the note symbol is always some "rounded" length.

But you can see the actual length of the sound represented by this note on the Info Line panel (select the note first). On this panel, you can also change the length of the note with one tick precision, change its pitch, start position, and velocity. These operations are done in the same way as in the Key Edit editor.

3.8. Length Selection

In order to write a note, select its length and click on the required line of the staff.
There are three ways to select the length of the note:

❑ Choose a value from the drop-down list of the **Quant** field. The cursor takes the shape of the selected length, and the corresponding icon is synchronously selected on the Score Edit **Toolbar** (Fig. 3.130).

❑ Values with the letter T are the triplets; values with a dot are dotted notes.

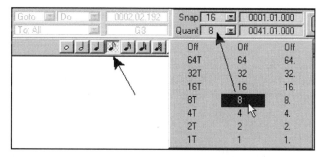

Fig. 3.130. Selecting the length in the drop-down list of the **Quant** field

❑ Click on the note symbol on the Score Edit Toolbar panel. You can do this with either **Arrow** or **Note**. (The same value is automatically set in the Quant field.)

❑ If you need to set a dotted note or triplet, click on the dot symbol or on the letter T. The cursor will take the shape of the selected length (Fig. 3.131).

❑ You can select the length with the keys from the *main* computer keyboard. We recommend using this method, since it is quicker. It differs from the two above in that the values in both the **Snap** and **Quant** fields (circled in Fig. 3.132) are changed *simultaneously*. So, if necessary, you can change the pitch of the grid in this way.

❑ The keys <1>, <2>, <3>, <4>, <5>, <6>, and <7> correspond to the series of lengths on the icons, and the <.> and <T> keys add a dot or triple symbol to the note (Fig. 3.132).

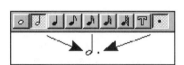

Fig. 3.131. Selecting the length on the **Score Edit Toolbar** panel

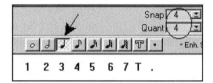

Fig. 3.132. Selecting the length using the keys

▶ *Tip*

You can also select the length on the keyboard and set it on the staves. Then, if another grid division value is necessary, press another key and move the length to the new place.

After the length is selected, click on the staff and the note will be set: it will be attached to the nearest authorized position in the Snap field.

3.9. Illustrations

Table 3.6 shows some quick operations with the notation, as well as examples of making work with the score more comfortable.

Table 3.6. Some Quick and Convenient Methods of Work

Name of operation	Illustration
Increase the scale on the screen: click in the right bottom corner of the **Score** window in the **Scale** field. If the values of the drop-down list are not suitable, enter a different one after double-clicking.	
Hide panels and increase the space for the score: click on the icons (bottom right). To navigate the pages, click the **Page** field.	
Listen to the notes when they are written and moved: click on the **Speaker** button on the **Status Bar** panel.	
Listen to the note: click on it with the **Magnifying Glass** tool.	

continues

Table 3.6 Continued

Name of operation	Illustration
Change the time, key, and clef, show notes of shorter length, make two staves, use polyphony, etc. for the whole part: double-click to the left of the staff and make the settings in the window that opens.	
Change the time, clef, and key signatures in the middle of the staff: call the **Clef ... (Score/Symbol Palettes)** panel, select the required icon, click on the score where you want to place the new value, make the settings in the window that opens, and exit using the **OK** button.	
Activate the staff (all operations are done on the staff marked with a black line in the beginning): click anywhere on it.	
Set a note in the score: click with the **Note** tool on the staff.	
Set a note in another voice: activate the staff (click on it with the **Arrow** tool), click on the number of the voice, and set the note.	
Select a note: click on it with the **Arrow** tool. Select several notes: click on each note with the **Arrow** tool, or frame them dragging the **Arrow** with the <Shift> key pressed.	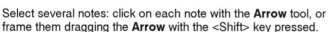 
Move a note: drag it to the new place holding it with the **Arrow** tool (horizontally or vertically). The rhythmical position depends on the value in the **Snap** field.	

Change the length of a note:

- Select the length (for example, with a number key on the keyboard), press and hold the <Alt> key, and click with the **Note** tool on the note in the score

- Select one (or several) notes, press and hold the <Ctrl> key, and click on the length icon on the **Score Edit Toolbar**

continues

Table 3.6 Continued

Name of operation	Illustration
Increase the length of a note because the next note is of the *same pitch*: glue them by clicking on the *first* one with the **Glue Tube** tool.	
Split a tied note into two notes of the same pitch: click on the last note with the **Scissors** tool.	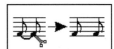
Delete a note: click on it with the **Eraser** tool. If you need to delete several notes, drag the tool without releasing the left mouse button.	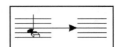
To avoid "unnecessary" notes when a note is set: hold the <Ctrl> key pressed, and you will not be able to set a non-harmonious note (e.g., in C-dur, the software *will not* insert notes with sharps and flats in the score).	
Insert a note in the middle of the score: activate the insertion mode with the **Insert** button and set the note as usual. The subsequent notation will be shifted to the right.	
Cancel an alteration symbol at a note (with a change in the pitch at the level of the MIDI event): press and hold the **Arrow** tool on the note.	
Add an alteration symbol to the note: shift the note up or down with the mouse (**Arrow** tool).	
Change the alteration symbol to the opposite one (enharmonic change): select the note and click on the required symbol on the **Score Edit Toolbar**.	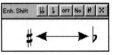
Insert a rest: select a length (as you would for a note) and click on the staff with the **Rest** tool. The whole score will be shifted to the left.	
Change a note to a rest: delete the note, and a rest will be set instead. The score is not shifted.	

continues

Table 3.6 Continued

Name of operation	Illustration
Delete a rest: erase it. The whole score will be moved towards the beginning. Change a rest to a note: click with the **Note** tool on it. The score is not moved.	
Change the note grouping: select *one* note and press the <Ctrl>+<Alt>+<G> key combination; to consolidate: select several notes and press the same key combination.	
Change the stem direction: select the note (notes) and press the key combination <Ctrl>+<Alt>+<X>.	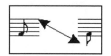
Move the cursor: • Grab the cursor with any tool and drag it along the score • Move the scrollbar on the **Transport** bar, press the scroll keys, or change the figures on the indicator panel • <Page Up> and <Page Down> keys • Set the cursor to the L and R locator positions with keys <1> and <2> of the additional keyboard (Set the L and R locators to the cursor position with the <Shift>+<1> and <Shift>+<2> key combinations on the additional keyboard.)	
Move the staff (up, down): click and hold the left mouse button to the left of the staff. After the staff is highlighted in black, hold the button and drag the staff to the new place. If the <Alt> key is held down during the operation, the space between *all* staves will be changed.	
Change the title of the score: click on the title and enter a new name in the window that opens. Close it with the **OK** button.	
Listen to a recorded melody: press the **Play** button on the **Transport** bar (or the <F12> key). Stop playback with the **Stop** button. To listen again: return the cursor to the beginning and repeat these operations. (You can also use hotkeys on the additional keyboard. See *Section 1.5.1*).	
Change the appearance of the bar line: double-click on the bar line and select the required variant in the window that opens.	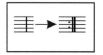

continues

Table 3.6 Continued

Name of operation	Illustration
Change the bar borders: click on the bar line and drag it to a new place holding the left mouse button pressed; to move the bars to another staff: click with the **Scissors** tool on the bar line (split the bars into 2 staves), and use the **Glue tube** (glue on 1 staff).	

This table presents only some of the capabilities of the note editor of the Cubasis Notation software. We have already covered many of them, and the rest will be considered below, including those that allow you to move notes from one staff to another, select a group of notes, change the MIDI sound using symbols, etc.

3.10. Editing Notes

3.10.1. Selecting Notes

Most of the operations in Cubasis Notation are done by first selecting notes, which you can then move from one voice (track) to another, copy, delete, etc.

There are several ways to select notes in the Score Edit editor.

A single note is selected by double-clicking on the note head. If there are tied notes of the same pitch, clicking on the first note selects both, and clicking on the second note selects only the second.

Selecting several notes

❏ Frame the notes. To do this, holding the left mouse button pressed, drag the **Arrow** tool across the score. This method is suitable for any adjacent notes, including those in different voices (Fig. 3.133).

❏ You can use this method to select other elements of the score as well.

❏ Note that the framed notes have a square on their stems — a marker. You can change the length of the stem by dragging this marker up or down.

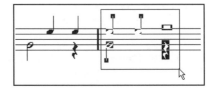

Fig. 3.133. Framing notes and score elements

❏ Click on the notes with the mouse cursor holding the <Shift> key pressed. This method is quite useful, since you can select distant notes (including those in different voices), and the method is suitable for any element of the score.

▼ *Warning*

After selecting (using any method), the majority of score elements can be moved by grabbing them with the mouse cursor. If you can't move them like this, you'll have to change the space between the score elements (see Table 3.5).

Group selection. The following methods of selection are applicable to *one voice only* (or a whole part if it is one-voice).

❏ Navigate through the notes using the <←> and <→> keys, holding the <Shift> key pressed.
❏ Double-clicking on the note while holding the <Ctrl> key pressed will select all the notes of this name *within one octave.*
❏ <Alt> + a double-click on the note selects all the notes of this name *in all octaves,* including other voices.
❏ <Shift> + a double-click on the note selects *all* the notes of this voice (or of the one-voice part).
❏ There is a universal method of selecting the whole score: check the Select All option in the Edit menu (or press the <Ctrl>+<A> key combination).

Undo Selection. In all the above methods, the heads of the selected notes are framed. To undo the selection, click on the score (but not on the selected elements).

If you need to *exclude* one or more notes from a selected group, click on the heads of these notes holding the <Shift> key pressed.

Selection with the To: menu options. When using this method of selection, the color of the notes is not changed, so you can understand what part of the score is selected only by the message in the To: field. You can also change the borders of the selected area in this field.

You can apply the commands of the Do menu to the fragment selected in the To: field.

This function is *very* useful.

With this method, you can select:

❏ The whole score (All Events).
❏ A loop in the editor (Looped Events): its borders are set either with mouse clicks or by entering new values in the fields indicated with the arrow in the illustration.
❏ A cycle between the locators in the Arrange window (Cycled Events); its borders are set by moving the L and R locators in the Arrange window, or on the Transport

bar in the Right Locator and Left Locator fields by clicking the mouse button or entering new values.

❑ Only the notes in these events (**Looped Selected Ev.** and **Cycled Selected Ev.**).

Fig. 3.134 shows that the **Looped Events** option (the area selected in the editor) is checked in the **To:** menu. The borders of this option are shown on the indicator board: from the first beat of the 10th bar to the first beat of the 11th. So the command selected in the **Do** menu will affect only this area.

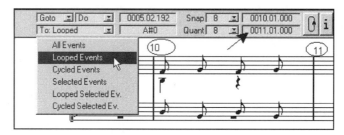

Fig. 3.134. Selecting a fragment of a score in the **To:** menu

The main operations that you can perform in an area thus selected are the following:

❑ **Fill** creates a chain of notes (according to the values in the Snap and Quant fields).
❑ **Delete** deletes notes.
❑ **Make Chords** sets chord designations.
❑ **Auto Grouping** groups the notes according to the "time configuration". This operation was done in the example (compare Figs. 3.134 and 3.135).
❑ **Multi Insert** sets the note symbols for *all notes* of the selected area.

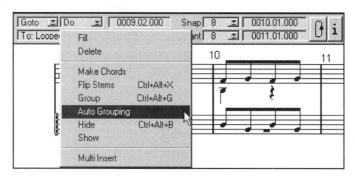

Fig. 3.135. Using the **Auto Grouping** command in the **Do** menu

3.10.2. Moving

Below is a description of notes selected in the usual way (any selection in the To: menu will be considered separately).

Moving with the mouse. The easiest way to move one or more notes is by dragging them with the mouse.

Grab the notes *by their heads* and move them to the new place. You can also move a group of notes by grabbing any of the notes. The Pitch/Transpose window can be used to trace the value of the move (indicated by the arrow in Fig. 3.136). Here you will see the number of semitones the composition was shifted by (12 semitones — an octave; positive value — augmenting, negative value — diminishing).

Remember that if you move horizontally, the authorized rhythmical position depends on the value in the Snap field.

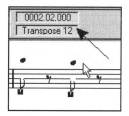

Fig. 3.136. The move value indicator

If you select notes on two different staves at the same time (e.g., frame them), you can move them simultaneously on two staves.

If you press and hold the <Shift> key, the notes will be moved *strictly* vertically *or* horizontally. This is very convenient, since you are able to retain the rhythmic or pitch position, respectively.

You may use the Info Line panel to move one note. Here, all the parameters of the selected note are shown, which you can change holding the mouse button pressed: scroll the values or enter a new one from the keyboard.

 Note

You can enter alterated notes in the **Pitch** field on the **Info Line** panel, but only those with the sharp symbol — # (<Shift>+<3>).

If the <Alt> key is held pressed during the move, the notes will be copied.

Moving in the Edit menu. You can move notes traditionally: first select, then copy (or cut), and then paste. Multiple pasting is available, e.g., into different parts (open in the Score Edit editor).

This is done in the Edit menu with the Cut, Copy, and Paste options, or with the: <Ctrl>+<X>, <Ctrl>+<C>, and <Ctrl>+<V> key combinations.

Pasting is done on the active staff and at the multitrack cursor position.
To activate the staff, click on it (a black line should appear at its beginning).
The cursor can be moved in several ways:

❑ By dragging with the mouse.
❑ With the <Page Up> and <Page Down> keys.
❑ With the sliders or scroll buttons on the **Transport** bar.
❑ By entering the necessary coordinates in the **Song Position** field on the **Transport** bar. This method is the most accurate.

▼ *Warning*

Only the most recent information is stored in the clipboard. So, after the material is copied, apply the insertion *immediately*, as it will be erased by the next material you copy.

Moving using the MIDI keyboard. This method of note editing has advantages that let you edit not only the pitch, but also the **Velocity** parameter of the notes.

The editing mechanism using the MIDI keyboard is the same as when using the key imprints in the Key Edit editor (*Sections 2.12, 2.13*).

Below are the main points. Fig. 3.137 shows the buttons for note editing using the MIDI keyboard.

Fig. 3.137. The buttons for editing notes
using the MIDI keyboard

After a note is edited, the next note is automatically selected. You can navigate through them using either the <←> and <→> keys or by clicking on them with the mouse.

The buttons marked with the numbers 1 and 2 must be pressed in any case (they provide for the connection with the MIDI keyboard, and the sound when moving in the score using the <←> and <→> keys).

Here are the combinations of buttons for various operations (Fig. 3.137):

❑ 1, 2, 3 — editing the pitch of the selected note
❑ 1, 2, 4 — editing the velocity
❑ 1, 2, 3, 4 — editing the pitch and velocity

Moving the pitch of the note with the MIDI keyboard can act as a quick method of editing the score.

1st variant. Create a chain of identical notes using the Fill command in the Do menu. Select the first note, and, pressing the keys of the MIDI keyboard, edit the pitch and velocity of the notes.

2nd variant. If different parts have the *same rhythm*, you can copy one part into different voices and edit the pitch of the notes in the same way from the MIDI keyboard.

Moving to another voice. This operation is available only when there is polyphony in the score: the **Polyphonic** option is checked, and the corresponding settings are made in the **Polyphonic Settings** window (Fig. 3.138, B).

You can move the notes from voice to voice without changing their rhythmic position — in the same bar.

Select the notes. Enter the **Score** menu, select **Staff Function/Move to Voice**, and in the drop-down list that opens, click on the number of the voice to which the notes are to be moved (compare Examples A and B in Fig. 3.138).

If the notes are not only to be moved vertically, but horizontally too (to another rhythmical position and another voice), do the following:

❐ Select the notes

❐ Cut them (<Ctrl>+<X>)

❐ Move the cursor to the position where you will paste them

❐ Paste the notes (<Ctrl>+<V>)

❐ While the inserted notes are selected, move them to another voice: select **Staff Function/Move to Voice** from the **Score** menu, and click on the number of the voice

➤ *Note*

The voice in the drop-down **Move to Voice** list to which the notes are moved must be active (black). Activation of voices is done in the **Polyphonic Settings** window (see details in *Section 3.2.3*).

Moving (or copying) *to another track* is done in the same way as it is "on paper": without affecting the MIDI event.

The main distinction is that you must open both tracks in the Score Edit editor. (Select the parts in the **Arrange** window with the <Shift> key pressed and press the <Ctrl>+<R> key combination).

Select **Move to Track** from the **Score/Staff Function** menu, and in the drop-down list, click on the track to which the notes must be moved. When selecting, keep in mind the name of the staff (Upper, Lower).

Strictly speaking, note quantization with the **Over Quantize** option in the **Functions** menu is one method of moving notes (see *Section 2.20*).

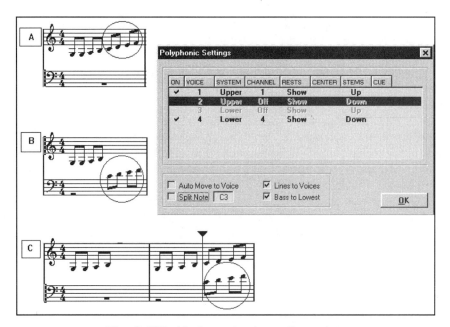

Fig. 3.138. Moving notes to another voice

3.10.3. Changing the Length

There are several ways to change the length. You need to understand that some of the methods affect *only* the inscription, while others affect *only* the sound. Some affect both the sound and the inscription.

To change *only the inscription* of the note, make the corresponding settings in the **Staff Settings** window in the **Display Quantize** or **Interpret. Flags** sections.

You can change *only the length of the note* on the **Info Line** panel by changing the length by several ticks in the **LENGTH** field.

How to *simultaneously* change the inscription and the sound is considered in this section.

Both methods are very convenient:

❏ Select the note (notes), press and hold the <Ctrl> key, and click on the required note symbol on the **Edit Toolbar** panel

❏ Click on the note of the required length on the **Edit Toolbar** panel, press and hold the <Alt> key, and click on the note (notes)

Fig. 3.139 (A) shows that if you want to change the length of a dotted note, press the length button and the dot icon. The letter T is for triplets.

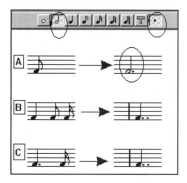

Fig. 3.139. Changing the length

If necessary, you can have double dotted notes in the score. For this, set three notes one after the other, each subsequent one being one half the length of the previous one. Then click on the first note with the Glue Tube tool, and the notes will be "glued" in two steps. Fig. 3.139 shows that these are quarter, eighth, and sixteenth notes (B). Or, you can join a length four times shorter to the dotted note, e.g., a sixteenth note to a dotted quarter (Fig. 3.141, C).

The Double Dotted Note

One dot next to the head of a note increases its length by 50%, a second dot increases it by 25% more. Therefore, the total length of a double dotted note is longer by 75% of its original length.

You can shorten tied notes *of the same pitch* by deleting the notes from the end to the beginning. Fig. 3.140 shows how a half note can be shortened by this method from Examples A to D. If you click on the first note, the whole length will be deleted.

Fig. 3.140. Changing the length of a tied note

You can also shorten the length of tied notes with the Scissors tool. When you click with the scissors on the last tied note, the tie will disappear, and each of the notes will be played separately: it stops being an addition to the previous length.

If you click on the note with the Glue Tube, the length of the note will be increased, since the next note will be glued to it.

Changing the length with symbols will be described in *Section 3.12.1*.

3.10.4. Deleting

Notes are deleted with the Eraser tool: use it to click on the note head, or drag the tool across several notes (thus erasing them).

Selected notes can be deleted with the <Delete> or <Backspace> keys. You can delete the notation of one of the voices using this method.

It is convenient to delete larger fragments of the score by selecting from the **To:** menu and then using the Delete command of the Do menu.

You can delete all of the material using the <Ctrl>+<A> key combination (select all), and then <Delete>.

3.10.5. The *Note Info* Window

The special Note Info window is intended for setting the note's appearance, and it is opened by double-clicking on the note head or using the <Ctrl>+<I> key combination.

▼ *Warning*

If there are two or more tied notes of the same pitch, you can only open this window by clicking on the *first* ("main") note.

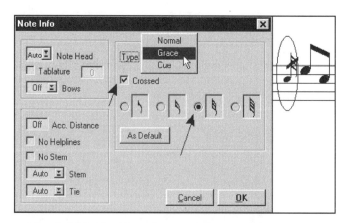

Fig. 3.141. The **Note Info** and **Grace Note** windows

You can select the appearance of the note in the right section (Fig. 3.141):

☐ Normal means a normal note.

☐ Grace means a note having neither the length nor the rhythmic position specified. If this option is checked, grace notes can have tails of various lengths: check the option indicated by the arrow. If the Crossed option is checked, their stems will be crossed. Grace notes are created only "on paper" in this software, without affecting the MIDI events.

Graces

Graces are melodic patterns that ornament the main notes of the melody. They are performed in time according to the length of the note they "decorate ", and so the *are not* within the beats of the bar. As a rule, grace notes have almost the same pitch as main notes: the difference may be only a semitone or a full tone.

One type of grace note is called a *vorschlag* (German for proposition). It consists of one or more notes. A short vorschlag is shown in small notes, while a long one is played for a longer time than the short one, and is designated by a length half as long as the main note.

In order to set a grace note, set the main note, insert the "regular" note for a grace of any length before the main note, and press the <Alt>+<Ctrl>+<Y> key combination, disregarding the tied notes that appear. A grace note will be created automatically. You can change its appearance by double-clicking on it and changing the settings in the Info Line window. The space between the grace notes are specified in the settings (*Section 3.4.2*).

Any note can be turned into a grace, and vice versa: check the option in the Type field.

☐ Cue — the note is *only graphically* smaller than the regular notes.

☐ The upper left section of the Info Line window is intended for selecting tablatures, note heads, and tie curves.

☐ If the Tablature option is checked, you can select tablature symbols in the adjacent field.

   Tablature — a system of writing music using letters and figures.

☐ For a six-string guitar, the tablature is written on six lines, denoting the strings. The strings are numbered from top to bottom (from 1 to 6).

☐ The figures show the *fret* on which these strings are to be pressed. Zero indicates an open (not pressed) string. As with a usual staff, the lines/strings of the tablature are divided into bars.

☐ A tablature is often written in combination with the staff (Fig. 3.142).

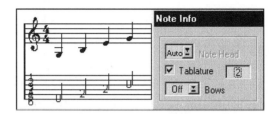

Fig. 3.142. Creating a tablature

❏ If you click in the Note Head field, a list opens in which you can select any form of note head (see details in *Section 3.2.9*).

❏ The drop-down list of the Bows field contains three options that allow you to tie the note *graphically*, i.e., without affecting its sound:

  • Off — no tie
  • Up — middle of tie is up
  • Down — middle of tie is down

The lower section contains fields for the following settings (Fig. 3.143):

❏ Acc. Distance is the distance from the note to the accidental (A).
❏ The No Helplines button undoes the ledger lines (B).
❏ The No Stem button hides the note stem, e.g., for scales or technical exercises (C).
❏ The Stem button sets the stem direction: Up, Down, Auto (D).
❏ The Tie button changes the tie direction: Up, Down, Auto (E).

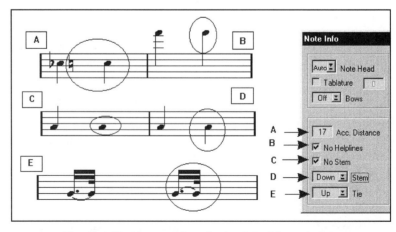

Fig. 3.143. Note settings in the **Info Line** window

3.10.6. Alteration Symbols

Alteration (from Latin *alterate* — change) means an augmentation or diminishing of the note by a semitone, tone, etc. without changing its name.

The alteration symbol is an integral part of the note's pitch designation, and so it is set automatically by the software. You can neither erase the symbol, since the note's pitch will be changed, nor simply add the symbol to the note.

In order to add an alteration symbol to a note, drag the note up or down with the mouse.

In order to cancel an alteration symbol, click on the note and hold the mouse button for a while, or move the note up or down.

> ► *Tip*
>
> It is important to note that to simplify positioning the note, you can hold the <Ctrl> key pressed: "unnecessary" alteration symbols will not appear, since you can set notes *only* within the key.

If you need to change the symbols for several notes, select these notes and move the whole group up or down.

Generally, the symbols are set automatically, and beginner musicians find these functions sufficient.

Apart from sharp and flat, the natural symbol — a cancellation symbol — is automatically set in the score, showing that no augmentation or diminishing is applicable to this note.

The key accidentals can be changed for the whole score in the **Staff Settings** window of the **Score** menu at the beginning of the staff in the **Edit Key** window (opened by double-clicking on the clef), and in the middle of the staff in the **Clef...** panel in the **Score/Symbol Palettes** menu (see *Section 3.2.2*).

You can change the settings for the appearance of the accidentals in Cubasis Notation. This is done in the **Score/Global Settings** menu in the **Global Settings** window.

We can conclude that it is better to use regular positioning of accidentals — **Regular** option, offered as default. The rest of the options are checked only if necessary.

Select the **Accidentals** category in the left part of the **Global Settings** window and click on one of the four icons in the right part (Fig. 3.144):

❏ **Regular** — accidentals are shown in accordance with the main rules: only at notes *outside of the scale*. With this mode active, accidentals are *not repeated* within the bar.

> ► *Note*
>
> Scales are dealt with in *Chapter 4*. Here we have the major scale from *D* (the *D*-dur key, 2 key sharps), and so its steps are the following: *D*, *E*, *F* sharp, *G*, *A*, *H*, *C* sharp.

❏ Help — the same as Regular, with the exception that the *accidental is cancelled* in the next bar.

❏ The accidental is not valid in the next bar in any case, so according to the rules, it is not set. Sometimes, however, it is set as a reminder for the performer.

❏ Not in Key — the same as Regular, but accidentals are repeated *even within the bar*. Remember that the accidental is valid for all subsequent notes of this octave *only* within the bar, and is not repeated in the bar according to the rules.

❏ All — *each* note has a "personal" key. The accidental duplicates the key signatures. Obviously, this option can be used for recording special exercises, as well as for beginner musicians or those with a "personal opinion" about accidentals.

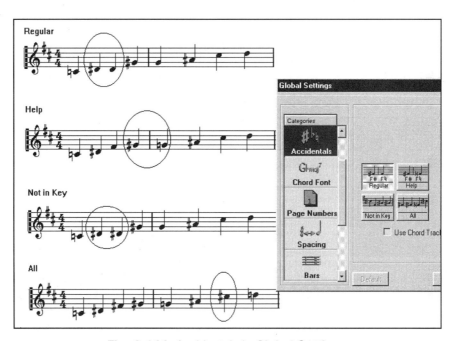

Fig. 3.144. Accidentals in **Global Settings**

Enharmonic shift. When speaking of accidentals, it is necessary to touch upon enharmonics. It should be noted that it is considered to be on somewhat of a higher level when it comes to the subject of notation, and beginners can probably do without it.

Enharmonics (from the Greek *enharmonios* — concurrent) is a different name for sounds *of the same pitch*, e.g., *C* sharp and *D* flat. Despite the physical sameness of the enharmonic sounds in the tempered scale, they sometimes bear an absolutely different expressive meaning.

So, you might ask, why this mess with the accidentals?

In answering, we'd like to highlight a few points: in simple cases, accidentals are used to denote the "black" keys (double accidentals are very seldom used), but an enharmonic shift is sometimes necessary (this topic is dealt with in *Chapter 4*).

There are 6 buttons on the Edit Toolbar panel that make it possible to perform an enharmonic shift — Enh. Shift.

Warning

Accidentals set by means of the **Enh. Shift** buttons *do not change* the pitch of the note. They record the same sound using the *selected symbol and, therefore, another note*.

For example, if you select the *E* note in the score and press the "flat" symbol on the Enh. Shift panel, the *F* flat note will appear, i.e., actually the same *E* note, but recorded with the use of the selected symbol and, as a result, a diminished *F* note.

We already mentioned that "sharp" augments the note by a semitone, and "flat" diminishes it. These symbols, however, can be doubled: a double sharp augments the note by a tone, and a double flat diminishes the note by a tone.

So, you may enharmonically shift *any* accidental in the Cubasis Notation software, but the sound will remain the same (this can be compared to saying the time: twenty to eight is the same as 7:40).

Fig. 3.145 shows examples of setting accidentals:

❐ A double flat and *F* double sharp are the same key — *G* (Example B).
❐ A natural is set when *one* or *two* accidentals are cancelled (Example C).
❐ *D* sharp and *E* flat indicate the same note (Example A).

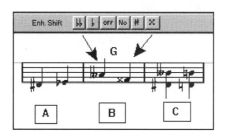

Fig. 3.145. The **Enh. Shift** panel

An enharmonic shift for one or two notes is done as follows: select the note (notes) and click on the button with the symbol image.

If you need to make an enharmonic shift for a large part of the score, select it in the To: menu and click on the correct symbol on the Enh. Shift panel.

The Off button switches off the enharmonic shift, restoring the previous variant.

The No button hides the symbol, *without changing* the pitch of the note. This means that the *G* sharp note with the symbol thus hidden (it will look like a *G* note in the score) still sounds like a *G* sharp.

In light of the above, we recommend that you use the Enh. Shift panel *only when an enharmonic shift is necessary.*

3.10.7. Rests

Fortunately for the musician, Cubasis Notation sets the rests, automatically filling the space around the notes.

Some important details to be remembered have already been described above:

❐ The minimal rest shown in the score depends on the settings in the Display Quantize field of the Staff Settings window (*Section 3.3.3*).

❐ If you check the Consolidate Rest option on the Switches section of the Staff Options window, rests will be consolidated into bigger ones (see *Section 3.2.6*).

❐ If there are many blank bars together in the score, you can record them as rests for several bars — a Multi Rest. These are described in *Section 3.4.1*.

Now let's consider operations with rests using the mouse. There are only a few:

❐ A rest can be erased by clicking on it with the Eraser tool. The subsequent material will be shifted towards the beginning by the length of the deleted rest.

❐ You can insert a rest. Select the Rest tool and the length of the rest. Selecting the length of the rest is done in the same way as for notes:

1. Press the <1>–<7> keys, the <.> button for a dotted note, and <T> for a triplet on the main keyboard.
2. Click on the icon of the required length on the Edit Toolbar panel.
3. Select the required length in the Quant field.

If you need to hide a rest (for example, for an upbeat), click on it and press the <Ctrl>+<Alt>+<B> key combination. Marks for hidden rests in the score are described in *Section 3.4.4*.

Hiding rests for the whole voice (part) is done via the Polyphonic Settings window (*Section 3.2.3*).

If you need to change the space between a rest and other elements of the score, change the settings in the Spacing window (*Section 3.2.3*).

3.11. Setting Symbols

Correctly positioned notes are, so to speak, the *words* of the text. In order for these words to be correctly understood and interpreted by the musician, they must form phrases and sentences, and be divided into paragraphs. They need to be semantically stressed, and have punctuation marks set. This means, in short, that you need to form the score.

This involves dynamic shades, accents, bows, repetition symbols, transposition by octave, special performance notes, etc.

All the symbols in the Cubasis Notation software can only be set graphically — as reminders to the musician. Some symbols, however, can be set so that they affect the MIDI sound of the score.

3.11.1. Overview of Symbol Palettes

The main operations with the score are done using the 6 panels available in the Score/ Symbol Palettes menu. Using these panels, you can set more than 100 symbols, write text, etc. (Fig. 3.146).

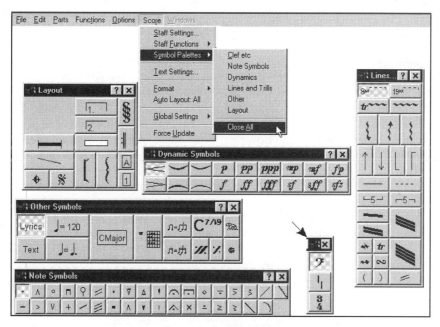

Fig. 3.146. The **Symbol Palettes** menu

We will not list all the symbols — they can be found in the program manual. It would be better to start with a description of these six panels, and just stress the most important points.

❐   Clef ... panel. These symbols set the clef, time, and key accidentals in the score (see the details in *Section 3.2.2*).

❑ Note Symbols panel. Used for designating performance techniques, e.g., tremolo, glissando, accent, bow down, open and close Hi-hat, etc.

   Some symbols of this and the next panel may affect the sound of the computer score. See details below.

❑ Dynamic Symbols panel. Contains symbols of the dynamic shades of performance that are *necessary* in any score.

   • Crescendo and diminuendo, which show a smooth increase and reduction in the force, are marked with special widening and narrowing symbols, respectively.

   • Ties denoting notes to be played legato (without breaks when going to another note).

   • Alphabetical designations of the dynamic shades: the force and volume of the performance, from pianissimo to fortissimo (see *Section 2.18*).

❑ Lines and Trills panel. These are special marks in the score. For example, using the quintole symbol (5 in brackets), you can designate *special rhythmical patterns* (duplets, quartlets, quintoles, sextolets, etc.).

Quintole — a rhythmic pattern played on one or several beats of the bar instead of the required four notes of *the same* designation. Figuratively speaking, it is a relative of the triplet. The latter, as the most common pattern, is designated automatically in the software.

   In order to change the default figure (5), click on it and enter another one (Fig. 3.152).

   It should be mentioned, however, that these patterns can be designated *only graphically*, since the software *does not allow* you to introduce more lengths in the bar than the number that are "fixed in time". In this case, the **Hide** option (<Ctrl>+<Alt>+<B>) can be used to hide "unnecessary" rests, bar lines, etc.

   Using the Line symbol, you can set a dotted border between the parts of the bar and the compound time for score readability (Fig. 3.147).

   The **Staff Separator** symbol is set as a "single" separator between the staves (Fig. 3.147). It can be set automatically — simultaneously on several staves: check the **Staff Separator** option in the **Page Mode Settings** menu (Score/Format).

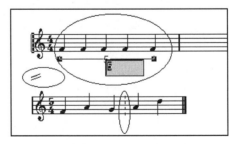

Fig. 3.147. Designating rhythmic patterns with the symbols
of the **Lines and Trills** panel

The Octave symbols (8--- and 15---) *graphically* move the notes one or two octaves up or down (depending on their position on the staff: upper or lower). This move affects *only the score*, and not the sound.

The Hand Indicator symbols (next to the arrows) are sometimes needed to mark which hand is to play the note.

The Beam symbols enable you to shorten the notation by replacing groups of notes with beams only: 1 beam means eighth notes, 2 means sixteenth, etc. Fig. 3.148 shows the notation thus shortened (the first bars of Examples A and B), and the way it is to be performed (the second bars of the examples).

Note that Beam is *only* a graphical symbol: it neither changes the notes, nor removes the rests. Therefore, the rests must be hidden beforehand (select them and press the <Ctrl>+<Alt>+<B> key combination).

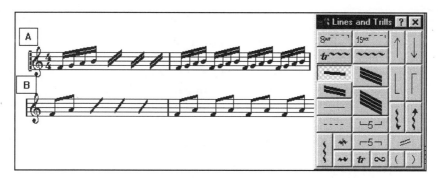

Fig. 3.148. Shortening the notation using the **Beam** symbols

❑ Other Symbols panel. It contains multi-purpose symbols. The Lyrics and Text symbols are intended for text insertion. The first one inserts the text, "linking" it with the note, and the second one allows you to position the text in any place of the score.

The Tempo symbol is very useful. It *automatically* shows the tempo in the place of the score where it is set. Remember that the tempo changes both on the Transport bar and in List Mastertrack.

The Scale Event symbol shows the scale (Fig. 3.149). See *Chapter 4*.

The Fret symbol enables you to write chords for guitarists.

Set a "blank" Fret symbol in the score, double-click on it with the Arrow tool, and enter the necessary values by clicking the mouse in the window that opens. Close the window with the OK button (Fig. 3.149).

The Repeat symbol denotes repeating bars (1 or 2 — according to the number of slanted lines). You can either set this symbol graphically or *replace* notation with it (see *Section 3.4.3*).

The Chord symbol allows you to set chords (see the details in *Chapter 4*).

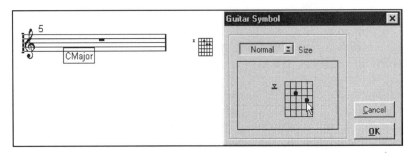

Fig. 3.149. The **Scale Event** and **Fret** symbols

The Pedal Down and Pedal Up symbols denote the pedal (press, release).

❑ Layout panel. Contains symbols mainly for designating the parts of the score.

Ending — ending symbols. They show that the part of the composition must be repeated several times with *different* endings.

In the example in Fig. 3.150 (staff 1) after the *a* bar, the first time you need to go to the 1st ending (bar *b*), and for the second time to bar *c*.

The ending mark can be corrected: enter a new value after a double-click.

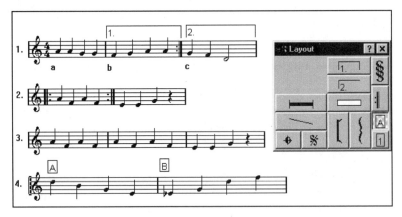

Fig. 3.150. The **Layout** panel

The Bar Lines symbol allows you to set the repetition sign (reprise): a bar line with two dots. Fig. 3.150 shows that Example 2 must be performed with a repetition: Example 3.

The Rehearsal mark symbols (letters or figures) are set so that musicians can easily find the necessary parts of the score during rehearsals for a simultaneous start. These symbols are changed *automatically* at every other setting or removal (Example 4 in Fig. 3.150).

3.11.2. Score Layers

Now let's turn to an important item necessary for work with symbols.

Symbols set by means of the six described panels can be positioned in *different layers* of the score, which depends on the symbol type.

If a symbol relates *directly* to a note, it goes into the Note Layer, and therefore, is copied, moved, or deleted *together with the note*. This concerns all the symbols of the Note Symbols Palette panel, the Dynamic Symbols panel, some symbols of the Lines panel (arpeggio, trill, quintole), as well as some symbols of other panels. In other words, it concerns all symbols having to do with the note.

If the symbol belongs to the score, it is inserted into the Layout Layer and remains "linked" to one place of the score, despite the notation changes: the time, key, and clef (Clef ... panel) are not changed. *All* the symbols of the Layout panel, the symbol of the octave transition (8--- and 15---) on the Lines panel, and some other symbols remain the same.

It should be mentioned that these layers are *not designated in the editor*; they are separated "implicitly".

And there is one more important issue. The Layout Layer is created for *each* score individually, and it *cannot* be divided into parts. In practice, this means the following: suppose you have a score for several tracks open. Symbols are inserted into this general score — for all instruments. If you then open a part of only *one* track, it will *lack* the symbols of the "general" score, and this can be explained by the fact that many symbols affect all the tracks at once (e.g., a "bracket" combining the parts), and cannot be divided.

3.11.3. Operations with Symbols

In practice, to invoke a panel, click on its name in the Score/Symbol Palettes menu. To remove a panel from the screen, click on the x in the upper right corner of the panel.

Close All closes all the opened panels.

The panel will be *replaced* with another one if you click on the Windows icon and click on the name of another panel in the menu that opens (indicated by the arrow in Fig. 3.151).

This menu is used to change the form of the panels: Rectangular, Horizontal, Vertical.

Panels may be moved around the screen in the usual way: grab at the name of the window and drag it to another place.

A very useful function is the <Ctrl>+<Alt>+<C> key combination. It allows you to *temporarily* hide the panels, leaving space for the score, and then restore them *with the same positioning on the score*.

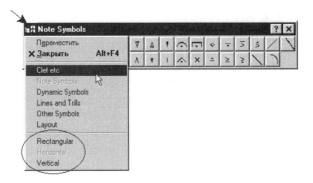

Fig. 3.151. Changing a panel's position

Below are the main principles of working with the symbols.

▼ *Warning*

If the notes are densely set, click on the **Auto Layout** option in the **Score** menu *before the symbols are set* (otherwise, some of them may be shifted). If necessary, before this operation is done, make the settings in the **Global Settings** menu.

It is very easy to set the symbols: open the panel, select the symbol (the tool is automatically changed to Pencil), and then click in the score.

To delete a symbol, erase it (click on it with the Eraser tool), or select it and press the <Backspace> or <Delete> keys.

If markers appear after clicking on the symbol with the **Arrow** tool, you can change the appearance of the symbol. Grab the marker and drag it to the new place. Fig. 3.152 shows with an example of a tie how you can change its form and borders.

If you just need to move the symbol with the markers, *without changing* its size, click and hold the Arrow tool on it: the markers will disappear, and you can move the symbol or hold the <Shift> key pressed when moving.

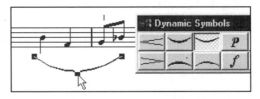

Fig. 3.152. The change in the symbol's appearance

You can click with the symbol belonging to the Note Layer (e.g., from the Note Symbols panel) in any place of the score, or directly on the note. In the second case, the symbol will be set at the fixed space near the note.

A symbol set by clicking on a note can be moved only *vertically* (Fig. 3.153).

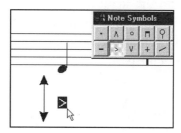

Fig. 3.153. The direction of moving the note symbol

Often, when symbols are set, you need to change the space between the staves. To do this, click and hold the **Arrow** tool to the left of the staff. When the latter is highlighted in black, move it up or down. If the <Alt> key is held down, the space between *all* the staves will be changed.

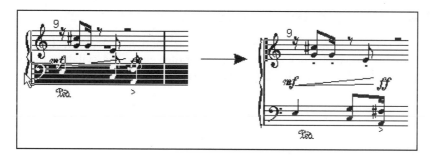

Fig. 3.154. Changing the space between staves

Symbol duplication. You can add the majority of symbols on the Note Symbols toolbar to several notes *simultaneously* (except for "single" symbols: fermata, etc.):

❏ 1st method:
1. Select the notes.
2. Click on the symbol of the **Note Symbols** panel.
3. Press the <Insert> key.
❏ 2nd method:
1. In the To: menu, select the area whose notes will have the symbols added.
2. Select a symbol on the Note Symbols toolbar.
3. Apply the Multi Insert command.

❏ 3rd method:

1. Press and hold the <Alt> key.
2. Click on a symbol of the Note Symbols toolbar.
3. Click on any note of the track and release the <Alt> key. The symbols will be added to all notes of the part.

You can set a symbol on several staves at the same time: *one under another* (in one rhythmic position). Press and hold the <Alt> key, and then click on the score. This method is very useful when you want to set dynamics, octave transition symbols, endings (1, 2), etc.

Many of the symbols can be copied (this is not applicable to the **Symbol Palettes** panel, ties, or bar lines). Press and hold the <Alt> key and drag the symbol to the new place.

Or, you can use the standard method: select the symbol, cut or copy (<Ctrl>+<X > or <Ctrl>+<C>), move the cursor to the required position, activate the staff with a click, and use the **Paste** command (<Ctrl>+<V>).

3.11.4. Lyrics in the Score

You can set words *exactly* under the notes as follows: select the **Lyrics** tool on the **Other Symbols** panel, click under the first note, enter the syllable, press the <Tab> key, then enter the next syllable, press the <Tab> key again, etc. After the entering is completed, click outside of the text.

You can edit these lyrics after double-clicking on a syllable. If a syllable is selected, you can move it up or down, delete it the <Delete> key, or erase it with the **Eraser** tool.

In all cases, when you need to add either letters or figures to a note, use the **Lyrics** symbol from the **Other Symbols** panel.

In order to add marks for the left or right hand to the percussion part, or to set fingering in a practice book, do the following:

1. Select all the notes above which this symbol is to be set. To do this, click on the notes holding the <Shift> key pressed.
2. Select **Lyrics** from **Other Symbols**.
3. Select the area in the **To:** menu (*always* with the word "Selected": **All Selected**, **Looped Selected Events**, etc.).
4. Click on any of the selected notes holding the <Alt> key pressed.
5. Enter the necessary letter or figure in the window that opens.
6. Press <Enter>, or click with the mouse outside of this field.

In this way, you can quickly "subscribe" the notes, so that these symbols are moved *strictly* together with the notes.

A text not linked with notes (e.g. the word "Tempo") is entered using the Text symbol.

The text settings are made in the windows opened in the Score menu by the Text Settings and Replace Text Font options.

The title of the score, name of the composer, and comments under the title are entered in the Score Title window opened by double-clicking either on the word "Composer" or on the default title.

3.12. Enlivening MIDI Sound

Below is a description of the symbols that affect the score.

3.12.1. Accents

One of the methods of changing the MIDI sound is to set "active" symbols in the score. You can accent notes using these symbols.

In the previous section, the graphic design of the score was considered, and all the symbols we covered were those intended for the musician.

The Cubasis Notation software allows you to set the 11 symbols of the Symbol Palettes panel in a way that can be understood and reproduced by the computer.

These symbols change the length of the note and its velocity, both in the score and on the MIDI event level.

Making the settings for the symbol is done in the Score menu in the MIDI Meaning window (Fig. 3.155). The necessary Velocity parameter and the length are set opposite the symbol in this window. The value is a percentage, from 25% to 200%, in steps of 25.

Check the Active option to activate the symbols. (If this option is checked, the MIDI Meaning window is invoked by double-clicking on any symbol.)

Fig. 3.155 shows the *quarter* notes *after* the symbols were set:

- ❑ The Staccato symbol makes a note shorter (bar 2).
- ❑ The Tenuto symbol makes a note longer (bar 3).
- ❑ One Accent symbol makes the note louder (bar 4).
- ❑ Another Accent symbol make the note longer and louder (bar 5).

Using the method of simultaneously adding symbols to notes, you can quickly edit the sound from the score.

You can set accents using the MIDI keyboard, recording only velocity to the notes. This makes the sound much more "live" than with a step of 25%, since more subtle shades are introduced manually. The details of the algorithm are described in *Section 2.17*.

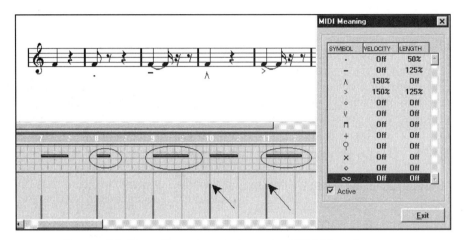

Fig. 3.155. The affect of symbols on the **MIDI Meaning** score

3.12.2. Dynamic Shades

The second method of enlivening the MIDI sound is done on a larger scale, and is related to the parameters of the dynamic shades.

In Cubasis Notation, you can make it so that most of the symbols of the Dynamics panel affect the sound by regulating the Velocity parameter.

The settings are made in the window opened by double-clicking on the symbol set in the score.

For alphabetical symbols (from triple piano to triple forte), the Process Dynamics window is opened (Fig. 3.156). Here, the borders of the start and the end of the symbol effect are set (in the Start and End fields), as well as the Velocity parameter.

In order to apply the settings only to one score, you should close the window with the This Staves button; to apply the setting to all scores, use the All Staves button.

These symbols are static: the volume remains the same for the period for which they are in effect.

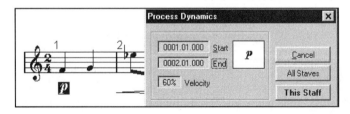

Fig. 3.156. Dynamic shade settings (alphabetical symbols)

Crescendo and diminuendo are intended for changing the dynamics in time while they are in effect.

After double-clicking on them, the Process Crescendo window opens (Fig. 3.157).

This window contains fields with the start and end coordinates of the symbol effect, the Velocity value in these points, as well as the End Velocity until end field. If you check the checkbox here, the Velocity value specified in the End Velocity field will be valid until the end of the part.

The area of application of the crescendo and diminuendo symbols also relates to one or all parts, depending on the button you pressed when you exited the window — This Staff or All Staves.

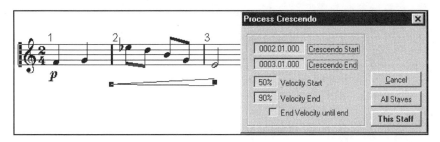

Fig. 3.157. Dynamic shade settings (crescendo and diminuendo)

The crescendo or diminuendo symbols of the Score Edit editor are handled by the software according to an intelligent algorithm that saves the previously set accents (Velocity). In comparison, the Line tool in the Key Edit editor positions velocity in one line, deleting the accents. This is another weighty argument in favor of the note editor that handles musical material "with care".

3.12.3. Tempo Changing

You can change the tempo at any place of the composition with any frequency and sequence. If you change the tempo by the beats of the bar, you can set a smooth slowing or acceleration.

This operation is done for the whole song (see details in *Section 2.19*).

Below we remind you of the main points (Fig. 3.158).

1. Set the cursor in the score at the point where the tempo changes. (The most precise way to do this is by entering a value in the Position Indicators field on the Transport bar.)
2. Open the List Mastertrack window in the Edit menu using the Mastertrack option.
3. Press the In button here, enter the required tempo in the newly created line, and close the window.

The change will be heard during the playback *only* if the **Master** button is pressed on the Transport bar.

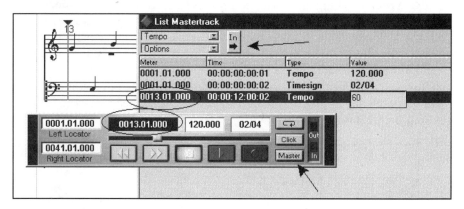

Fig. 3.158. Changing the tempo in the **List Mastertrack** window

3.12.4. Computer Swing

If you set the notes in the Score Edit editor using the mouse or the Fill option in the Do menu, they are positioned at accurate rhythmic positions.

This "mechanicalness" is impossible to hide with any special effects, timbres, etc.: you will always end up with a computer, "machine" performance.

If you employ rhythmic "enlivening" and supplement it with the methods mentioned above — adding dynamic shades, accents, tempo motion — then the computer music will sound very much like a "live" performance.

The result might be called computer swing.

We propose that you use the following method.

1. Select some notes in the Score Edit editor. (Separate notes can be selected with the <Shift> key pressed, and a chord can be framed.)
2. Open the Key Edit editor (the <Ctrl>+<E> key combination). The key imprints *selected* here correspond to the notes selected in the Score Edit editor.
3. Set the **Off** value in the Snap field to move the key imprints *by several ticks*. For convenience, set fine grid divisions in the **Quant** field (select 32).
4. Press and hold *any* of the selected key imprints before the "hand" appears.
5. Press and hold the <Shift> key so that the notes can only be moved horizontally.
6. Move a group of selected notes *by several ticks* to the right or to the left (when the shift is major, the notation in the Score Edit editor will be changed).
7. Go back to the Score Edit editor (using the <Ctrl>+<R> key combination).

If you reasonably apply this operation to *several* of the selected groups, shifting them slightly in the reverse direction, and then "enliven" the dynamics of the score using the methods described above, the "computerized" sound will be somewhat eliminated.

At the end of this review of the Score Edit editor, we'd like to concentrate on some of its similarities with the Key Edit editor.

3.13. Score Edit and Key Edit Comparison

As we already mentioned, many operations in the Score Edit editor coincide with those described in *Chapter 2* (the Key Edit editor). So, in order not to repeat ourselves, we refer you to *Chapter 2* for details on some of the methods.

❑ Step recording — *Section 2.13*
❑ Changing the tempo — *Section 2.19*
❑ Cycle recording — *Section 2.22*
❑ Quantization — *Section 2.20*

We'd also like to remind you of some useful methods.

❑ You can switch between editors using the <Ctrl>+<E> and <Ctrl>+<R> key combinations.
❑ Switch between windows using <Ctrl>+<Tab>.
❑ Switch between voices using the buttons with the numbers of voices on the Edit **Toolbar** panel. (The voice numbers of the *active* staff appear.)
❑ In order to simultaneously work with several parts in the Score Edit editor, select several parts in the **Arrange** window, and then open the editor for them (using the <Ctrl>+<R> key combination).
❑ The preset settings will be applied to all tracks opened in the Score Edit editor if you close the **Staff Settings** window with the <Alt> button pressed.
❑ If you need to place several parts opened in different editors on the screen, do the following:
   1. Open the Score Edit editor for the first track, and select, for example, the **Stack** option from the **Windows** menu.
   2. *Without closing this window*, open the Key Edit editor for another track, and select the same **Stack** option from the **Windows** window.
   3. If you don't need the **Arrange** window any more, minimize it (without closing it!) and position the remaining windows as you like by dragging their borders or by pressing the **Stack** option again (the windows will be arranged automatically).

❏ You can set the notes for a percussion part using the Fill option in the Do menu. To do this, select the values in the Quant and Snap fields, and then select the area in the To: menu and apply this command.

Select the notes (e.g., press the <Ctrl> key and double-click on one of the notes).

Grab the selected note with the mouse and move the whole chain to the required height. Enliven the part using the methods described above.

A percussion part can also be entered from the keyboard; you can look for new rhythmic sequences using rhythmic quantize, cycle recording, etc. (*Sections 2.20* and *2.22*).

We are sure that after some experience working with Cubasis Notation, you will find suitable solutions. In our opinion, the main thing is to understand the main working principles and to feel free to experiment.

The next chapter deals with experiments in the area of scales and the ways of searching for interesting melodic patterns.

3.14. Score Printing

You can only print a score from the Score Edit editor. To do this, select the Print or Print&Page option from the File menu. When one of these options is selected, a window is opened in which the user can make the necessary settings.

Since the printing operation is simple and done just as you would usually print a document, we will remind you here of just a few practical issues.

❏ You can hide unnecessary elements of the score (e.g., the default Composer inscription) in the usual way: select the element you want to hide and apply the Hide command from the Do menu (the Show command returns *all* the hidden elements). See details in *Section 3.1.4*.

❏ If there are notes hidden in the score after the Hide command is applied, *they will still sound, but will not be shown when the score is printed*. You can check for hidden elements by putting a check in the Hidden field of the Show Invisible (Score/Global Settings/Show Invisible) window. See details in *Sections 3.4.3* and *3.4.4*.

❏ You can optimize the score layout automatically by using the Auto Layout:All option of the Score menu.

❏ See details on the distance between score elements in *Section 3.4.2*.

❏ If necessary, you can have the note heads be in color when printed. To do this, click on the Edit Colors (▤) button and select the required color from the drop-down list (or edit it in the Colors window opened by selecting the Edit option). The color of the notes in the area selected in the To: field will be changed. Thus, you can highlight in color, for example, voices. Remember that in order to select all the notes of one voice, just click on any of its notes with the <Shift> key pressed.

❏ Use the fields of the System (Score/Staff Settings/Staff Options) section to change the scale, the distance between the lines, or the number of lines (or to hide them altogether when the figuring is printed). See details in *Section 3.2.7*.

❏ Sometimes, before the score is printed, it is good to make some marks especially for the musicians. This can be done not only with the accepted symbols (described in *Section 3.11.1*), but by simply adding text using the Text symbol. See details in *Section 3.11.4*.

❏ The **Real Book** option allows you to print the score without clefs on all lines (except for the first one).

❏ When different methods of transposition are used, you can print the score in the selected key, regardless of its real key. See details in *Sections 3.2.8* and *4.3.2*.

❏ The use of the CUE command, which enables you to graphically reduce the size of the notes, is described in *Section 3.2.3*.

❏ Methods of printing grace notes are described in *Section 3.10.5*.

Thus you see that the printing capabilities of the Cubasis Notation software are very wide and diverse.

CHAPTER 4

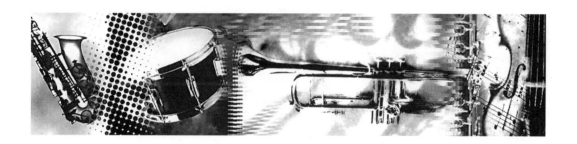

Chords and Scales

J ust as words are made up of syllables, chords are made up of intervals. The interval structure is seen in the chords, so you have to first grasp the idea of intervals in order to read the alphanumeric chord symbols (figuring).

4.1. Intervals — the Basis of a Chord's Formation

Intervals serve to measure the distance between notes in a chord. You can easily form a chord from *any* note if you know the interval structure of this chord.

An interval is the distance between the notes (from the Latin *intervallum* — space, distance). Since the minimal distance between notes in the tempered pitch is semitone, the intervals are measured in semitones or tones. A tone is equal to two semitones.

As we mentioned, only the white keys have independent names, the black keys being derived from them. You cannot name a black key unless you refer to a white one. It is this circumstance that makes it possible to easily determine intervals in any situation.

An elementary method of determining an interval is the following: *count the distance between the names of the white keys* within the interval, inclusive — from the lowest note to the highest.

For example, *C* and *D* up is a second (the names of two notes are used). There are two names of white keys between *C* and *D* flat, and so this interval is also a second. (They differ, however, in the number of semitones; this is considered below (Table 4.1).)

The names and designations of the intervals follow a clear logic: these are the numbers:

1 — Prime (unison) (from Latin *"prima"* — first)
2 — Second
3 — Third
4 — Fourth
5 — Fifth
6 — Sixth
7 — Seventh
8 — Octave

It is the numeric symbols that are used in the alphanumeric chord symbols (from here on out referred to as *figuring*).

In the majority of cases, it is sufficient to just know *simple* intervals. These are the intervals *within one octave*. Remember that an octave is the distance between *any* of the closest notes with the same name (not necessarily *C* notes).

Fig. 4.1 shows the scheme of interval formation up from the *C* note. You can see that *only* eight intervals lie within an octave, since there are eight names of the white keys, inclusive.

The same scheme is used to form intervals from *any* note — *up or down.*

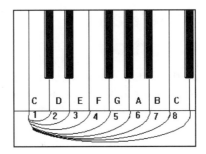

Fig. 4.1. Interval formation (up from the C note)

Depending on the number of semitones, intervals have specified names (Table 4.1).

Table 4.1. Simple Intervals from the C Note up

Name and abbreviated designation	Number of semitones	On keyboard	Example in notation
Perfect prime	0		
Minor second	1		
Major second (M 2)	2		
Minor third (m 3)	3		
Major third (M 3)	4		

continues

Table 4.1 Continued

Name and abbreviated designation	Number of semitones	On keyboard	Example in notation
Perfect fourth (P 4)	5		
Augmented fourth (A 4) (tritone)	6 (or 3 tones)		
Diminished fifth (d 5) (tritone)	6 (or 3 tones)		
Perfect fifth (P 5)	7		
Minor sixth (m 6)	8		
Major sixth (M 6)	9		
Minor seventh (m 7)	10		
Major seventh (M 7)	11		
Perfect octave (P 8)	12		

❗ Tritone

Two intervals (the augmented fourth and the diminished fifth) are often called "tritone", since both of them contain three tones.

If you switch the places of notes of any interval, the distance between them will be changed. In music, this change is called "inversion".

Inversion of a simple interval — the raising of one note up or down an octave so that the top note/bottom note relationship is reversed.

Understanding the logic of inversion simplifies understanding intervals.

For example, from the *C* note up to *D* is a second. If these notes are reversed, you will have an interval from *D* up to a *C*. Now, there are already *seven* names of the white keys between these notes, and therefore this is a *seventh* interval (Fig. 4.2).

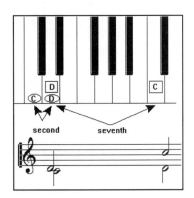

Fig. 4.2. Second-seventh inversion

Thus, if the notes are reversed within an octave, pairs of intervals occur — prime-octave, second-seventh, third-sixth, fourth-fifth.

When the intervals are inversed within an octave, the "sum" of their semitones is always equal to 12; minor intervals are inverted into major ones, diminished into augmented, and perfect into perfect (Fig. 4. 3).

No key signatures (accidentals) can affect the "main" name of the interval, but they can change the "second part" of the interval name: e.g., make it diminished or augmented, etc.

Below are the examples of such special cases, so that in the future, no accidental can prevent you from identifying the interval.

Intervals can be either narrowed or expanded using symbols. If a symbol *moves one note away from another*, then the interval is augmented; if the notes *get closer to each other*, the interval is diminished. Fig. 4 shows a *major* third from *C* to *E* (Example A). If you set the notes apart — e.g., augment the upper note — then you will have an *augmented* third: *C — E* sharp (Example B).

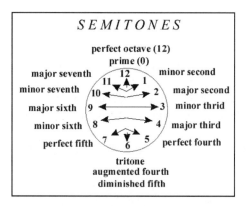

Fig. 4.3. Interval sizes in semitones and their inversion

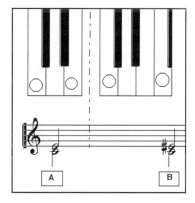

Fig. 4.4. Augmented intervals

Augmented or diminished intervals (except for tritones) are actually just variants on the names of the "common" intervals, being their enharmonic substitution.

Different names of notes of the same pitch is called in music enharmonics (from Greek *enharmonios* — concurrent). Example B in Fig. 4.4 is the enharmonic change of the fifth interval: from *C* to *F*.

Thus, by bringing the notes closer to each other or separating them, you can get an *augmented* interval from any *major* one, and a *diminished* interval from any *minor* one. Using this method, you can also make augmented or diminished intervals from perfect ones.

Finally, enharmonics can be illustrated by a joke-like question: what is the interval between "*C* seven-times-flat" and "*D* five-times-sharp"? The answer will comply with the rules — a second, since only *two* names of the white keys are used, but this facetious second is very, very much augmented by the number of semitones. So, the "life-saver" that we offer when the intervals are to be identified is to remember the names of the *white keys* in this interval.

Practical methods of identifying intervals. If you count the semitones every time you play the MIDI keyboard, you will have no time for the music itself. Therefore, you need to learn to determine the distance between the keys with your fingers. This takes nothing but practice, in which each musician works out his or her own techniques.

The following observations may be of use in the beginning.

- ❏ Two adjacent keys are a minor second, and a key and the one a key away is a major second.
- ❏ If there are one or two notes between the outermost notes, then this is a third interval (minor or major, respectively).
- ❏ Perfect fourth and fifth are intervals that can be easily seen on the keyboard, since in the majority of cases they consist either of *two white* keys, or two *black keys* of the piano (except when there are *H/B* or *F/F* sharp notes in the interval).

▶ *Note*

The fifth interval may help beginner musicians to build a triad, easily find the sixth interval, etc.

- ❏ The sixth interval is always a little broader than the fifth: if by a semitone, then it is minor sixth, and if by a tone, then it is a major sixth
- ❏ The seventh interval is slightly narrower than an octave: by a semitone (major seventh) or a tone (minor seventh)
- ❏ Some people may find it easier to identify a broad interval via its inversion

For example, in order to identify the interval from *C* to *B* (up), it is easier to "mentally" move the *C* note up (Fig. 4.5). Then you will have two neighboring notes: *C* and *B*. The distance between them is a semitone, so it is minor second, and its inversion is the source interval (from *C* up to *B*) — a major seventh.

We did not use the example of a seventh interval just by chance, since it is this interval that serves as the "border" of the most commonly used chord in modern music — the seventh chord, considered in the next section.

In order to "feel" intervals, you must play with them as you would with building blocks — learn to build any interval up and down from any note. Then you need to learn to build two and three intervals, and soon your knowledge will turn to skill, and you will master chord formation and start to understand figuring.

Now we'll say a few words about intervals in notation.

An amateur may say that a musician playing from music is a "superman", since he or she can decode the meaning of small and very similar "hieroglyphs" on the spot. This is only partially true. A musician playing from music doesn't scrutinize *each* note, but is guided by the distance between them. This is similar to reading, in which we don't scrutinize each letter, but grasp words, phrases, sentences or even pages at one glance. And anybody can learn to play from music. The thing is that not everybody is aware of some simple tricks.

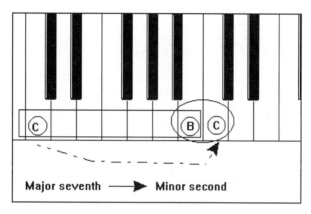

Major seventh ——▶ Minor second

Fig. 4.5. Using inversion to identify the interval

One of them is to determine the distance between the notes (intervals) "by appearance" (Fig. 4.6).

The notes of *absolutely all* intervals can only be written in two ways.

❑ One note of the interval is *on the line*, and the other is *between the lines* (Examples A, C, E in Fig. 4.6). This concerns all "even" intervals: seconds (2), fourths (4), sixths (6), etc.

❑ Both notes are written *on the lines* or *between the lines* (Examples B, D, F in Fig. 4.6). The concerns all odd intervals: thirds (3), fifths (5), sevenths (7), etc.

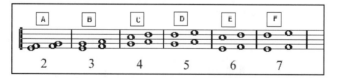

Fig. 4.6. Intervals in notation

If you are aware of this, it is sufficient to just look at one of the notes and determine "by eye" the distance to the other. The second note is determined at once: it is always *adjacent* notes, since they can not be positioned one above the other (Example A). If both notes are written on neighboring lines, then this is a third, after skipping a line a fifth, and skipping two lines a seventh, etc.

To conclude the topic, it is worth mentioning that intervals can be wider than an octave; these are called "compound intervals". For example, a *nona* (from the Greek — ninth) is from the *C* note up to *D* of the next octave. A nona is the distance between the outermost notes of a ninth chord.

Now we'll move on to constructing chords from intervals.

4.2. Chords and Figuring

The system of alphanumeric chord symbols is constantly developing, and unity has yet to be achieved. Therefore, you may run into different symbols for the same chord, for example, in jazz music, pop music, and musical literature. Since this book deals with Cubasis Notation, we will consider the variants of the chord symbols used in this software.

In Cubasis Notation, it is possible to identify chords in the notation and record them in the form of figuring to be used later as a guideline, either from the screen or as printouts.

Remember that the **Make Chords** command of the **Do** menu is intended for creating figuring (for the notes selected in the **To:** menu). Removing the staves is described in *Section 3.2.7*, in the explanation to Fig. 3.76, Example A.

Tertiary chord position. Usually, a chord (from the late Latin *accordo* — agree) is a consonance of notes that are positioned or that *can be* positioned in thirds.

In practice, the second part of the definition means the following. Suppose you have simultaneously pressed several notes in different registers: *C* in bass, *E* in the middle, and *G* in the upper register. In order to identify the structure and name of the chord, you need to make these notes closer to one another (any repetition of the same note is counted as one big note). In this example, we will get a chord whose sounds are positioned in *thirds*: *C, E, G* (Fig. 4.7).

 Note

If the notes were not set in thirds (for example, *E, G, C* or *G, E, C*), then this would be an inversion. This will be considered later.

Such a positioning of tertiary chord notes is called the *main position*.

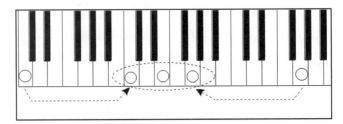

Fig. 4.7. Moving notes into one octave to identify the chord structure

If, as a result of such an operation, there are *three notes* in a chord positioned by thirds, such chord is called a *triad*; if there are 4 notes it is called a *seventh chord*, and if there are 5 notes it is a *ninth chord* (Fig. 4.8).

Numbers are usually assigned to the notes to make it possible to show the augmenting or diminishing of each note in the chord.

These numbers correspond to the *interval designations* from the first note to each subsequent one: 1 — prime, 3 — third, 5 — fifth, 7 — seventh, 9 — ninth (Fig. 4.8).

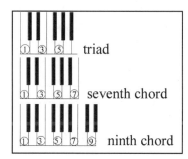

Fig. 4.8. Types of chords

Chords with a tertiary structure can be at any position in the "musical environment", and the numbers assigned to notes are retained. It is these numbers that are shown in the figuring. The Cubasis Notation software adds flat and sharp symbols to them. These symbols show that that the note with this number is either diminished or augmented by a semitone.

Now we'll turn our attention to chord symbols in the figuring of Cubasis Notation.

Triads. Triads differ by the thirds they consist of, and this affects the symbol.

The most widely spread triads are major and minor (Fig. 4.9):

❏ The major triad has a major third at the bottom and a minor third at the top (A).

❏ The minor triad is the opposite: the minor third is at the bottom, and the major third is at the top (B).

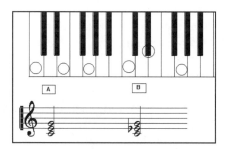

Fig. 4.9. Major and minor triads

A major triad is designated in the software by *one letter*: the name of the first note of the triad. If the note has a symbol (e.g., sharp or flat), then the symbol is written beside the letter (Fig. 4.10).

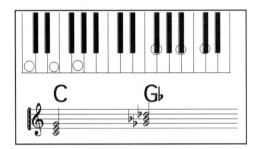

Fig. 4.10. Designation of a major triad

A minor triad is supplemented with a "minor symbol" — minus, or the letter m (Fig. 4. 11). If necessary, the user can change this symbol in the Chord Font tab of the Global Settings window.

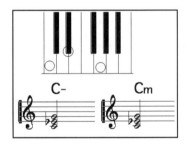

Fig. 4.11. Variants of designating a minor triad

Triads can not only be major or minor, but also *diminished* — consisting of two minor thirds, and *augmented* — consisting of two major thirds. Both possess unique harmonic colors.

The outermost notes of these triads make a diminished or augmented fifth, respectively. These "peculiar fifths" are marked in the figuring: the software sets either a flat (diminishing) or sharp (augmentation) symbol beside the number 5 (Fig. 4.12).

It is very important to understand that in *figuring*, the flat and sharp symbols denote *only the fact of diminishing or augmenting the note with this number*, i.e., they show the *size of the interval* with this number, and not the alteration symbol in notation.

So, Fig. 4.12 shows that a diminished triad in figuring is marked with the flat symbol beside the number 5: a diminished fifth. However, there may not be a flat symbol in the notation (the last chord).

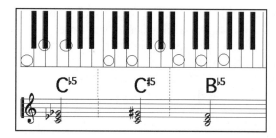

Fig. 4.12. Designating diminished and augmented triads

All the types of triads are the foundation of the more complicated chords: seventh chords, ninth chords, etc. (see Fig. 4.8). So, figuring in Cubasis Notation may have flats or sharps beside the number 5 not only when indicating a triad. A flat or sharp symbol beside the number 5 cues the musician that the chord contains a diminished or augmented triad, respectively.

Chord inversion. Chord inversion is considered below using the example of a triad.

The position of a tertiary chord — when all notes are set by thirds — is called the main position.

If there is some tone other than the root one in the bass (not the note marked with number 1), then this chord is *inverted.*

Fig. 4.13 shows, using the example of the *C* major triad, the way the software indicates inversion: the name of the bass note is hyphenated from the chord symbol.

Note

Compound chords are inverted in a similar manner — the bass note is designated with a letter.

If you invert any tertiary chord, the notes there will not be positioned strictly by thirds. Consider the example of a major triad. First, we'll move its bottom note an octave higher, and then its middle note. As a result, we have two variants of the triad's inversion (Fig. 4.13).

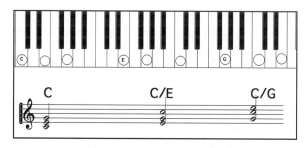

Fig. 4.13. Triad inversion

Inversions are easily detected in the figuring of Cubasis Notation: the first letter is the triad, and the second (slashed) one is the bass note.

In music, inversions are used together with main chords, and experienced musicians have no trouble with them.

All inversions, including those of triads, have their own names that show the peculiarities of their interval structure (Fig. 4.13):

❑ The first inversion of a triad is called a *sixth chord*, since a sixth interval is between the outermost notes.

❑ The second inversion is a six-four chord. This name implies two intervals: fourth (from the bottom note to the middle note) and sixth (from the bottom note to the top note).

In order not to get tangled up in the variety of chords, do not take inversions as separate chords. Figuratively speaking, inversions are different sides of one object. For example, if you look at a book, its appearance will be different, depending on your perspective — from top, side, or front. But despite the spatial position, the attributes of the object will remain the same. The same with notes: the names of the notes making a chord *never change* with inversion.

▶ *Tip*

In practice, the "fulcrum" used in triad inversions reminds us of the position of the main tone (the first *lettered* note in figuring, and the one numbered "1" in tertiary structure). It is at the bottom in the triad, on top in the first inversion, and in the middle in the second inversion (Fig. 4.13).

The best method of mastering the science of chords is step-by-step. First you should know the triad and its inversions, then the seventh chord and its inversions. Then all the rest of the chords (ninth chord, etc.). Usually, it is often sufficient to know just the first two stages.

We should note that it is much easier to understand the structure of chords if you think of them as within a scale, since it is the distance between the scale steps that governs the chord structure. Scales are considered in the next section. Here, the chord structure is considered without scales, since the pure structure of the chord is shown in figuring without any scales whatsoever.

Seventh chord. Figuratively speaking, a seventh chord is a "triad plus a third" (Fig. 4.14). The name of this interval comes from the interval between the outermost notes — a seventh.

We know that there are four triads: major, minor, diminished, and augmented. Seventh chords are formed by adding various thirds to them. It should be mentioned that not all of the possible combinations of triads and thirds are actively used in modern music.

Like that of triad, the structure of a seventh chord is also shown in figuring.

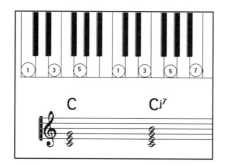

Fig. 4.14. Comparison of a triad and a seventh chord

Different musical trends, countries, and schools have "special" symbols for the most common kinds of seventh chords. In Cubasis Notation, you can choose the one you are accustomed to.

The settings are made in the right part of the Global Settings window after the Chord Font category is selected (Fig. 4.15). To apply the settings, close the window with the OK button.

► Note

The designation of a minor triad is set in the **Minor** section.

The Chord Size field is used to set the font size of the symbols.

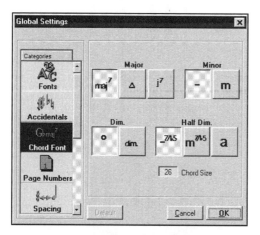

Fig. 4.15. The **Global Settings** window.
The **Chord Font** category

Table 4.2 shows symbols of eight different seventh chords in Cubasis Notation. The last column contains the name of the section in which the symbol is changed.

 Note

You can build the seventh chord in various ways: you can add the seventh of the **main tone** to the triad, or the third of the **fifth tone**. The table shows both methods, and you can choose the one you like most.

Table 4.2. Symbols of Eight Differently Built Seventh Chords from *C* and *B*

Structure	On keyboard	Notation	Variants of symbols and name of section
Major triad and minor seventh of the main tone (or the minor third of the fifth tone)			C^7
Major triad and major seventh of the main tone (or major third of the fifth tone)			C_{maj}^7 C_Δ C_j^7 **Major**
Minor triad and minor seventh of the main tone (or minor third of the fifth tone)			Cm^7 C^{-7} **Minor**
Minor triad and major seventh of the main tone (or major third of the fifth tone)			C^{-j^7} Cm^{j^7} **Minor**
Diminished triad and diminished seventh of the main tone (or minor third of the fifth tone)			$B_{dim.}$ B° **Dim.**

continues

Table 4.2 Continued

Structure	On keyboard	Notation	Variants of symbols and name of section
Diminished triad and minor seventh of the main tone (or major third of the fifth tone)			$Cm^{7/\flat5}$ $C^{-7/\flat5}$ Ca **Half Dim.**
Diminished triad and major seventh of the main tone (or augmented third of the fifth tone)			$Cj^{7/\flat5}$
Augmented triad and major seventh of the main tone (or minor third of the fifth tone)			$Cmaj^{7/\sharp5}$ $C\Delta^{\sharp5}$ $Cj^{7/\sharp5}$ **Major**

Like a triad, a seventh chord also has inversions, which are made similarly: the bottom note is moved an octave up.

The inversions of seventh chords look like inversions of triads:

❐ The notes are also positioned in thirds.

❐ The interval structure is also shown in the name (the interval from the *bottom* note to the next notes is taken into account).

❐ They are designated in the same way in figuring: the bass note is written as a letter after a slash (Table 4.2).

Table 4.3. Inversions of Seventh Chords: Structure and Symbols Using the Example of the Major Seventh Chord Built from the C Note

Name of chord	On keyboard	In notation
Seventh chord (main position)		$Cmaj^{7}$

continues

Table 4.3 Continued

Name of chord	On keyboard	In notation
First inversion — six-five chord		C_{maj}^7/E
Second inversion — four-three chord		C_{maj}^7/G
Third inversion — four-two chord		C/B *)

* For the sake of clarity, the four-two chord in Cubasis Notation is designated as a triad and a bass note.

If you need to edit the chord symbol in figuring, click on the name of the chord, select the new symbols in the **Edit Chord Symbol** window, and close the window with the OK button (Fig. 4.16).

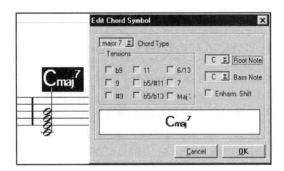

Fig. 4.16. The **Edit Chord Symbol** window

You can change the symbol of the chord type in this window by selecting the required value in the Chord Type field (Fig. 4.17). You can also edit the name of the root note of the chord in the Root Note drop-down list, and change the name of the bass note by selecting the required letter from the Bass Note field's drop-down list.

If the note symbols available in these lists are not suitable, you can change them enharmonically by placing a check in the Enharm. Shift field. Thus you can set, for example, the note symbol with a flat instead of a sharp in the figuring.

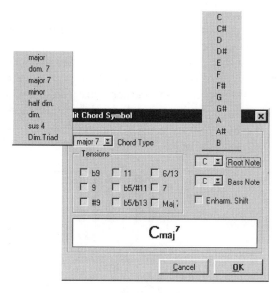

Fig. 4.17. Drop-down lists for editing chords in the figuring

The fields in the Tensions section are checked automatically (Fig. 4.18). Here, variants of chord steps are shown: from 9 up, as well as some of their combinations.

You can also check the boxes manually, which will affect the chord symbol in the figuring.

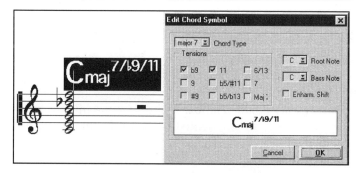

Fig. 4.18. The **Tensions** field

And now we'll give you just a little more about chords.

If all the "root" notes of a scale are set by thirds, you will have a chain of seven notes: *C, E, G, B, D, F,* and *A*. Thus the total number of tertiary chords is five.

We have considered two types of chords: the triad and the seventh chord. They consist of 3 and 4 notes set by thirds, respectively.

Three other "big chords" consist of 5, 6, and 7 notes set by thirds; these are named by the interval between their outermost notes: the ninth chord (9), the decimal chord (11) and the undecimal chord (13).

It is not uncommon in music to have not all the notes of a chord be played, but just *some* of them. If a chord is identified by its fragments, its name may be interpreted differently, and thus theoretical disagreements are possible when identifying a chord.

The Cubasis Notation software "intelligently" identifies chords, depending on the context, trying to designate them as simply as possible. The figuring in Fig. 4.19 shows a seventh chord with an "addition": the sixth step (see more details on steps in the next section).

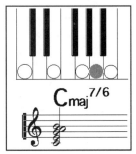

Fig. 4.19. A variant of a chord symbol

The conclusion that can be drawn here is that the "frightening" chord symbols in the figuring help a competent musician see the structure of these chords.

- ☐ The first letter is the root note designation (the main tone).
- ☐ The letter after the slash is the bass note (or additional step).
- ☐ Numbers are the numbers of the notes in the chord. They correspond to the interval by which these notes are separated from the main tone in the main position of the chord: 1, 3, 5, 7, 9, etc.
- ☐ Flats and sharps beside the number make clear the interval structure of the chord (a sharp before a 5 is an augmented triad within the chord, a flat before a 9 is a minor ninth, etc.).

Figuring has many advantages: it is concise, clear, shows a complex chord structure, provides freedom for improvisation, etc.

But you should remember that figuring is just a symbolic designation of harmonic colors and is not as detailed as the notation. It doesn't show the octave the chord must be performed in, or its length, texture, the details of voices, etc. So, figuring is by no means literal: if there is a major or minor triad above the bar, then that means you should press and hold for the whole bar.

Figuring is nothing but the "harmonic frame" of a composition. It helps performers to improvise, but they are the ones who must introduce variety and additions using the available means of expression. The more experienced and talented the musician, the more interesting is a performance guided by figuring.

4.3. Scales and Scale Quantization

There are 21 scales in Cubasis Notation. Among them are major, minor, Oriental, Chinese, Japanese, Indian (Raga–Todi), Hungarian, and others (Fig. 4.20).

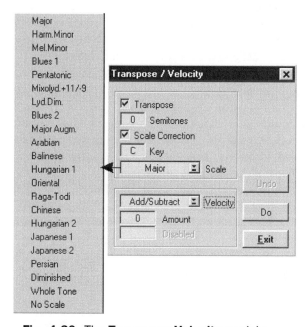

Fig. 4.20. The **Transpose Velocity** module

All these scales are available in the Transpose/Velocity window (Functions menu). This window has the Scale Correction function, which will from now on be referred to as *scale quantize.*

Scale quantizing allows you to "correct mistakes" made within a scale, or change material by moving it to another scale. The scale quantize function may not only help to "get your bearings" within a scale, but can also provide you with some interesting creative ideas as well.

Below is a brief overview of scale for those who are not very well acquainted with musical theory.

4.3.1. Scale and Key

Imagine some very simple melody without the very last note. Even if you have never heard this melody before, you will feel that it has been interrupted before its time, and may very well be able to guess what the last note is supposed to be.

This example shows that there are some "laws" in the music world that are understood by all people.

The contemporary system of music is a range of sounds in a certain ratio among themselves. Some of these sounds are stable (a melody could be said to rest upon them) and unstable sounds gravitate to them, "anxious" to become stable. The transformation of an unstable sound into a stable one is called *resolution*.

Scale is the "relationship", or the interconnection of musical sounds based on the dependence of the unstable sounds on the stable ones.

Figuratively speaking, scale is the "rule of the game", and according to this rule, you can "move only by permitted steps" positioned at a certain distance from each other.

The sounds of a scale are called its *steps*. These are designated with Roman numerals, from unison (I) (the first and the most stable sound) up (II, III, etc.).

There is a *strictly specified* distance between the steps in each scale.

In tempered harmony, this distance is *always* divisible by a semitone — the minimal distance between sounds.

One of the most widely spread scales in contemporary music is the major scale. It is called Major in the software, and has the following structure: Tone + Tone + Semitone + Tone + Tone + Tone + Semitone. This distance between the steps is retained when a major scale is formed, beginning from any note.

For example, if you make a major scale from the *C* note, then all of its steps will fall on the white keys (Fig. 4.21). This scale is very convenient for beginners to play; the main idea is not to touch the black keys.

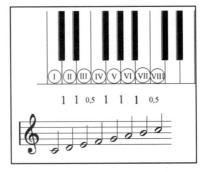

Fig. 4.21. A major scale from C

Fig. 4.22 shows a major scale from the *D* note. The figure illustrates that there are six white and 2 black keys. It is important to remember that the formula for constructing any scale remains the same, no matter what the root note is. So, the distances between the steps in a major formed from *D* are also the same: 1; 1; 0.5; 1; 1; 1; 0.5.

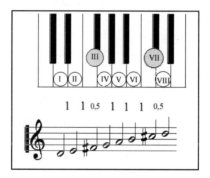

Fig. 4.22. A major scale from *D*

Another widely used scale is minor. It has the following structure: Tone + Semitone + Tone + Tone + Semitone + Tone + Tone.

If you form a minor scale from the *A* note, then all its steps will be found only on the white keys (Fig. 4.23).

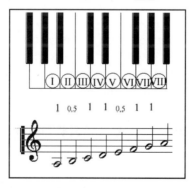

Fig. 4.23. A perfect minor from *A*

Both scales — major and minor — have varieties. Here we only show their perfect types.

In order to avoid confusion, we need to define the concepts of scale, tonic (key note), and key.

A scale can be formed from *any* note; the note it is formed from is called the *tonic*.

No contradictions occur in any scale except for major and minor. This means that, when speaking about these scales, people usually talk about "such-and-such a scale" from "such-and-such a note".

However, the major and minor scales formed from certain notes are often called *key*. The key of *C* major is the major scale from the *C* note. The key of *A* minor is the minor scale from the *A* note, etc.

Now we'll say a few words about "relationships" in the musical world. Keys may be very close to each other, and this is determined by the number of identical notes within them: the more identical "genes", the closer the relatives.

Sometimes the notes included in two keys fully coincide. This occurs, for example, with *C* major and *A* minor. The notes in these keys are the same, but the major and minor scales rest upon different tonics: *C* and *A* (compare Figs. 4.21 and 4.23). Such keys are called *relative*. The tonics of relative keys are a minor third apart from each other (major at the top, minor at the bottom). Relative keys are of the first degree of relation.

The more identical notes there are in the keys, the more chords they have in common. Consequently, the wider are your options of shifting from one key to another, so-called *modulation*.

Finally, a bit more information about the benefits of scale.

The sequence of a scale's steps forms its *gamut*, and beginner musicians do not spend their time playing gamuts for nothing: apart from everything else, they master scales formed from different notes, "memorizing with their fingers" the positions of their steps.

Knowing a scale's steps enables you to easily form chords, since all their notes are positioned *only* on the scale's steps.

The topic of harmony and computer technology is very interesting indeed, and we plan to consider it in more detail in our next book.

4.3.2. The *Transpose/Velocity* Module.
21 Creative Scales

This section deals with the main principles of scale quantization, called Scale Correction in the software.

The slogan of the scale quantization might be: "All notes — to the scale steps!" Literally, it means that no matter what notes there are in a part, after scale quantization, all of them will be positioned on the steps of the selected scale — the "permitted pitch positions".

If the reader knows the theory of scale only slightly, Cubasis Notation will be of help.

This process recalls rhythmic quantization, but there is one crucial difference. When rhythmic quantization is applied, the notes are set to the *nearest* rhythmical positions. When scale quantization is applied, the transition is done in accordance with an intelligent algorithm: notes are moved to the scale steps, but *not necessarily* the nearest ones — they are moved to the ones that the software "deems the most suitable".

Scale quantization makes computer the "electronic co-author", offering its own melodic and harmonic patterns. Thus, when you place a musical part (or its pieces) in different scales, you may come up with some very interesting variants on the theme's development, which later you just need to edit and use in your composition.

Scale quantization can be applied to both whole parts and their pieces. Cutting parts (and pasting them) is done in the **Arrange** window. You can also apply these operations to just selected notes (see below).

Remember that you can edit a part (also after scale quantization) in the cycle playback mode. See the details on that in *Section 2.22*.

The scales available in Cubasis Notation are quite diverse, both in the number of steps and in the distance between them (Table 4.4). Thanks to this, each scale has its own unique melodic and harmonic colors.

 Note

The scales shown in the table are formed from the *C* note, and in two cases, for harmonic and melodic minor, from the *A* note. This is done to be able to conveniently compare them with the perfect minor in Fig. 4.23.

Table 4.4. Scales of the Transpose/Velocity Module in Cubasis Notation

Scale	On keyboard (with distance between the scale steps)	Comments*
Major	1 1 0.5 1 1 1 0.5	Seven steps within an octave. Perfect major. Distances between them — one tone, one semitone.

continues

Table 4.4 Continued

Scale	On keyboard (with distance between the scale steps)	Comments*
Harm. Minor (Harmonic minor)	1 0.5 1 1 0.5 1 0.5	Seven steps within an octave. Distances between them — one tone and one semitone. In harmonic minor — the most common minor — the seventh step is augmented.
Mel. Minor (Melodic minor)	1 0.5 1 1 1 0.5 1 0.5	Seven steps within an octave. Distances between them — one tone and one semitone. In a melodic minor, the sixth and seventh steps are augmented.
Blues 1	1 0.5 1 0.5 0.5 1 0.5 1	Eight steps within an octave. Distances between them — one tone and one semitone.
Blues 2	1 0.5 0.5 1.5 1 1.5	Six steps within an octave. Distances between them — one and a half tone and one semitone.
Pentatonic	1 1 1.5 1 1.5	Five steps within an octave. Distances between them — one tone and one and a half semitone.

continues

Table 4.4 Continued

Scale	On keyboard (with distance between the scale steps)	Comments*
Mixolyd. +11/-9 (Mixolydic with augmented 11 and diminished 9 steps	0.5 1.5 1 0.5 1 0.5 1	Seven steps within an octave. Distances between them — one semitone, one tone, and one and a half tone. Actually, −9 and +11 take the place of "regular" steps in this scale: they diminish the second and augment the fourth.
Lyd. Dim (Lydic diminished)	1 0.5 1.5 0.5 1 1 0.5	Seven steps within an octave. Distances between them — one semitone, one tone, and one and a half tone.
Major Augm (Major with augmented triad on 1st step)	1.5 0.5 1.5 0.5 1.5 0.5	Six steps within an octave. Distances between them *alternate uniformly*: one and a half tone and one semitone.
Arabian	1 1 0.5 0.5 1 1 1	Seven steps within an octave. Distances between them — one semitone and one tone.
Balinese	1 0.5 2 0.5 2	Five steps within an octave. Distances between them — one tone, one semitone, and two tones.

continues

Table 4.4 Continued

Scale	On keyboard (with distance between the scale steps)	Comments*
Hungarian 1	1 0.5 1.5 0.5 0.5 1.5 0.5	Seven steps within an octave. Distances between them — one semitone, one tone, and one and a half tone.
Hungarian 2	1.5 0.5 1 0.5 1 0.5 1	Seven steps within an octave. Distances between them — one semitone, one tone, and one and a half tone.
Oriental	0.5 1.5 0.5 0.5 1 1 1	Seven steps within an octave. Distances between them — one semitone, one tone, and one and a half tone.
Raga-Todi (Indian)	0.5 1 1.5 0.5 0.5 1 1	Seven steps within an octave. Distances between them — one semitone, one tone, and one and a half tone.
Chinese	2 1 0.5 2 0.5	Five steps within an octave. Distances between them — one semitone, one tone, and two tones.

continues

Table 4.4 Continued

Scale	On keyboard (with distance between the scale steps)	Comments*
Japanese 1	0.5 2 1 0.5 2	Five steps within an octave. Distances between them — one semitone, one tone, and two tones.
Japanese 2	1 1.5 1 0.5 2	Five steps within an octave. Distances between them — one semitone, one tone, one and a half tone, and two tones.
Persian	0.5 1.5 0.5 0.5 1 1.5 0.5	Seven steps within an octave. Distances between them — one semitone, one tone, and one and a half tone.
Diminished	1 0.5 1 0.5 1 0.5 1 0.5	Eight steps within an octave. Distances between them — one semitone and one tone.
Whole Tone	1 1 1 1 1 1	Seven steps within an octave. Distance between them — one tone.

continues

Table 4.4 Continued

Scale	On keyboard (with distance between the scale steps)	Comments*
No Scale		Transposition option — moving all notes to another pitch without changing the scale.

* The eighth step is considered to be a repetition of the first step: VIII = I.

Now we'll consider the Transpose/Velocity window, where the scale quantization and dynamic range handling is done (Fig. 4.24). The window is invoked in the Functions menu using the Transpose/Velocity option or the <Ctrl>+<H> key combination.

Warning

You can undo all the operations of the **Transpose/Velocity** module *only once!* To do this, invoke the window again and press the **Undo** button, and then close it with the **Exit** button.

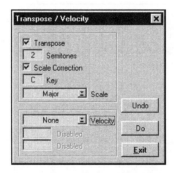

Fig. 4.24. The **Transpose Velocity** window

This window consists of two sections. The upper section allows you to shift notes by scales using one of four variants: transposition, scale change without a tonic change, quantization when shifting the "scale pattern", and the simultaneous change of scale and tonic. Below are examples.

Transposition. Transposition moves all notes to another pitch *without changing* the distance between them.

In order to transpose notes, check the box in the Transpose field, and using the mouse button, select the number of semitones in the Semitones window (negative — diminishing, positive — augmenting). Then press the Do and Exit buttons one after the other. Upon doing this, both the MIDI events and the notation are *simultaneously* moved (see *Section 3.2.8* for details on other types of transposition).

Warning

In order to avoid accidental application of scale quantization during transposition, uncheck the **Scale Correction** box, or select **No Scale** from the list of scales.

Fig. 4.25 shows that after the notes were transposed by 5 semitones (Example A), they were moved up (Example B). This can seen in both the Score Edit and the Key Edit editor.

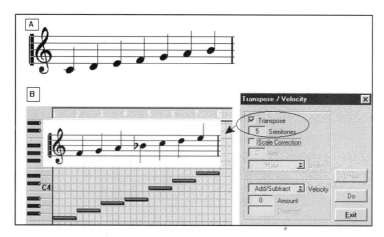

Fig. 4.25. Transposition via the **Transpose/Velocity** module

Scale change. This function moves the notes to the steps of the selected scale, and the distance between the notes is *changed* in accordance with the new scale (Fig. 4.26).

To change the scale, check the **Scale Correction** box. Then select the scale in the drop-down list of the **Scale** field, and press the **Do** and **Exit** buttons.

Important! The value in the **Key** field indicates the note the scale is formed from.

The source example (A) in Fig. 4.26 is done in the *C* major key. The tonic of this scale is *C*. The **Raga-Todi** scale is also formed from the *C* note (this is shown in the **Key** field).

Note

In Table 4.4, the **Raga-Todi** scale is also formed from the *C* note. You can trace the logic of scale quantization by comparing Fig. 4.26 and example 15 in Table 4.4.

Quantization while shifting the "scale pattern". The scale can be formed not only from the *C* note but from any other note as well. If the "scale quantization pattern" is shifted, then the result of applying the **Scale Correction** function will be different.

In order to understand the logic of the software, create the Indian scale Raga-Todi from the *G* note ("on paper") (Fig. 4.27).

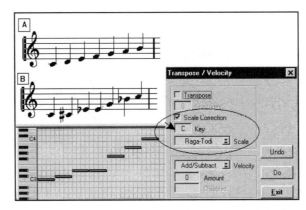

Fig. 4.26. Changing the scale via the **Transpose/Velocity** module

You know its "formula": 0.5, 1; 1.5; 0.5; 0.5; 1.1 (Table 4.4, Example 14).

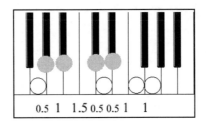

Fig. 4.27. The **Raga Todi** scale from *G*

Now specify the alphabetic designation of the *G* note in the Key field of the Transpose/Velocity window. The software will form the Raga-Todi scale from *G*, and quantize accordingly. The result of such quantization will differ from the previous example, since the notes of the source example will appear on *other* steps of the scale: compare Example B in Figs. 4.26 and 4.28.

Simultaneous change of scale and tonic. If you need to *transpose* the material and simultaneously perform scale quantization in a new scale-key, change the values in the Semitone and Key fields.

Fig. 4.29 shows a *single transposition operation* from the *C* major key to the *E* major key — the material was raised by four semitones and further quantized by the Raga–Todi pattern from the new tonic (E). The number of semitones is shown in the Semitones field, and the tonic of the new scale is specified in the Key field (Fig. 4.29).

Another important point is that scale quantization can be applied *selectively* — to *certain* notes. This method will considerably diversify the results. Select some notes in the Key Edit or Score Edit editors, invoke the **Transpose/Velocity** window, make the necessary settings, and press the Do and Exit buttons. You can select notes with a frame, or click on them with the <Shift> key pressed.

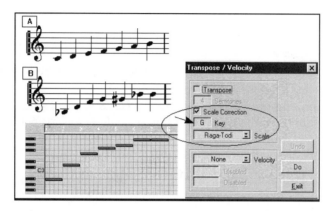

Fig. 4.28. Scale quantization using
the **Raga Todi** scale formed from *G*

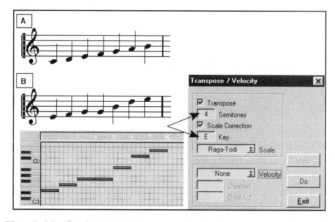

Fig. 4.29. Scale and tonic change via **Transpose / Velocity**

Fig. 4.30 shows that in the first case, scale quantization was applied to the whole material (Example A), and in the second case it was only applied to three selected notes (Example B). The last four notes in the second example remained the same.

Let's now take a look at the second section of the Transpose / Velocity window. It is intended for volume compression and expansion. The interface of this section may differ, depending on the value selected in the **Velocity** field (Fig. 4.31).

❑ None — no operations are done (Example A)

❑ Compress/Expand — compression/expansion (Example B):

   • Ratio — compression/expansion ratio as a percentage: if more than 100%, then volume expansion takes place; if less, then compression.

- Center — the central **Velocity** value, regulating compression and expansion. If Ratio is more than 100%, then the values exceeding the central **Velocity** value will be increased, and those less than the central value will be decreased.
- ❑ **Add/Subtract** — simple addition or subtraction of the value specified in the **Amount** field (Example C)
- ❑ **Limit** — limiting the **Velocity** values to a certain range, with the upper and lower borders specified in the **Upper** and **Lower** fields, respectively (Example D)

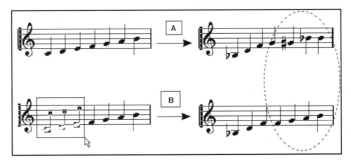

Fig. 4.30. Applying scale quantization to selected notes

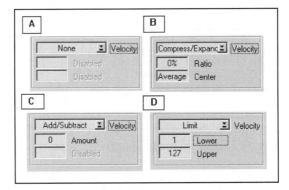

Fig. 4.31. The **Velocity** section of the **Transpose/Velocity** window

Experimenting with the Transpose/Velocity module may suggest to you some fresh melodic and harmonic ideas.

CHAPTER 5

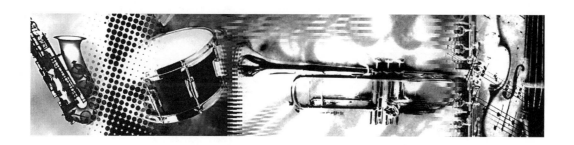

Quality MIDI Converting into Audio with VST Instruments

V ST instruments (Virtual Studio Technology) are a special variety of audio processing plug-ins.

The virtuality of these instruments lies in the fact that they can not be physically touched. In everything else, they look like real musical instruments: we can see them, hear them play, tune them, switch the programs, select the timbre, etc. Unlike real instruments, however, their handles and keys are placed in a virtual environment: on the screen (Fig. 5.1).

Fig. 5.1. The PRO-52 virtual instrument

VST instruments have many advantages.

❑ First, the quality of the sound and their capabilities compare well with those of their "real brothers".

❑ Second, they are mobile, do not occupy much space, and are less expensive. Therefore, you can often replace them, remaining at the forefront of audio technology.

❑ Third, they are integrated directly into the Cubasis VST software. This enables you to play a MIDI part using a special integrated application (a plug-in) called a VST instrument. Then you can mix the MIDI sound thus received with audio tracks on the virtual mixer (**VST Channel Mixer**). This is an extremely important advantage of VST instruments, since it enables you to transform *MIDI into Audio without a loss of quality* (re-recording MIDI into Audio is done via the sound card).

❑ Fourth, thanks to VST instruments, both MIDI parts and Audio tracks can be processed in real time with *all kinds of virtual effects* (Insert and Send).

❏ Fifth, you can play VST instruments in real time by pressing the keys of the regular MIDI keyboard. This is possible, however, only if your sound card supports professional ASIO program interfaces. (Two such sound cards — M-Audio Audiophile 2496 and SB Audigy — were considered in *Chapter 1*).

❏ Sixth, if you have no special sound card, virtual instruments can still be used for playing *previously created* MIDI parts.

By default, VST instruments are placed in the **Program Files/Steinberg/ Cubasis VST/Vstplugins** folder.

There are several demo VST instruments supplied with the Cubasis VST software. If necessary, the user can always connect professional models, for example, the PRO-52 VST instrument shown in Fig. 5.1, or the HALion virtual sampler.

VST instruments are files with the DLL extension (Fig. 5.2). Files with the FXB extension are placed in separate folders, and also contain program banks (sometimes called *timbres* or *patches*) for each instrument.

Fig. 5.2. VST instrument files

The instruments installed are loaded by default together with Cubasis VST.

The **VST Instruments** command of the **Audio** menu opens the virtual instrument rack, which consists of 4 sections (Fig. 5.3). There is one VST instrument switched on in each section.

▶ *Tip*

Since some VST instruments require many resources, it is best to unload them if you don't use them.

The interface of VST instruments looks like that of the virtual effects considered in *Chapter 1*.

The **POWER** buttons (indicated by the arrow in Fig. 5.3) are used for switching each of them on/off.

Connecting and unloading a VST instrument is done by selecting a command in the drop-down list (Fig. 5.3, Example A). It is opened with a click on the field with the name of the VST instrument (or with No VST Instruments when no instruments are loaded).

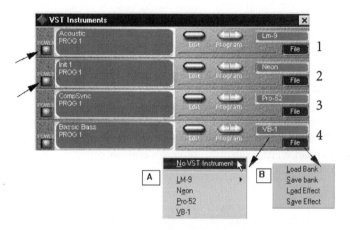

Fig. 5.3. The virtual rack for VST instruments

When you click on the **Edit** button, you open the VST instrument window. The double **Program** button is used for program (timbre) switching.

The drop-down list (B) is used for loading and saving separate programs and banks. This is done in the same way as with the plug-ins (see *Section 1.15.2*).

Each loaded VST instrument creates a virtual MIDI port.

In order to assign a MIDI track to a virtual port, click in the field of the Output column and select the name of the port (Fig. 5.4). The name of the port coincides with that of the virtual instrument. There is a number near the port showing the number of this VST instrument in the virtual rack (compare the number of PRO-52 in Figs. 5.3 and 5.4).

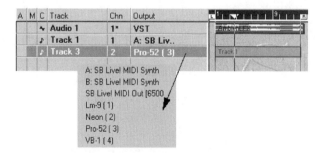

Fig. 5.4. Selecting a virtual port for the VST instrument

If the MIDI track is thus assigned to a virtual port, then the signal coming from the corresponding VST instrument can be mixed with the Audio tracks in the virtual VST Channel Mixer (using the <Ctrl>+<*> combination of additional keyboard keys).

Remember that you can change the size of the VST Channel Mixer by dragging the borders. This is shown in Fig. 5.5.

❏ On the left, there are channel strips for mono and stereo audio channels (marked with a 1 in the illustration).

❏ Then come the channel strips of the VST instruments (2).

❏ Rightmost is the Master section (3).

Each VST instrument is represented in the mixer by a virtual MIDI port (the input) and the channel strips of the VST mixer (outputs). Some VST instruments, such as the HALion virtual sampler, have several outputs.

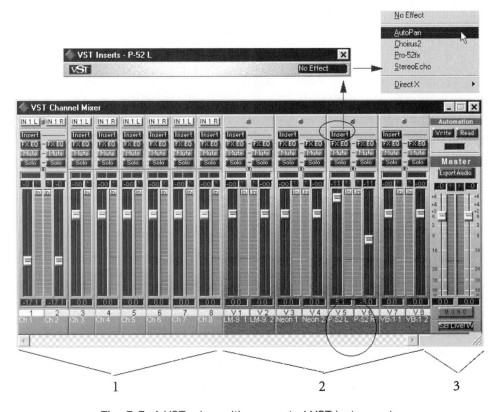

Fig. 5.5. A VST mixer with connected VST instruments

Note that PRO-52 is third in the drop-down list and the third among the channel strips of the VST instruments (Fig. 5.4).

The channel strips of the VST instruments are the nearest to the Master section (3). You can connect a plug-in to each output of the VST instrument. To do this, click on the Insert button and select the name of the effect from the drop-down list. The virtual mixer is described in detail in *Section 1.15.1*, and setting up Insert effects is covered in *Section 1.15.2*.

The same VST instrument can be connected to *several* sections of the virtual rack. And each of the duplicated instruments can have different programs and a different Insert effect connected. For example, loading two HALion samplers will provide 32 virtual MIDI channels and 24 outputs in the VST mixer.

A	M	C	Track	Chn	Output
			Audio 1	1*	VST
			Track 1	1	Pro-52 (1)
			Track 3	2	Pro-52 (3)
			Track 4	3	Pro-52 (2)

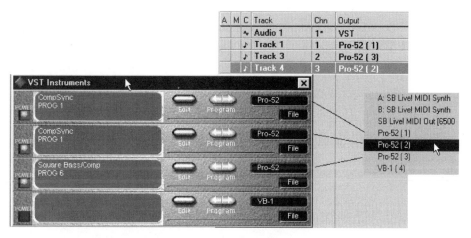

Fig. 5.6. Connecting several identical VST instruments

Finally, another very important issue needs to be mentioned. The Export Audio operation described in *Section 1.16* is applicable to MIDI tracks assigned to VST instruments.

In other words, one of the functions of the Export Audio operation is the virtual procedure of converting MIDI into Audio without losing quality. Cubasis VST recalculates the MIDI track (tracks) in the audio file and imports it to an audio track (if the Add created file to current song option is checked in the Export Audio File window), with respect to audio processing and automation.

Note that VST technology allows you to ignore the quality of the integrated MIDI synthesizer of the sound card, since *it is not used* for VST instruments. The one thing the VST technology requires from the sound card are the specialized ASIO drivers to allow you to comfortably perform on the VST instrument in real time.

Below are the stages of creating a musical composition on the computer.

- ❏ Creating the *MIDI project* in Cubasis Notation and Cubasis VST
- ❏ Recording *audio tracks* in Cubasis VST
- ❏ Converting MIDI into Audio
- ❏ Processing in the external audio editor
- ❏ Mixing, Export Audio
- ❏ Mastering and burning the Audio CD in WaveLab 4.0

In the next chapter, we describe the final stage.

CHAPTER 6

Creating an Audio CD

6.1. Destructively Processing an Audio File

The Cubasis VST software is intended for beginner computer musicians who wish to quickly master musical technologies on a simple level with a decent result.

The "simplicity" of this software is revealed on all levels, including the structure of the virtual mixer, which is considerably simplified compared to the professional version, Cubase VST.

Undoubtedly, this fact restricts the capabilities of audio processing in Cubasis VST. But there are simple solutions that will allow you to perform some very high-quality audio processing in this software.

There is a special class of applications intended for professional audio processing. Their capabilities have recently been expanded to such an extent that the result now depends only on the fantasies and ingenuity of the user.

The main difference is the fact that they let you do the processing not only in real time. This means that even a relatively "weak" computer can handle the task. Of course, this method requires more effort from the user, and you have to take into account that in this case, the material is processed destructively (changing the original material). But in the end it is definitely worth it.

6.1.1. Connecting the Audio Editor

In order for it to be possible to use the audio editor together with Cubasis VST, do the following:

1. Open the Audio Preferences window in the Audio menu using the Preferences option.
2. In the Wave Editor field of this window, show the path to the executable file of the audio editor — for example, wavelab.exe. You can do this either from the keyboard or by selecting it in the Browse for Wave Editor window that is opened by clicking on the Browse button (Fig. 6.1). As a rule, audio editors are placed in the Program Files folder.
3. Check the Segment Range Selection option if WaveLab (from Steinberg) will be used as the audio editor. In this case, the entire audio file that contains the selected segment will be opened in the editor.
4. Complete the operation with the OK button.

After these operations are completed, the audio file will be automatically loaded in the audio editor. All you will have to do is double click on the required audio clip in the arrangement window.

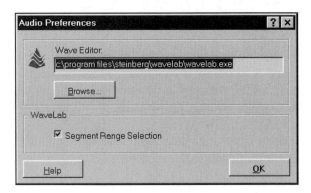

Fig. 6.1. Connecting the audio editor

> ## Warning
>
> For both applications to perform together correctly, you'll need to uncheck the **Play in Background** option in the **Options** menu of Cubasis VST. Otherwise, you will not be able to save the file edited in the audio editor with its original name — i.e., the automatic re-import of the edited audio file will be impossible in Cubasis VST.

The following sections deal with the methods of processing audio clips in the audio editor. Here we had quite a dilemma facing us, actually. On the one hand, we wanted to provide the reader with information on the most powerful audio editors: WaveLab 4.0 and Sound Forge 6.0 (http://www.sonicfoundry.com). But since they are professional-level, a detailed description would hardly be relevant to this book. Therefore, we decided to concentrate only on the issues that will enable musicians to master the above software on their own.

6.1.2. Processing Audio Clips in the Sound Forge 6.0 Editor

First of all, the Sound Forge editor should be connected to Cubasis VST, as we described above.

One possible appearance of the Sound Forge window with an audio file loaded is shown in Fig. 6.2.

You can simultaneously work with several audio files in the Sound Forge editor, each of them opening in separate windows with the same name. If there are several windows opened at the same time, then, according to the Windows interface, the active window is the front one.

The Effects menu contains many algorithms of destructive processing typical for professional audio editors. Each algorithm (effect) contains an interface window of settings (Fig. 6.3).

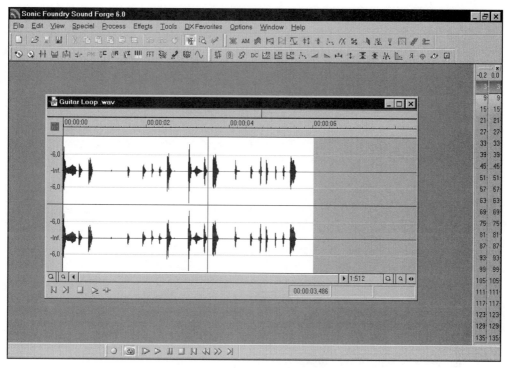

Fig. 6.2. A possible appearance of the Sound Forge 6.0 editor window

The basic widgets are the Bypass and Real-time checkboxes, the drop-down **Preset** list, and the buttons in the right part of the window:

❑ Save As saves the current setting as a preset. Further on, the preset will be available in the Preset list.

❑ The Delete button deletes the current preset from the list. Presets with the [Sys] mark relate to the system and cannot be deleted.

❑ The Preview button is the audition mode for applied processing. If the **Bypass** option is checked, then the "dry" (not processed) signal is heard in the **Preview** mode. When you check and uncheck this option, you can compare the sound. If the **Real-time** option is checked, the processing is done in real time. Of course, this is a very convenient function, giving you the impression of working with a hardware effect processor. The **Real-time** option should be unchecked only for very weak computers where real-time processing is hard to perform. In this case, the editor will do preliminary processing of the fragment, and then will play it back in cycle mode from the RAM of the computer.

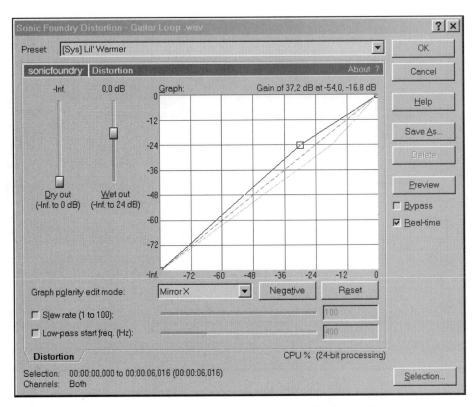

Fig. 6.3. An example of applying the **Distortion** effect

❑ Selection is the button that opens the Set Selection window (Fig. 6.4). In this window, you can specify the area of the audio file that is to have destructive processing applied.

❑ The purpose of the OK, Cancel, and Help buttons is the same as usual.

If you first select an area in the audio file window and then open the effect window in the Effects menu, *only the selected area* will be heard in the Preview mode. If there is no selection made, the processing will affect the whole file. You can change the borders of the selected area in the Set Selection window in Preview mode using the Play/Stop buttons.

The Start, End, and Length fields determine the borders of the selected area, while the unit is selected from the Input format drop-down list. The Custom line should be selected in the drop-down Selection list.

The Snap Zero button snaps the borders of the selected area to the nearest zero points. This function will free the recording from too much clicking, since the area processed by the effect will start and end at a point of zero amplitude. The Snap Time button snaps the borders of the selected area to the nearest integer values on the time scale (Fig. 6.5).

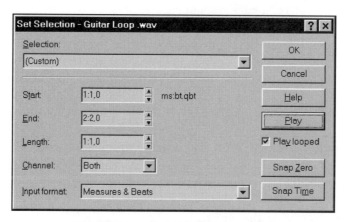

Fig. 6.4. The **Set Selection** window

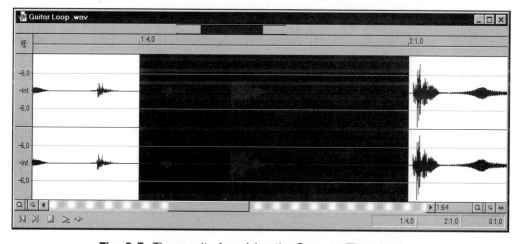

Fig. 6.5. The result of applying the **Snap to Time** function

In many cases, it is more convenient to select the fragment *before* the effect is called from the Effects menu. To do this, use the commands of the Edit/ Selection menu, or the hotkeys.

❐ The Snap to Time command (or the <T> key) shifts the right edge to integer values step-by-step (Fig. 6.5).

❏ The Snap Edge to Time command (or the <Shift>+<T> key combination) snaps the edges to the nearest integer value of the time scale. When this operation is performed, the *direction* in which you make the selection matters: when it is from left to right, the right edge is snapped.

❏ The Snap to Zero command (or the <Z> key) snaps to the zero points. Applying the command again widens the selected area to the next point of zero amplitude.

❏ The Snap Edge to Zero command (or the <Shift>+<Z> key combination) snaps the edge to a zero amplitude point. The direction of the cursor move also matters during selection: if it was from left to right, the right edge will be snapped. Applying the command again shifts the edge to the next point of zero amplitude.

Let's consider a few more useful hotkey combinations that accelerate work with the editor.

❏ <↑> Zooms In on the time scale

❏ <↓> Zooms Out on the time scale

❏ <Ctrl>+<↑> full Zoom In

❏ <Ctrl>+<↓> full Zoom Out (complete view of the audio file)

❏ <Shift>+<↑> increases vertically

❏ <Shift>+<↑> reduces vertically

If an area is selected, the <Ctrl>+<↑> key combination performs the **Zoom to Selection** operation. It can also be performed with a double-click on the vertical **Level Ruler**, whose scale is in percents or decibels. If it is in decibels, the waves are automatically scaled vertically.

The destructive processing method described above has a considerable disadvantage: it cannot control several effects simultaneously. You can get around this, though, by using effect chains with real-time processing.

To do this, you will need plug-ins capable of working *only within the other main applications*, e.g., audio editors or multitrack virtual studios.

Such plug-ins are present in Sound Forge 6.0, developed by the Sonic Foundry company. These plug-ins belong to the DirectX standard, which is supported by the Sound Forge 6.0 editor.

Since the range of plug-ins is constantly expanding, and many modules can be installed on the computer, the developers of Sound Forge 6.0 have provided the special DX Favorites menu. Here you can specially sort plug-ins so as not to get confused.

The easiest way to do this is to sort the connected modules by their names. Do this with the Recreate by Plug-In Name command in the **DX Favorites** menu.

Later on, you can easily create additional folders and sort the plug-ins according to their functional features, such as reverberation units, equalizers, compressors, etc. Select the Organize option from the DX Favorites menu and make the additional manipulations in the Organize Favorites window (Fig. 6.6).

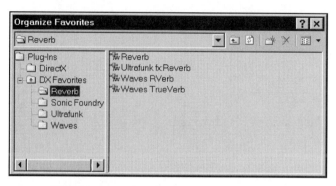

Fig. 6.6. The **Organize Favorites** window

The structure of the Organize Favorites window recalls Windows Explorer. Thus it is very easy to create a new folder — named, for example, Reverb — and drag the icons for the reverber plug-in from the other folders. As a result of this operation, the Reverb submenu will appear in the DX Favorites menu.

In order to use the algorithm of the connected module for destructive processing, select the area and call the plug-in from the DX Favorites menu. This procedure is the same as that of using the algorithms of the Effects menu.

We already mentioned that chains of the plug-ins is the most efficient method of audio processing. The performance of modern computers enables you to do the most complicated audio processing in real time.

To use this method, there is a virtual device in any window containing an audio file — the Plug-In Chainer — which is opened with a special button (Fig. 6.7).

The user chooses whether to make this module separate for each window, or common for a number of windows. This depends on the state of the Share Plug-In Chainer option in the Options menu. If it is checked, one general module will be configured for all windows. This is convenient when you need to quickly apply *the same* processing to different audio files.

This powerful module has a very simple interface (Fig. 6.8). A list of the presets can be found in the top of the window. Each of them contains the full configuration of the plug-in chain. The functional buttons are on the right.

❑ The Bypass button is used for bypassing the entire processing of the module.

❑ The Preview button enables you to control real-time processing with the effect setup. Here you can freely select any area of the audio file. (For further continuous playback, the Loop Playback button on the Transport bar should be pressed).

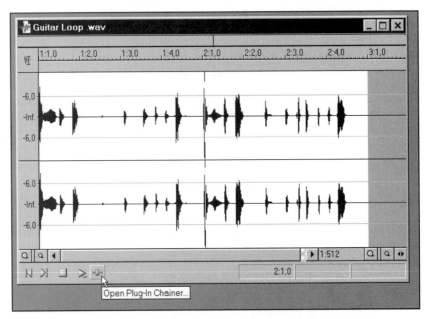

Fig. 6.7. The button opening the **Plug-In Chainer** module

Fig. 6.8. The **Audio Plug-In Chainer** window

❑ The Process Selection button makes all the processing destructive.

❑ The Ignore Tail Data button ignores the additional audio data (tail) that forms as a result of the work of some plug-ins, such as the **Waves True Verb** reverber, where a certain numeric value or **Auto tail** is set in the **Tail** field. If the **Ignore Tail Data** button is pressed, the tail of the reverberation will be cut off.

❑ The **Mix Tail Data** button mixes the additional audio data with the original. This mode imitates the performance of a mixing console with a Send effect connected to the additional Aux bus to which a send route was organized. In this mode, the tail of the reverberation is a natural fading background for the original signal.

❑ **Insert Tail Data** replaces the original data with the additional audio data. For example, in this mode the tail of reverberation will replace the sound of the original audio file.

❑ The **Save Chain Preset** and **Delete Chain Preset** buttons control the saving and deleting of the **Plug-In Chainer** module presets.

❑ The **Add Plug-ins to Chain** button opens the **Plug-In Chooser** window, which has a structure similar to Windows Explorer. Using the **Add** and **Delete** buttons, you can easily create the necessary plug-in chains.

❑ The **Remove Selected Plug-In** button deletes the selected plug-in (visible in the **Plug-In Chainer** window) from the chain.

During this creative process, you may need to change the order in which the plug-ins are connected, since this affects the sequence in which the audio processing algorithms are applied. This is done by simply dragging the blocks containing the names of the modules (Fig. 6.9). The module on the left is the first in the chain, the first to process the sound.

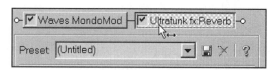

Fig. 6.9. Dragging modules in the chain

The **Plug-In Chainer** window displays the widgets of the currently active module: the rectangular block with its name is pressed (selected). If you uncheck this block, the connected module switches to the Bypass mode, i.e., is completely *bypassed*.

You can change the *processing bit depth* in the **Audio Plug-In Chainer** window. To do this, right-click in the **X-bit Processing** field (where X is the number of bits) and select the parameter from the pop-up menu (Fig. 6.10).

The larger the selected parameter, the more accurate the processing and, consequently, the better the quality of the final audio.

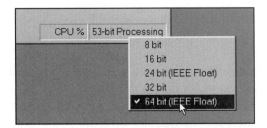

Fig. 6.10. Setting the processing bit depth

The Sound Forge 6.0 audio editor is the latest professional software for the PC. Therefore, 64-bit mathematics with floating-point number format is used. We are not going to consider this serious topic here, but simply dwell on some important practical issues.

❑ The audio files that Cubasis VST works with have the 16-bit integer format. In order to obtain the best sound quality, processing is to be done with a resolution *exceeding* that of the original audio file. The powerful Sound Forge editor and *professional plug-ins*, such as those from the Waves company, provide such a service.

❑ To preserve quality, try to do all the main processing using just one chain of plug-ins — in *one operation of the destructive editing*, since saving the interim results reduces the final quality.

 Note

You can save the interim result in the Sound Forge 6.0 editor as a 64-bit audio file, but we are not going to dwell on this topic in detail.

❑ Check the signal level *at the output of the chain*. For control over this, you have Play Meters with the Clip clipping indicators.

Generally, the algorithm for using Cubasis VST and Sound Forge 6.0 together goes as follows.

1. The montage of the composition is done in Cubasis VST.
2. Audio clips are imported one by one into Sound Forge 6.0 for audio processing.
3. After processing in the editor, each audio file should be saved with the Save command in the File menu.
4. If several files are processed simultaneously, it is very convenient to use the Share Plug-In Chainer option of the Options menu. Thanks to this option, the same

plug-in chain can be used for a group of audio clips of the same type. And some of the settings of the included plug-ins can even be changed for some of the clips.

5.   Then, the final mixing of the composition is done in Cubasis VST.

6.2. Processing Audio Clips in the WaveLab 4.0 Editor

WaveLab 4.0 from Steinberg is a high-class professional audio editor. The use of even just some of its features allows a beginner to get high-quality results.

Like Cubasis VST, the WaveLab 4.0 editor can interact with the sound card via a specialized ASIO driver. Use this feature if your sound card allows you to.

When the editor is connected, *always* check the **Segment Range Selection** checkbox in the **Audio Preferences** window of Cubasis VST. The segment in the audio file imported to the editor will be *automatically* selected, which will make it possible to edit only this segment without affecting neighboring segments of the audio file (Fig. 6.11).

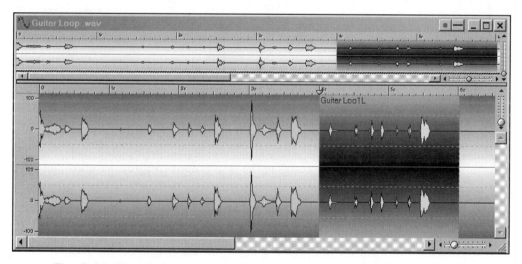

Fig. 6.11. The window of the imported audio file with the selected segment

After the editor is installed, it needs to be set up.

All the main settings are made in the **Preferences** window (which is opened with the **Preferences** option in the **Options** menu). There are ten tabs in this window, among them one named **General**. If you check the **Cubase compatible keyboard commands for cursor positioning** checkbox found on it, then, just as in Cubasis VST, you will be able to control the **Transport** bar of the editor from the additional keyboard. The hotkeys will also be the same for both the software and the editor, which is also important. We recommend that you do this to make it easier to work with both programs at once.

Select the specialized ASIO driver from the **Playback/Record** drop-down list on the **Audio Card** tab of the **Preferences** window (Fig. 6.12).

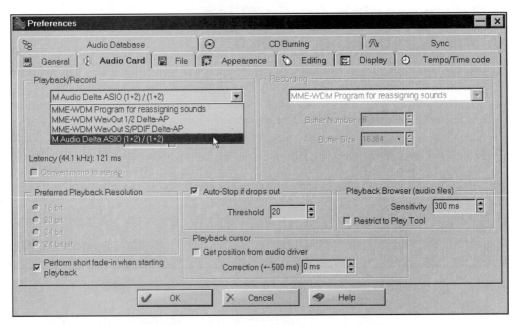

Fig. 6.12. Selecting a specialized ASIO driver

Then make the following settings in the ASIO **inputs/outputs** window that opens:

❑ If there are several inputs and outputs on the sound card, assign the input and output, or check the **Limit to 2 inputs** and **Limit to 2 outputs** checkboxes.

❑ For less powerful computers with a slow graphic subsystem, we recommend that you check the Do not use **gradient backgrounds** option on the **Display** tab. This function will eliminate graphic excesses in the software's design.

One of the advantages of the WaveLab editors has always been a Master section with *several* plug-ins connected. As a result, you were able to process the sound in real time via a chain of the plug-ins. This advantage can hardly be overestimated, since it allows you to control the result in *real time*, which saves the user from experimenting with pressing the Undo and Redo buttons. Those not familiar with this problem should know that in many audio editors of previous generations, *only one plug-in algorithm* could be applied for one operation.

Therefore, we will give special attention to audio processing using plug-in chains.

Fig. 6.13. The Master section

Fig. 6.13 shows the Master section of the WaveLab 4.0 editor. It consists of three windows.

❑ The **Effects** window, used to connect VST and DirectX plug-ins

❑ The **Master** window, used to control the level, indication, and mono/stereo conversion

❑ The **Dithering** window, used for final processing of the audio data when the bit capacity is changed (this is described below)

You can change the appearance of the Master section with a special button (shown with the arrow in Fig. 6.14).

❑ One click on this button opens/hides the window.

❑ A double-click opens the selected window and those below.

❑ Clicking with the right mouse button opens only the selected window, minimizing all the rest.

❑ There are eight slots in the **Effects** window for connecting plug-ins (Fig. 6.15). Processing is done one-by-one, from the top down: the uppermost plug-in is the first to process the sound.

❑ Connecting plug-ins is very simple (Fig. 6.15).

Fig. 6.14. The button for controlling the window

Fig. 6.15. Connecting plug-ins

1. Click in the slot or on the button with its number (shown by the arrows in Fig. 6.15).

2. Select the connected plug-in from the drop-down list.

To the left of each slot there are two buttons: the **On** button switches the plug-in on/off (click with the left mouse button), whereas the **Solo** button leaves only the processing of the selected plug-in, putting all the rest of the plug-ins in the Bypass mode.

The widgets in the WaveLab 4.0 editor are multifunctional. For example, each of the connected plug-ins has its own control panel with all the necessary controls for setting the parameters.

Since this panel is quite big in some of the plug-ins, the option of quickly opening and minimizing these panels is provided in the editor interface. This is done by clicking the *right* mouse button. If you click the **On** button, the control panel of the effect will be either opened or hidden, whereas if you click the **Solo** button, the control panel of this effect will be opened, and *the panels of the other plug-ins will be closed.*

In the slot, the name of the plug-in with the open control panel is highlighted in blue.

You can change the order of the plug-ins by simply dragging them from one slot to another. This operation can be done *during playback* as well. Since the order of the plug-ins affects the sequence of the processing algorithms, this method considerably expands creative potential.

The control panel of each effect contains the **Bypass**, **Mute**, and **Preset** buttons. The function of the **Bypass** and **Mute** buttons is no different than what it is normally: bypass and mute an effect. The **Preset** button opens the path to the controlling the preset. It is the same for all VST applications from Steinberg, and was described in *Section 1.15.*

The **Global Bypass** button is found in the bottom of the **Effects** window. If you click on it, you will bypass *all* the connected plug-ins.

The nearby **Presets** button opens the **Master Section Presets** window, which is used for saving the general configuration presets of the plug-in chains. This function allows you to save and then return to a sound that you have obtained with the settings of a specific plug-in chain.

You can create your own preset collection for typical cases of sample processing, e.g., a special chain of plug-ins for bass (or vocal) sample processing. The presets are saved in the MasterSectionPresets.set file. The path is the following: C:\Program Files\ Steinberg\Wavelab\Presets\MasterSection.

Using previously saved preset chains can make work with Cubasis VST and WaveLab 4.0 most efficient.

You can control the signal level in the **Master** window. If clipping occurs, you should reduce it immediately.

The **Mono** button allows you to estimate the compatibility of stereo processing with a mono mode.

After finishing setting up the plug-in chain, save the file processing destructively. To do this, use the **Render** button, which opens the **Rendering preferences for...** window (Fig. 6.16).

In the described case — minimal use of the WaveLab 4.0 editor — you don't need to make any settings in this window. If the file area was previously selected, the radio button in the **Range** section is in the **Selection** position.

If the whole audio file is processed, this switch should be in the **Whole file** position.

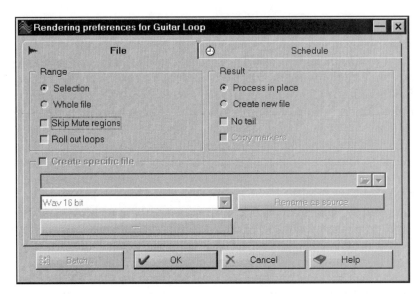

Fig. 6.16. The **Rendering preferences for...** window

If you are using Cubasis VST and WaveLab 4.0 together, the Result section's radio button should be in the **Process in place** position. The processing is then applied to the *loaded* audio file. Save the processed file with the **Save** command in the File menu and return to the Cubasis VST window.

6.3. Eliminating Digital Distortions. Dithering

The bit capacity of an audio file imported from Cubasis VST is 16 bit. The WaveLab 4.0 editor performs processing with a large resolution. The capacity of the processing is a very important parameter for the sound quality. We will not dig too deep in this topic, but just give some practical recommendations. You can find details on preserving the digital audio quality in *Chapter 8* of our book *Live Music on Your PC*, A-LIST Publishing, 2002.

And so we connect the plug-in chain to the Master section in order to get the most interesting, high-quality sound. To preserve the quality, a very high bit capacity is needed, which is provided by the audio editor together with many plug-ins. After the processing, however, the bit capacity should be reduced to the initial value (16 bit), since the file goes back into Cubasis VST. This process — bit capacity reduction — is characterized by digital distortions called *quantization distortions*. To eliminate them, the special *dithering algorithm* is used (Dithering).

Dithering should be the last in the algorithm chain applied to the audio file (therefore, the **Dithering** window is at the bottom of the Master section).

Select the dithering processor from the drop-down list of the **Dithering** window, e.g., UV22HR. A 16-bit digit capacity should be specified in its control panel (the 16 button should be pressed), and the **Normal** button should be pressed as well (Fig. 6.17).

Now, ask yourself a question: why should you use the dithering algorithm? You can find the answer in the special **Bit Meter**, opened in the **Analysis** menu with the **Bit Meter** option (Fig. 6.18).

If the vertical columns of the bit meter occupy a range of 24 bits (not 16), then the dithering algorithm is necessary.

Fig. 6.17. The **UV22 HR** dithering
processor window

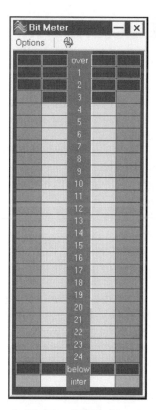

Fig. 6.18. The **Bit Meter** window

 Note

The measurements should be done in the **Monitor playback** mode, activated with the option of the same name in the **Analysis** menu.

Using the bit meter, you can easily test plug-ins from other manufacturers. Some of these plug-ins (most of which are now obsolete) use 16-bit algorithms that are *unable* to provide professional quality.

 Note

If the **below** segment of the indicator is lit, then the algorithm performs processing with a bit capacity exceeding 24 bits. The **inter** segment shows that the data cannot be expressed in 24 bits in the right scale, since the processing is done in floating-point format. This is typical for professional plug-ins.

6.4. Mastering in WaveLab 4.0. Burning a CD

The main task of mastering is to obtain the highest quality possible on a specific commercial carrier. In other words, mastering is kind of a special, high-quality audio processing with album montage and further CD cutting according to the Red Book standard.

At the stage of audio processing, you should ensure that listening to the album is comfortable. All compositions should be equal in volume and frequency characteristics so that the listener doesn't have to play with the knobs to correct these parameters.

The WaveLab 4.0 audio editor is the only software that uses the special Meta Normalizer algorithm, which enables you to *automatically* equalize the volume of all compositions on the album. Besides which, it is armed with special means of simplifying the process of equalizing the frequency characteristics of the compositions.

We recommend that you use the simple mastering algorithm described below for performers that sing with a "minus" phonogram (with the vocal excluded), as this may help to avoid the very widely spread problem of constantly having to balance the adjustment between the voice and the phonogram for every composition.

The algorithm offered consists of the most necessary and simple operations, which you can always change or add to.

Suppose there is a folder in which you store your audio files in 16-bit and 44,000 Hz format, which were gotten as a result of the **Export Audio** procedure in Cubasis VST (described in *Section 1.6*). These files are the compositions from which we will create the Audio CD.

To start, we need to create a virtual editing environment — audio montage. To do this, enter the File menu, select the New option, and apply the Audio Montage command.

Then set Sample Rate to the 44.1 kHz position in the **Audio Properties** window that appears.

Then load the original audio files. This is done as follows:

1. Click with the right mouse button on the virtual Audio Montage track and select the Insert file(s) command.
2. In the Select file(s) window that appears, choose the folder with the original files, select them, and press the Open button.
3. Another Insert audio files window will appear, in which you are to set the radio button in the How to layout the files section to the Line up on the current track position.
4. Press the OK button, and the files will be imported as parts into Audio Montage.

The order in which the clips are linked should correspond to the sequence of the tracks on the future Audio CD. You can drag the clips one over another, creating, if necessary, a virtual crossfade (Fig. 6.19). Do this by grabbing at the clip in its lower part.

Fig. 6.19. Dragging clips in Audio Montage

After the composition order is set, we recommend that you save the file in the mono configuration created in Audio Montage. This is done in the File menu with the Save option.

All processing in the Audio Montage window is virtual — i.e., *it does not affect the original audio files.* Thus you can freely clip the edges of the clips or make a smooth volume change in the start or end of the compositions with the Fade In or Fade Out commands. This is done by dragging the markers as shown in Fig. 6.20. You can also easily change the borders of the clip by dragging them in this window.

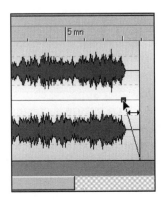

Fig. 6.20. The Fade Out process

If you want to create a curve of a certain form according to which the volume will change, click on the **Fade In/Out** marker with the right mouse button. Then select one of the offered variants (standard presets) in the **Fade-in ROM presets** or **Fade-out ROM presets** submenu of the pop-up menu that appears.

After these operations are completed, press the following buttons in the Audio Montage window: first the one that says **CD**, and then the magic wand of the CD Wizard.

If virtual crossfades are not used, you can leave the default settings in the CD Wizard window.

In order to automatically set the markers at the points of the crossfades, check the **Create markers at crossfade points** function. It will help you to create a CD with continuous audio — a non-stop CD.

With this operation completed, the step of montage can be considered complete, and we can now move on to audio processing. The Q parametric equalizer VST plug-in will be sufficient for equalizating each clip.

You can connect VST plug-ins to each clip in the Audio Montage virtual environment. To do this, click with the right mouse button on the clip, and check the **Add effect slot** function in the pop-up menu. Then press the **Effects** button in the window that appears, and select the required VST plug-in from the list.

Below is an example of connecting two plug-ins with simple interfaces, and some comments on their use. Fig. 6.21 shows the Q equalizer's connection to the first slot.

We recommend that you connect the **MultiBand Compressor** to the next slot (Fig. 6.22).

Using this chain of two connected plug-ins, you can perform separate equalization and multiband compression of each clip.

The maximum number of bands in the **MultiBand Compressor** plug-in is five. If you want to increase the number of bands, simply move the border: drag the outermost (right or left) marker of the frequency band border to the center.

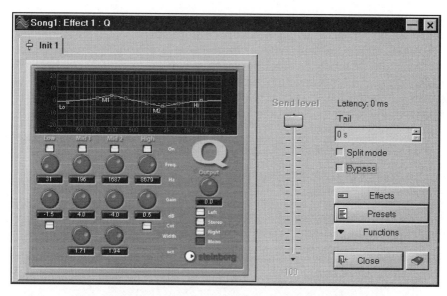

Fig. 6.21. An example of the **Q** equalizer's connection

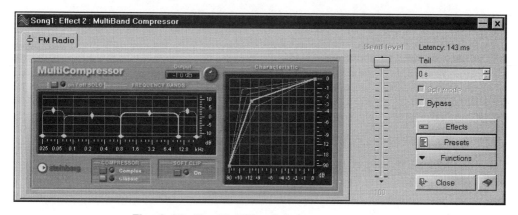

Fig. 6.22. The **MultiBand Compressor** effect

Each frequency band is controlled by three markers: two determine the border of the frequency range, and one determines its level.

You can build the compression amplitude curve by points for each frequency band. The Characteristic display shows the active curve for the selected frequency band. Each click on the curve adds a new point, whereas each click with the pressed <Shift> key deletes it. The points are dragged with the mouse. This is how you build the amplitude curve.

Use the **Complex** button in the **Compressor** section to switch on a mode that gives less distortions when signal dynamics are compressed.

For each clip included in Audio Montage, the equalizer and multiband compressor settings should be made. During mastering, you need to control the RMS (Root Mean Square) level, which best corresponds to the volume perceived by human ear, and you also should control the spectrum with the spectrum analyzer. These two tools are available in the fourth version of WaveLab (Fig. 6.23).

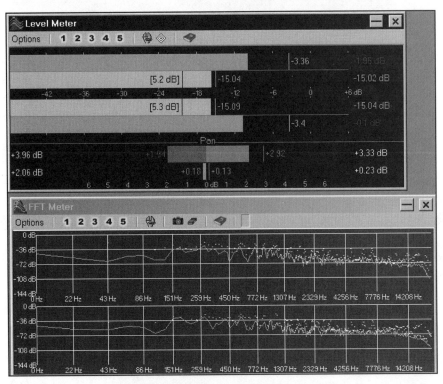

Fig. 6.23. Level Meter and **FFT Meter**

There is a special **Analysis** menu for opening them, and also a Meters toolbar. The blue columns on the Level Meter indicator display the RMS level.

Thus, at this stage of work with the project, you can correct mixing errors having to do with frequency. Those fond of wide, loud sound can increase the RMS level using the multiband compressor.

Despite the above advice, keep in mind that the best sense is a sense of proportion, and so it is hardly worthwhile to neglect the sound's harmony, even for the sake of fashion. In most cases, an overcompressed sound will tire the listener instead of making him or her willing to listen to this music again.

The next step in mastering is to use the Meta normalizer algorithm.

To call this algorithm, press the Edit button in the Audio Montage window and select the Meta normalizer command from the Special menu.

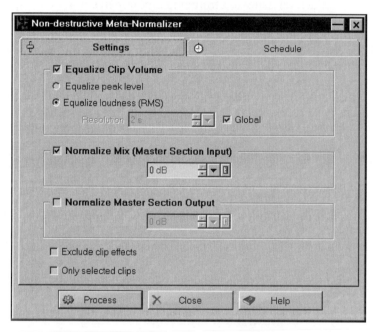

Fig. 6.24. The **Non-destructive Meta-Normalizer** window

The Equalize Clip Volume, Normalize Mix (Master Section Input), and Global functions should be checked in this process' settings window (Fig. 6.24). The radio button should be set to the Equalize loudness (RMS) position. If you do so, the algorithm will measure the RMS level of each clip, and then virtually equalize them so that the level never exceeds 0 dB at the Master section input. The process starts after the Process button is pressed.

Note that the Exclude clip effects function should be unchecked, since the Meta normalization algorithm should take into account the virtual processing of the clips with the effects.

▶ *Note*

Other settings of this algorithm are also possible. See the software's user guide.

After the Meta normalization process is completed, the volume of the clips — and consequently the tracks of the future Audio CD — will be equalized.

You can increase the general RMS level even more if you use Waves RCL (www.waves.com) as a Master section DirectX plug-in effect, or the Peak Master plug-in of the editor. It is best to set the Out Ceiling parameter of this plug-in equal to −0.20 dB and increase the level using the Input Gain parameter.

The UV22HR module with the 16 and Normal parameters should be loaded in the Dithering window of the Master section.

Then do the final controlling of the clips both by ear and using the meters of the Analysis menu.

Now you can start to burn the Audio CD. Press the CD button in the Audio Montage window, and then press the Write CD button.

You need to check the Render to temporary file before burning option in the Write CD window that appears (Fig. 6.25), and specify the writing speed and number of copies.

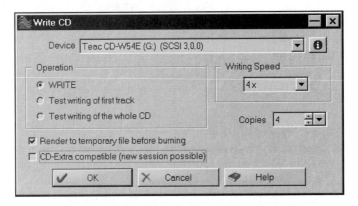

Fig. 6.25. The **Write CD** window

Since WaveLab converts the *whole* virtual project into a big temporary file before burning starts, there will be sufficient space on the hard disk for this operation.

Note

The burning device — the CD recorder — is displayed in the **Device** list. If you press **i**, you can easily get the information on its capabilities in the **CD Recorder** window that appears.

We do not recommend that you do the burning with an unchecked Render to temporary file before burning checkbox, since the CPU has a huge load on it during the complicated audio processing calculations, and less powerful computers may fail.

We will note once again that the mastering technology described in this section is not the only possible one. These are but the first steps into the complex and interesting world of mastering. For users interested in results of higher quality, we recommend the iZotope Ozone module (www.izotope.com)(see our book *"PC Virtual Digital Audio Workstation with SAWStudio, Nuendo, & Samplitude Producer"*, A-LIST Publishing, 2002).

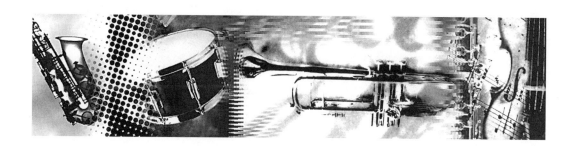

Notation Reading Exercises (Cubasis Notation and the Score Edit Editor)

The Computer as a Musical Simulator

The computer can be used as a *musical simulator*, providing invaluable assistance in mastering notation to *all*: to those of different ages and educational backgrounds, those who were taught music in their childhood, and those who are just now learning it in adulthood. In this respect, the computer is truly an indispensable "little helper" to all those who don't plan on going to music school, but who want to *independently* master the mysteries of notation and get some experience in reading a score, including for work with musical software.

The exercises in Folder 3 — "Musical simulator", are aimed at acquiring basic notation reading skills:

- ❏ Using notation to *learn to read and reproduce rhythmic patterns* consisting of straight lengths (half notes, quarters, eighths, sixteenths), including dotted notes and dotted rhythm. Much attention is paid to the exercises with triplets.
- ❏ Understanding *various meters* (simple 2/4, 3/4, 3/8, straight compound 4/4, 4/8, 3/4, 6/4, 6/8).
- ❏ *Reading music* in the treble and bass clefs.
- ❏ Recognizing accidentals and *alteration symbols* (flats, sharps) during a performance.
- ❏ Playing in *different keys*.
- ❏ Adapting a score *according to the key*.
- ❏ Playing separate parts (with the left and right hands), and the whole score with *both hands*.

Nothing but Notes on the Screen

When the exercise is being performed, the score should be opened on the screen in the Score Edit editor *for all parts of this exercise*. This is done by default, but if the editor is accidentally closed, select all parts in the **Arrange** window (click on each of them holding the <Shift> key pressed), and then open the editor using the <Ctrl>+<R> key combination.

For the most convenient positioning of the score on the screen, all the upper bars are minimized, and the scale *inside* the page (Score/Staff Settings/Staff Options) is enlarged in the **Size** field.

It is best to enlarge the page scale as well. This is done in the **Window Zoom Factor** field in the bottom right corner of the window — Scale 135% | Page: 1 ☐☐. Remember that after double-clicking, you can enter any value, including the convenient scale of 135%. Next to it is the field for page selection, and the rightmost **Show/Hide Status Bar** button returns the upper bars to the screen.

If the **Transport** bar overlaps the notation, you can move it aside (with the mouse), or hide it (with the <F12> key).

In all exercises, the upper line is named **Teacher:** this is the reference template. The lower line of the score is named **Pupil.** It is the lower line that you *should not forget to activate* before starting any of the exercises (by clicking on this line) in order to perform all further operations.

To render assistance to beginners, colored notes are used in the exercises: those with key symbols — sharps and flats — are highlighted in red and blue, respectively. In scores intended for playing with both hands, green denotes the right hand part, and brown the left hand part. All the explanations are provided in the algorithms.

Comfort while Performing the Exercise

Tempo. Using exercises will be more fruitful if the correct tempo is selected at each stage. Don't be afraid to play slowly. Only practice can improve your rate of reading notation. The main task in this first stage is to learn to play rhythmically. Increase the tempo gradually in accordance with *your* progress. The tempo can be changed any time (including during the performance). You can do this in various ways — e.g., using the <−> and <+> keys on the additional keyboard, or by entering a new value on the **Transport** bar.

Continuity of Performance. In the offered settings, after the exercise is over, the cursor returns to the beginning so that you can repeat the exercise several times in a row. Cycle playback is switched off with the ▭ (Cycle) button on the **Transport** bar.

Metronome. When you see the exercise for the first time, it is best to play with the metronome (which is activated in all exercises). The metronome is switched off with the **Click** button on the **Transport** bar. If necessary, you can change its settings — volume, timbre, and number of intro bars — before recording in the **Metronome** window opened by double-clicking on the **Click** button.

Cursor, Recording, and Playback Control. Each exercise has two variants of performance: in recording and playback modes. These modes are switched on and off by buttons on the **Transport** bar or with the keys on the additional keyboard (Play — <Enter>, Record — <*>, Stop — <0>).

The editor can be moved with the slider on the **Transport** bar or with the <Page Up> and <Page Down> keys of the keyboard. The <1> and <2> keys on the additional keyboard set the cursor at the start and the end of the exercise, respectively. The recording always starts from the left locator (L). Therefore, if you want to start the recording from somewhere other than the first bar, move the locator first. To do this, set the editor cursor to the recording start point and press the <Shift>+<1> key combination on the additional keyboard.

Active Staff. It is important to remember that *you have to select the lower (empty) Pupil staff (click on it) before you start to perform the exercises.* If you fail to do this, and the recording is made on the staff with the example, select the Undo option from the Edit menu or press the <Ctrl>+<Z> key combination. If *more than one* wrong operation has been performed, close the exercise *without saving the changes* and open it again.

Deleting the Recorded Training Part. The number of training parts you can record is unlimited. You can delete the recording using any of the methods described in this book. For example, double-click on a note (on the lower line) of the part to be deleted (holding the <Shift> key pressed) and press the <Delete> button. Or you can undo the last operation with the <Ctrl>+<Z> key combination. After that, you can repeat the training recording.

Timbres of the Instruments. You can change the timbres with which the instruments play the **Teacher** and **Pupil** parts, if you want. To do this, exit the editor and make a selection in the **Arrange** window (the **Patch** field of the **Inspector** panel), or change the channel settings in the **Chn** column of the multitrack.

In exercises 1A—13A, the training part of the lower staff is deliberately assigned to the Channel 10, so that only the *percussion instruments* sound during the rhythm playback.

Score Adaptation. For training purposes, various settings of the score display are used in the exercises for the **Pupil** parts. You can see them in the **Staff Settings** window (Score/Staff Settings menu). Despite the fact that they help you to play correctly, note that it is important to *hold all the lengths* during the recording (not to play staccato). This pertains to the A exercises, even though the sound of most percussion instruments is quite short.

Sequence of Exercises. It is recommended that you perform the exercises in order (1A — 1B — 1C; 2A — 2B — 2C; etc.). If it is too difficult to play from music at the beginner stage, you can try exercises 1—13 A first, and then go to the B exercises. When starting a new exercise, it is very useful to repeat the previous ones.

Like learning words, the skill of reading notation is made up of two components: *a)* the pupil should faultlessly recognize the length and pitch of the notes (the necessary information is given in the present book), and *b)* he or she should be able to do it quickly. Both skills are gained *with practice only.*

Before the exercises are performed, you may listen to them, carefully looking over the notation as you do. It is very useful to analyze the score with the playback deactivated and determine the most convenient fingering for a certain piece. If you want, you can indicate the numbers of fingers under the notes as it is done in music textbooks. The procedure is described in *Section 3.11.4* (finger numbering on both hands goes from thumb (1) to little finger (5)).

MIDI Keyboard Position. There is yet another very important issue. Real musicians do not *look* at the keyboard when reading music. So, if possible, get into the habit of playing, looking *only* at the notation. In this respect, it is very important to conveniently position the MIDI keyboard when performing the exercises: not too far from the screen or the computer keyboard.

Exercise Performance Algorithms

The offered set includes 96 exercises. They are compiled from 48 exercises in each of two modes: playing and recording. These exercises consist of 16 basic musical fragments, each of them having three modifications (A, B, C).

❐ A exercises 1–13 are aimed at reading and reproducing the rhythm of the notation.

❐ B exercises 1–13 are aimed at mastering playing from music.

❐ C exercises 1–13 is the reading of notation for *more complicated material* .

❐ Exercises 14, 15, and 16 are aimed at playing with both hands.

The starting position for beginning all exercises:

❐ The Score Edit editor is opened for two tracks (**Teacher** and **Pupil**).

❐ The lower (training) **Pupil** staff is activated.

❐ The cursor is at the beginning of the exercise.

"Playing Rhythm" Exercises (1A — 13A)

1. Activate the **Pupil** staff (Fig. A.1). To do this, you can click on the treble clef or press the <↓> key.

2. Switch on the playback mode (the **Play** button on the **Transport** bar, or the <Enter> key on the additional keyboard).

3. According to the notation of the **Teacher** part, play the rhythmic pattern on the MIDI keyboard: reproduce the corresponding lengths, pressing any (*different*) keys on the MIDI keyboard synchronously with the computer sounds. The tempo is selected individually.

4. Stop playback after you can confidently perform the exercise without mistakes (with the **Stop** button of the **Transport** bar or the <0> key of the additional keyboard).

5. Return the cursor to the start of the exercise (the <1> key of the additional keyboard) and move on to the "Recording rhythm" exercise.

"Recording Rhythm" Exercises (1A — 13A)

1. Switch on the recording mode (with the **Record** button on the **Transport** bar, or the <*> key on the additional keyboard).

2. Listen to the introduction, and, as in the previous exercise, play the rhythmic pattern, pressing *any* keys on the MIDI keyboard (Fig. A.1). The lengths should be held (not released prematurely, despite the brevity of the percussion sounds).

3. Stop the recording (with the **Stop** button on the **Transport** bar, or the <0> key on the additional keyboard).

4. Compare the resulting recording with the reference template. If there are discrepancies in the rhythm, erase the recording (double-click on one of the notes of the recorded part with the <Shift> key pressed, and press the <Delete> key) and repeat the exercise.

5. When you can perform the exercise with confidence and without mistakes, close the exercise without saving.

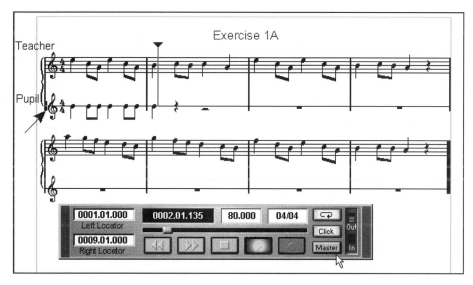

Fig. A.1. The "Recording rhythm" exercise

"Playing Melody" Exercises (1B – 13B, 1C – 13C)

1. Activate the Pupil staff.

2. Switch on the playback mode (the **Record** button on the **Transport** bar, or the <Enter> key on the additional keyboard).

3. According to the notation of the **Teacher** part, play the melody on the MIDI keyboard synchronously with the computer sound. The parts in the treble clef are played with the right hand, and those in the bass clef with the left hand. The notes with key symbols are highlighted in color: sharps are red and flats are blue.

4. Stop the playback after you can confidently perform the exercise without mistakes (the Stop button on the Transport bar or the <0> key on the additional keyboard).

5. Return the cursor to the start of the exercise (the <1> key of the additional keyboard) and move on to the "Recording melody" exercises.

The C exercises differ from the B excersizes in key, scale, or clef.

"Recording Melody" Exercises (1 B — 13B, 1C — 13C)

1. Switch on the recording mode and play the melody after the introduction.

2. Stop the recording and analyze the result. If there are discrepancies, erase the recording and repeat the exercise.

3. When you can perform the exercise without mistakes, make the task more complicated in the exercises with red and blue notes: take away the color prompt of the key symbols. To do this, select the Teacher part (double-click on one of its notes holding the <Shift> key pressed), and then, using the Show/Hide Status Bar button, return the Status Bar to the screen, press the Editor Colors button, and select Black from the drop-down list. Then hide the Status Bar panel again.

4. Repeat the recording.

5. Analyze the resulting score (determine the key) and adapt it accordingly: set the key symbols on your own in Pupil using either the settings of the Staff Settings window or the Clef ... panel (the Score/Symbol Palettes menu). See the details on the keys in *Section 3.3*, and on changing key symbols in *Section 3.2.3*.

6. Close the exercise without saving the changes.

"Playing with Two Hands" Exercises
(14 A, B, C, 15 A, B, C, 16 A, B, C)

1. Open an A exercise, activate the Pupil staff, and in the Play mode play synchronously with the computer. First play the part of the right hand (green), and then the part of the left hand (brown).

2. Record this exercise (as described in the "Recording melody" algorithm) and exit it without saving.

3. Open the B exercise of the same number. Play first the right hand part, and then the left hand part. The computer will play the other part at the same time.

4. Record the part. Exit the exercise without saving.

5. Open the C exercise and play the score with both hands without the computer playing. Then record it on the training Pupil track.

The exercises on the computer are helpful, since any new area of knowledge can be mastered in its live tempo, and therefore, there is no need to be in a hurry or upset if you fail to obtain the desired results right away. Remember that practice makes perfect.

The basic key of the major part of the A exercises we deliberately chose to be *A* flat, since on the one hand it has no key symbols, and on the other hand the accidental symbols appear in the score when the steps of the harmonic and melodic minor are increased.

The offered exercises can be modified: you can change the scale, key, and the rhythmic base. You can also create your own exercises, in doing which the algorithms of rhythmic and scale quantization may come in handy.

The authors are planning to put information on modification of exercises (algorithms and examples) on the site: www.alistpublishing.com.

APPENDIX B

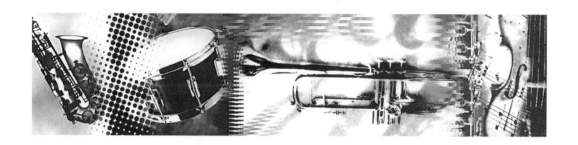

CD Description

Folder 1. Metronomes of Compound Meters (Cubasis Notation and Cubasis VST)

This folder contains 14 songs with training metronomes used for mastering playing with compound meters: 4/4, 4/8, 5/4 (3+2), 5/4 (2+3), 5/8 (3+2), 5/8 (2+3), 6/8, 6/4, 7/4 (3+2+2), 7/4 (2+3+3), 7/4 (2+2+3), 7/8 (3+2+2), 7/8 (2+3+3), and 7/8(2+2+3).

Cubasis Notation uses songs — files with the ALL extension. Files with the PRT extension are to be used in Cubasis VST. The time signature should be set accoding to the chosen PRT file using the **Transport** bar.

To use them, it is necessary to save the file (the metronome template file with the ALL extension) with the selected meter on the hard disk in a separate folder with a new name.

Switch off the metronome on the **Transport** panel (with the Click button). Instead of it, the track that has the strong beat and *relatively strong beats* stressed according to the meter will sound.

Folder 2. Presets for Score Adaptation (Cubasis Notation)

This folder contains 8 songs with settings for adaptation of various types of scores.

In order to use them, you need to save the file on the hard disk with another name, and make the recording in it. Each song contains settings of 7-15 presets: 7 system songs (mandatory), and several offered by the authors. The Normal ALL song includes all presets. The preset settings are described in detail in Tables 3.3 and 3.4 (*Section 3.3.1*).

Folder 3. Musical Simulator (Cubasis Notation)

The folder contains exercises (songs — files with the ALL extension) that you can use to teach yourself how to read and play music with both one and two hands, in various keys, meters, and the treble and bass clefs.

The exercises are geared towards readers familiar with the information set forth in the book. They can be performed by people of any age, both those that know notation and those that don't.

To perform the exercises, copy the songs to the hard disk in a separate folder, connect the MIDI keyboard, and make the necessary settings described in the book. Then go through the working algorithms offered in the "*Notation Reading Exercises*", *Appendix A*. (Author of the method and exercises — Vera Trusova, musiclive@ratrunner.com).

Folder 4. Virtual Mixing (Cubasis VST)

This Demo folder contains a demo song with an example of a project with audio clips.

Copy the Demo folder to the root directory of the C drive, and open the Demo.all file in Cubasis VST. Do a practice mixing of the demo project using the information in *Chapter 1*. The Recycle folder contains an example of a project that uses Recycle files. Copy the Recycle folder to the root directory on disk C and open the Recycle.all file in Cubasis VST.

Folder 5. Audio (Examples of Projects Produced Using the Described Software)

This folder contains files used to demonstrate a final product created with the Cubasis Notation and Cubasis VST software. To mix the compositions, the projects were imported into the Steinberg Nuendo software (see our book *"PC Virtual Digital Audio Workstation with SAWStudio, Nuendo, & Samplitude Producer"*, A-LIST Publishing, 2002). During mixing, the virtual sampler HALion was used, as well as other VST instruments. Audio processing was done in the Sound Forge 6.0 and WaveLab 4.0 editors. Mastering was done in WaveLab 4.0.

The compositions from "Seven Stories from LanoLine" demonstrate:

"Story 1" — cycle recording technology, editing methods, options of VST instruments.

"Gateway" — example of combining improvised and computer technologies, use of the virtual studio technology (VST technology).

"Terrible talks" — an example of a composition with variable meter. (As an exercise, you can select parts and determine the meters on your own.)

Evgeny Medvedev — composition, arrangement, sound processing, sound-design, mixing, and mastering. E-mail: mt_authors@pisem.net, musiclive@ratrunner.com.

Dmitry Nazarychev — guitars, composition, and arrangement.

Index